Dear Zoe || Love Dad

Our Journey from IVF to the NICU to your 1st Birthday

Ryan Richardson (aka Dad)

Dear Zoe || Love Dad

Dedications

I dedicate this book to my wife. Without your love, support, and guidance, I would not be the father that I am today.

I dedicate this book to Zoe's grandparents. Thank you for all the help and support that you have offered through the multitude of challenges we faced. Zoe is lucky to have all of you in her life.

I dedicate this book to all parents who have struggled with infertility. My hope is that you find success by whichever means works for you and your family.

I dedicate this book to all parents who have had a child go through the NICU.

Finally, I dedicate this book to children everywhere. Truly, there is nothing more special than a baby. May you grow up to make the world a better place.

Dear Zoe || Love Dad

Copyright © 2011 by Ryan Richardson

All rights reserved. No part of this book may be reproduced or transmitted in any form without the expressed written consent of the author. Author can be contacted at dearzoelovedad@gmail.com.

Front cover photography by Stevi Webb

This book is a non-fictional account of my experience. I have however changed the names of the medical staff as well as friends and family in order to respect their privacy.

ISBN – 13: 978-0-9849997-1-2
ISBN – 10: 0-9849997-1-X

First Edition

Contents

Introduction to the Reader   6

Introduction to Zoe   8

Part I – Letters to Zoe

IVF	11
Pregnancy	75
NICU	107
Home	169

Part II – Reflections

Introduction	340
IVF: Round 1	341
NICU	362
IVF: Round 2	378

Dear Zoe || Love Dad

Dear Reader – An Introduction

I began this book as a way to capture the adventure that my wife and I were undertaking in pursuit of a child. Even before the process began, I couldn't help but assume that our journey was going to be filled with many ups and downs. We weren't sure whether fertility treatments, surgeries, or adoption would eventually play a role. What we did know was that we were committed to having a child together and starting a family.

"Mom, what was I like when I was little?" was a common question that I have asked numerous times. It was this question that made me decide that what I should really be doing was documenting the journey for my unborn child. Regardless of the method or the length of the journey, our child's story started the day my wife and I decided that we wanted to expand from a 2 to 3 person family. At the time, I had no idea that this seemingly innocuous decision would greatly enhance my relationship with the daughter I have been so fortunate to have. Writing to my unborn child, my embryo, my fetus, my baby, and now my toddler has been extremely rewarding. It made the writing personal, emotional, and real. Writing to someone who you know doesn't comprehend language can be odd at times. Throughout the book, you will notice that there are days when I write to her and I seem to be talking to an actual baby. Others, I write knowing that she will read these words at a much older age. I have purposely chosen to not "edit" these seemingly incongruent voices because I am very conscious of not wanting to strip away the "rawness" of what I was feeling. There were days when I thought of my unborn child as being completely able to comprehend complex thoughts and words. It was a connection that I have never been able to accurately explain as it is far from rational. Other days, especially when I actually saw and held her, my view of her was much more accurate. Clearly, she was still unable to understand my words but I was compelled to write in a more "child-friendly" style.

The various trials and tribulations that my wife and I faced as we went through the fertility process and then the NICU made me think that maybe I should turn these entries into a book that could be shared with other couples. Many days were hard. Feelings of isolation from friends and family were commonplace as they simply were unable to comprehend our situation as first-time parents desperately wanting a healthy baby. It dawned on me as I perused some literature written about what to expect as you go through IVF or the NICU that many works lacked a sense of authenticity. There are certainly some generalizations that can be made about the process, but each mother and father would be experiencing these tough times in their own unique way. What I longed for was not "general" information culled from many sources, but a real story. Such a story would have its limitations as comparisons to my situation would be limited by definition. On the flipside, an acknowledgement of these limitations would free me from the trap of thinking that my situation should be like what is "typical" for a parent in my shoes. I just wasn't ready to accept that my or any other family would have a "typical" situation. Empathy is not an easy emotion to fully cultivate. This thinking led me to want to share my experience that others could read and make their own decisions about its relevance to their lives.

Finally, I wanted to give a dad's point of view. No one questions the ability of a woman to be a parent. This view is so ingrained in our society that its power can be seen throughout the court system where a mother's rights often trump those of a father. The stereotype of the aloof dad is slowly being eroded, but it still exists. Speaking with my male co-workers and friends, I realized that this stereotype couldn't be further from the truth. Many men want to be a great, caring parent. Sharing my experience will hopefully give a voice to these men who also think the sun rises and sets with their kids.

Nothing would make me happier than to know that this book helped individuals who are going through the fertility process, caring for a child in the NICU, or simply enjoying life as a parent.

Dear Zoe || Love Dad

Dear Zoe – An Introduction

Zoe, I could never have imagined how much joy and happiness you would bring to my life when your mommy and I decided that we wanted to have a baby. Your arrival has had such an enormous impact on every facet of my life from the mundane, how I spend my time, to the profound, who I strive to be. I knew that the journey to bring you to this world would be filled with various trials and tribulations, but there is no way I could have understood how you would fundamentally change who I am. The last two years have been the best days of my life; each day being bringing a full range of emotions. Thankfully, I decided to record our journey as I never want to forget the smiles, tears, and sleepless nights.

At first, I wanted to write so that you would understand the process involved as we went through IVF. Soon, I discovered that writing to you helped keep me calm through the trying times. I learned to make sense of my emotions as the words filled the pages. My entries went from simply detailing events to recording my most sincere emotions. Too often, I have held my true thoughts and feelings to myself. Your birth made me realize that I never want you or your mom to wonder how much I love you.

Through writing to you, I was able to start our relationship well before you were even alive. You were still in heaven with all the other little babies when this book began. Then, you decided to come down from heaven and spend a little time in the hospital before making your way into your first home… your mom's stomach. Even before you were implanted in your mom's tummy, I loved you. I didn't need to wait until your first soccer game to be your biggest cheerleader as I prayed and prayed that your implantation would succeed.

When I learned that mommy was pregnant, I was in utter amazement. It was the happiest moment of my life… a moment that left with paralyzed with joy. As I watched your grow from a blinking light to a three dimensional fetus with arms, legs, and big nose. My love only increased. I was a dad, the greatest title a man can have. The three of us were a happy family. The clock was ticking as to when you would finally arrive giving me the chance to do what I had wanted to do since I first learned your mom was pregnant… that is, hold you in my arms.

You arrived five weeks early, a welcomed surprise for a daddy who was ready to see his little girl. All of our bonding through my writing definitely prepared me for your first day in the NICU when mommy was too sick to see you. I might have been a first time dad who didn't know a whole lot about babies, but I did know that I loved you with all my heart and that I would do anything for you. You might have been connected to a breathing mask and had a web of wires

Dear Zoe || Love Dad

connected to you, but you were the most beautiful sight my eyes had ever seen. It definitely wasn't the plan to have me be the first person to hold and care for you; I guess I just lucked out in the end.

We spent three weeks in the NICU watching you grow from a five pound baby too young to open her eyes or use a bottle to a healthy seven pound baby ready for home. I always knew that your mommy would be the greatest parent a child could have, but seeing her stay vigil by your side was something that I will never forget and with this book, you won't either. We are both so lucky to have her in our lives.

Finally, you came home where you have brought nothing but happiness to your mom and me since. Though tired at times, never has the sight of you failed to bring a smile to my face. It wasn't long before I realized that even though you were dependent on me and your mommy for all your physical needs, I was the one who often needed you. There is nothing better than quietly rocking you to sleep after a long stressful day at the office.

As you read the entries, you might realize that I have changed over the last 24 months. Looking back, how could I not. I started the process as one person and have ended up today being someone different. Someone better I believe.

While going through IVF, my focus was on being strong and supportive for your mom as she encountered many different challenges. As we progressed through her pregnancy, my focus changed from protecting mommy to being amazed by you. I nervously awaited each doctor's appointment as you developed in mommy's tummy from 6 cells to a little girl. When you were sick and in the NICU, my assertive/ aggressive side emerged as I needed to protect you. There was no way that you weren't going to get the absolute best care. Your mom and I each had our own roles to play; mommy was providing the love and support and I was providing the protection. Finally, you came home, and my aggression turned to the purest form of love that exists in this world. Love between a parent and a child.

Over the last two years, you have taught me more about life than just about anyone I have ever known. I realized several things which I believe are making me a better person. First, I realized that everyone has a parent who hopefully loves their baby young or old the way that I love you. If I want everyone to be nice to you, then I should do the same for others' babies as well. Second, I want nothing more than to be a person of whom you can be proud. Third, people are naturally hopeful and good. So many people ranging from strangers to family members have wished you well. Maybe things don't need to change when people get older. Maybe I should treat everyone with the same hope and love

Dear Zoe || Love Dad

that I see in others when they are around you. Finally, I could learn a lot from the lessons I plan to teach you. If I would never let you tease a classmate who didn't have as nice a house as you do, then why would I judge anyone who might be less successful than me? Rather than judging or competing with others, maybe I should help them.

I think with this introduction, you are ready to read your story. I love you little girl.

Dad

IVF

Dear Zoe || Love Dad

Dear Angel – May, 2009

I wanted to let you know that I already love even though I still haven't met you. Your mom and I have been waiting to ask God for a baby, and we finally think that the time is just right. I know that you are probably having a great time up in heaven with all the other little angels, but we hope that you will consider joining us down here on earth.

I just finished getting my masters degree in Business Administration from the University of North Carolina. Your mom and I are now in the process of moving to Hershey, PA where I will be taking a job making chocolate. Well, I won't exactly be the one making the chocolate, but I will be working for a chocolate company. Doesn't that sound like a cool job? Your mom and I had always planned on having a baby after I finished school, and the time has finally come. Now that I think of it, your mom has probably planned on having a baby as soon as we got married. Being the conservative guy that I am, I was able to convince her that we should wait until our lives were more stable. I'm not sure how stable I feel having just taken a new job, but I can't wait any longer. Your mom is such a beautiful person that I know it is a great time to bring a little baby into our family. With the decision made, your mom and I set our plan in motion.

Our first step in our efforts to have you was to go to the doctor in order to ensure that we were healthy enough to have a baby. Sometimes people have a hard time having a baby no matter how hard they pray. Of course, God can make anything happen, but we want to give Him as much help as possible given He does have a pretty big world to shepherd. We hoped that we would be given a clear bill of health, but we were also prepared to do whatever the doctor recommended.

Your mom sure didn't waste any time getting us an appointment once I said I was ready to have a baby. Like I said, I had told her that I thought we should wait until I finished school and had a job. Well, school had only been out for a few days when I found myself in a doctor's office with your mom. The doctor checked both of us to make sure that our bodies were ready. The doctor said that we might have to pray harder than other couples, but he thought that with a little prayer and a little luck that everything would work out fine. Mommy was a little sad that we might have to wait awhile to have a baby, but I left happy knowing that our voyage to having our very own child was now underway.

Dear Angel – July, 2009

We went to Europe with my mom and dad to celebrate my graduation. We were so excited to go see all the beautiful art work in Italy and enjoy some great food. The doctor had told us that we would need to pray extra hard if we wanted to have a baby, and luckily, we were headed to the land of the Pope. I couldn't think of a better place to start praying for you to come down from heaven; things seemed to be working out perfectly. My mom had always told me that you get three wishes whenever you go to a new church, and if there is something that Italy has a lot of, it is churches. There seemed to be a gelato shop, a pizza place, and a church on every street. Every day, we would stop at a new church and ask God to give us a baby. As the four of us prayed for you to come down to join our family, I felt so close to you, your mom, my parents, and God. I had prayed throughout my life, but never before had I prayed about something so important. It sure hasn't taken long for me to realize how special the chance to be a dad really is. Weeks earlier I had been nervously sitting in the doctor's office wondering whether I was ready. Now, I was praying for you to come down and be my baby with every ounce of faith I had.

We met one woman in Italy who told us that there is a special statue at one of the churches in Rome where you can pray to Mary for her intercession. My mom found out its location and we headed off to see this special statue. We walked into the church and it was absolutely beautiful. There were statues and paintings showing the great works of the church. I looked to my right and I saw the statue about which the woman had told me. Your mom and I walked over to the statue and looked at all the pictures of little babies. There was a tradition that if God allowed you to have a baby after praying at this statue that the parents should come back and place a picture or baby booties on the wall next to it. Seeing all the baby booties and pictures made me so happy. I was filled with hope that your mom and I would be able to have a baby in the near future.

Dear Angel – August, 2009

When we returned from our trip, your mom quickly found a doctor in Hershey who she believed could help us try and have a baby. We had come back from Italy, packed our things, and driven to Hershey since I last wrote to you. Now that we had said our prayers to Mary (at every church in Italy☺), we thought that we should also seek the assistance of doctors. God made all things and all people, and sometimes He wants us to get help from the people he created. Mommy and daddy thought that this was one of those times, and we therefore wanted the help of those people that God had given the intellect and drive to become doctors.

Your mom found a doctor who had done her training at Harvard, the same college that I had attended. Your mom was anxious to have a baby, and she knew that picking a doctor that I would like was a good first step. You will learn that I am someone who is not easily impressed, and your mom knew that not every doctor would meet the high standards that I desired for this most important project.

We met Dr. Magnuson, and she was very kind. We left her office knowing that we had met someone who would play a very significant and special role in our lives. There would never be anything that your mom and I do that would be as important as having you. We needed to find the right person to help us, and I believed we had just met her. Dr. Magnuson was clearly intelligent, but she had many other qualities that made me believe in her. She was confident; she was straightforward; she was caring. Ultimately, God would be deciding whether you could come and live with us, but I think Dr. Magnuson will be a great partner in this process.

Even though we had each gone through some tests in North Carolina, Dr. Magnuson recommended that we each do some additional testing. Rather than be annoyed that I was going to be subjected to more tests, I was pleased by how thorough she was being. Dr. Magnuson thought that more tests would arm her with the knowledge needed to eventually recommend a plan of attack. She gave us the names of some other doctors with whom we would need to meet. I really don't like going to the doctor, but there is nothing that I wouldn't do for you. Things were moving really fast, but I was confident that we were making all the right decisions.

Dear Angel – September, 10

We just got back from another appointment with Dr. Magnuson. We received the results from some of the tests that had been run on your mom. We were waiting to see whether simply praying for a baby was the best plan or whether there was something that the doctors could do to help us. After the tests came back, Dr. Magnuson said that she thought that your mom should have a surgery to remove something called a cyst that was growing inside her. It was going to be important to remove the cyst because it happened to be on a part of your mom that plays an important role in making babies. If you were going to come all the way down from heaven, we definitely wanted to make sure you would have a comfortable home in your mom's tummy.

It was hard learning about this issue even if I did my best not to show it. Dr. Magnuson said that the surgery would be fairly minor, but it was of little solace. I never like to hear that mommy has a problem or that she needs surgery; I hate the idea of her being in any pain. I kept my fears to myself so that I would not make your mom concerned. The time for me to be strong had arrived.

Dear Zoe || Love Dad

Your mom is very courageous, and the thought of surgery was not frightening to her. She was sad however when she heard this news because she had always hoped that she could get pregnant through prayer alone. I didn't have time to be sad or worried however. My job is to take care of your mom the same way that I will take care of you.

When I saw that she was sad, I assured her that she and I WOULD have a baby. There was no stopping us even if it meant praying for years or doing many medical procedures. I told your mom when we got married that we were going to have a baby and I don't go back on my word. Also, I wanted a baby just as badly as a future father could. I was going to say "just as badly as mommy," but mommies have a special relationship with babies that I really believe daddies just can't understand.

[My determination to have a child is why I am able to write to you right now even though I don't quite know you. How and when I will become a parent is still a mystery, but I truly believe it will happen. These letters will therefore help you know how much your mom and I have always loved you.]

Dr. Magnuson told us that if your mom had the surgery that our chances of having our prayers answered with the arrival of a little baby would increase. The surgery was going to be laparoscopic which meant that it shouldn't cause your mom much discomfort. There are always risks with any surgery which meant that the decision could not be made lightly. I was confident in what our decision would be, but it was important to let your mom think about it for a few days.

After mommy had some time to think about things, her sadness went away as she continued to focus on her goal of having a baby. I think that the initial shock of needing medical assistance was what caused her to be upset. It is definitely not true, but she was upset that there was something wrong with her. I tried to tell her that she couldn't be more wrong. She was going to be the perfect mother because she was willing to do whatever it took to bring you into this world. If the doctor would have told her that she needed to ride a bicycle from Hershey, PA to Los Angeles, CA in order to have a baby, she would have been at a bicycle shop later that day. You are going to be very lucky to have a mother as wonderful as my wife. Not only is she full of love, but she is also very tough. Love and toughness are two qualities that all great mommies have.

It didn't take long for us to agree that mommy was going to have the surgery. I tried to stay positive by telling her that with each appointment, we got one step closer to having a little baby in our arms. We had to understand that there were going to be tough times and happy times. I was confident that if we just always remembered that the end goal was to have a baby then we would find the strength we needed. My mom always said that God would not give us more than we could handle, and I continue to believe this is true.

Dear Angel – September, 16

Today was the day your mom's surgery. I didn't want to tell your, but I was really nervous. There was nothing that I could do in this situation except pray. Not being able to protect your mom while she was in the special room called the "OR," where they would be taking out the cyst, was very challenging. Only doctors and nurses were allowed in the OR, and I had to wait outside. We were only separated by a few doors and a few hundred feet, but the distance felt much greater. Even though I wanted to be right there with mommy, there was nothing that I could do. Actually, it probably was a good that I had to wait outside as I can be a little squeamish when it comes to blood.

We needed to be at the hospital at nine which meant that your mom and I would be leaving our house around 8:00 a.m. On the way to the hospital, I couldn't stop talking.
"Everything is going to be okay."
"Dr. Magnuson is a very smart doctor who will take great care of you."
"I will be right next to you when you wake up in the recovery room."
"This was yet another step in reach our dream of having a baby."

Finally, your mother looked over at me and said, "I know I am going to be fine. Are you okay?"

Your mom knows me too well, and she could tell that I was a nervous wreck. I thought that I was being very strong for my wife by reassuring her that everything was okay, but in reality, my constant reassurance made it abundantly clear to her just how nervous I was. Your mom is my life; of course I would be scared. Well, at least I tried. I told you that she was strong.

We got the hospital and checked in at the front desk. Mommy was given a bracelet which meant that she was now officially a patient. I don't like hospitals in general, and being there because mommy was going to have surgery made it even worse. After checking in at the front desk, a very nice man showed your mom and me the way to the office where we would wait for Dr. Magnuson. I couldn't help but think about what a difficult job he had; he was the person who was in charge of greeting people at a very difficult time in their lives. I don't remember his name and I probably won't see him again, but I really did appreciate his kindness on that difficult morning.

Dear Zoe || Love Dad

Dr. Magnuson came and got your mom and took her back to the OR where she would have the cyst removed. I asked how long the procedure would take, and Dr. Magnuson said that it would be about an hour. I told your mom that I loved her and that I would see her when Dr. Magnuson was finished. I told Dr. Magnuson to take care of her and went to the waiting room.

I had packed a bunch of magazines, a book, and a computer so that I would have something to do while I was in the waiting room. With mommy being wheeled back to the OR, I opened up a magazine. I quickly learned that it was impossible to read when you were worried about someone you love. I stared at the pages, but I just couldn't concentrate. I could see the words on the pages, but I couldn't comprehend anything. My mind was on your mom's well-being. My hope that the magazines would take my mind of off things was dashed as I felt so helpless sitting in the waiting room.

Time was moving so slowly. I tried to just close my eyes and relax, but I was having very little luck. When I first opened my eyes, I thought for sure that 20 minutes had passed. When I actually looked down at my watch for confirmation, I was off by about 15 minutes. The first five minutes took forever, and I knew that this was going to be a long hour.

An hour finally passed, but there was no sign of Dr. Magnuson who promised to come tell me how things went as soon as she was finished. Your mom had now been in surgery for an hour and fifteen minutes. Many doctors had come to the waiting room to meet with other people who had family in surgery. Each time the door opened, my stomach fluttered with anticipation. Doctor after doctor would enter the room and say, "everything went great" to a nervous family member. When would it be my turn to hear these words and escape this tortuous wait?

In my heart, I knew that everything was going to be fine, but my mind kept wondering and imagining the worst. Finally, the door opened to reveal Dr. Magnuson. She walked over to me and I was trying to figure out how things had gone by the expression on her face. Did she look nervous because she had bad news to tell me? Did she look happy because things had gone better than expected? While I was trying to "read" her facial expressions, she continued moving forward until she was standing right in front of me. I waited for her to tell me that "everything had gone great" just as all the other doctors had told the other families. These words didn't come however. She simply said, "Let's go in this room to talk."

Now, I am not a skinny man as you know, but I popped up out of my seat as if it were on fire. We walked into the room with my heart pounding. She closed the door and said, "Everything went well." Phew! The tension built up over the last hour and fifteen minutes was finally released.

As we talked, I kept wondering why she hadn't at least given me the good news in the waiting room even if she wanted to give me more details in private. I understand the concept of patient privacy, but she almost had a new patient to take care of as I was moments away from having a heart attack.

She went on to explain that she had to remove two cysts rather than one. She detailed all the other things that she had unexpectedly needed to fix during the operation. Your mom had something called endometriosis which had led to a lot of scarring inside her tummy. She then pulled out a sheet of paper that had a bunch of pictures. Apparently, she was able to use a special camera to take pictures inside of mommy's tummy and she wanted to explain what she had done. I looked at the pictures, but to be honest, I couldn't begin to tell you what I was looking at. All I cared about was the answers to two questions; (1) was mommy okay and (2) were we closer to having a baby. All the details weren't failed to capture my attention after having been so nervous the last hour and a half.

When pressed to answer those two questions, she said that your mom was doing well and that we were closer to having a little baby. I then asked what she recommended that we do next if we want to have a baby as soon as possible. Mommy had already told me that there were a few procedures that we could try from taking medicines to something called IUI to something called IVF. Being the businessman that I am, I had actually calculated the cost of each procedure and the probability that each would lead to having a baby (It is amazing what information you can find on the internet these days). I was so committed to understanding our best option that I actually sent my excel spreadsheet to a former statistics professor to make sure that my math was correct. Your mom told me that I was acting crazy and that I should let the doctors decide. I think she was both right and wrong. Yes, I was acting crazy, but I wasn't going to let the doctors decide until I had all my questions answered. Having you was too important to me to let anyone make the decision except for mom and me because no one could possible care as much as we did. Also, I must admit that trying to make the process as rational and logical as possible was my way of "gaining control" over something that I knew was ultimately in the very capable hands of God. The doctors might be able to help, but only God would be able to grant me a baby.

Dr. Magnuson said that she believed that our best option was to go through IVF and to start the procedure in the very near future. She said that now that your mom had been through the surgery to remove the cysts and the endometriosis that she was in her best physical shape to have a child. Your mom was still recovering, but she would have been very happy to know that Dr. Magnuson was giving me this advice. I have been thinking that we should just keep praying and my calculations had reinforced this belief, but mommy has always said that she believed we would eventually have to do IVF.

With my questions answered, I was now able to go and see your mom. The doctors had given her medicine that would make her go to sleep so that they could do the surgery without her feeling any pain. I walked back to where she was, and she was still sleeping. I was very happy to once again see her after what had felt like a very long operation. I called over to a nurse and asked him how she was doing. He said that she was recovering very well; the doctor had already told me that she could go home as soon as she was able to go to the bathroom and eat something. Going home was not my main focus; I simply wanted to make sure that she was not in any pain.

Your mom looked so peaceful that I didn't want to wake her even though I was anxious to give her the report on how her surgery had gone. She had undergone this operation in the hopes that she would be better prepared for a baby, and the doctor said that she had definitely accomplished this goal.

When her eyes started to open slightly, I took her hand and softly said, "Your surgery went great." Your mom looked back at me and said, "It did?" She was so tired that before I had a chance to give her more details, her eyes shut and she went back to sleep. Rather than wake her, I just went back to reading a magazine. Knowing that mommy was fine, I was actually able to concentrate on reading, a simple task that I couldn't do just two hours previously.

Mommy woke up a second time, and I once again told her that everything went well as I am not sure she would even remember our first conversation. I told her that we couldn't leave the hospital until she had used the bathroom and shown that she could eat and drink something. The nurse brought mommy some graham crackers and some ginger ale. Knowing that your mom would want to leave, I gently encouraged her to take a bite of the graham crackers. She was still taking medicine to help with the pain, and I didn't want her stomach to hurt because she was taking medications on an empty stomach. She put the graham cracker in her mouth and took two bites. When I didn't hear the expected crunching of the cracker in her mouth, I looked to find what I thought was one of the funniest sights that I had ever seen. She was still holding the graham cracker up to her mouth, but she had actually fallen asleep. The graham cracker was resting in between her lips, but she was just too tired to chew. It was so cute.

Dear Zoe || Love Dad

Now, I have been really tired in my life, but I don't think that I have every fallen asleep with food pressed up to my mouth. I took the cracker out of her hand to ensure that she wouldn't choke. I then gave her a small sip of the ginger ale so that she could wash down whatever cracker she had managed to break off before drifting off.

An hour passed and your mom continued to have trouble staying awake long enough to eat. She wanted to leave, but I had to tell her that she also needed to use the restroom before we left. When I told her this, she looked back at me quizzically. She told me that she had already gone to the bathroom before I had made it back to the recovery room. Convinced that lethargic wife was mistaken, I went to find her nurse. To my surprise, he corroborated her story. I later learned that mommy had fallen asleep in the bathroom too, and upon waking, had to call the nurse from the bathroom phone for help.

With your mom accomplishing all she needed to get done, I helped her collect all her belongings and then wheeled her out to the car. I drove extra carefully on the way home because I didn't want mommy to wake up or be in pain. Once we got home, I helped her up the stairs and into bed. I took care of her and made sure she was comfortable. I never got a chance to tell her about her surgery, but I bet she will want to know as soon as she wakes up tomorrow.

Dear Angel – September, 29 2009

I had told mommy about the conversation Dr. Magnuson and I had after her surgery. She was thrilled to hear that Dr. Magnuson was thinking that we should do IVF. Your mom wants a baby so badly that she had always favored this method. In her mind, IVF was the only choice at this point. I didn't tell her my fear of starting with the best option because I realized that there was no reason to add stress to her life. In the end, I had to accept that this process, the process of having a child, was going to be extremely stressful regardless of the approach. We both want you to come down from heaven to be our baby so bad. In the end, there would be little solace if we chose a different method first and it failed. Any failure would be tough even if another, better option still remained.

Today, your mom was having a follow up appointment with Dr. Magnuson to make sure that the surgery had gone okay. I wanted to go with your mom so that she and I could once again discuss whether we should do IVF. I knew that Dr. Magnuson was recommending this course of action, but I wanted to make sure that I had all the information I could collect before we settled on this particular course of action. On the other hand, your mom didn't have any questions for Dr. Magnuson. When Dr. Magnuson had said she recommended IVF, your mom had heard everything that she wanted to hear.

Dear Zoe || Love Dad

Dr. Magnuson checked mommy and said that your mom was doing great. It was now time to discuss our options. The first option was to continue praying like we had been without any medical assistance. What made this approach attractive was that it was FREE and it would not be physically taxing on mommy. The second option was called artificial insemination which would be around $4,000, but it would not cause your mom any real pain. The final option was IVF which was the most effective, but it was also the most expensive and the most time-consuming. I wanted Dr. Magnuson to give me probabilities of our having a baby with each method. She wouldn't give me numbers which was frustrating because after going to Business School, I love numbers. I figured that I could multiply the probability of each method by how much it cost to arrive at the actual value of the procedure. I also wanted to calculate whether two rounds of artificial insemination were actually more effective and less expensive than one round of IVF. I wanted to see whether my previous calculations were still accurate now that I could use actual numbers and not assumptions based on my internet research.

I tried and tried to have her put percentages with each method, but she wouldn't budge. She would only say that IVF would give us our best chance to have a baby in the near future.

I also asked her whether we should try IVF now because your mom just had her surgery. She confirmed that the sooner we tried the better; your mom was now in the best physical condition to carry a child. When I asked her whether the effects of the surgery would still be in effect in six months, she said she couldn't say. I was getting frustrated because I didn't know how I was supposed to make a decision if the doctor was giving such vague answers. Mommy and I will have a baby, but I wanted to be smart about everything so that I could put my wife and your mom through as little physical and emotional stress as possible. I also wanted to save money so that we could buy a house once we learned she was pregnant.

We left and told the doctor that we would call her back with what we decided. I already knew what mommy was thinking. I tried to explain my position to your mother, but she didn't want to hear it. Your mom was so focused on having a baby that as soon as she heard that IVF was our best chance, she stopped even considering other options. I love your mommy so much and one of the reasons is because she makes decisions on feelings whereas your daddy is always making decisions based on rationality. It may be frustrating at times, but life is a lot more exciting since I met your mommy.

Dear Zoe || Love Dad

I haven't told mommy yet, but I am pretty confident that we are going to do IVF. If mommy wants to do IVF, then this is what we should do. I know that your mom is going to be an amazing mother, and I think that I already need to start trusting her mothering instincts.

Looking back – October, 2011
It was about this time that I also realized that I had to let go of my calculations and embrace the emotional elements of this process. I had to admit to myself that I was scared to do IVF as the first option because I knew that it would in fact give us the best chance. It wasn't about the money. It was about admitting that I desperately wanted a baby and there would never be any guarantee that this would occur. As long as IVF was an option to be pursued in the future, I could maintain a certain amount of hope. I couldn't help but fear the day that IVF didn't work. What would we do next? I was 95% sure that I was going to suggest to your mom that we moved forward with IVF, but one question still lingered in my mind. What impact would a failed IVF attempt have on your mom?

Dear Future Baby – October, 5 2009

Your mom and I decided to meet with the "official" IVF doctor to discuss the process in more detail. Your mom hoped that he would provide me with the final pieces of information that I was seeking not knowing that there wasn't any information that I truly needed. What I needed was to take the leap of faith. You are only supposed to schedule an appointment with this doctor if you have decided that you are going to proceed with IVF. I think your mom scheduled the appointment to put a little more pressure on me. She surely is determined. Hopefully, he won't care that we are not yet 100% sure.

Dr. Palmer walked into the room, and I let him know that we were almost positive that that we wanted to do IVF, but I still had some questions. He was more than willing to answer all my questions; he even gave percentages. He said that last year, 40% of the women who went through IVF at his clinic were able to have babies. I was disappointed that this number was not higher, but I at least had the information I had been seeking. (It was close enough to the numbers that I had found on the internet when I was first doing my calculations that I didn't feel compelled to redo my spreadsheet.)

He walked your mom and me through what the IVF process would entail. I was shocked to learn how complicated this procedure was going to be. Mommy had to take shots twice a day for about six weeks, and guess who was supposed to give them to her? If you guessed me, you are right. I hate the sight of blood, I don't like needles, and I don't ever want to see mommy in pain. What a terrible

Dear Zoe || Love Dad

job this would be. I thought to myself, "Can I really do this?" Then, I thought about how much I want to have you, and I realized that I could overcome almost all my personal weaknesses for something this important to me.

Besides the shots, we would need to go to many doctors appointments over the next few months. There would come a time when mommy and I were going to the doctor every single day. Finally, she would need to have two more "procedures" before we would know whether you were in her tummy or not.

I tried to pay attention to all the details, but there were so many things rushing through my mind. I knew that I had married a woman who would be a great mommy, but was I going to be a great daddy? I wondered if I would have had so many questions about IVF if I were more confident in my abilities to take care of a baby. Maybe there were more reasons to why I had originally been opposed to starting with IVF than I had thought.

There were so many facts, emotions, and insecurities being brought to light by this process. I tried to remain confident that everything would work out and I would be a great dad. But in that doctor's office, I was just overwhelmed. I couldn't concentrate on any one thing as the deluge of facts and emotions engulfed me.

Mommy and I left, and I told her that we could talk later, but I was 99% sure we should go with IVF. I knew that any other answer would have led to major disappointment on her end, and I don't like disappointing your mom.

I always knew that I would love my baby with all my heart, but I had to admit to myself that I was scared of this reality. Hearing Dr. Palmer talk about our needing to schedule our first appointment forced me to really think about being a dad in a very real way. There was a big difference between wanting to be a dad and actually taking the steps to become a dad in the next 10 months. Was I ready?

I knew that I could learn how to feed a baby or change his/ her diapers. What really scared me was whether I would be able to handle seeing you, my baby, upset and knowing that I couldn't always guarantee your happiness. I wasn't just having a baby, I was having baby who would go to middle school, high school, and college. Life can be hard sometimes, and even though you are still an angel in heaven, I am already sad thinking about hardships that you, like every other person, will face. If you were going to be leaving heaven, I needed to make sure that I was going to provide a great life here on earth.

Dear Zoe || Love Dad

The more I thought about the situation, the more I realized that I was ready. No, I wasn't going to be the perfect father, and I would need to lean on mommy for a lot of help. But, I knew that I was going to do my best. God had made all of us and if He thought that all people could handle some hardships in life, then who was I to question Him. Of course, I will always worry about you, but I have faith that you will be just fine.

Here we go! I was going to have a baby – fingers crossed.

Chances of IVF are now 100%. I can't wait to tell your mom; I bet she will never have loved me as much as she will when I tell her that I want to initiate the IVF process.

Dear Angel – October, 28 2009

The journey begins today. Your mom and I had to go meet with a nurse named, Janet. She was going to show mommy and me how to administer the shots your mom will need to take to get ready for your arrival. With daily injections, going to the doctor for all the shots was too impractical. I never wanted to be a doctor or nurse, but I was willing to learn certain medical skills to get mom prepared to have a baby. I had already told myself that I wasn't going to let my fears of blood or needles stop me from having you; now, I just need to be as brave as I told myself I would be.

Janet walked us through all the various shots that mommy would need to take over the next few months. There sure were a lot. First there was a medicine called Lupron that she would take for 22 straight days. Janet showed me how to draw the medicine back into the syringe and how to get out any air bubbles. I told her that I already knew how to do this because I like to watch medical shows on TV. Your mom laughed which made me happy because I didn't want her worrying about all the shots she was going to be taking. The Lupron shots were to be given in mommy's tummy which sounded pretty scary to me, but your mom didn't seem the least bit concerned. She is a very strong woman, and her desire to have a child has only fortified this strength.

The next medicine that your mom would be taking was called Follistim which she would be taking twice a day for twelve days. The Follistim was to be administered via a syringe that looked just like a pen. Janet explained how to turn the bottom of the pen and change the needle. It was pretty confusing to be honest. I hope that mommy understood it. The needle for the Follistim was very thin, just like the needle for the Lupron. I was beginning to think that this wasn't going to be so bad. Your mom would probably tell you that it wasn't going to be bad at all for me because she and not I was the person getting the shots.

Dear Zoe || Love Dad

The next shot was called HCG, and it had to be given at exactly 8:00 p.m. on the night before mommy's first procedure. This shot was HUGE! When Janet pulled it out of her kit to show us, I started laughing because this thing was ridiculous. Your normally brave mother looked as if she had seen a ghost because her face went pale with fear. Janet started talking to me about how I would need to mix the medicine before giving it to mommy, but I couldn't pay attention. All I was thinking about was how big the needle was. I thought to myself that there was no way that I would be able to give this shot to your mom. I would be way too nervous that I would hurt her. Janet said that it wasn't going to be that painful for mommy, but I am not sure that I believed her. I finally realized that I needed to have Janet stop talking and start over with how I was supposed to mix the medicine. This shot was crucial, and I had no idea how to mix it because I had been so distracted. Janet went back over how to mix it, and she even said that she would draw a circle on your mom's hip so that I would know exactly where on your mom's body the shot needed to be given. I guess I would have time to worry about this later; maybe having practiced with the other shots will have given me confidence that I can handle it. I hope so because I wasn't ready at that moment.

The final set of shots contained a medicine called Progesterone, and these shots were supposed to help you grow once you were in mommy's tummy. Janet said that these were the shots that hurt the most because the medicine was really thick which meant the needle had to be pretty wide. She also said that mommies usually didn't complain about this medicine because it was for their babies, and mommies love taking care of their children. Although what she was saying was true, I bet the mommies would rather take care of their babies without having large needles plunged into their sides.

We left feeling pretty overwhelmed. Your mom was rightfully nervous as she was about to become a pin cushion. I on the other hand was overwhelmed with the thought that I could become a father if all things go well. With Janet talking about mommy taking Progesterone if she did in fact have a baby in her stomach, the reality of our journey took another step to fully solidifying in my mind. My wife was and is such a strong person that I actually wasn't too worried about her having to take all the shots. She wants you too badly anything to let anything scare her.

Dear Angel – November, 4 2009

All the medicine that mommy will be taking arrived today. It was a huge box with nothing but medicine and needles! Your mom took all the medicine and supplies out of the box to make sure that we had everything we needed.

Dear Zoe || Love Dad

Organizing the medicines and needles was actually more difficult than I had thought. Some medicines needed to be refrigerated while others could be stored at room temperature. There were liquids, powders, self-contained medicine pens. Arranging the medicine was hard, but organizing the needles was next to impossible. First, I didn't know why we had so many. Did they send too many? Had I not understood Janet correctly? Second, how do I know what gauge needle to use? Did a higher number mean a wider or smaller needle? The process hadn't even begun and we were already overwhelmed. I guess I still have time to figure it out. I think I might need to call your Aunt JoJo for some help; she is a doctor.

When Janet had gone over everything with us, I never imagined that simply organizing the medicine and shots would cause so much anxiety. We hadn't even start administering the shots and I was mentally exhausted. I just wanted to make sure that I do everything correctly so that your mom and I would have the best chance of having you. I got the feeling that this is going to be a very draining process.

Slowly but surely, I am beginning to understand what is making me so nervous all the time. It wasn't the decision on which method to purse, it wasn't the thought of giving your mom the shots, and it wasn't organizing the shots. You know what it is? It is my hope to have YOU! Never before have I wanted something or in this case someone☺ so badly. With each day, I was becoming more ready to be a dad. Actually, I was more than ready; I WANTED to be a dad. I wanted to hold you in my arms, feed you a bottle, and teach you how to play sports.

Knowing that there was nothing that your mom and I could do to accelerate the process, I was going to just try and focus on what I could control, giving mommy her medicine. Although this was my plan, I had a feeling that executing this strategy was going to be quite the challenge.

Dear Future Baby – November, 9 2009

The process officially begun this morning as mommy had her first appointment at the hospital. All the evaluating of options and ordering of medicine was now over; it was finally start to kick this process into high gear. I was very excited.

We were told that the doctors begin seeing patients at 8:00 a.m. in the morning and that they saw patients in a first come first serve manner. Mommy is working as a teacher, and she wanted to be the first patient seen so that she could try and be at school by 8:30 a.m. Because she wanted to be seen first, your mom arrived at the hospital very early; it was not later than 6:30 a.m. when she took her place

Dear Zoe || Love Dad

in the waiting room. I had work as well today, and mommy suggested that I meet her at the hospital at 8:00 rather than show up at 6:30. She was very considerate saying that she didn't want me to be too tired during my work day.

I arrived around 7:45 a.m. I walked into the waiting room, and it was very tense. We are both usually very loud and talkative, but this morning we sat silently. Nobody was talking in the waiting room which made me very uncomfortable. Mommy told me that she was the first person to arrive which meant that we would be seeing the doctor first. Before we went to see the doctor, I took a check for $8,500 to the front desk. See how much I love you; I paid $8,500 for a 40% chance to have you☺ I am sure this will be the best money I have ever spent.

After giving the check to the receptionist, I went back to sit next to your mom. Finally, a nurse walked into the waiting room and called the first patient. Surprisingly, the first patient wasn't mommy. I figured that there must be some patients who weren't in the IVF cycle which is why they were being called first. The next nurse walked into the waiting room only moments later, and I started to stand, but once again, she failed to call your mother's name.

I turned to your mom and asked her whether she was really first, and she assured me that she was. Given the stress that I was feeling from paying the big check, embarking on this important journey, and sitting in a silent room with other nervous people, I started to get very agitated. I'm sure I was just nervous this morning because I know how much your mom and I want to have you, but these other factors weren't helping. My stomach was in knots as I continued waiting for our name to be called.

Mommy leaned over to me, and she told me to go ask the front desk what was happening. I could tell that she was getting stressed by both long term thoughts – are these doctors going to help my prayers be answered- and short term thoughts – am I going to make it to school on time. I couldn't do much to make mommy feel better about her long term worries because I was experiencing these same anxious thoughts. I could however address the second concern. I politely asked the woman at the front desk why my wife had not been called as she was the first person to arrive.

The receptionist said that your mom was fourth on the list. I informed her that she was mistaken as your mom had told me she was here first. The receptionist then said that your mom must have gone to the waiting room before checking in with the front desk. Her comments made my heart beat faster as I didn't like that she was implying that it was your mom's fault. Knowing that your mom was already having a tough day made the receptionist's comments that much more frustrating. It is always very upsetting when I think someone is treating mommy unfairly. I calmly told the receptionist that it was not my wife's fault that she went to the waiting room because none of the staff was present when she arrived. Your mom had simply done exactly what she had been told by Janet when we met to discuss her shots. The receptionist looked back at me and said that she can't do anything about it.

Now, I was getting more and more mad. My blood was boiling. I love your mom more than anything, and I hated her having more stress than was necessary. I asked the receptionist whether she wanted your mother to "wait" at the desk in the future if the staff hadn't arrived rather than sit in the room labeled "patient waiting room." (My dad often told me that no one likes a smart aleck, but I managed to forget this lesson this morning.) She said that there was no way she could have known someone was in there. Is she really giving me these nonsensical excuses? I told her that I was willing to solve her problem for her. Actually, I said, I could give her two solutions to the problem right now. First, you could walk into the waiting room when you arrived and see whether any patients had arrived. If the answer was yes, you could simply ask in what order they arrived. Second, you could leave a signup sheet at the desk where people could right down their initials or code name (privacy concerns) if there was no one at the desk. Needless to say, she was not amused by my attempt to help.

I decided that getting into an argument with the receptionist would only upset your mom further. Plus, I didn't want to cause a commotion that might upset the other patients who were most likely feeling the same level of stress as we were. It was an unfair and unfortunate decision, but I just had to let it go.

We had been pretty happy these last few weeks after we had finally decided that IVF was our best option to have a little baby. I think that we felt some relief at finally making the decision. But beginning the process had brought a whole new set of emotions and feelings. When mommy gets stressed, she gets sad. When I get worried, I unfortunately get angry. I try very hard to manage my emotions, but it is no easy task. I am sure that I will have a conversation with you someday about how to act when someone treats you unfairly.

Walking back into the room, I tried to appear calm for your mom's benefit. My body and mind however were still as tense as they could be. How could this receptionist be so rude when she knew that amount of pressure that your mom and I were feeling on this first day of the IVF cycle? Why wouldn't she simply apologize for the inconvenience her team had obviously caused?

I told your mom that we were now second on the list. She seemed confused, and I told her about my conversation. She was frustrated, and I was partially pleased

Dear Zoe || Love Dad

that she was able to take her mind off the real reason we were here. As we sat there, a woman who appeared to be a patient walked into the waiting room. Your mom immediately told her that her name might have been called when she had left the room to go to the bathroom. I looked at your mom and smiled. Even though she should have been in front of this woman in line, your mom was still courteous enough to let her skip in front. When I told her that it was very nice what she had just done; she just said that all the women must be nervous and she felt bad for this woman who was their without her husband. What a special mom you are going to have.

This morning was not turning out how I expected. I planned on telling the doctor about how we had been treated, but I figured the worst was now over. I was wrong as one of the nurses decided to tell mommy that many of the other women have jobs too when she overheard your mom tell me that she was nervous about getting to work on time. Your mom wasn't even talking to her, but this nurse felt compelled to inject herself into our conversation. The only good thing about this comment was that mommy was no longer sad as her face became flushed with anger. She told the nurse that she was not talking to her, and I couldn't help but laugh. Your mom has so much love in her heart, but she is definitely no shrinking violet. The nurse had picked the wrong time to get on your mom's bad side.

As we waited in the room where we would be meeting the doctor, your mom was almost in tears and my heart was pounding with frustration. The altercation with the nurse now seemed less funny to me as it became clear how upsetting it had been to your mom. The nurse had managed to re-stoke the fire.

I have a feeling that there will be many more highly emotion mornings as we go through this process. The stakes are simply too high to remain calm. Maybe I was overreacting this morning to these slights, but nothing gets me going like seeing your mother upset.

When Dr. Palmer entered the room, I couldn't help but tell him about how upsetting it was to be treated so inconsiderately this morning when we not only handed the hospital a check for $8,500 but also began the most important journey of our lives. He was so kind as he listened and reassured us. He even took the additional step of not charging us for the appointment.

After all the drama of the morning, it was finally time to actually do what we came here to do; get mommy checked out by the doctor. The doctor needed to see whether her body had prepared itself to have a baby. He took out a magic wand which allowed him to see inside of mommy's tummy. He moved the wand around looking for evidence that she was ready, but unfortunately, her body had not been listening to her mind and heart. She was definitely ready to have a baby, but her body was going to need a little more time.

Mommy was really sad to hear this news, but Dr. Palmer did a great job of making her feel better by telling her that he was going to give her medicine that would solve this problem. He also said that it was time to start taking the shots about which we had learned so much. Your mom was to start taking 25 ml of Lupron for the next 10 days.

I kissed your mom and gave her a big hug. I told her that everything was going to be okay. We walked out of the hospital in the crisp fall weather hand in hand. There was a certain closeness between us that we had never felt as we both walked silently thinking about having you in our lives. The silence was broken when we arrived at the parking garage, and I told your mom to drive carefully to work even if meant she would be late. I hopped in my car and headed to work as well. I was happy to be starting, and I said a little prayer that your mom would have a good day.

I knew that I would need to be able to regulate my emotions during this process. I needed to be the calm, level-headed one. I was going to have to put my feelings aside and be the rock that your mom could lean on. Between the medicines and the hope of a child, she was going to be feeling emotions she had never experienced. The last thing she needed was my adding any additional stress. She had always calmed me down in the past when I was concerned about money, school, or any other issue; it was now my time to return the favor. This morning had been really tough on me. The arguments with the receptionist and nurse were unexpected and unnecessary. As I drove to work, I knew that my focus had to be on the future and not the past. Like I said before, I just had to let it go.

I drove home from work excited about your mom's first shot. I wasn't looking forward to her having to get poked with a needle, but I was excited about beginning IVF. As soon as I walked through the door, I asked your mom whether she was ready to get the shot. She wisely said that we should wait until 7:00. She wanted to establish an easy to remember routine. When the time for the shot finally approached, I went to the container where we were storing all the syringes and needles. Your mom decided that she would give herself the first shot, but she wanted me to get everything ready.

It seemed like very simple arrangement. The only problem was the fact that I have a condition called Obsessive Compulsive Disorder (OCD). Having OCD makes me worry about many things not the least of which is germs. This condition added a certain layer of complexity to the process. I got the Lupron out of the refrigerator and cleaned off the rubber top with alcohol just as I had been taught. I then cleaned off the rubber top again with another alcohol swab just to be extra careful. When I began to clean it a third time, mommy said, "Ryan!" in a very stern voice, and I knew it was time to move on. I then screwed the needle onto the syringe. With the Lupron bottle turned upside down, I slowly filled the syringe with 35ml of medicine. I over-filled the syringe because I knew that I would be pushing some medicine out when I got rid of all the air bubbles.

I depressed the needle to get rid of the extra medicine. With 25ml in the syringe, I was ready to hand over the needle to her. Unfortunately, my OCD got the better of me again and I started flicking the syringe over and over again trying to guarantee that there were no air bubbles remaining. After several flicks with my finger, I decided that there were still air bubbles, and I started the process ALL OVER AGAIN!

Your mom was not happy, but she knows me well enough to know that my OCD is not something that I can really control all the time. I took out the alcohol swab and repeated the steps that I had just completed. I will save you from having to listen to the play by play again, but by the end, I was happy that there were no air bubbles this time.

Knowing that the syringe was ready, mommy lifted up her shirt to expose a small area of her tummy. She had been given the choice of taking the shots in her stomach or her thigh; she decided that the stomach was a better place. She took one of the alcohol swabs and cleaned the "injection site." She took the syringe from me with her left hand and gently pinched her stomach with her right. She slowly moved the needle close to her skin and said, "One, Two, …" Fearing the pain associated with the shot, she stopped before getting to three. I asked whether she wanted me to give her the shot; she said that she would be fine. She went again, "One, Two, …" I listened for "Three" but once again, she had gotten too nervous. She had never actually given anyone let alone herself a shot before, and it was turning about to be a little more challenging than she expected.

I once again offered my services, but I was pleased when she refused them. I knew the day would come when I would be giving the shots, but I was happy for that day to be in the future. She placed the needle against her skin, and a small dimple was created as the skin resisted being punctured. Without a countdown, she pressed the needle until it broke through the skin and the small indention that had been formed while the skin withheld the needle rose back to its normal shape. She took the plunger and slowly depressed it causing the medicine to go into her stomach. We had been told to leave the needle in for about five seconds to make sure that all the medicine was transmitted. Because we were so cautious, we left it in for ten seconds.

I was so proud of mommy. She had done it. I knew that there would be nothing that she wouldn't do for you whenever you finally arrive, and I am beginning to understand that there was nothing your mom wouldn't do for even a chance at having you.

Looking Back – February, 2010
As I reflected back on this day months later, I had the following observation. Going through the IVF process was a very unique medical procedure. There were two elements in particular that struck me as odd. First, was the fact that you were a part of a "cycle" which had many different patients all wanting the same thing – a little baby. Second, you would see many different doctors throughout the "cycle" as they took turns seeing patients each morning.

The whole situation felt terribly strange at first. We were looking for help in creating a baby, the greatest gift a husband and wife could ever receive. The process was so personal to us because we wanted a child, but the way we were treated was very impersonal. You lined up with other women (first come first serve) who needed to be seen only to be rushed in and out by whatever doctor happened to be "on." I am not sure what I expected, but this process was certainly not it.

Dear Angel – November, 23 2009

Your mom and I had are second appointment today. We were both really excited when Dr. Palmer told us that mommy's body was reacting positively to the medicine. He saw signs that her body was preparing itself to have a baby which meant that we could move onto the next phase in the process… even more shots. He told your mom to continue taking Lupron and to start taking a medicine called Follistim. The Follistim had to be given twice a day. This medicine was supposed to make mom grow big follicles that would eventually house eggs. Your mom needed to make eggs if she wanted to have a baby. She wants to make sure that you will have a nice home when you come down from heaven. It is just like a mother chicken who lays eggs when she wants to have little baby chicks. I don't know if your mom will be happy that I compared her to a chicken, but this was the best analogy I could think of tonight.

Since the last time I wrote to you, there has been a slight change to our shot routine. I think it is something you might want to know when you are older as it is a good example of how much your mom and I love each other and you.

Dear Zoe || Love Dad

I still prepare the shots, and yes, I still sometimes start over if I think the shot is not "just right." The big change is in who gives the shots. After a few days of giving herself the shots, your mom started having a hard time. She was having a difficult time overcoming the very real human instinct of not causing oneself undo harm. Finally, she realized that it was my time to start helping her. The actual event that finally led to this revelation was quite funny. She started the counting that would always precede her actually giving the shot. Each time she reached three, she failed to muster the courage to thrust the needle into her belly. It took several false starts before the needle made its way to her skin. Right before the needle was to pierce her stomach, she must have hesitated and slowed down. The lack of force caused the needle to literally "bounce off" her tummy. We both started laughing, and she suggested that I need to take over.

I had been confident that I could handle shot duty while I had been watching mommy the first few days. Now that it was my turn, I actually got pretty nervous. I didn't want to hurt her in any way, and I was scared that I would do something wrong. Thoughts flooded my mind about hitting a nerve, a blood vessel, or some other important part of your mom's anatomy. She looked at me, and said, "You need to do it for me; let's go." Her words of "encouragement" helped me get of my fears. She wasn't in the mood to listen to any of my irrational OCD-induced fears. It was her time to be the center of attention, not mine.

I took the needle and bent down so that my face was staring at mommy's tummy. I remember Janet saying that you should go fast and with some strength in order for the needle to go in easy. Janet's advice might have been correct, but as I stared at your mom's stomach with a needle in my hand, the last thing I wanted to do was quickly thrust a needle into her. Was hard and fast really the way to go?

I held the shot with my index finger and thumb as if I was getting ready to throw a dart. I counted one, two, three … but just like mommy's first try, I stopped. I guess I would make a horrible nurse. I told myself that Janet had taught me what I needed to do and that your mom and I were doing this for a chance to have you. When I thought about having you, I found the courage to start over. One, two, three … I quickly moved the shot into mommy's tummy. Your mother was so sweet as she said that it didn't hurt at all. I pushed the plunger down to give her the medicine, and just like that I had given my first shot. Mommy said that she preferred my doing it which meant that this might have been my first shot, but it certainly wasn't going to be my last.

Dear Zoe || Love Dad

Now that you know about giving my first shot, I can continue to tell you about today. The routine tonight was changing as there were now two not one shots to give. I first gave mommy her shot of Lupron, which by this point had become very easy for me to give. Janet was right; going quickly and without hesitation was the key to making it as painless as possible. There was however one problem. Your mom's tummy had been used as a giant pin cushion, and it was starting to show the effects. Because she was getting shots every single day, her stomach was starting to get black and blue bruises all over it. It was getting harder and harder to find a spot on her stomach where she had fresh skin that wouldn't be sore when I gave her the shot. Your mommy is so amazing; she never complained even though I knew that getting shots every day had to be challenging.

With the Lupron shot out of the way, it was time for the Follistim shot. Because I had never given this shot, I needed to read the directions as to what I should be doing. The Follistim came in its own little pouch that we had placed in the refrigerator upon its arrival. I remember from my training session with Janet that Follistim had a pen that you twisted to set how much medicine would be given. I read and re-read the directions to make sure that I was going to be giving the shot properly. I placed the cartridge which contained all the medicine into the pen and screwed on a needle. I then twisted the pen until it was set to give your mom the correct dose. With everything ready, I found a non-bruised spot on mommy's tummy and gave her the medicine. She said that this shot hurt when the medicine was injected. It seemed to have a burning feeling which as you can imagine is not very pleasant.

I feel bad for your mom because she is experiencing not only the stress that comes from wanting to have you so badly, but she is also experiencing the physical pain that comes from preparing her body. I tell her that I am proud of her so that she knows how amazing and brave I think she is. I know my comments don't make all the pains go away, but I hope that they make her feel better for at least a moment.

Dear Angel – November, 28 2009

Mommy and I had another appointment today. I don't know if I already mentioned this or not, but all of our doctor's appointments are actually at the hospital. It is kind of weird going to the hospital so much when neither mommy nor I are sick. As we walk through the hospital, I can't help but be filled with all kinds of emotions as I pass people. There are some people who are obviously sick, and I say little prayers hoping that they get better. Other people are there visiting sick people whom they love, and I thank God for all the good health in my family. The process of trying to get your mom ready to have you is already highly emotional, and the long walk through the hospital has only caused me to think more and more about how special the gift of life is. As hard as it is seeing patients young and old in the halls of the hospital, I do think it is a great way to tacitly reinforce both the beauty and fragility of life. I know that I have been thinking a lot more about what we are doing in asking God to send you down from heaven to be our child.

Hopefully someday, you will be here and get a chance to meet your Aunt Jo, who is a doctor. She has been a really great supporter of ours as we go through this process. She mentioned to me that the only people at the hospital who are patients and not sick are the people who are having babies. I guess when I get sad walking around the hospital, I try to think about all the joy that people get from seeing babies. Maybe someday I will walk you out of the hospital and all those people who are sad will get a little moment of joy from seeing you.

When it is our turn to see the doctor, mommy and I were pleased to see Dr. Magnuson. She has been our doctor from day one, and I have confidence in her ability to provide your mom with the best care possible. After exchanging a few words, Dr. Magnuson got out the magic wand and began to look inside mommy's tummy to make sure the medicines were working properly. The images from the wand showed up on a little TV screen, and I was able to see what she was doing which was very exciting. Because I am not a doctor or nurse, I had trouble understanding exactly what I was seeing because the pictures were not very clear; they were nothing like the TV's we watch at home. Dr. Magnuson however did an excellent job of explaining what she was seeing. She said that she could see some follicles which was a very good sign. In order for your mom to have eggs, she will need her follicles to grow. Dr. Magnuson measured each of the follicles by calling out numbers to her assistant.

The numbers didn't mean much to me, and I therefore asked Dr. Magnuson whether she was happy with mommy's progress. She said that everything looked great. Were very excited and relieved by this news, and I think that it made your mom happy to know that the pain of the shots was at least being rewarded with some progress.

I had told myself that I was not going to try and think too much about our chances of having you at this point in the process, and I am pleased to say that the plan is actually working. Your mom and I just try to concentrate on what we can control which is giving and receiving the shots. I spend my time worrying about whether I can give your mom her shot in the most painless manner possible. My desire for a little baby is growing stronger every day, but I know there is nothing more that I can do besides pray and give mommy her shots.

Dear Zoe || Love Dad

(For when you are older: Even though the process is stressful, I am finding that mommy and I are getting very close. Of course, we were already close, but there is something very special about going through this process. I love your mom very much and I love her more and more as I see her courage and strength come out so clearly on a daily basis. I feel much closer to God too as my helplessness and vulnerability are almost cathartic. I realize that only God can help me have you, and it feels nice to be reliant on a higher being and not simply myself. I have always felt pressure to be perfect or to use the talents that I have. With everyone always telling me that I can do anything because I am so smart or gifted, I have often struggled with the thought that I haven't done enough. Have I really lived up to my "potential?" The words are always said with kindness, but they unfortunately bring pressure as well. I already know that I will tell you how much I love you and how confident I am in you. If these words start to make you feel more stressed than supported, you know you can talk to your dad.)

Dear Angel – November, 30 2009

We had another doctor's appointment today. I get so nervous every time that we go to the doctor because I just want our appointment to go well so badly not only for me, but especially for your mom. She is taking so many shots and putting herself through so much both physically and mentally that I worry about her and her reaction to the news we will find out from the physician. Some of the medicines that she is taking can have the potential to make her feel even more emotional than she normally does. There is an expression that you will learn, "adding fuel to the fire," which comes to my mind as I write this. Your mom is already the most empathetic/ emotional person I know, crying daily about something she sees, hear, or reads. It is one of many of her qualities that make me love her so much. Even though I often write to you telling you how difficult the process is for your mom and me, I hope you know that there is nothing we wouldn't do to have you. We love you already, and we will continue to do whatever it takes to have you even if our prayers are not answered during this cycle.

Mommy and I are becoming very proficient at the shot routine each morning and night, and it is starting to feel "normal" just like brushing your teeth or taking vitamins. Don't get me wrong, I will be happy when this process is over and I can only imagine how happy your mom will be. The nice thing about the shots is that it at least allows your mom and me to feel that we are "doing" something every day to bring you into this world rather than just waiting around helplessly.

Dear Zoe || Love Dad

Today, we saw Dr. Palmer for our appointment. Your mom and I were happy to see him because he has always been very kind to us. After answering a few questions, it was time for Dr. Palmer to get out the magic wand to look inside mommy's tummy.

He was able to find several follicles which was a really good sign. The magic wand isn't able to see eggs, but having follicles usually means that there are eggs being made which is exactly what we need to bring you down from heaven and into your mom's tummy. We were thrilled with this news.

Having gone to so many appointments your mom and I are beginning to understand everything that we are seeing on the monitor. This new found ability has been both a blessing and a curse. I like being able to see the follicles and their progress, but it is also very stressful because sometimes I get nervous that I am not seeing what I should be seeing. Often, my not seeing something can be attributed to the magic wand not being in the right place. Unfortunately, because I am not a doctor, I don't get to use the magic wand and maneuver it for a better shot. Eventually, the doctor has always found what he/ she is looking for and I can then take a huge sigh of relief.

Dr. Palmer thinks that the "retrieval", when the doctor takes the eggs from the follicles, could be within the week which is very exciting. Even though your mother doesn't complain, it is clear that taking the medicines is becoming difficult for her. Her stomach continues to be bruised and finding places to give her shots becomes harder and harder every day. Her stomach is also starting to get bloated as the follicles enlarge and press against her tummy. I don't know what she is feeling, but her bruised and bloated stomach looks very painful. I know that she is looking forward to the "retrieval" as it will signal the end of the shots that are causing her follicles to enlarge. I too am anxious for this day because I will be glad for her to get a reprieve from the daily shots in the abdomen.

Dear Angel – December 2, 2009

Mommy and I are going to be going to the doctor every single day from now until the retrieval. It has been really nice spending time with your mom every morning before I go to work. Before we started this process, she and I didn't usually see each other until I got home around 7:00 o'clock. It feels great to be going through this process as a team, and we are growing closer and closer every single day. We both definitely have a role in this process. Your mom arranges all the appointments and makes sure that I know where I need to be, and I do my best to ask as many questions as possible to ensure that we are getting the best care possible. This arrangement is working great as I am definitely more assertive than your mom and she is much more organized than me.

Dr. Palmer does his examine, and it is clear to him, your mom, and me that mommy's follicles are continuing to grow. The follicles are able to grow on both side of a woman's tummy. For some reason, your mom's left side has the majority of the follicles. She has many follicles on her left side – I think seven – but she only has two on her right side. Being the worrier that I am, I inquired as to whether he was alarmed by this development. Dr. Palmer said that this is not abnormal at all, and he remains confident that we will be able to get a lot of eggs from the follicles he is seeing. I was relieved by his reassuring answer especially because your mom was in the room to hear our conversation.

Sometimes I wish that the doctor and I could speak in private because I don't want mommy to have to worry about anything except for taking her shots and getting rest. This process is hard on me, but I get strength from believing that I am taking care of your mom as best I can. It feels really good to take care of someone you love. Also, my stress level is usually lowered by my asking questions whereas your mom often gets more nervous. Half the time, I ask questions about issues that she never even considered.

When I asked Dr. Palmer how many eggs he believed your mom had made, he would only say that he believed that she would be in the normal range which is between 4 and 20. Knowing that we were getting close to the end of this process, we inquired as to when he thought the retrieval would be. He thought it could be as early as Saturday or Sunday. I'm ready, and I know your mom is ready. Each day the growing follicles and daily injections are making her more and more bloated. The bloating has recently been accompanied by some pain on her left side due to the many follicles growing and pressing against the walls of her tummy. Having a baby sure is hard work for a mom. Yet, she doesn't complain; she is just too excited about the chance of having you.

Dear Angel – December 3, 2009

When your mom got ready to go to the doctor this morning, she noticed another change to her body. She couldn't button her pants! The medicines have been working so well and her follicles are getting so big that her pants just wouldn't button. Even though I thought the situation was quite humorous, I was nervous that your mom would be upset. I was definitely relieved when she started laughing and headed upstairs to put on a flowing dress which would provide her swollen tummy with all the room it needed.

Dear Zoe || Love Dad

My excitement about the upcoming retrieval had put me in a really good mood. I decided that I would have a little fun with your mom as we waited for the doctor. She jumped up on the patient table as she always did when we went back into the patient room. Usually I sit in a chair right next to her, but today I decided to sit on the rolling stool reserved for the doctors. I picked up the magic wand that the doctors use to look inside mommy's tummy with my right hand and pretended to punch buttons on the big computer with my left. Your mom started laughing, and I was glad that I could break the tension that we always feel as we wait hoping for a positive report. Seeing that she was enjoying my joke, I started calling out the numbers that always accompany her exams. I said, "Okay, first follicle is 11 by 7. Second follicle, is 6 by 9."

Before I could get any further, I heard the door start to open. It was Dr. Magnuson. She looked pretty surprised to see someone in her chair. I told her that I had been to so many appointments that I was pretty sure that I could do the examine myself. She laughed, and then told me to get out of her chair☺

The sight of Dr. Magnuson always brings a smile to my face. My nerves immediately begin to calm as she has earned my trust and respect with the great care she has provided to your mom over the last few months. It only seemed fitting that she would be with us during this final week before the retrieval. She did her examine was very happy with what she saw. The follicles continued to grow at an appropriate rate, and she confirmed that she expected the retrieval to be Sunday.

If the retrieval was Sunday, then your mom would need to get her HCG shot tomorrow! As soon as I figured this out, I immediately asked Nurse Janet for a refresher course. She wanted to wait until the actual day it was to be administered. I had the feeling that Janet and the other nurses needed to keep the line of patients moving which is why explaining the shot today, with the chance of having to explain again tomorrow, didn't seem to be a priority.

I was frustrated initially, but I decided that there probably was no use in worrying about giving the HCG shot for the rest of the day as well as all day tomorrow. Your mom and I had actually done a pretty good job of just focusing on what we needed to do each day. We knew what we would be doing this evening as far as shots went, and I guess that was enough.

Dear Angel – Morning of December 4, 2009

Today should be the day that I give your mom her HCG shot. Although I have become pretty adept at giving shots, I am apprehensive about this particular one.

Dear Zoe || Love Dad

It is the most important shot I will ever give. There have been three different concerns running through my mind this morning.

First, this shot needs to be given exactly at 8:00 p.m. There is no way that I would forget, but the need for such precise timing only serves to show how fragile and delicate this whole process really is. I have tried to keep the fragility of the process out of my mind. We were told the odds were 40%, but it is hard not to think your chances are better.

Second, all of the shots that mommy has been getting thus far have been in preparation for this shot. The HCG shot will really set this process in motion. Once your mom gets this shot, we MUST do the retrieval in 36 hours. The process has certainly been real from the beginning, but this shot is definitely a big, important step.

And finally, the needle is HUGE! I have been nervous about giving your mom this shot since Janet first showed it to us in our pre-treatment meeting weeks ago. I don't think that I have ever seen a needle this big. I will definitely take a picture of the needle for you so that you will always know how much your mom sacrificed for you☺

Dear Angel – Night of December 4, 2009

Sitting in the waiting room felt different today. I knew that this would be one of the last times that I was sitting in those chairs waiting to see the progress of the follicles inside your mom's tummy. We were at one of our final pre-implantation appointments. Hopefully in the future, I would be waiting in those chairs waiting to see you growing rapidly in your mom's tummy.

Janet called us back to the patient rooms where she had us fill out forms regarding the retrieval. We asked whether she could put a mark on mommy's hip where I should give the HCG shot like we had discussed originally, and she said that she definitely would before we left. I really wanted Janet to draw this circle on your mom because Janet's original directions, as to the proper placement of the shot, were not totally clear to me. She had said that the shot went into the hip, but when she pointed to the spot, it looked like she was pointing at your mom's butt. Janet kept telling me that there was nothing to worry about. It was easy for her to say, she was a medical professional specializing in the IVF process. I however was a businessman. Your mom had undergone weeks of daily injections to prepare her body for this moment which would all be for not, if I failed to administer the shot correctly. If mommy had a "target" on her, then I figured our chance of success would be greatly enhanced.

Dear Zoe || Love Dad

Before Janet had a chance to mark your mom, the doctor came through the door to see us. Janet said that she would come back at the end of our appointment so that we had nothing to worry about. Well, I might disagree with the use of the word "nothing" as we were about to embark on the most crucial part of our journey to date.

The doctor was someone we had never seen previously. With my nerves already on edge, I was hoping to see Dr. Palmer or Dr. Magnuson. Not only had we grown comfortable with each of them, but we also knew they had the greatest knowledge of your mom's physical progress. Your mom and I knew from the beginning that we would see different doctors, but it had worked out thus far that only Dr. Magnuson and Dr. Palmer were on call when we had appointments.

I tried to think positively and convince myself that this new doctor must be very talented; I mean, she did go through many years of schooling and residency to qualify her for her current position. She introduced herself as Dr. Johnson, and she had a very warm and pleasant demeanor. She reminded me of someone's grandmother with her tender heart.

Unfortunately, I did notice a cut on her face which seemed very fresh. This was definitely not what I needed this morning as my fear of blood and germs started to overwhelm me. My OCD started to get bad which often is the first indication to me that I am really nervous and stressed. I tried my best to combat the worries in my head as today was not the day to be ruminating about irrational, invasive thoughts. I needed to be "present" for mommy.

Dr. Johnson got out the magic wand and began to examine your mom. She saw that mommy's follicles had continued to grow, but less quickly than expected. She then said something that came as a big surprise to us. In her opinion, our retrieval should be Monday rather than Sunday. What? We had mentally been preparing for a Sunday retrieval and a Friday HCG shot. My emotions were already all over the place this morning. The thought of postponing meant another day and a half of anxiously waiting for the HCG to be given.

The temporary stress of waiting an additional day paled in comparison to our desire to maximize our chance at getting many healthy eggs. After the initial shock, your mom and I were fine and said that we just wanted to do whatever we needed to do to have the best retrieval possible. Dr. Johnson said that although she believed we should wait until Monday, she did want to consult with the rest of the team later in the day get their perspectives and ultimate alignment. I was glad she was going to involve the other doctors reasoning that the collective wisdom of 16 years of medical school would be better than her

Dear Zoe || Love Dad

four☺ Plus Dr. Magnuson and Dr. Palmer would be at this meeting, and they had a much greater understanding of our situation.

We walked out to our cars as we had so many times. I asked your mom how she was feeling given the unexpected news. She said that she would be fine. I gave her a quick kiss before she headed to work.

I went to work and tried to focus on my various assignments. As a general rule, work helped keep my mind off of the stressful situation at hand. I don't know what I would have done if my schedule weren't so busy since starting my new job. Rather than add an additional layer of stress, work has actually been a welcomed distraction. My bosses Mike and Jeff have been unbelievably supportive throughout this process. Both are parents who can appreciate what your mom and I are doing. They have allowed me to start my day with your mom at her appointments even if it meant my being late. They have also worked with me to scale back my travel significantly so that I am available not only for your mom's appointments, but also for the daily shot administration.

The day was winding down when I got a call from your mom. It was around 3:30, and she said that Dr. Johnson had just called and said that the team decided that they wanted the retrieval to be moved back to Sunday. I had forgot to mention this earlier, but you're your mom had given the doctors some blood to analyze at the appointment. When the results came back, her hormone levels led the doctors to switch the retrieval back to Sunday rather than waiting until Monday. The doctors thought that the potential benefit of letting the follicles mature did not justify risking a less favorable hormone level. You might not care about this level of detail, but who knows, some day you might be going through the same process. Regardless, I want you to know everything about how you entered our lives.

I was a little surprised and caught off guard. My day had been spent trying to NOT think about the HCG shot knowing that there was only so much stress I could take. Now, the HCG shot was going to be hours away. I of course knew that there might be a chance I would be receiving this call. Dr. Magnuson and Dr. Palmer had been caring for mommy for such a long time that I thought that they would definitely have a strong influence at the doctor's summit that afternoon. I had suppressed these thoughts successfully however which led to my initial shock. I didn't tell your mom I was shocked for fearing of adding to the anxiety I knew she must have been feeling. I simply told her that I was excited to be moving forward before hanging up the phone.

Five minutes hadn't even passed when I received another call from your mom. Since we had talked, she remembered that Janet had not marked the spot on her

Dear Zoe || Love Dad

hip where the HCG shot was to be given. When Dr. Johnson told us that the retrieval was going to be postponed for a day, Janet had decided to not mark mommy's hip surmising it could be done at tomorrow's appointment. Your mom asked me whether I knew exactly where to give the shot. I told her that I thought I had a pretty good idea, but I was far from "sure." The inflection and cadence of your mom's voice changed as her nervousness increased. I could hear her anxiety building all the way through the phone. She had done an amazing job of staying calm and strong throughout this process, but we were both clearly struggling today.

I asked your mom where she was because I could tell that she was in the car. She said that she was fairly close to the hospital. I decided that there was no reason that we should both endure this anxiety about the "marking" when we could do something about it. I suggested that she come to my office and pick me up and so that we could go to the doctor's office and ask someone to quickly draw a circle on her hip. It would be a simple request. Mommy didn't think this was such a great idea at first because we didn't have an appointment, but I was able to convince her. We were soon headed to the hospital.

I had your mom call the doctor's office as we drove toward the hospital. She explained the whole situation to the administrator who answered the phone. I was expecting mommy to receive a very sympathetic response given our unique situation, but to my surprise and frustration, she was told that there was no one at the office that could help her. The unwillingness of this administrator to help us infuriated me. I was unable to help but feel that she was trying to prevent me from having the best chance at having YOU! I was really mad. How could she not want to help us? How could anyone not want to help give a couple the chance at the greatest gift anyone could ever-receive… a beautiful baby? I told your mom that we were still going to go up to the office in person because I wasn't going to let anything or anyone stand in my way from getting the help we needed.

As we walked through the hospital, I could feel my pulse start to race as my frustration grew with each step. I had made this walk so many times in order to get to this point where mommy was ready to have her eggs retrieved, and someone's willingness to jeopardize all of our time, money, energy and strength by not helping to correct a situation that THEY caused made me as mad as I had ever been!

Your mommy was and still is not very confrontational, and I could tell that she was equally frustrated but much less ready for a verbal altercation. I told her that I was not going to be rude, but I really needed help right now. My parental instinct was already being developed, and I was not going to let anything negatively impact my family if I could help it.

I reached the lobby and spoke to the woman who had told mommy that no one could help us. I re-explained our situation and asked her to please help us find someone in this BIG, HUGE hospital that could answer the questions we had. We weren't asking for a doctor specifically as we knew that nurses, residents, interns, etc... would be able to provide the information that we needed. She said that there were no doctors or nurses who could help us. I told her calmly that I couldn't really believe this given the fact that we were in fact standing in a hospital at 4:30 p.m. on a weekday. I told her that I wanted her to either call someone or find someone who had the authority to help us.

I am remaining composed as getting angry at her would not help my cause, but controlling my emotions was getting harder and harder. She left her desk to go and find someone. When she returned, she said that there were no doctors or nurses; they had all gone home for the day. I once again explained to her that I didn't need one of the doctors or nurses that were specifically associated with this particular practice. I said that any doctor in the ob/gyn or labor and delivery department would suffice. She refused to digest my words as each comment was met with a quick excuse. I tried my best to explain that we had the shot and we know how much medicine to give. We only need help knowing how to give an intra-muscular shot. She continued to be unhelpful as she unsuccessfully tried to convince me that only the four doctors and two nurses who worked with the IVF patients were qualified to draw a circle on mommy's hip.

I just wanted to scream. At this point, my frustration was at an all time high as I tried my best to maintain at least a semblance of control. I said, "This is absolutely insane! We are in the middle of a hospital with thousands of doctors, nurses, and other medical professionals who are perfectly capable of administering an intramuscular shot, and YOU are preventing me from speaking with them."

She said that she couldn't help me. I told her that I was extremely disappointed that she was not willing to make the extra effort to go beyond the most basic elements of protocol to assist someone in need. Sensing that this woman was not going to be the answer, I told mommy that we needed to leave to find an alternative plan.

We walked through the hospital frustrated by every white coat (this is what doctors and nurses wear) that we saw. On the way to the car, I told mommy that we should go to the other ob/gyn office that was located a short distance from the hospital. I was pretty confident that I could have found out how to give an intramuscular shot on the internet or by calling Aunt Jo, but once we initiated this process of finding a doctor in person, it seemed like it is the only viable option.

We headed over to the other office only to find that it was closed. All of the verbal wrangling with the administrator at the other office and the long walks to and from the hospital parking lot had cost us time. We were about to move onto plan "C" when mommy saw two women exiting the elevator who were wearing nurses outfits. Mommy ran over to them and quickly explained our situation. They were very sympathetic and told us to go to an office on the third floor which was still open.

We entered the office and told the woman at the front desk that we needed to quickly have someone mark the spot on your mom where she would be receiving an intramuscular shot. She was very kind, and she went in the back to find, "Little Mary." Little Mary emerged from the back and said that she would be more than happy to help. We told her the story, and she apologized that we have had to go through so much. She said that our request was very reasonable and very easy to address. Within a minute, Little Mary had marked your mom and we were good to go.

I can't explain how much affection mommy and I had for Little Mary at this moment. I guess you appreciate people more when they are helping you with either your child or your attempt at having a child. With the crisis averted, mommy and I headed home.

You might think that after the day that we have had that mommy and I would take it easy for the rest of the evening. Well, this wasn't the case.

Your mom had planned a Christmas party with our friends Jim and Kelly. She had already made plans with them to go to Costco to pick up supplies this evening. I tried to rationalize this plan telling myself that it would keep my mind off of things and that it would be uplifting to see my friends. In reality however, I thought this was the last thing that I wanted to be doing. Today had been so exhausting; all I wanted to do was sit on my couch and relax. Knowing me, I would have probably sat on the couch and stressed out about the shot and the impending retrieval, but I would rather be stressed in the comfort of my own home than in the aisles of Costco.

We hadn't been home for more than ten minutes when they arrived at our house. I would have been happy to see them, but in the very short time since Little Mary marked mommy and the knock on our door, I realized that I had another question that I needed answered tonight.

Dear Zoe || Love Dad

Because we left the doctor this morning not thinking that today would be the day of the HCG shot, I had failed to ask all the questions that I normally would have wanted answered. Thankfully, we had been able to have the placement of the shot issue resolved, but I realized that I wasn't sure whether mommy was supposed to continue taking the Follistim shots as well as the HCG. I thought to myself, "Not again. What I am I going to do now that it was after hours?"

Mommy was excited to see Jim and Kelly and she told me that I needed to get my jacket because we were about to leave. I told her that I wasn't leaving until I figured out whether she was supposed to take Follistim tonight or not. We had come too far to make any mistakes. Knowing that the HCG shot had to be given at 8:00 p.m. exactly (not 7:50 or 8:05) made me think that everything needed to be very precise from this point forward. What if the Follistim shot interfered with the effectiveness of the HCG? What if we had to start all over again?

I couldn't stop these questions from entering my mind, and mommy's insistence that we leave was only making me more stressed. I felt under attack by the barrage of thoughts swirling in my head.

The questions continued. Would taking the Follistim change mom's hormone levels in a way that made the retrieval less effective? The doctors had convened for a long meeting and made their decision based on all different types of information including mommy's hormone levels and the size of her follicles. Who was I to be making this decision?

I tried to reach a conclusion on my own. Yes, she should take the Follistim because it would make the follicles bigger which is why Dr. Johnson had wanted to wait another day for the retrieval. No, the Follistim would change mommy's hormone levels and make her body less receptive to the implantation.

I quickly realized that I wasn't going to be happy until I was able to speak with a medical professional or at the very least find published information giving me the answer. I told mommy that she would need to wait. Jim and Kelly could sense my stress and they were very kind saying that they would be more than happy to go to Costco without us. Mommy kept telling them that this was not necessary even though I thought it was a great idea. I think that mommy was stressed too, and she wanted to go to Costco because that would make her more relaxed whereas it was having the exact opposite impact on me.

I went to the drawer where we keep all of the information about the IVF process. I looked and looked, but I just couldn't find any information regarding whether she should take Follistim tonight or not. I am not a big believer in using the internet to find valid and sound medical advice, but in my desperate state, I fired up my machine and began searching in vain for an answer. As I am writing this to you, I think you can probably feel my stress as I relive this anxious moments.

Mommy said that we really needed to leave because she was hungry. I said, "How can you be worried about a burrito at a time like this?" She was not happy with me at all. I have tried so hard to remain strong for mommy, but tonight my stress was getting the better of me. I hated feeling that I should have been more prepared. I hated not knowing what to do. At this moment, I was trying to figure out how to make the best of the situation and come up with a solution. Mommy knows that I love her, and I decided that I needed to continue focusing on making the best decision for both of us even if it meant that she was going to be frustrated with me in the short term. I did however need to be mindful of not making mommy any more upset than she already was. Between the shots, today's adventure, and her deep desire for a baby, I knew that her body and mind didn't need any more taxing.

I remembered that there was a number to call for after-hours questions, and I decided that this was our only hope. I promised your mom that we could leave as soon as I was able to locate this number; a decision which I believed to be a happy compromise. We could leave and go to the store with our friends, and I could get the answer that I needed.

I made the call and I was disappointed that the after-hours number was routed through a call center in Alabama. Could this day get any worse? First, the administrators at the hospital wouldn't help us and now I needed to leave a message with a tech in a completely different state who would then hopefully get back to me. I tried my best to remain cool. The clock was ticking toward 8:00 p.m. I told the tech our situation, and I explained that this matter was urgent due to the fact that I needed to give your mom her shot in less than two hours. The tech told me that I should expect to hear from someone in an hour. Her understanding of urgent was apparently quite different from mine.

I gave my cell phone number to the tech, and the four of us headed to Chipotle for a burrito before our shopping trip at Costco. Jim and Kelly continued to tell me not to be so worried, but no words from a lay person could soothe me at this time.

Waiting for a call from a complete stranger somewhere in Alabama was terrible. I felt completely helpless as we continued to creep closer and closer to 8:00. If you couldn't tell, my OCD had most definitely reared its ugly head as I became more and more irrational and panicked with each passing second. I told mommy to call her brother, your Uncle Tait, because he was as close to a medical professional as I figured I could find. He was a dentist, an occupation which is definitely quite different than a fertility expert, but I knew that he did have an understanding of how medicines interact with each other. For some reason, your usually "know it all/ control freak" uncle was unwilling to provide an answer. He also wasn't willing to call his friend who actually was an ob/ gyn doctor. I was so mad. This was certainly not your future-dad's finest hour.

I then decided to call your Aunt Jo because she was essentially a doctor. She was finishing up her fourth year of medical school, and I was hoping that if she didn't have an answer that she might be able to get one from one of her friends or teachers. I explained the situation to her as I stood outside of Chipotle. Mommy was inside glaring at me, and I could tell I was going to be in trouble. She came outside and told me I was being ridiculous and that I was making her extremely nervous. Great, I thought to myself. Not only was I not being strong for mommy tonight, but I was actively making her upset. I didn't know what to do. I felt strongly that finding an answer was the best thing for her, but I had to weigh this benefit with the negative of contributing to her anxiety.

I told Aunt Jo that I needed to go inside but that I wanted her to call me if she was able to find an answer for me. I went inside and tried to eat my dinner, but I wasn't hungry. My stomach was in knots, and for one of the first times in my life, I just couldn't eat.

The four of us went to Costco to pick out all the things that we were going to need for our Christmas party. To be honest, I can hardly even remember what we decided to get. Jim and I would separate from mommy and Kelly because I thought that mommy might want to rightfully complain to Kelly about her husband's crazy behavior. If I wasn't able to be as supportive to mommy as I would like, then the least that I could do was get out of her way and let Kelly fill that void.

We finished shopping and got back in the car around 7:10. We were now fifty minutes away from the time when I would need to give mommy her HCG shot. I looked at my phone over and over again, but no one had called. I began to think about what I would do if I didn't hear back from the nurse in Alabama; a situation that was becoming more and more likely. Kelly then gave me a suggestion. See, Kelly works at the hospital and she had a number that she calls to page a doctor when she needs to speak with him or her. She said that maybe I should call this number. Now, I try to be a very ethical person because some day I want you and your siblings to look at me with pride. I wasn't sure that using this number was the "right" thing to do, and I definitely did not want Kelly to get in trouble. I did however need an answer.

Dear Zoe || Love Dad

After taking a few minutes to think about the situation, I asked Kelly for the number. I called the hospital and waited for it to ring. When someone answered, I said, "please connect me with the ob/ gyn resident on call." I was so nervous because I wasn't sure that I was actually supposed to be calling this number. The woman then said, "Will you please provide the patient's name." I gave her mommy's name and waited while she paged the doctor. I couldn't believe it. This plan actually seemed to be working.

Moments later, a voice on the other end of the line said, "this is Dr. Stevens." I told her that I needed to know whether my wife should take her Follistim shot along with her HCG shot tonight. I could tell that Dr. Stevens seemed slightly confused by the fact that I was able to reach her in this manner. I think she was expecting a medical colleague not a panicked husband on the other side of the line. I had however explained how desperate I was when she answered, and I think my panic motivated her to solve my problem rather than ask questions. She asked me to hold as she consulted another physician. Being on hold frightened me because I knew that if the call was dropped that getting through to her again might be difficult. This was my one and only shot. When she came back on the line, I was so happy and relieved. She said that mommy should not take the Follistim. I could actively feel the stress leaving my body. I couldn't believe it; I had finally gotten my answer, and I had thirty minutes to spare.

By the time we got home, we had around 15 minutes before mommy was to get her shot. I found the HCG medicine and read the directions regarding how it should be mixed. Next, I laid everything that I would need out on the kitchen table and then watched the minutes go by on the kitchen clock.

The needle was just as big as I remembered, and I was nervous on mommy's behalf. At a few minutes before 8:00, I mixed the medicine and prepared the syringe. I used the alcohol swab to clean mommy's hip where Little Mary had drawn the circle. Finally after our two adventures, it was finally time to give mommy the shot. I asked her if she was ready, and she said that she was as ready as she was going to be. I tried to mimic the swift, shot-giving motion, honed over the last three weeks hoping that this method of minimizing pain would work for this shot as well. The needle pierced mommy's skin, and she hardly reacted. I wasn't sure if she was being tough or whether I had just done a great job. I pushed down the plunger forcing the medicine out of the syringe.

Finally, our night could be over. I kissed mommy and told her that I loved her. I said that I was sorry for making her upset. She knew that I just wanted to do what was best for her. I got the sense also that she was happy that I was so committed to this process. She already knew that I wanted to be a father, but today, she was given a little more evidence.

Dear Zoe || Love Dad

The clock has started; retrieval is in 36 hours.

Dear Angel – December 5, 2009

We woke up early to go to the doctor to discuss the retrieval that was going to take place tomorrow. Mommy and I were so happy that yesterday's stresses were over. We were looking forward to making today a much better and more relaxing day. Your mom had more blood work completed to make sure her hormone levels were still where they needed to be. After finishing the blood work, we headed back to the patient room.

Moments later, Dr. Jones entered the room. He asked mommy how she was feeling, and she said that she was a little nervous and very much bloated, but overall, she was doing fine. He asked whether we had any problems with the HCG shot. Little did he know that this simple question was going to lead to such a long and passionate response.

I told him that Dr. Johnson had thought that the retrieval was going to be on Monday rather than Sunday which led to Janet not marking mommy for the shot. Not wanting to go through every detail, I jumped to the front desk attendant telling us that there were no doctors in the hospital who could explain how to give an intramuscular shot. You could see his face tighten as his frustration with his staff grew. He asked what time we had been up at the hospital. When we told him around 4:30 pm, he looked even more frustrated. He told mommy and me that he had been in his office at the hospital until 6:30 last night. He also said that he was on call for situations just like the one we experienced. Dr. Jones had a very similar reaction to Dr. Palmer's on our first day of IVF when we complained. He apologized profusely because after spending years working with IVF patients, he certainly knew what a challenging and emotional experience this whole process was. We thanked him for his concern.

We then told him about our Follistim issue and our difficulty in reaching an after-hours doctor. Once again, he said that the system was not working as designed. He apologized for the stress that this event must have caused. The good news he said was that it really wouldn't have mattered if we took the Follistim shot or not. Mommy kept saying to him that she didn't want to be seen as a complainer (this concern never even entered my mind, a people-pleaser I am not), and he reassured her that he was sincerely concerned with how his patients were doing. Mommy and I have found that the doctors are extremely caring toward the patients; unfortunately, not all the nurses, techs, and administrators have this helpful outlook.

Dear Zoe || Love Dad

He told mommy to take it easy and get plenty of rest. I decided to tell him about the Christmas party which was taking place at our house later that night. He said that in all of his years of working with IVF couples, he has never had anyone have a party the night before their retrieval. I wasn't exactly sure what to make of his comment initially, but he followed this statement by saying that he thought it would be a good way to keep our minds off of tomorrow's big event.

Mommy and I left the hospital, and I said my first of many prayers that day.

We spent the day relaxing at home and getting ready for our party. I have never actually thrown any parties as an adult, and I couldn't believe that my first was going to be the day before mommy's retrieval. Mommy had done an amazing job decorating our house, and the Christmas spirit could clearly be felt. You can probably guess what mommy and I wanted for Christmas – to bring you down from heaven and into our family of course.

Our friends started to arrive, and I was actually glad to have a momentary distraction. I had told my friends Jim, Kelly, and Jeanne that mommy was scheduled to have her retrieval the following day and that I might need their help in "kicking people out" if they decided to stay too long.

The more I thought about this party, the more I started to believe that having a Christmas party the night before our retrieval was very fitting. Throughout this whole process, mommy and I have prayed every day for a chance to be parents. If there was anyone who would understand this insatiable desire for a child, it would be God and Mary who had their own son, Jesus. Hosting a birthday party for Jesus who was going to help us tomorrow seemed like a good way to say thank you.

The party was great, and our friends definitely lifted our spirits. When the clock hit 9:45, I looked at Jim and tried to communicate that it was going to be about that time when I needed his help in getting everyone out the door so that mommy could get some rest. Fifteen minutes later, I shut the door behind our last guest.

Mommy and I headed upstairs for what we hoped would be a restful night.

Dear Angel – December, 6

The retrieval had finally arrived. All of the shots that mommy had been taking and all the appointments she had attended were in preparation for this day. I was surprised when I woke up to my alarm because I would have thought that my anxiety would have woken me up at least one time during the night. I looked at mommy and said, "Alright, here we go!"

We were both very excited and very nervous. Mommy was given a special pill called Valium to take at six in the morning. This pill was to help her relax because she was going to be having all the eggs removed from her tummy. Even before taking the pill, mommy had a very tranquil disposition this morning. She has been so strong throughout this process that I shouldn't have been surprised, but I was nonetheless.

While mommy was getting ready, I ran downstairs to make sure that it had not snowed or iced while we were sleeping. Because mommy and I grew up in the South, neither one of us is very comfortable driving in the snow. The clear, snow-free driveway and streets were a very welcomed sight. At least, we would not be having any trouble getting to the hospital.

I went back up stairs to tell mommy that it had not snowed and that I was ready to leave whenever she wanted. She asked whether I wanted to eat, but I was not hungry in the least. The only thing on my mind was getting mommy to the hospital safely and supporting her through the retrieval.

Because mommy had taken the pill to relax her, I drove to the hospital. We decided to say a prayer together as we drove. We asked God to be with us as we were taking this important step in our journey. Mommy and I have been so fortunate throughout our lives that we thanked Him for all the gifts he had already bestowed upon us. We ended the prayer by once again asking Him to bless us with a baby. Mommy then took out the prayer card that we had gotten in Italy and read the prayer aloud like she did every morning. I listened to the words and let them really resonate. I was extremely emotional as we prayed together. I had never felt closer to God or mommy then at this time.

I was asking God to send me a baby, to create a life. I realized that there could be no greater gift than the gift of life. As I prayed, I actually started to appreciate all the visuals around me that I usually take for granted. The trees seemed different. The horses on the horse farm were more impressive and brilliant. My view of the world was literally changing as I thought about what I was really asking. I was asking for a life. Mommy and I not only wanted a baby, but we wanted a middle school student, a teenager, and a future parent. None of this will probably make sense to you until you are much older; it may not make sense to you until you want your own baby. But, I wanted to tell you because the chance of having you has already had a tremendously positive impact on me.

Dear Zoe || Love Dad

Mommy and I got to the hospital parking lot, and we took the long walk to the hospital entrance. It was very early on a Sunday morning, and it felt that we were the only ones going to the hospital. It was quiet and serene. We had made it.

We checked in at the front desk and then were quickly ushered back to what looked like an operating room. Mommy put on a special gown and hopped up on the bed. The nurses put a needle in her arm so that they could give her more medicine to relax. Because mommy was going to be having minor surgery, the nurse made me put on a special outfit too. It was made of blue cloth that covered all my clothes. The nurses said that it would help make sure that mommy would not get an infection. After I got dressed in this special sterile jumpsuit, the nurse said that I wasn't finished. She handed me a special hat, booties for my feet, and a mask to cover my face. Mommy thought that I looked really funny, and she asked that I bring her the camera. I was glad that mommy was not very stressed; I guess the Valium was working. I on the other hand was a wreck as the realization that mommy was going to be having a medical procedure started to set in. I was completely focused on the situation at hand; my mind was quiet, a very rare occurrence for an OCD sufferer.

We heard a knock on the door, and two women walked into the room with a big metal cart. They introduced themselves and said that they were embryologists. They were the women who would be looking for the eggs when Dr. Jones performed the procedure. Shortly after they entered, a young female doctor who was going to be assisting Dr. Jones came to ask mommy how she was feeling. Mommy had been given more medicine through her IV, and she was starting to get very drowsy as she lied in bed. The young doctor said that Dr. Jones had just arrived and that they would be beginning shortly.

I went to my chair which was positioned right next to mommy's head. Dr. Jones was ready to start. I said one more quick prayer and then kissed mommy on the forehead and told her that I loved her. I got back into my seat and took a hold of mommy's right hand; her left was clutching the Italian prayer card.

Dr. Jones explained the procedure which involved puncturing the follicles and capturing all the liquid and hopefully eggs inside them. His assistant would then put the fluid in vials and hand them to the embryologists via the incubator (on top of the metal cart I mentioned) they had brought into the room. The embryologists would then take the vials of fluid and look at them under a microscope and call out when they found eggs. Janet was also in the room. She said that there was going to be a time delay from when the follicle was punctured to when I would hear the embryologists call out that they had found eggs. She said that finding the eggs was not always very easy and that I shouldn't be alarmed if many follicles were broken prior to my hearing the embryologists call out 1, 2, 3, etc…

Mommy wasn't really able to pay attention to the explanation that Dr. Jones and Janet had given me because she was so tired that she could hardly keep her eyes open. Dr. Jones was ready to begin, and I squeezed mommy's hand so that she knew I was right there with her. I looked at the monitor and could see the needle and vacuum making their way to mommy's follicles. Dr. Jones started on mommy's left side because he knew that Mommy had many eggs on this side. He maneuvered the needle until it looked as if it was pressing one of the large follicles. The needle moved forward, and I saw the follicle collapse right as I felt mommy squeeze my hand. I looked over to see mommy clinching her jaw and squinting her eyes. I hated seeing her in so much pain knowing that there was nothing I could do. It was clear from the collapsing of this first follicle that each puncturing would result in extreme discomfort.

Dr. Jones's assistant transferred the first vial to the embryologists, and I anxiously waited to hear whether they had found any eggs. I waited and waited, but I heard nothing. Dr. Jones continued to fill up vials that were subsequently passed through the incubator, but still I waited. My anxiety had been high several times during this process, but I can't explain how scary and awful these first few minutes were. I wanted there to be eggs so badly. Dr. Jones had collapsed 5 or 6 follicles, and the embryologists still hadn't found one egg. The sight of mommy in pain combined with my anxiety about finding eggs was almost at an intolerable level when I heard, "One." Janet looked at me and said, "They found the first egg." Suddenly, I heard, "Two." A huge sense of relief washed over me.

Unfortunately, it didn't last long as I knew that we wanted many, many eggs. Mommy was coming in and out of alertness, and she was very worried when she heard "two" because she thought she would have many more. I told her that it takes a lot of time for the embryologists to find the eggs because I didn't want her worry. I however was still feeling very tense as Dr. Jones broke more and more follicles without any corresponding shouts from the embryologists.

It seemed like many minutes passed before I heard, "Three." Dr. Jones was almost finished, and I definitely was hoping for more than three eggs from mommy's left side. "Four." Thank you, God. The embryologists were still working even though all of the follicles had been collapsed. By the time the embryologists had finished their search, they found seven eggs from the follicles on mommy's left side.

Dear Zoe || Love Dad

Dr. Jones said that he was now going to move onto mommy's right side which we knew had way fewer follicles. He used the magic wand to try and find the follicles, but he just didn't see anything. He looked at mommy's records and then went back to looking. Once again, he found nothing. He was ready to stop looking figuring that the follicles had been too small to produce eggs when I said to him, "I saw two large follicles on Friday on this side. I had been seeing that at every appointment for weeks. Is it really possible that they just went away?"

I think he was surprised by my assertiveness, but he once again moved the wand looking for follicles. Suddenly, a very familiar image appeared on the screen. He had found the four follicles which I was describing. I took mommy's hand and told her that she was doing great and that Dr. Jones was almost finished. You could see the pain in her eyes as she squeezed them shut every time the needle punctured another follicle. Janet was able to giver her some more medicine half way through the procedure, but I knew that the only true respite would come when the last follicle had been drained.

By the end of the procedure, the embryologists had found a total of ELEVEN eggs. Seven had come from the left side and four had come from the right. When I told mommy what had happened when Dr. Jones had gone to the right side, she was shocked. She was very thankful that I had been there to advocate for her.

With the procedure over, Janet told us that we would receive a call tomorrow letting us know how many eggs had turned into embryos which are the smallest babies you can have. It was time for you to decide whether you wanted to come down from Heaven and join our family. We would also be told when the embryos would be put back into mommy's tummy so that they could hopefully grow into little babies.

I asked about how I should take care of your mom, and Janet said that mommy needed to drink a lot of water and keep her legs up for the next couple of days. She also said that mommy needed to take a Medrol pill every night for the next three nights. Finally, mommy needed to start taking her progesterone shots as well.

Mommy was still very drowsy, and we needed to wait until mommy could stand on her own before heading home. I too was really drowsy and the low light and soothing music of the operating room weren't helping the situation. I kept telling mommy that I wish I head a nice big bed to lie in like she did rather than this small stool. I was trying to be cute and playful, but it wasn't exactly working. Janet heard my complaint, and she said that I was a real piece of work. I guess my joking had crossed over from amusing to annoying. She and mommy then started laughing, and I realized that hopeful daddies don't get a lot of sympathy in this unit.

Your mom took a nap as soon as we got home. She was able to do a lot of resting during the day even though I kept forcing her to drink water and keep her legs elevated. It was getting close to 7:00 p.m., the time when we were to take the Medrol and progesterone, when we made an ill-timed discovery. Mommy and I could not find the Medrol. Mommy had thought that she had received all the medicine that she needed in her first big shipment. She had gone through all the items to make sure that each medicine on the packing label was actually contained in the box. What neither she nor I did was make sure that the packing label had all the medicines that we would need. I couldn't believe it. Was this really happening to us?

Mommy was so stressed. She was getting mad at herself for not checking more closely, and I tried to reassure her that it was not her fault in the least. I said that she needed to remain calm because her body and mind had already been through a lot that day. I had mommy call the company that sent the medicine to tell them that they hadn't sent the Medrol and that we needed it. We figured that calling the company/ pharmacy would be easier than trying to track down a doctor after hours again.

Mommy was able to quickly get someone on the phone. They were very helpful, but they said that Medrol needed to be prescribed by our IVF doctors because not all patients got this medicine. I was so mad. How could these doctors let us leave the hospital today without making sure that we had all of our medicine? Why didn't they write us the prescription?

I needed to solve the problem rather than get mad. I told mommy that I would make the call to the after hours number again. I went through the same procedure as I had on Friday night. I waited and waited for them to call back, but I got nothing. I tried calling the number that Kelly had given me as well, but I couldn't get through this time. I was thinking of any and all ways that I could get Medrol for mommy tonight, when I tried the hospital number again. This time, I was able to get through. I explained the situation, and a resident was able to call a prescription into a pharmacy that happened to be open 24/7.

I got back to the house right at seven and in time to give mommy the Medrol pills. The pharmacist had asked about insurance, and I said that I didn't care what it costs. I just needed those pills. Mommy took her pill and it was now time for the progesterone.

Dear Zoe || Love Dad

I took at the needle that I had been using for the Lupron shots and prepared to give mommy her progesterone. The progesterone was a very thick medicine, quite different from the Lupron. A very odd thing was happening when I tried to draw the progesterone into the syringe; the plunger would be pulled down as if there was a vacuum in the progesterone vial. I tried over and over again, but I was not able to get the medicine into the needle. I explained the problem to mommy, and we decided to try another needle.

I went to our box of IVF medical supplies and got out a different needle and syringe. When I took out the needle, I was shocked. This needle was not only long like the HCG shot needle, but it was also EXTREMELY WIDE. There was no way that I could put this in mommy's hip. I was nervous and didn't know what to do. I wanted to show mommy the needle so that she could verify that it was the correct one, but I didn't want to scare her with its size. I thought that it might hurt less if she never saw it.

All of a sudden, I let out a small laugh, something I do when I'm nervous. Mommy turned her head around to see the largest needle either of us had ever seen. She looked at me and said angrily, "This is not funny." I felt terrible because it wasn't funny to me either; I was just so nervous because I knew mommy needed this medicine and I knew that ultimately I needed to give it to her.

She said that I just needed to give it to her. I cleaned off her skin with an alcohol wipe, and pressed the shot against her skin. The quick motion that I had developed with the other shots was going to be a challenge given my current state of mind. I had no other choice but to give mommy the shot, and she was getting more and more mad the longer I took. Finally, I moved the needle forward, but I had not applied enough pressure and it didn't initially break the skin. I kept pressing until I heard mommy yelp. My immediate reaction was to pull the needle back. When I looked down, mommy was bleeding from where the needle had been. Her yelp had been triggered by the needle finally breaking through the skin.

She said it really hurt, but she was glad it was over. Uh, Oh! She had not realized that I pulled the needle out before giving her the medicine. When she screamed, I got nervous and pulled the needle out without ever pushing down the plunger. We were going to have to do the whole thing over again. I told her the situation, and she was definitely not happy with me. I asked whether I should go and get some ice to numb the area, but she said to just do it again.

This time, I tried not to hesitate. I plunged the needle into her other hip. I gave her the medicine and another stressful day was over.

Dear Zoe || Love Dad

Dear Little Angels – December 7, 2009

I woke up this morning knowing that today would be the day that we found out whether mommy's eggs had been turned into embryos, which is another word for Angel Babies. Embryos are angels that come down from heaven and decide whether they want to go back to heaven or stay here on earth. I know this is probably difficult to understand, but you will learn that many things are hard to understand in this world such as calculus and the Holy Trinity. For now, just trust me.

Without any embryos, mommy and I would need to start the whole process over from the beginning. We knew that we would go through this process as many times as it took, but we were definitely hoping to have a little baby sooner than later.

It felt weird driving to work in the morning because for the first time in what seemed like forever my first stop was not the hospital. Mommy didn't need to go to the doctor this morning which made her quite happy. She was finally able to get some rest after our tough weekend. A nurse would be calling mommy later in the day to tell her whether any embryos had decided to come down from heaven to see whether they liked things here in Pennsylvania.

Even though I was at work, I wasn't getting much work finished. My mind continually drifted back to yesterday morning and mommy's retrieval. I tried to tell myself that we had a good chance of having embryos because mommy had so many eggs. There was nothing more that I could do at this point; I just needed to wait for mommy's call.

I was hoping that we would have at least three embryos in case a couple of them decided that they would rather be back in heaven. I figured that the more embryos we had, the better chance of our having a baby.

Throughout this process, all the attention has been on mommy because she was taking the shots and she was producing the eggs. Today however, I was also feeling nervous because after mommy's retrieval, I had to go to the hospital as well. When parents go through IVF, mommies supply the eggs, but daddies have to go and say special prayers over the eggs in order for them to change into embryos.

Mommy had done her part. After putting her body through so much pain with the daily shots and the resulting bloating and cramping, she had produced eleven eggs. Now, it was my turn assist in the process. I felt feelings that I had not really experienced during the last several weeks. My attention had always been on mommy as I tried to support her and love her as best I could. Sometimes mommy would get sad and wish that she could just have a baby by praying rather than having to go through this process. She would question herself as a woman because she thought women were supposed to be able to have babies without all the assistance from the doctors. I always reassured her that I loved her more than any person in the whole wide world, and I thought she was absolutely perfect the way she was. She would always say that she appreciated what I was saying, but it was still "really hard."

Today was my day to experience all these thoughts. What if my prayers didn't change the eggs into embryos? What was wrong with me? Was I going to disappoint your mom?

Your mommy wants nothing more than to be a mother. I can understand this feeling because she is going to be the most loving and caring parent a child could ever have. I think God sent your mom down from Heaven with a little special ability that would make her a great mom. She has a special connection with all kids. I desperately wanted to make this dream come true for HER as well as for myself. Mommy always told me that she would love me no matter what, but it was now my turn to empathize with the words, "really hard."

I said prayers at my desk when my anxiety was getting out of control. When I received a call from mommy later in the day, I knew that she was about to give me the most important news that I had ever received. It was clear from her voice that she was not crying, and I took this to be a very good sign. She said, "We have 5 embryos!" I felt a jolt of energy course through my whole body. I was at once relieved that my prayers had worked and ecstatic that my chance of having a baby was closer to becoming a reality. Mommy was so happy, and she thought that five was a very good number.

She continued to tell me that the "implantation" was going to be on Wednesday and that I needed to tell my boss that I would not be at work. The reality of the situation had not fully set in as I hung up the phone. Having been so anxious throughout the day, I was having a hard time processing and truly accepting the news that I just heard. I thought, "So, I don't need to worry about my prayers over the eggs not working? We have embryos?" It was even harder to concentrate at work for the rest of the day because I was just so happy. I tried to not get too excited because I knew that the process was still very much not over, but it was hard not to celebrate this little victory.

There were so many hurdles that mommy and I would need to jump over before we could hold you in our arms, but we were getting there slowly but surely.

Dear Zoe || Love Dad

Dear Angel Embryos – December 9, 2009

Mommy and I woke up in a great mood. We were both excited to get to the hospital for the implantation. The good news, regarding mommy's eggs turning into embryos, had finally settled in my mind. I realized that I was already a dad because angel embryos were living beings that mommy and I created with a little help from the doctors and a lot of help from God. The more I thought about these embryos, the more amazed I became.

I began thinking about how amazing this journey had already been. The creation of the embryos was both extremely complicated and elegantly simple. Your mom produced eggs and I said my prayers and angel embryos were created just like that. I had no idea how the angels knew to come down to our hospital to become embryos. Nor could I comprehend how these tiny embryos would know how to grow all their fingers and toes while living in mommy's tummy.

I got so wrapped in thinking about the process of creating a life that I wasn't nervous during the first part of the drive to the hospital. Mommy on the other hand had started to think about the importance of today's procedure. She knew that it wasn't going to hurt at all and she knew that she had done everything she possibly could to create a comfortable home for the embryos. Still, I think she wished there was something she could do or say to guarantee that one of the embryos would decide to stay here in her tummy rather than go back to heaven. I told her that all she could do was pray and try to be as relaxed as possible. I figured that her taking care of herself would in turn take care of the embryos.

It had snowed last night, and our drive was beautiful if not completely peaceful. I tried to convince mommy that the snow fall was a very good sign. She wasn't exactly sure why I thought that, and to be honest, I didn't know either. I was just trying to put mommy in a good mood. We were pretty quiet on the drive just listening to music and thinking our own thoughts. When we heard a song on the radio from Lady Gaga, a popular music artist, I told mommy that this was another good sign. For some reason, mommy seemed to readily accept this explanation whereas she had been less than convinced about the snow fall. See, we had heard songs by Lady Gaga on the morning of the retrieval which had gone well, and mommy thought that hearing one today must be a good thing. I didn't really care whether my or mommy's logic made any sense, I was just glad that your mom had positive thoughts.

We made the very familiar walk from the parking lot to the hospital entrance. Because it was a Wednesday morning, the hospital was much fuller than it had

Dear Zoe || Love Dad

been during out last visit on Sunday morning. I hardly even noticed anyone as I made my way up the elevator to the IVF check-in.

We only waited in the reception area for a few minutes before we were taken back to the same room where mommy had had her eggs retrieved. Mommy and I once again got ready by putting on sterile gowns, booties, and hats.

The embryologists were the first people to knock on our door. We invited them in and they explained that they would be putting two embryos into mommy's tummy. The head embryologist explained that the reason we had waited three days to do the implantation was to see which embryos decided to grow the biggest. She said that some embryos looked like they really wanted to go into mommy's tummy whereas as some of the others were taking things slow and trying to decide whether they wanted to stay here or go back to heaven.

The embryologist was kind and explained what had been happening with you and your fellow embryos over the last few days. She had been monitoring your growth very closely so that she would be able to recommend which embryos were to be placed in mommy's tummy. We thanked her for taking such good care of you and the rest of our little embryos; we then told her that we agreed with her recommendation to implant the two embryos that were the biggest and healthiest. She said that she would take care of the other embryos until mommy was ready to put them in her tummy too. See, mommy and I have decided to start by implanting two embryos. We will than wait to implant the other embryos at a later date. We don't want all of the embryos getting too crammed in mommy's little tummy; it is already going to be a tight squeeze.

She walked out the door, and mommy and I smiled at each other. We were about to implant two of our little embryo children in her stomach. I had a hard time believing this was really happening. It was AMAZING.

We heard another knock on the door, and the embryologist walked back into the room. This time she was carrying a small metal box. She said, "Say hello to your babies." I will never forget this moment as it was the first time that anyone had ever said that I had a baby. It felt wonderful. Of course, I couldn't talk to you or play with you, but I still was your dad. I didn't realize that I would be overwhelmed with such a strong feeling of love. It was a kind of love that I had never experienced, and it is not easy to explain. I love your mommy and my parents very much, but my feelings toward you were different. My love was comprised of feelings of pride, hope, joy, and many other things wrapped into one. I just didn't realize that I could feel so close to you when you were so tiny that you could only be seen in a microscope. Well, parent hood really is going to be different.

Dear Zoe || Love Dad

Dr. Johnson and Janet then walked into the room and said that they were so happy that we had two babies to implant. I think they asked mommy how she was feeling, but I honestly don't remember. My eyes and thoughts were focused on the little metal box that was housing you. Dr. Johnson apologized for what had happened on the day of the HCG shot because she had been the one who told us that the retrieval was probably going to be Monday. I very much appreciated her comments, but I told her that it was not her fault and that we were just glad that everything had been going well since that appointment.

She sat down in a small stool and asked the embryologist to bring you and your sibling over to the table to her right. She took out a long wand that she was going to use to place you into mommy's tummy. I wasn't exactly sure how you were supposed to stay on this wand and not fall off, but Dr. Johnson said that she would be sure you were in the right place before we left the hospital.

Mommy was ready, and she told Dr. Johnson to go ahead and start the procedure. The embryologist opened the metal box and you hitched a ride on the special wand. You could see the concentration in Dr. Johnson's eyes as she looked at the monitor and tried to find you a nice home inside mommy's tummy. After she was pleased she had found just the right spot, she withdrew the wand. She then looked down on the wand to make sure that you had stayed in mommy's tummy. When she verified that you did, it was onto your sibling.

Once again, she took out the wand and put your sibling into mommy's tummy. When she checked to see if your sibling had stayed inside mommy's tummy, she was disappointed to find that your sibling had decided to stay on the wand. I tried to tell mommy not to worry, but I was petrified that something was wrong. You guys are so tiny that I was afraid that any misstep would hurt you. I asked Dr. Johnson, "Is the baby okay?" I didn't want to ask this question in front of mommy because I didn't want her to worry, but I just couldn't help myself.

Dr. Johnson said that this was very normal and that I should not be concerned. I had to take her word for it, but I still had a pit in my stomach. She tried again, and this time she was successful. Both of my babies were now resting in mommy's tummy.

Mommy and I waited in the room for only a short time before Dr. Johnson said that we were free to go. She said that it wasn't important for mommy to continue lying on her back. Now that you were safely in her tummy, your mom could return to her normal day to day activities. Knowing your mommy, she would have stood on her head for hours if Dr. Johnson had said that would help you guys grab onto her tummy and find a place to stay for the next 9 months.

Dear Zoe || Love Dad

Mommy got dressed, and we headed out the door. The whole procedure only took around ten minutes. They had told us that the implementation would be quick, but I still couldn't believe how quickly we were finished. It would take longer to get a hamburger at McDonald's than it took to place two babies in your mom's stomach. It was just crazy.

As we walked out, Dr. Johnson, Dr. Jones, and Dr. Magnuson were standing in the hallway talking. They all said hello and wished us good luck. I said, "Don't wish us good luck. Tell our little embryos good luck as they are the ones that now need to do all the hard work." They laughed and I think they appreciated that I was able to remain upbeat during this difficult time.

We were about to leave when Dr. Johnson said, "I just know this is going to work." Mommy and I were both shocked and pleased. We were shocked that she, a doctor, would express such a positive outlook knowing full well that the odds were against us. We also couldn't help but be pleased that she thought we were going to have success. Moments later, she said, "That was my personal not professional opinion. You are both so sweet that I really pray that you will have a baby."

Mommy and I looked at each other and smiled. Dr. Johnson was so sweet. I think that she was meant to be our doctor today because we needed someone positive. We needed to stay strong over these next two weeks when you and your sibling were deciding whether to stay here or not.

We thanked her and headed to the car.

Mommy and I were both hungry and we decided to go to one of our favorite places to eat to celebrate this momentous occasion. It was a very funny meal. We both realized that it was pretty hard to come up with conversational topics after just undergoing the most important medical procedure of either of our lives. Talking about work or mundane things such as the bills or movies just didn't seem important or interesting. WE HAD JUST IMPLANTED OUR TWO BABIES INTO MOMMY!

Mommy and I drove home and decided to take a nap. I lied in bed staring at the ceiling. I prayed again asking God and Mary to help you and your little sibling find a place to live in mommy's tummy. I then tried to talk to you.

I said, "I love you so much. Please fight your hardest to hold onto mommy's tummy and grow. Your mommy and I want to have you here with us more than you could ever know. I know that it is scary and dark inside mommy's tummy, but I know you can do it. Be strong and keep fighting. Love you, dad."

Dear Embryo Babies – December 13, 2009

Mommy and I went to see Uncle Ryder and Aunt Jo this weekend in New York City. Even though I didn't want to go, I had an amazing time. Thinking about you and how you guys are doing in mommy's tummy has been very hard on me. These past couple of days has definitely been the hardest part of the process thus far. I was used to going to the doctor every day and celebrating small "wins." When the doctor would measure mommy's follicles with the magic wand and see that they were growing, I was able to set aside my worries until the next morning. Since the implantation, there have been no reassuring doctor appointments. Mommy and I have been left alone to console and support each other. I desperately want to know what you are doing. Are you finding a comfortable place to live in mommy's tummy? Are you growing like you should be? Have you decided to stay here or go back to heaven?

I have been so tired these last few days because my mind is never at rest. I want mommy to be pregnant so, so badly. When mommy said that she wanted to go to NYC, I said that I just didn't know if I could handle this bustling city with so much on my mind. When she told me my schedule for Friday was going to be dropping her car off in a far away town, go to work, pick up her car, and then go to the train station, I wanted to go even less. I tried to tell her that I just wanted to sit at home on the couch all weekend. She said that we needed to go to New York and enjoy ourselves and try to keep our minds from worrying. Reluctantly, I agreed because she really is the boss these days.

We arrived on Friday night, and I must admit that it was nice to be in the city. Christmas was right around the corner and the city had many holiday decorations that really put me in the Christmas spirit. Of course, the only gift I want this year is for mommy to be pregnant. The store windows were filled with elaborate Christmas scenes, and I was excited to spend the weekend with Uncle Ryder and Aunt Jo.

We spent all day Saturday walking the city in the pouring snow. If mommy wanted to give our minds a break from worrying about the implantation, then she picked the right place to visit. There was at least a part of my brain that was forced into thinking about how cold I was and how hard it was walking on the slippery city streets while trying to make sure your mom didn't fall.

I hope you know that there was also a part of my brain dedicated to you. We didn't once stop thinking about how much we wanted to have you in our lives.

Dear Zoe || Love Dad

When I say that we tried to stop worrying, what I mean is that we simply tried to focus on the positive things that we could control such as making sure mommy was relaxed and eating well. We never once stopped hoping and praying for you to be in our lives.

As we walked the city, we made a special stop at the biggest church in all of New York. Mommy and I went inside and lit a candle and asked for God to help you and your little sibling latch onto mommy's tummy so that you could grow safely into a little baby. It was a really special moment standing in this magnificent church and praying with mommy for your continued development knowing that you and your little sibling were right there with us. We prayed for strength and understanding. We didn't know what God's plan for us would entail. Of course, we hoped His plan is for you to stay in mommy's tummy, but we know that God makes the ultimate decisions not us.

We also prayed for Aunt Jo's mommy who is very sick. She has a disease called cancer, and she has been fighting it for many years. Aunt Jo's mom is a very sweet lady who has remarkable strength. I prayed for you to have some of the strength that she has had as she has fought this awful disease so that she can spend more time with her family. Like her, I want the two of you to fight.

After saying our prayers, we decided to go to a basketball game in Madison Square Garden. Because your daddy works for a big company that was sponsoring the game, the four of us had front row seats. When you are older, I will take you to Madison Square Garden to see a game too if you would like.

One of the teams playing was Gonzaga which is a Catholic school. Mommy noticed that they had a priest, a man who is an expert at saying prayers, with them. As he walked on the court, mommy asked whether she should call out to him and have him come over and pray for our babies. I started laughing and said that I didn't think she should really get one of the participants to leave the court, but I definitely appreciated her thinking.

It was a great weekend, and I was glad that I went. Uncle Ryder and Aunt Jo wanted to hear all about all the things that mommy and I had been doing in order to try and have you be our baby. Their support was very comforting to us. You know that there are so many people that are excited that mommy and I are trying to have you. (Not to put any pressure on you of course☺) Love you.

Dear Embryo Babies – December 22, 2009

The last two weeks have been the hardest of my life. They have probably been really hard for you too. You came down from heaven where everything is perfect and you have a lot of angel friends to a dark tummy where you have to fight to find a nice home in mommy's tummy.

My ability to stay calm and take things one day at a time completely eroded over the last week especially as we approached the day when we would find out whether mommy is pregnant or not. New York was a nice distraction, but since returning, it is very hard not to fixate on whether you are going to be joining our family permanently or whether you are going to go back to heaven with all the other angels. You know that I will always love you no matter what you decide. I do however want you to be my child more than you could ever imagine.

Each day has gotten progressively more stressful for both mommy and I because we continue to look for signs that mommy is pregnant. The doctors and nurses said that many women don't experience any noticeable changes during the two weeks post-implantation regardless of the baby's decision to stay or go to heaven. I have honestly tried my best to believe this statement, but it is very difficult. I continue to wonder whether mommy should be feeling sick, hungry, or sore; any one of these symptoms would have given me hope that you were in fact staying in her tummy permanently.

Over the last week, my OCD has started to get the best of me. For the first time during this entire process, I just haven't been able to fight off my worrisome thoughts. Hours upon hours have been spent worrying about what could be going wrong. My weakness led to my consulting the internet for answers for the first time since mommy and I started this process (I'm not counting looking for instructions regarding whether to give mom the Follistim on the night of the HCG.). My goal was to find "credible" information stating that mommy's without any symptoms after implantation still can be pregnant. The internet has both good and bad attributes, and one of its bad attributes is that it has a lot of unreliable information. I knew that if I searched long enough I could find information to support any conclusion that I wanted. Each time I would find information confirming that many pregnant women don't experience any noticeable symptoms, I would decide that the site wasn't credible and the search would continue. I just couldn't help myself this last week as I was willing to do anything to help me maintain a positive outlook.

From day one, mommy and I have been told that there was only a 40% chance that you would decide to join our family. To be honest however, I have never really thought of this process not working. As mommy and I have continued to grow closer to each other and more importantly to God, my confidence in our being given a baby has steadily risen. There are so many other mommies and daddies that we have met going through IVF, and I bet that they too have a hard time believing that the process won't work. Staying positive was much easier in the beginning when the results of the pregnancy test were weeks away. Now that we are only a day away from the test, my confidence has been severely shaken.

The biggest reason that my confidence is not as high as it once may have been is probably due to the fact that my love for you and my desire for you to join our family grow every single day. Also, I have realized that I have what it takes to be a father.

Helping mommy throughout this process and having to overcome my fears and anxieties has convinced me that I truly am ready to be a dad to a little new born baby. Mommy was born ready, but I knew that it would take me some time. For weeks, I have tried to protect and advocate for your mommy. Whether it was administrators skipping her in line or doctors failing to give her all needed prescriptions, I did what was needed to get her the best care possible. Loving and supporting her has brought out a side of me that I didn't know I had. Now more than ever, I know that I can love, support, and advocate for you if you decide to join our family.

I also realized during the last week that going through this whole process with mommy makes it both simultaneously much easier and much more difficult. It is easier because I have my best friend, mommy, who knows what I am experiencing. We tell our friends and family what we are going through, but I don't think you can really understand all the emotional highs and lows unless you are actually going through the process. Mommy knows by looking at me whether I am having a good or bad day. On our wedding day, she and I committed to love and care for each other and never has this been more evident than during the last couple of months.

Alternatively, it is also very hard going through this process with your mom because I have to juggle my own emotions while trying to help mommy cope with hers. There have definitely been days during this last week where I have had my own fears, but I never share these with mommy. I want to show nothing but strength in front of her. With her emotions on edge from all of the shots that she is taking, I don't feel that I can lean on her right now. On the days when my fears have been high and I give into my compulsion to scour the internet for positive answers to my questions, I have to wait until she goes to bed. Normally, mommy is the rock that I lean on, but I just don't think it is fair for her to fulfill this role right now.

Finally, I have also had to force myself to think about what happens if we don't get the news we want tomorrow. I think that through prayer and faith that I will be okay, but I don't know about mommy. Thinking about how upset she would be terrifies me. I don't know if I could console her. I pray that I don't have to find out, but I am trying to prepare myself in case I do. I think it would be possible through love and hope, but I'm just not sure.

Tomorrow is the day.

Dear Embryo Babies – December, 23 2009

I woke up knowing that today would be like not other I had never experienced. If we find out that mommy is pregnant, I am sure it will be the greatest day I have ever known. If on the other hand, mommy is not pregnant and you and your sibling have gone back to heaven, then mommy and I will face a loss on scale I have never experienced.

Even though I knew I might be getting the greatest news a person could receive, I wasn't feeling very upbeat. My stomach was in knots, and I could hardly function as my mind was completely consumed with thoughts about mommy's impending test results.

The optimism that I had managed throughout this process was now gone. Mommy wasn't feeling any symptoms suggesting that she was pregnant. And even worse, she was starting to feel as if she was producing new eggs, a sure sign that she was not pregnant. I told mommy that she needed to think positive. I even admitted to my use of the internet which had clearly claimed that many women don't have any symptoms. I desperately wanted to make mommy feel better. I didn't even believe the words I was saying as most of the information I found online suggested that mommy would be feeling at least something!

We got in the car and drove to the doctor for our 8:15 appointment. Mommy and I didn't talk much as we both sat silently wrapped up in our own thoughts and emotions. With each minute, my hope dwindled more and more. I wasn't really prepared for the way I was feeling. There had been such a precipitous drop in my level of confidence over the last couple of days. Today, even the drive felt so different. The snow wasn't as white and the sky was less blue and magnificent. If I were feeling so low, I couldn't imagine what mommy was going through. She has always been much more emotional than I.

We made the familiar walk to the hospital in the cold crisp air which felt less refreshing and more bitter this morning. Mommy had her blood drawn by the nurse and then we headed back to the office to speak with Dr. Palmer. I was glad to see him as he was someone with whom I had always had a lot of confidence. He asked how we were feeling, and I told him that we were just a little anxious. I wasn't going to tell him how upset I really was because I was still trying to be strong for mommy.

Dear Zoe || Love Dad

The conversation that followed only served to heighten my fears. For the first time in this process, he spoke to us about what we would do if mommy wasn't pregnant. As you know, I always knew this was a possibility, but hearing a doctor say it out loud was awful. There was no hiding from the issue. There was no more fooling myself that our odds were somehow better than everyone else's. My mood continued to drop as he spoke. I thought to myself that if I could hardly handle his *talking* about the possibility of mommy not being pregnant, what was I going to do if we got the call this morning saying that mommy *actually wasn't* pregnant? He continued to discuss the plan, but I didn't really pay attention. I couldn't; I was in my own world. We thanked him for all of his help and wished him a merry Christmas.

Mommy and I walked back to our car, and I decided that I could no longer pretend that everything was okay. I needed mommy's support. We had gone through this process together and there was no one else living who could understand what I was feeling except for her. When she said, "I don't think I'm pregnant," I said for the first time, "I don't think you are either."

She looked surprised as I had always refuted these negative thoughts. I decided that the best thing now was to be honest with mommy and tell her that I didn't think she was pregnant either. If we were to receive this bad news, we both needed to be prepared. I couldn't hide from these emotions, and I couldn't handle them on my own. I needed mommy to help me cope as I had always tried to help her.

I told mommy that I loved her more than anyone in the whole world and that I was so proud of her for going through this process. I said that I have never wanted anything as badly as a little baby with her because I know that she is going to be a wonderful mother. I then told her that we WOULD have a baby whether it was this time, after another IVF attempt, or through adoption.

I think mommy felt closer to me knowing that I was struggling with emotions just as she was. She knew that she was not alone in fearing the results today. Hopefully, knowing that I was 100% committed to having a child with her provided a momentary respite from the sadness we were feeling.

We decided that we would go to a fancy hotel and treat ourselves to a nice breakfast. Neither of us wanted to go home and just wait. Maybe a breakfast buffet could provide temporary relief from our negative and anxious thoughts. We were definitely wrong. I love breakfast, and I can honestly say that it was the worst breakfast of my life. The food was amazing, the view out the windows was gorgeous, and the service was outstanding, but nothing was going to be able to elevate my mood this morning except for a positive test result.

Mommy and I decided that we would both call our moms and tell them that we were fairly positive that mommy was not pregnant. Mommy's mom told her that it everything was going to be okay, but your mom said you could hear the sadness in her mother's voice. She wants a grandbaby almost as bad as mommy and I want a baby. My mom told me to stay positive because she still believed that mommy was pregnant. I wasn't surprised by this reaction as my mom doesn't have a pessimistic bone in her body. She is a woman of extreme faith, and I know that she believes that all her prayers for you and your sibling's implantation will be answered.

There were many kids running around the restaurant, and there smiles and laughs were the only thing that could bring me moments of joy. I can't really describe the sadness I was feeling as it was a completely new emotion. It was almost a feeling of no emotion. My ability to feel hope had been momentarily stripped away as I sat there eating food which had seemingly lost all taste.

I sat there thinking about our journey, and I couldn't imagine going through everything again. I thought about writing another check for $8,500, going to appointment after appointment, giving mommy shots every day, etc...

We paid our bill and drove home. I walked around the house feeling extremely uncomfortable in my own skin. Watching TV was too passive. Doing work was too involved. I knew that we were within hours of finally finding out once and for all.

I went up stairs and went to the bathroom. I was only in there for a few minutes when I heard the phone ring. At first, I assumed it was your mommy's mom just calling to check in on her. It didn't take long however for me to realize that it was not mommy's mom as mommy's tone was much more formal than it would have been if it were her own mother.

I will never forget what I heard next. Mommy started yelling, "Are you serious? Are you serious? Are you sure? Shut up, are you kidding? Ryan, I'm pregnant. I'm pregnant." She was crying as she ran up the stairs screaming, "I'm pregnant."

I was sitting down when I first heard mommy screaming that she was pregnant. My breath was literally taken away. I think I skipped a breath as all my brain could do was process this news. I was in such a state of shock that I couldn't move. Within moments, I raised my hands to my face and closed my eyes. I said a prayer to God thanking him for the greatest gift I had ever received.

She opened the door and tears were streaming down her face as she hugged me. She continued, "I can't believe it. I'm pregnant. I'm %$@# pregnant." She was so happy that she started swearing. I have never seen someone in such a state of joy. It was truly indescribable. She was crying and screaming, "I'm pregnant" even though she was still on the phone with the doctor's office. I kissed her and told her that I loved her very much.

She was still on the phone, and I told her to make sure that she asks what we did next. Finally, she calmed down long enough to get the instructions about when the doctor would want to see us again. Mommy left the room, but I couldn't get up just yet. I continued sitting in a state of blissful shock for minutes.

Both my body and mind were exhausted from the three months of stress. Every day, I had prayed and hoped for this. I had been to all of mommy's appointments, I had given her the necessary shots, I had argued with nurses and doctors on her behalf, etc... My whole life had been consumed with this process. Finally hearing the news I had desperately wanted had just overwhelmed me. How does one react when he receives the thing you want most, I thought to myself.

I finally made my way downstairs to hug mommy who was also dealing with her own emotions. She was crying and repeating, "I'm pregnant." I know that I will never forget those fifteen minutes starting with the phone call to our sitting on the couch with each other just quietly celebrating. For a brief moment, everything in our life was perfect. For someone like me who suffers from OCD and anxiety, it was such a tremendous feeling to not have any fears or worries. I was simply in the moment. I was on the couch with my wife who I loved with all my heart and you, my beautiful baby, were right there with us.

Your mommy was ready to call our parents as they had been nervously awaiting an update. I asked her whether she could wait just a little longer. I was so content and thankful that I didn't want anything to disturb the peace I was feeling. She agreed, and the three of us sat there on the couch as happy as could be.

It wasn't long before we needed to call our moms to let them know the good news. I told mommy that I didn't want to play any jokes or make them wait. We called mommy's mom first. As soon as she said hello, mommy yelled, "I'm pregnant." It was great being able to share good news as mommy's mom immediately started crying with happiness. Her reaction was not too unlike your mom's as she too was quickly overcome with emotion.

Next, we called my mom. I told her that mommy was pregnant as soon as she answered. Her reaction was very different than mommy's mom. My mom said calmly, "I knew that she was. I have been praying for this." By the time you are able to read this, you will probably have learned that your grandmother's religious convictions are so strong that she doesn't experience fear or anxiety like most people. She always thinks that God will take care of her and answer her prayers. She has a faith like no one I have ever known. We talked for a few minutes, and it was clear that she was thrilled with the news even if she was expecting it.

It was pretty hard to wipe the smile off of my face for the rest of the day. Mommy and I were actually flying to North Carolina that night for the Christmas holiday. I had just received the greatest Christmas gift of my life, and it came two days early. Knowing I was having a little baby even outranked the blue roller skates with red wheels which had formerly seemed destined to hold the top spot for life☺ I was excited to see my parents and brothers and sisters in person so that we could celebrate as a family.

Mommy and I called our friends Jim and Kelly to tell them the good news as well. They had been such great friends to us throughout this process. Without family in town, they had been our emotional support every step along the way. They were so happy to hear the good news, and they asked if they could stop by the house as they headed back home to Michigan for the holidays. Mommy told them that it would be great as long as they made it before we needed to leave for the airport.

When I learned they would be coming over, I first thought to myself that they are such good friends that they probably wanted to give us a present. They are both so nice that it wouldn't have surprised me if they took time out of their last day in town to make a special stop at a gift shop. As I thought more about it however, I began wondering whether there was some other reason they wanted to stop by the house.

They knocked on the door and we all hugged in celebration of your successful implantation. We talked for only a few short minutes before they said that they wanted to show us something. Kelly then reached into her pocket and pulled out a sonogram picture, which is a picture of a little baby inside a mommy's tummy. Kelly was pregnant too! We all hugged again as there was now even more reason to celebrate. They explained that they had known for a couple of weeks but that they didn't want to say anything until we found out whether your mom

Dear Zoe || Love Dad

was pregnant. They are so thoughtful and considerate. As they left, I was filled with happiness as there is nothing more exciting than the news that someone is going to have a baby.

Mommy and I packed the rest of our things and headed to the airport. When we arrived to my parent's house, I hugged my mom and yelled it's a Christmas miracle. I was saying it in a joking manner congruent with my personality, but deep down, I meant it. God had given mommy and me the greatest gift, and it was a miracle that you were able to find your way from the little metal box to a safe spot in mommy's tummy.

It was time to talk to you. Even though you don't have ears, I think you can hear me. "My little baby, thank you so, so much for your willingness to come down from heaven and be my child. I already love you with all my heart. It is going to be so hard to wait for you to grown and mature in mommy's tummy because I want to meet you now. You just need to continue to fight and grow, grow, grow so that you are big and healthy. Love you, daddy."

Dear Zoe || Love Dad

Pregnancy

Dear Zoe || Love Dad

Dear Baby, December 28

Mommy and I made it back home after our Christmas trip to North Carolina to see my family. Everyone was so happy to learn the good news that mommy was pregnant. Christmas felt totally different to me this year as I knew that there was nothing under the tree that could even remotely compare to the gift I had just received. It seems like every minute of the day, I think about you in mommy's tummy. I pray that you continue to fight to hang on in there and find a nice home for the next nine months.

Even though it has been five days since I found out that mommy was pregnant with you, the pure joy and happiness has not worn off one bit. My life has changed so much already; I can't even imagine what it will be like when you are in my arms.

Mommy went to the doctor today to get her blood work completed. The results came back, and mommy has an HCG count of 1614 which the nurse said is right where it needs to be. From talking with some other people who have gone through this process, mommy and I think that this HCG level means that there is only one baby instead of two. We still hope for two, but we knew all along that this was not the most likely outcome. If one of the babies decided to stay in heaven, mommy and I will be sad, but we understand. The little angel will look after you from heaven. Before mommy and I started this journey, I could never have imagined how much I already love you. You may still be microscopic, but you are my baby and I am your daddy. I will always be there for you, and I know your mommy feels the same way.

I think you might have already started taking some of mommy's nutrients as she has told me that she has been feeling tired these last few days. Unfortunately, she is also having some headaches as her body prepares to nurture you for the next nine months. Normally, having headaches and feeling tired would be very much unwelcomed, but your mommy is in great spirits as she would do anything for you. She desperately wants to be a mother, and a few headaches are certainly not going to detract from the unadulterated joy she is feeling.

I love you and keep growing, okay!

Dear Baby, December – 31

Today was a really big day for your mommy and me. We went to the doctor for our first appointment since learning that the implantation had worked and that you were in her tummy. We would also be finding out today whether mommy was going to be having one or two babies.

Dear Zoe || Love Dad

I woke up this morning feeling very nervous. Learning that mommy was pregnant was the greatest news that I had ever-received, and I was so happy to be a father. Over the last few days, I started to worry however that something might happen and you might decide to go back to heaven with your brothers and sisters. When mommy and I first started this process, the doctor told us that even if mommy got pregnant there was a chance that she could have something called a miscarriage. A miscarriage is a big word to describe when a baby goes back up to heaven to be with God. Even though the chances of mommy having a miscarriage were low, the thought of her not being pregnant scared me to death.

When Dr. Magnuson walked through the door, we were happy to share the good news with her. She already knew of course, but it was nice to tell her and thank her in person for all that she had done to help us get to this point. She took the time to congratulate us before she started the exam. Mommy hopped up onto the table and Dr. Magnuson once again pulled out the magic wand which would allow all of us to hopefully see you.

Dr. Magnuson moved the wand back and forth, and my heart was racing. I don't ever remember a time when I had been this nervous. This appointment was turning out to be the hardest one yet. Having never been a dad before, I didn't know what I was supposed to be seeing. All kinds of negative thoughts flooded my mind as it seemed to me that Dr. Magnuson was having a hard time locating the baby with the wand. I looked at Dr. Magnuson face to see whether she was having a negative reaction, but her face was like a mask – unchanged. I had grown so accustomed to seeing the big follicles which each doctor found with ease that my nerves grew more frayed with each passing second. It seemed like forever when Dr. Magnuson' voice cut through my panic. She said, "Do you see that little light? That is the sack that holds the baby." YES, you were okay.

I could only see one sack, and Dr. Magnuson had not mentioned anything about another sack for the other baby. I was thrilled at the sight of the first sack, and I knew that it was a long shot that we would be having twins, but I still held out some hope. Dr. Magnuson said that there was only one sack which meant that the other baby had gone back to heaven. My emotions had gone from fear when I thought she couldn't find you to euphoria at the sight of the sack to sadness at the knowledge that one baby had gone to heaven.

I wasn't sure how to feel as we walked back to our cars through the cold, brisk wind. The odds were against us even having one baby, and I was so thankful that mommy was pregnant. But, there was still a feeling of considerable sadness and loss that we wouldn't be having twins. I know that God has a plan for all of us, and I know that He has done what is best. It might be a while but I am sure that I will meet this baby in Heaven some day.

This entry shouldn't end on a sad note because your mommy and I still feel amazingly blessed. And, you bring more joy to our lives than you could possibly imagine – especially since you don't yet have a fully formed brain☺ Your mommy is already a great mom as she is devouring all kinds of literature on what she should be doing with regards to pre-natal care. She was disappointed to learn that she should not be having cold cuts as we often go to a local restaurant that has the best turkey grinders we have ever had. Part of being a parent is making sacrifices; there will be a day when both mommy and I need to make sacrifices. For these next few months however, mommy will be the one with the greater burden. We both love you and we continue to pray for you every night.

Dear Baby – January, 7

At our last appointment, Dr. Magnuson told mommy and me that we could come back in one week or two weeks. She said that she hoped to be able to see the heartbeat on the monitor at the next appointment, and she wasn't positive you would be old enough after only one more week. The goal of the next appointment was to see your tiny heart beating on the monitor. Mommy and I weren't sure what to do. Let me explain.

Mommy and I have been nervous throughout the whole IVF process. At first, we were concerned about whether we were giving the shots correctly. Then, we worried that the follicles wouldn't produce enough eggs. Next, we were apprehensive about whether the eggs would fertilize. Finally, we had to undergo the longest two weeks of our lives as we waited to see whether you were going to be able to find a nice home in mommy's tummy. For some reason, I had though that I would be more relaxed once I learned that mommy was pregnant. Truthfully, I have been just the opposite.

The big change is that I went from being a *hopeful* parent to an *actual* parent, and I already worry about you, my little baby. When I think about the journey you are undertaking – growing from just a few cells in a hospital lab to a full grown baby inside mommy – I can't help but worry. You are undergoing such a complex transition that it just amazes me. I try to tell myself that everything is okay and I pray to God for comfort. After all, it is He who created this beautifully complex process.

Ultimately, we decided that we would come back in a week even if we knew we might not be able to see the heartbeat. The hardest part of the process thus far has simply been not knowing what was going on with you from day to day.

Dear Zoe || Love Dad

Mommy and I used to go to the doctor every single day, and we would leave knowing whether everything was progressing properly or not. Even if I was worried that something was wrong, I would be able to ask the doctor in less than 24 hours. In some bizarre way, your mom and I had been spoiled by the IVF process where constant updates were the norm. Now, mommy and I have to wait a week or two. I just wasn't ready to wait a full two weeks yet.

Dr. Magnuson reminded us when she first walked in the door that we should not panic if we didn't see the heartbeat just yet because you are right on the cusp of when your heart beat should be visible. Even though Dr. Magnuson gave us this warning, I knew that I would be an absolute basket case if we failed to see your heart beat. Dr. Magnuson had already explained that seeing your heart beat would be a very, very good sign. She told us that baby's who develop a heartbeat have an excellent chance of making it to a live birth.

Dr. Magnuson took out the magic wand and started looking for the sack inside of mommy's belly. It wasn't long before I could see a little sack, and it had a small flashing light inside of it. It was your heart beat! You had grown a heart that was beating away. I was relieved and amazed at the same time. You were so small and yet you had a working heart. Mommy and I had been to all the major museums of Italy, but I don't think that I had ever seen something as beautiful as the flickering white dot on the monitor. Dr. Magnuson then said that she was going to try and listen to the heart beat. She said that it was unlikely because you were so small, but moments later we heard a whooshing sound that was pulsating very quickly. She had done it; she had captured your audible heart beat with the computer.

Your heart beat was 128 beats per minute which was right where it was supposed to be. Dr. Magnuson informed us that everything looked great, and I felt as if the weight of the world was lifted off of my shoulders.

Nothing in my life had ever been as terrifying as the few seconds before Dr. Magnuson started to use the magic wand to look for your heart beat. I knew that I was moments away from learning whether my greatest love, you, was okay or not. For a few brief moments after seeing the flickering light on the screen, life seemed so perfect. All the fears and worries experienced over the last week were gone in an instant. See how happy you already make me.

The nurse came into the room and told us that you were due on August 29, 2010. It sure does seem like a long time to wait to see you, but I am sure I can make it. Now, you keep growing, and I am proud of you for growing such a strong heart.

Dear Baby – Morning of January, 14

Dear Zoe || Love Dad

Today, we should be having our final appointment with Dr. Magnuson before we are "released" to another ob/gyn. You might think that I would be less nervous before this appointment after seeing your heartbeat last week, but it is not the case. I don't know whether our having to go through the IVF process has made me more nervous than other parents or whether my OCD is the cause, but each appointment brings with it extreme anxiety. I still pray every day for your well being, and I am usually able to think positively. On the days of our appointments however, my nerves get real bad. I guess when you love someone so much, you always worry about them even if there isn't a great reason. Maybe you will read this when you get older, and it will help you understand why your mother and I have certain rules that you may think are overprotective. We have been dealing with the "good" stress of being a parent even before you came down from heaven.

Dear Baby – Evening of January, 14

The appointment went great, and you continue to do everything that you need to do. It was amazing how much you have grown in just seven days. You look to be at least twice as big as your were last week. We listened to your heart beat again, and it is just the sweetest sound a parent could hear. At 158 beats per minute (about the same rate as your dad's right before our appointments☺), your little heart is working very hard which we learned is typical of babies your age.

We had to say good bye to Dr. Magnuson because she needed to help other couples bring down babies from heaven via IVF. You are doing so well that we no longer need the assistance of a fertility specialist. Dr. Magnuson will always hold a special place in my heart as the doctor who had the greatest role in helping us have you. From performing mommy's surgery to encouraging us to consider IVF as a first option, her confidence, compassion and skill were on display. I hope she knows how important her job is; I actually can't think of anything that would be more important.

Dr. Magnuson asked us whether we knew which ob/gyn we wanted to see at the other office. I looked at her and said, "I trust you, and I want you to tell me the absolute best ob/gyn available." She looked at me and kind of smiled because she has learned that I typically expect the best care and that I am also willing to ask for it directly. She then said, "They are all very good." Before she could continue, I said, "I know that you need to say that since you work with them, but I want the best doctor for my wife and baby. I don't need a good doctor, I need the best doctor. The doctor that you would go to if you were in our shoes." I felt that she really cared for your mommy and me; the three of us had really been a team in making the decisions up to this point. I was confident that she would

Dear Zoe || Love Dad

eventually give me her recommendation. She said, "I think you should see Dr. Crosby who is the chief of the department. I will make you the appointment."

We said our goodbyes. I guess you, me, and mommy are just normal patients now. It is going to be weird going to another office because I have grown so comfortable at the current location. Even with all the trials and tribulations we had faced at this office, it still had been the place where mommy got pregnant. It was therefore very special to me. It will also be very different being amongst other families who didn't go through IVF. In the IVF waiting room there was definitely a sort of camaraderie. You might not have always talked to each other, but there was nonetheless an implicit if unstated bond. Everyone in the waiting room wanted desperately to have a baby and we all shared the same hopes and fears. Today, I will pray for all these families that they too can experience the happiness that your mother and I have felt since learning that she was pregnant.

You keep fighting. Love, dad

Dear Zoe – January 18, 2010

Today is a big day for your mom. At approximately 7:30 p.m., I gave your mommy her last shot of progesterone. Even though she would take these shots for the rest of her life let alone pregnancy if it would make you healthier, she must be relieved that this nightly ritual has ended. I know that I am relieved, and I was the one injecting not getting injected. With each shot, your mommy's hips have grown more sore and tender. I alternate hips and look for virgin skin with each injection, but she is simply running out of room. Her hips are bruised and swollen. The needle needed for this medicine is also so wide that you can see little scabs where the skin was healing from an injection. I had begun to lose my nerve. Knowing that each shot got more painful for your mom made giving each shot more painful for me. Your mom sure is tough.

The bond between your mom and I has never been stronger. I don't know whether my giving her shots has played any role in this, but having a nightly ritual together has been nice. If the giving of shots had played a role, then I bet mommy would recommend she give rather than receive the shots in the future.

Dear Zoe – January, 28

We met mommy's new doctor today, and I am glad to report that you are in good hands. Not only was Dr. Crosby very intelligent, he was also equally caring and compassionate. I am very happy that I demanded a clear recommendation from Dr. Magnuson after having such a positive experience at our appointment today. In speaking with Dr. Crosby, we told him that we would like for him to be mommy's doctor throughout her pregnancy rather than switching from doctor to doctor with each appointment. (Some parents like to meet all the doctors so that they will have met the doctor who ultimately delivers the baby, but we were told that the delivery of the baby is the easy part.) We made this decision because mommy and I think that you will get better care if you have one doctor who charts your progress from start to finish. After going through IVF, I don't want to have the same experience as we did during the egg retrieval where I was educating the doctor. I may be bright, but even I recognize that I'm not a doctor.

We spent the first half of our appointment with Dr. Crosby asking him general questions. He answered them all confidently and with a touch of humor, something I can easily appreciate. He did bring up one thing that I hesitate to tell you because it is something more appropriate for mommies and daddies rather than babies or kids. I guess I will write it down but ask you to skip this part if you are reading this before you reach high school.

(Dr. Crosby spent a lot of time talking with us about genetic testing. I wasn't exactly sure why he was offering this service at first because you were already alive in mommy's tummy. I had heard of parents getting these tests prior to praying for a baby to make sure that they could have a healthy baby, but wasn't it a little late? As he continued to discuss this option, I realized why he was asking. All you need to know is my answer. "We have no need for any testing unless it could uncover something that we could help treat in the womb. We would NEVER do anything to hurt our baby." I already love you so much that all I can think about is helping you live as full and complete a life as possible. Living a full life means different things for different babies, but I have to have faith that God will always help your mommy and I provide the best life possible for you.)

With the question and answer portion of the appointment over, it was time for the fun part, seeing you. It has been awhile since your mommy and I had seen you, and I was very excited to lay my eyes on you again. Dr. Crosby took out his version of Dr. Magnuson' magic wand and laid it against mommy's tummy. As always, my heart momentarily stopped as I nervously awaited a sign that you were doing okay. Hopefully this nervous feeling before each appointment will subside as mommy's pregnancy progresses, but knowing me, it won't. Dr. Crosby moved his special wand across mommy's belly until you appeared on the monitor. I couldn't believe it; YOU WERE A BABY! Of course you were a baby, but now, you actually looked like a baby. Whereas before I could only imagine your little head, legs, and arms, now I could actually see them. Granted, you are still really, really small and you don't look like a mini version of mom or I, but you look like a baby, a very little non-fully formed baby at least. Your heart was firing away, and I can't help but think that it must be tiring for you inside mommy's tummy with your racing heart and incredible growth.

Intellectually, I knew that you would be growing arms and legs. I even knew what the ultrasound images might look like at various ages. But, the actual experience of seeing you, my child, go through these stages of development was a completely new and mind blowing experience. In my high school biology class, I learned how human life is created and how babies grow. We were supposed to be amazed by the miracle of life, but to be honest, I just processed this information the same way that I processed the material from my other classes. I memorized the various stages, and regurgitated the material back on my exams. Now that I am actually seeing my own child go through this process, "miraculous" almost seems like an understatement. I have no idea how you know that it is time to take some of mommy's food and energy and make yourself a leg or an arm. You must be really brilliant because I know that I couldn't all of sudden decide to make a new limb.

I am just amazed by you. You are so tiny, but yet you have a little heart that beats faster than mine. You don't have a fully formed brain, but yet you can complete tasks such as growing a functioning arm – something MIT bio-engineering grad students haven't mastered. I guess my high school teachers were right; the creation of life really is a miracle.

Dear Baby – February, 18

Mommy has gained two pounds since our last appointment which means that you should continue to feel free taking some of her food☺ She is eating enough for both of you. I am too, but unfortunately we can't share our meals until you are out of mommy's tummy.

Everything is going very well according to Dr. Crosby. I have even noticed that some of my IVF-related anxiety, that I had thought might never go away, has started to diminish. Hopefully this trend will continue and I can free up the 10% of my brain that has been dedicated to worrying about IVF and you for the last several months. (Of course, I will always worry about you because you are my child, but I am talking about the irrational/ non-productive worrying. It's hard to really feel joy and happiness when you are so worried; I want to get my fears under control so that I can allow myself to really experience the beauty of becoming a dad.) Each time I have the chance to hear your little heart beat, I allow myself to get a little more optimistic.

Unfortunately, we didn't have an ultrasound today which meant that I couldn't see you. It turns out that most of our appointments moving forward will only require a special machine that allows us to hear your heart beat. We will however have at least one more appointment where I can see you; at this appointment, I even get to find out whether you are a little boy or little girl. Just so you know, it doesn't matter to me one bit.

Dear Baby – March, 1

I was very excited today because you and your mommy were returning from a trip to Texas to see your grandparents. (I hope you enjoyed not having to take your shoes off or unpack your bag at airport security because this might be your last chance☺ Don't worry, I will explain this to you are older if the policy changes and you no longer understand what I meant by that statement.) Your first airplane ride was not the most exciting thing that happened today however. Mommy said that for the very first time, she was able to feel you kicking. I am so jealous. Now, there are not many things that have taken place since we started this process (surgery, shots, egg-retrieval, etc…) that have made me jealous, but having this special bond with you is one. To be clear, I am jealous of the BOND with you, not the actual carrying of you. If I am being perfectly honest, I must admit that the whole living inside of mommy's tummy sounds a little gross to me. You seem to like it however which is all that really matters.

It was great to see mommy again; I always miss her when she is gone. You must be getting bigger because mommy has definitely developed a little baby bump. She has even had to start wearing special clothes that expand at the waist. I think she looks beautiful of course, and I am sure you will think the same once you get a view from the outside rather than the inside.

Keep kicking away because it helps me know that you are alive and doing well. Mommy just loves the feeling too. Have a nice night.

Dear Baby – March, 18

Once again, I am jealous of your mom. She not only gets to feel you kicking, but today she also got to SEE you for a whole ten minutes. You might be wondering how I missed seeing you since I go to all of your appointments. Well, here is the story of what happened. It is actually pretty funny.

Your mom had something called kidney stones when she was in college; she describes the experience as being exceptionally painful. She told me that the pain she experienced with her last kidney stone was like nothing she had ever experienced. Last week, your mom started having some discomfort in her back. Her first thought was that she must have a kidney stone as she often fears the worst. She immediately instituted her anti-kidney stone regimen which basically boils down to drinking as much water as possible. I have no idea whether this "regimen" works or not, but I see no need to question it or tell her otherwise. She always panics when she thinks she is getting sick. Now that she is pregnant, she is even more concerned. She therefore wasted no time in scheduling an appointment with her doctor.

She called the office and spoke with the receptionist who told her that she would need to get an ultrasound prior to her appointment. As your mom told me the whole story, she said that she needed to get a rectal ultrasound. Now, I was very shocked that the doctor wanted a rectal ultrasound as "rectal" refers to your bottom not your kidneys. When I quizzed mommy, she said that she wasn't sure either, but she was willing to do whatever it took to make sure that you and she were okay. In my mind, I quickly thought of a possible explanation, but I wasn't ready to share with mommy just yet.

Days went by, and I said nothing to mommy about her impending rectal ultrasound. Surprisingly, she wasn't the least bit worried. Finally, I couldn't take it anymore. One thing you will learn as you get older is that your mother is not exactly the most detail-oriented person. When you throw in her ADD, many times facts get distorted when she is recanting a story. I asked your mother what type of ultrasound she needed again. "Rectal," she replied. I said do you think that maybe you misinterpreted what the receptionist said. "No, I'm pretty sure she said rectal."

I asked, "Do you think that it makes much sense that the doctor would be doing a rectal exam for a possible kidney stone?"

"I don't know. But, I just want to make sure that everything is okay with the baby."

Finally I said, "Do you think that the receptionist might have said 'renal' rather than 'rectal.'?" She looked at me and quickly replied, "Yeah, that is what she said. "Do you know what renal refers to?" I asked.

"No."

I had waited long enough. I said, "'Renal' is the adjective you use to describe the kidneys. You need a 'renal' not 'rectal' exam."

We both laughed as mommy is quite capable of laughing at herself.

Now that you know the story, I can tell you about her appointment. Your mom met with the technician who was going to be performing the ultrasound. The tech scanned her kidneys quickly, and it was clear that there were no stones to be found. The tech, who had noticed that mommy was pregnant, then asked mommy whether she would like to see her baby. Your mom jumped at the chance, and she was able to see you for ten whole minutes as the tech had taken a liking to her. Your mom is so nice and friendly that it seems that wherever we go, she gets treated extra special. Her smiling face, affable demeanor, and Southern accent all contribute to her being loved by pretty much anyone she meets. She seems to get exceptional treatment on a regular basis. I bet people will be extra nice to you as well because I am sure you will be sweet like your momma.

Your mom said that you were moving all over the place during the ultrasound. Unlike before, you were now moving your whole body, not just your feet. If I would have known that I would have gotten a chance to see you, I would have gone to mommy's appointment with her. She is so lucky.

Dear Baby Girl – April, 5

Today was another big day. I had been looking forward to this appointment since I last had a chance to see you. At today's appointment, we were going to find out whether you are a little boy or a little girl.

My mom and dad, your grandparents, have been in town helping us celebrate Easter and your mommy's birthday. It just so happened that this seminal ultrasound appointment coincided with their trip. Both my mom and my dad are excited to meet you, and they both feel very privileged that mommy and I asked them to come to the appointment today. I wouldn't have had it any other way as I know that they will both play a very big role in your life.

The morning started out great as you woke mommy up with some strong kicks. I had to go to work prior to your appointment, but I must confess that you rather than work were on my mind all morning. Time passed so slowly as I waited to leave for the hospital. Eleven a.m. couldn't arrive fast enough.

We went to the hospital where we had gone through all of our IVF appointments. The walk from the car sure felt different today. I was more excited than scared. We went back to the room where the ultrasound would be performed and mommy hopped up on the table and exposed her belly which is becoming more rotund by the day. Your grandmother was right there next to the table as she didn't want to miss anything, but your granddad maintained his distance. I don't think he knew exactly what he should be doing.

Dear Zoe || Love Dad

A young female doctor entered the room and introduced herself as Dr. Thomas. She said that she was going to be taking all the pictures of you. There were many different "shots" that she needed to get, and we should expect for the appointment to last about 45 minutes. I was thrilled to learn that I was going to be able to look at you for 45 minutes as our previous ultra sounds only last 2 or 3 minutes. Considering this might be the last ultra sound of mommy's whole pregnancy, I told Dr. Thomas that she should feel free to take her time.

She squirted some gel on mommy's tummy and then began. You had grown a lot since I last saw you. As she moved the magic wand, it was very easy to see your arms, head, legs, and bottom. No longer did I need to use my imagination to create these appendages as they were very much developed; I was even able to see the various bones that make up your limbs. Dr. Thomas asked whether we would like to know whether you were a boy or girl, and mommy and I both yelled, "Yes" in unison. She said that she would tell us once the appointment had finished. I tried my best to figure out your sex as you flashed on the screen. (For the record, I thought you were a boy throughout the exam.)

Dr. Thomas was very thorough as she took her time to make sure that she was getting all the images that she needed. There was another doctor, Dr. Stein, who would be looking at all the images in order to determine whether you were developing properly. He needed to see images of your brain, your heart, your kidneys, your lungs, and all your appendages. Dr. Thomas was having a difficult time getting just the right shot of your heart as you were facing away from mommy's tummy. At one point, she said, "your little baby just isn't cooperating." Being your number one fan, I took umbrage with this comment and said, "Well, it isn't exactly like she knows what you are trying to do." Your mom laughed as she realized how protective of you I would be.

Dr. Thomas continued to try and get the shot of your heart that she needed. She asked your mom to roll onto her side. Then she started to push down on mommy's belly. To me it looked like she was pushing fairly hard, and I said, "don't hurt the baby!" She assured me that you were very much protected by mommy's tummy and the amniotic fluid contained within. Your mom started laughing again because she had never seen me so protective of anything or anyone. You continued to face towards mommy's spine, and Dr. Thomas said that she would show Dr. Stein the pictures that she already took hoping they would in fact suffice. She wasn't confident that she was going to get any better ones.

Before Dr. Thomas left the room, she asked whether we were ready to find out your sex. Anxiously, we said, "Absolutely." She looked at us and said, "You are having a little girl."

I was so excited. I didn't have a preference before these words left her mouth, but once she said you were a girl, I felt that I wouldn't have wanted it any other way. I was going to have a little girl. My mind almost immediately wandered to hair bows, little cute patent leather shoes and a closet full of pink clothes. (See, I have two little sisters which is why I know little patent leather shoes.) I am definitely going to spoil you.

Dr. Thomas excused herself from the room and said that Dr. Stein would be coming to speak with us. Dr. Thomas had been clear from the beginning that she was not allowed to tell us whether everything looked "normal or good" due to her status an intern. I had tried to read her facial expressions (as you know I like to do) throughout the scan, and I hadn't seen any harbingers of bad news.

My excitement over seeing you and learning your sex had tempered the stress I usually feel during one of your appointments. As we waited for Dr. Stein, my thoughts slowly transitioned from patent leather shoes to questions about your health and development. Each minute without a knock on the door fed my fears. Dr. Thomas sure had been concerned with getting better shots? Did she see something? What was taking Dr. Stein so long? Did he see something abnormal? Maybe he had to see another patient? No, Dr. Thomas would have told us if he needed to see another patient.

There was nothing I could do but wait.

Finally, the knock on the door arrived. An older man wearing Bose headphones around his neck walked into the room. His face gave away nothing as it was utterly expressionless. He introduced himself as Dr. Stein. With a very flat affect, he said everything looked okay, but he needed us to come back so that he could check out a few more shots of your heart and your head. WHAT! Panic engulfed me.

What did he mean when he said he needed more images of your head and heart? Were things okay or not? The head and the heart are the two most important parts of a little baby. I tried to remain calm as I asked, "Why do you need more pictures of or head and heart? Is there something that is causing your concern? Is there something wrong with my baby?" He looked back at me with the same blank expression, and said, "I need more pictures because I couldn't see what I needed to see."

The floodgates in my mind immediately opened unleashing a torrent of questions. What did he mean? Was he not wanting to alarm me before he was positive there was a problem or was he simply a poor communicator? Was he

Dear Zoe || Love Dad

looking for four chambers in your heart and he could only see three? Could he not see what he needed because it wasn't there or because the pictures were not clear?

I asked him specifically whether there was an issue with the images due to your position or whether there was an issue with your anatomy. His expression never changed as he said that he needed more pictures. What was wrong with this guy, I thought to myself. Could he not sense my distress? He said, "Everything looks okay."

In my high state of arousal, "okay" was not going to do. I was used to hearing Dr. Magnuson or Dr. Palmer saying that everything was fantastic or perfect. What the heck did "okay" mean? All of a sudden, my mom, sensing my frustration, inserted herself into the conversation. She started to explain to me what Dr. Stein meant by his use of the word "okay." Without hesitation, I told her that I was having a conversation with Dr. Stein, and I needed him to tell me what he meant rather than have her interpret. The tension in the room rose as I was not only nervous about you, but now, I had just stood up to my mom in a way that I had never previously.

Finally, Dr. Stein explained that everything with your anatomy looked "okay" meaning good or normal. We needed to come back because mommy's spine was casting a shadow over your heart which made it difficult to see what he needed. Furthermore, he explained that he did not have any concerns at this point.

Whoa! I was exhausted from the emotional roller coaster I had just taken. I calmed down and told my mom that I did not mean to be rude, but I needed to hear from the doctor directly. I'm a dad now, and it is my job to insure your well-being. She said she understood, but I couldn't help but wonder how the exchange would change our relationship. I felt more like a dad than a son for the first time in my life. My quick retort may very well turn out to be a seminal moment in my life; the moment I gained a new-found confidence in myself.

Let me explain.

When I was little, probably five or six years older than you are now, I used to wonder what my mom or dad would do when they go scared. See, I would go to their room at night if I had a bad dream, and they made me feel safe. It amazed me how the simple sight of them could make me feel better. No longer due I sneak into my parents' room for comfort, but they still serve this protective role for me. Whether I have problems at work, trouble with my neighbors, or medical concerns, each issue seems a little less severe after a call home.

Dear Zoe || Love Dad

This safety net has been great and I will be forever grateful for their love and support. That being said, their support had made me question how strong I could be on my own. I want to know that I can take care of you and your mom by myself. Even when I was a kid, I used to wonder what my parents did when they got scared. Who would they go to? At the doctor today, I realized that I am ready to be your safety net. Something has happened to me over the last few months. God just gives special powers to parents I guess.

We went to the receptionist and scheduled another appointment. Although I would have loved to have gotten all the pictures we needed and left without any doubts as to your development, I was excited that I would be seeing you again in two weeks.

Next week, will you please show us your heart and your head. I don't know if my heart and head can handle another appointment like todays☺

Dear Baby Girl – April, 14

Today was yet another milestone. I have heard your hear beat and seen your image, but only your mom has been able to actually *feel* you. That was until tonight. We were having another mundane evening of watching TV when your mom grabbed my hand and placed it on her stomach. Moments later, I felt a little movement tickle my palm. It was you; I felt you kick. Wow, what an amazingly weird feeling.

Every step of this process impacts me in unexpected ways. It is hard to explain, but feeling you in mommy's tummy made you seem more real to me. I knew this was going to be hard to explain, and I find my last sentence clumsy at best. Of course, you have been real to me since we received the call saying that the eggs had fertilized. What I am trying to say is that there is something really unique about the tactile experience of feeling *you* kick in *my* wife's stomach.

By looking in books or scanning the web, it was not difficult to find images of babies in utero or sound files of beating hearts. Seeing your images and hearing your heart beat was a totally different experience of course, but I had an idea of what to expect. Also, there was a certain distance created by having to view you on a monitor or hear you through speakers. There was still a distance between us in these experiences as high-tech machinery still played a necessary role.

Tonight, the experience of feeling you was so special. It was just very different than these previous interactions with you. First, there were no doctors or nurses

Dear Zoe || Love Dad

with whom I was sharing the moment. Rather, it was just the three of us, me and my two girls, sitting in our home. Second, the lack of machinery erased the barrier between the two of us. Finally, it was the first time that I interacted with you when I wasn't filled with fear. Usually, I hear or see you as a part of a "check-up." I never expected to have this moment with you and your mom tonight; my mind was free. It was a surprise, an amazing surprise.

I spent the rest of the night with a big grin on my face as I could feel your presence in the room like never before. It really felt like the three of us were sitting there watching TV together as a little, nuclear family.

Dear Baby Girl – April, 19

Today was round two of your "long ultrasound" where the doctors were to make sure that you were developing properly. After our first attempt where Dr. Stein had just about caused me to have an aneurysm, I was a little less excited than your mother. Your mom woke up this morning thrilled that she was going to be able to see you again. I too was excited to see you, but my main thought processes were reserved for worrying about your head and your heart.

Oddly enough, your mom had her family in town this weekend. Maybe God wanted to make sure that both grandmothers had a chance to see you. There were actually four generations of women in the room during the ultrasound. There was you, your mom, her mom, and her mom. You are definitely lucky to have this many generations alive and well. As we waited for the tech, it was amazing to me that your grandmother and great grandmother had never even seen this type of ultra sound as the medical field has progressed so much since they were having their children. Hearing this made me especially happy that they were going to be able to share this moment with us.

A different tech walked into the room, and I was disappointed that we weren't going to be seeing Dr. Thomas again who I had liked even though I felt she pushed down on you too much. She turned on the machine, and it was immediately apparent that you had decided to look back at mommy's spine once again. She moved the wand over mommy's tummy, but she was struggling to get the pictures she needed. Your mom rolled onto her side to see whether this would cause you to move, but you were perfectly content in your current position and remained still. The tech started to press down hard on mommy's tummy trying to cause you to move, and she succeeded, kind of. As she pushed down, I saw your little, tiny hand push back as if to say, "Leave me alone." Normally, I would have started laughing, but I was concerned again that the tech was pushing too hard. I said, "Obviously, she doesn't want you pushing so hard. You should stop."

Dear Zoe || Love Dad

Everyone in the room seemed a little shocked as your mother and her family was much less assertive than I. The tech said that it wasn't hurting the baby which made me feel a small sense of relief, but I was still frustrated. I said, "It might not be hurting her, but she is clearly annoyed. Maybe we will just have to come back again."

The tech stopped pushing so hard and asked your mom to roll back the other way. I thanked her and said that she could try other methods to cajole you into moving, but pressing against you was not something that seemed to be working. The tech continued to move the wand for about five more minutes before giving up. You were just not interested in moving; I think you might have been taking a nap. Knowing how much your mother hates being woken up, I shouldn't have been surprised by your lack of willingness to get up and move.

The tech said that she would show the pictures to Dr. Stein to see whether she had gotten the necessary pictures. She said she was very confident and neither was I.

As we waited for Dr. Stein to enter the room, my anxiety was much lower than last time knowing that there was most likely a problem *with the* photographs not *what was in the* photographs. The tech had been right. When Dr. Stein returned, he said that he still needed more shots of the heart but that he was able to see everything he needed with regards to your head.

Overall, today was a good appointment. We came wondering about your head and your heart and left only wondering about your heart. Don't get me wrong, your heart is very important, but with so much stress, I am going to allow myself to celebrate this good news for at least a day.

I guess we also learned that you don't like people disturbing you when you are resting.

Dear Baby Girl – May, 3

I woke up hoping that a third time really would be a charm. Although I love seeing you on the ultrasounds, I really wanted to go to bed tonight knowing that your heart was healthy. Given our struggles during the last two appointments, your mom has been looking on the internet for information regarding ways to make you move (in case we can't get the pictures we need). She found one method which we thought she should try. Basically, she planned on drinking a really cold drink if you were not in a position where you heart could be easily photographed. Apparently, drinking something cold would make you move because your home, mommy's womb, is located near her stomach. When the cold liquid would start to fill her belly, you would naturally want to move away from it. (I know that cold water is an effective way to wake someone up after having experienced it directly from your grandmother one morning when I was particularly slow getting ready for school. The experience was unpleasant enough that I still remember that morning after more than 25 years.)

With drink in hand, your mommy jumped up on the table. We had yet another different ultrasound tech. She was very sweet, and it was clear from before she even started that she was confident she would be getting all the necessary pictures. Her confidence was comforting as I was ready for success. The wand moved across mommy's stomach revealing you and more importantly your heart. The technician quickly took many pictures knowing that this moment might not last forever. The whole procedure only took about two minutes as you were in a perfect position. She sent the pictures off to be read by one of Dr. Stein's partners as Dr. Stein had the day off.

The tech left the room, and it was only mommy and I in the room (no family in town this time). We were both very happy that we finally got the pictures we needed, and we nervously awaited a positive report from the doctor. It was amazing how much bigger you had gotten over the last four weeks. The technician focused on your heart because she was trying to be efficient as possible, but your profile and limbs were by far the most developed that I had ever seen. Your mom and I spent some time talking about how beautiful you were and how much we wanted to meet you in person. My positive attitude was challenged however as the doctor failed to knock on the door in a very timely manner. At our previous appointments, Dr. Stein usually came knocking within two or three minutes. When I looked down at my watch, it had been around five minutes and there was still no doctor.

With fear having entered my OCD-inflicted mind, there was little hope that I could ward off negative thoughts. I've learned through this process that as soon as I have one fearful thought or anxious moment that it is very difficult if not impossible for me to snap out of it without a clear reason. Minutes passed and I could do nothing but worry. Why was he taking so long? He must have seen something that he didn't like because there was nothing wrong with the pictures this time? Did you need to have surgery? The questions wouldn't stop. I was worried about your heart even as mine was racing and about to explode out of my chest. Five minutes turned into ten minutes, and I was exhausted mentally and physically.

Finally, the door opened revealing a doctor that we had never seen at any of our past appointments. He walked toward me and introduced himself, but I don't even remember his name as exchanging pleasantries was not at the top of my priority list. He then said, "Everything looks great. I was able to see all four chambers of the heart beating as they should. I have zero concerns."

I was so happy that I could have hugged him if I weren't still frustrated that he made us wait for such good news.

I am very proud of you. Thank you for growing such a perfect, little heart and for your willingness to finally show it to us☺

Dear Baby Girl – May, 4

I am going to tell you this story, and you are going to have to eventually tell me whether it is true or not. By the time you are able to read this, you will know that your mom will sometimes exaggerate or "enhance" her stories. I think that what I am about to tell you might be one of these instances. On the other hand, I might just be jealous that I had to work while she was staying at home enjoying spending time with you. Here is a quick version of what happened.

I was at my desk when your mom called and said, "I just saw the baby kick."

I said, "What do you mean? How do you see a baby kick? Don't you mean you *felt* the baby kick?"

"No, I saw her. I felt her kicking, and it was the strongest that I had ever felt. It was so strong that I looked down at my stomach, and I could actually SEE her kicking."

I decided that I would let her to continue to believe that she saw you kicking, but between me and you, I have my doubts. It would take a pretty strong leg to move mommy's taught skin out of place. How big could your muscles even be at this point? You spent all day suspended in amniotic fluid just floating and relaxing.

I was excited to come home tonight because I was hoping that I too would be able to see you kicking if this really was possible. After we had dinner, your mom told me to feel her stomach because you were kicking again. Sure enough, I could feel either your little feet or your little hands. (I always talk about you kicking, but for all I know you might have been punching. For some reason, society always talks about babies kicking rather than kicking and punching. If you have been punching all this time, I apologize☺) I then started to stare at your mom's stomach to see whether I could see these movements as well. Could

Dear Zoe || Love Dad

I? No, there was no way. Each time you kicked however, your mom would say, "Did you see that?" and I would say, "No."

Only you really know the truth, but thank you for making your mom so happy tonight. With all the stress that she has been under throughout this process, I was thrilled to see the excitement on her face as she *saw* you kicking.

Dear Baby Girl – June, 10

We didn't have a doctor's appointment today, but I did want to give you an update. See, I just wanted to let you know that I, the world's biggest worrier, have actually been doing pretty well since your last ultrasound. I didn't want you to think that I was always in a panic☺

The IVF process really had an impact on me and how I have viewed the whole pregnancy. When your mom and I first learned that we would probably need help from not only God but also doctors, I hadn't realized the emotional stress that would accompany this pregnancy. No longer did I view having a baby as a simple process where you just pray for a little child and voila, nine months later you had a baby in your arms.

I didn't realize how strong you were going to have to be. There were so many challenges you had to overcome if you wanted to stay here on earth and be our baby. Each day seemed to bring on a new obstacle. You went from being only 6 cells when you were first placed in mommy's tummy to the 4 pound baby you are now. At each step, the odds were against you (40% chance of a successful implantation, 20% chance of miscarriage, etc…) and I have often let fear and anxiety get the best of me. With so many doubts swirling in my head, I haven't done a very good job of enjoying the more mundane yet fun side of this pregnancy such as figuring out what we should name you or how we should decorate your room.

I'm finally at a point that I think I can do this. Seeing you so well developed in your last ultrasound really calmed me down. You are doing great, and I think I should be confident that you will continue to do well. It has been with this mindset that I have been living for the last week, and I can tell you that it has been very, very nice. My obsessive thoughts are not completely gone, but they are a lot more palatable. My major obsessions this last week have been focused on things such as which stroller to buy or what color to paint your room.

Coming down from heaven to stay in mommy's tummy has probably been a pretty big adjustment. I assume that you have been pretty pre-occupied with the whole growing of essential organs, but if you were worried about what your new life would be like, I am happy to give you an update. Well, I can at least update you on all the material possessions you will be getting.

Your mom bought a book called "Baby Bargains" which basically lists every product you could ever need for your new child. Along with the items, there are short write ups that rate the products. My new favorite activity is to look through the book marking all the large items (stroller, crib, changing table, bouncer, etc…) that you will need. Of course, you will only be getting items with an "A" rating because I want you to have only the best and more importantly safest products. I am starting to drive your mom crazy as I have extended my research from the book to the internet as well. I think if I ask her to look at another product review that she just might stop talking to me.

Fortunately for her, I think we know what we are getting you with regards to your bedroom furniture, your rocker, your bouncers, and your high chair. We did have one argument over your mattress which I think highlights the difference between the two of us and our future parenting styles. Even before the mattress, we did have one other disagreement regarding your bedding which involved bumpers. After some effort, I was able to convince your mom that even though the pink, furry bumpers that she bought for your crib looked nice that they needed to be taken out of the crib as soon as you came home. See, experts recommend only "breathable" bumpers to prevent babies from suffocating. I knew she would eventually come around because she would never let anything happen to you. [There is no way that I can explain "breathing or suffocation" to you given the fact that you don't currently have lungs or access to air. You will have to trust me. Writing this paragraph has made me realize what an enormous change you are going to undergo when you leave your mom's tummy. Right now, there isn't even a way for me to explain what it means to see, breathe, hear, taste, etc… Having a baby really is amazing.]

Our next disagreement was not so cut and dry. Basically, there is something called SIDS that causes babies to die. No one can really explain what happens to the baby, but all of a sudden the baby just stops breathing. Although there is no clear explanation as to the cause, there are a few things that might help prevent it including, placing babies on their back, having a fan in the room, and buying a very firm mattress. We agreed on the first two conditions, but we had different ideas about the third. We went to the store, and I selected the Baby Bargains' top-rated mattress for preventing SIDS. I showed it to mommy, and she said it was way too firm. It was hard to disagree with her because even all 225 pounds of me could hardly cause it to depress when I sat down on it. I tried to hold my ground by saying that Baby Bargains had recommended it, but she wasn't budging. We decided to ask the woman who not only owned the store but who had also been in business for about forty years to help provide some clarity. She said that the mattress your mother picked out was just as safe even if it was a little less firm. Not being one to back down easily, I said, "I will have my baby sleep on a slab of marble if that is what it takes to make her safe." As the words came out of my mouth, I knew that you would not be getting the mattress that I picked out. I had just proven that I was going to be a little crazy with regards to your safety, and I should probably trust your mother to provide more rational answers.

Your mom and I are already falling into our respective parenting roles. She will probably show her love by making sure that you are happy and comfortable. Although these things are important to me as well, my love for you will be shown by protecting you and making you safe. Hopefully, we will balance each other out and you will be the most loved and protected baby the world has ever known. You are too young to complain now, but I can only imagine the disagreements you and I are going to have when you are in high school.

With the mattress situation resolved, the only outstanding item, which your mother has graciously given me complete autonomy over, is your stroller. I think she felt bad that I lost the mattress argument. Well, I am here to let you know that you shouldn't worry because you will be riding in style. Weeks of research has led to my decision to get you an UPPABaby Vista stroller in bright red. This stroller is amazing as it can accommodate you when you are a little baby fresh from the hospital until you are a big girl going to kindergarten. I would go through all the features, but rather than tell you, I should probably just let you experience the smooth ride generated by this aircraft quality aluminum built carriage with the solid foam and rubber wheels. Okay, I am a little obsessed, but I want you to have the best. There is one feature that I think you will definitely like. The seat can be changed so that you either face forward or backward. For you, this should be a true win/ win as you can either look forward and explore the world or look back and stare at your beautiful daddy☺

Dear Baby Girl – June, 17

Your mom stepped on the scale at the doctor's office today, and she had gained 30 pounds since we first learned she was pregnant. Dr. Crosby thought that she might gain another ten before you joined us. I was worried at first that your mom might be concerned about gaining so much weight so quickly as most women aren't necessarily thrilled with the changes to their bodies, but I was pleasantly surprised by her attitude. Rather than look at each pound as being one that would need to be lost once you were here, she has seen each pound as being beneficial to you.

Dear Zoe || Love Dad

Dr. Crosby said that everything was going perfectly which means that I have a surprise for you. You are going to Hawaii tomorrow! I didn't want to tell you until I knew for sure that you would be able to go, but with a clean bill of health, the three of us are off to Maui for a wedding. Normally, there would have been no way that I would have agreed to go so far away for a wedding, but this was going to be a fairly unique wedding.

Here is the situation. When your mom and I got married, my sister, Alyssa took a liking to mommy's brother, Tait. After two years of dating, they decided that they wanted to get married too. If you are having a hard time following, don't worry; this is a very odd situation. What this means for you is that when Alyssa and Tait have kids they will be double cousins, meaning that you will share the exact same set of grandparents. Because your mom and I are related to both the bride and the groom, we wanted to make every effort possible to attend.

I asked Dr. Crosby over and over again whether he was sure that it would be safe for both you and your mom to fly all the way from PA to Hawaii, and he said not to worry. My dad however wasn't so sure about this whole thing. If you think I worry a lot, wait until you meet your grandpa. He was so nervous in fact that he made my mom, your grandma, go to the medical supply store and create a special carry-on bag with things such as gauze and alcohol wipes in case you decided you wanted to be born thousands of feet above the ground. He also asked her to read up on how to deliver babies. I wish I could tell you that I was joking, but I am not. Now, do you understand why I wanted you to get the rock hard mattress?

Dr. Crosby only gave your mom two basic instructions which were to drink lots of water and to get up every forty five minutes to walk around. He then followed up this statement by saying that she probably didn't need to use a watch because she would be going to the bathroom that much anyways. I think he is definitely correct because your mom needs to use the restroom all the time these days. As you have gotten bigger, mommy's tummy has definitely expanded, but her insides are still getting crowded. Right now, you will sometimes push up directly against her bladder which makes her run to the bathroom; a sight I think I will always find very funny.

With the final approval, we went home and finished packing. With your grandma in charge of the early delivery kit, we were free to pack our carry-on with plenty of snacks. When you are travelling with a very pregnant woman, you definitely need to have snacks and I managed to fit week's worth of snacks into our bag.

Dear Zoe || Love Dad

Dear Baby Girl – June, 26

We made it back from Hawaii, and I am very pleased that you are still safely inside mommy's ever-expanding tummy. There was no need for the early delivery kit. The only thing of note about the flight was when your mom thought I might have gone a little overboard in talking with a stewardess.

When we first got on the plane headed for Hawaii, I told the stewardess that your mom would be getting up every 45 minutes to which she said, "that will be fine as long as the fasten seat belt sign is off." At which point, I said, "Like I said, she WILL be getting up every forty five minutes. I don't care whether the fasten seat belt sign is on or off. She needs to do this for both her and the baby's safety." I don't know what has come over me, but my protective instincts are in full effect these days. Your mom gave me a stern look, but the stewardess quickly retreated from her earlier position.

Once we arrived, Hawaii was beautiful and relaxing. Every day that we were there, your mom and I would talk about how we can't wait to take you to Hawaii someday. We want to take you to the pool and teach you how to swim. We want to take you to a luau and show you the pretty dances. We want to pick flowers and put them in your hair. I could go on and on, but I hope you realize that you were always on our mind.

I was very happy to see your mom relaxing with her friends and family. Sometimes it has been hard going through the IVF and pregnancy process without having our families close by. For your mom, it has been especially challenging at times because she is so close to her family. Our relative isolation hasn't been all bad however. We have been forced to really rely on each other and we have gotten closer with each step along the way. In Hawaii, your mom had the best of both worlds, a supportive husband and a wonderful family.

Your mom looked beautiful and confident in her maternity swimwear. Whenever I would go to the pool, she would be surrounded by several people as if she were holding court. I think she loved the attention, and I have a feeling you will be just like her. I always picture you in my mind as being a little version of your mom – blond hair and light eyes. I think of you as having the same outgoing, bubbly personality as well. I guess I will find out soon enough, but being a little mini-version of your mom would definitely not be a bad thing as she is an amazing woman.

Even though your mom is looking beautiful, the changes to her body are starting to challenge her physically. Each night in Hawaii, she complained about pains in her back and hips. Her back has continued to ache as the muscles compensate for the new found weight in her stomach. Her hips remain sore as they have been forced to widen to accommodate your growing body. On one particular night in Hawaii, your mom kept asking you to move to another side of her tummy as you were "all balled up." I looked at her and said, "I'm sorry that you hips and back hurt, but you need to make more room for my little baby. She probably doesn't want to be all balled up; she just doesn't have any room."

Luckily, your mom started laughing as she found my serious response amusing. What I said was ridiculous as if your mom could magically grow her stomach and hips so that you would have more room. I was just picturing you all contorted in her tummy. If anyone should be complaining it was you.

I guess I should be honest with you. Your mom was not the only one complaining in Hawaii. Many nights your mom's complaints are met by my whining, "I don't want to rub your back; I'm watching T.V." Given all that your mom has been through over the last year, I really should be more agreeable to the few requests she has had during this pregnancy.

Dear Baby Girl – July, 8

It is hard to believe that you are going to be in my arms in about 7 weeks. It was only a year ago when your mom and I were praying for you to come down from heaven and join us as we toured through Italy. Those days seem like a very long time ago rather than a just a year as it is hard to imagine my life before we started asking God for you. The last year has been by far the best of my life because it was filled with so much emotion and love. Sure, it was stressful having to always be concerned about you, but I would go through it and much, much more to be able to have the feelings of love I have for you and your mom. I just can't even imagine what it will be like when you are finally in my arms. It is such an exciting time for me not knowing how my life will change.

I do have one exciting update for you. Remember how I told you that people just seem to be nice to your mom? I was telling you about how your mom got to see you when she went for her renal ultra sound. Well, something very similar happened again this weekend. Here is what happened.

Our friends, Kelly and Jim, had found a place called "Womb with a View" where you could pay $100 to get a three-dimensional ultra sound of your baby. Even though I don't always have the most respect for the medical community, there was no way that I was letting someone without medical training give mommy an ultrasound in a store located within a strip mall. Yes, I wanted to see you, but I was smart enough to know that putting myself in that position might have caused me to have a panic attack. What if I saw something that I thought

Dear Zoe || Love Dad

looked odd? There would be no one to answer my questions. Your mom agreed that getting this ultrasound was probably not the best idea. I don't know whether she shared my same concerns or whether she just knew that I couldn't handle it and would therefore drive her crazy. I never really asked her.

Anyways, your mom learned that Kelly and Jim were going to in fact get an ultra sound of their daughter. She decided that she would just accompany Kelly and Jim to their ultra sound because she wanted to see Kelly's baby. I stayed home as I thought the whole thing was a little weird. I couldn't decide what I thought was more odd, the strip mall ultra sound or the viewing of another couple's ultra sound.

Two hours later, your mom stormed into the house and yelled, "Look at our baby! She is so beautiful." It took me a second to comprehend what was going on as it was Kelly's baby who was supposed to be photographed, not you. It turned out that Kelly's baby was in an awkward position for pictures when they first started the scan. The tech told Kelly to go and drink something cold and that they would then start over again in fifteen minutes with the hope that her baby had moved. The technician then looked at your mom and said, "While we are waiting, would you like to see your baby." "Of course," your mom answered.

Your mom pulled out the two pictures that she received from the technician and they were shocking. The machine they were using was much more sophisticated than the one at the hospital which as I think about it is a little disturbing. Anyways, the image was three dimensional and I could clearly see your eyes, nose, mouth, and limbs. It was astonishing how clear the image was. I just kept staring at you.

I continued looking at the image and asking your mom what certain things were. There is a tube called the placenta which connects you to your mom while you are in her tummy. This tube is really remarkable because it enables you to get all your food and oxygen from mommy. In the photograph, this tube was in front of your face slightly which obstructed the view of your face to some degree, but I could see your features as never before. You are so beautiful. I wish I was a better writer so that I could describe what it was like seeing you so vividly, but I am only capable of telling you that it was amazing.

Fortunately, I did not see anything that caused me any concern. My initial fears of having questions without a doctor to answer them turned out to be invalid, at least in this case. The only real question I had was about your nose. See both your mom and I have "great" noses in my opinion. They are both on the average to small size with no bumps or curves. When I looked at the picture of you more closely, it seemed that your nose was very large and wide. Previously, the concerns I had during your ultra sounds revolved around important things such as the development of your heart and brain; I guess I really have grown more optimistic during the last month. Here I was worrying about your nose, and my worries were cosmetic. I felt bad even asking, but I did inquire whether this was normal. Your mom started laughing because Jim had said the same thing about their baby. I am happy to report that the answer was "yes, this is normal." In these particular images, the nose often appeared large and flat due to it pushing up against something.

Don't worry; I will love you more than you will ever know regardless of what you look like. I actually do mean it when I say I will love you more than you can imagine. I have never loved someone as much as I love you. Having you has allowed me to love more deeply than I knew possible.

Dear Baby Girl – July 22

Your mom and I had another one of our birthing preparation classes tonight. Because we are going to be first-time parents, we thought that we should take classes to make sure that we knew what to do when it was finally time for you to come out of mommy's stomach. We have already taken classes on pain management, feeding, and CPR. Even though I wasn't always thrilled to have to go to a 3 hour class after spending all day at work, there is nothing that I wouldn't do for you and your mom. I want to be the best husband and dad possible which meant that I needed to arm myself with certain knowledge. Your mom is such a natural with kids that she probably didn't even need to attend the classes, but I was glad that she came with me. She was just born with all the right parental instincts.

Our first class was about pain management. You don't really need to know the specifics, but getting you out of your mom's stomach might be a little painful for mommy, not you. Now, mommy is tough, but she is also not foolish. Even before the class, she was confident that she wanted something called an epidural which is a pretty amazing treatment. A doctor will put a small tube next to her spine which shoots out medicine so that she can just relax and enjoy the whole birthing process. The class was taught by two very nice men who only solidified your mom's belief that an epidural was the way to go. I found the class very interesting; actually, I might have found it too interesting as your mom started to get annoyed by how many questions I was asking. In my defense, I wanted to make sure that I knew all the potential risks because I don't want anything happening to my two girls! I love you guys way too much.

Dear Zoe || Love Dad

Our next class was about feeding. I thought I understood this process, but in reality, I was completely clueless. It seemed pretty easy to me, mommies make milk and babies latch on and eat. Turns out, it is not so simple. The first thing I learned is that not all babies know what to do when they are first born. Eating outside of the womb requires new skills such as latching and sucking which are very different than just relaxing in mommy's tummy getting foods through the umbilical cord.

Let me back up for a minute as I realized that you probably don't know that your mom will continue to produce all your food even after you are outside of her stomach. You will learn that your mom has many amazing talents; one of these talents is the ability to make food for you when you are first born. Moms really are special people, but by the time you read this, you will already know that. I learned way too many things to tell you now, but I will point out two things that very much surprised me. Moms are so smart that they are able to produce different food depending on when you are born. If you for example decide to come early, mommy will make a special type of milk specifically formulated for premature babies. This milk will have all the nutrients that you need at this stage of development. Don't ask me how this happens because I don't know, but God really did a great job when He designed your mom. I learned one other thing that you will be glad to hear. Apparently, you are going to want to eat every couple of hours. I was shocked because I only eat three times a day, and I weigh over 200 pounds. I figured little babies might eat even less given how little they are. Fortunately for you, you want have to go hungry now that I took the feeding class. It turns out that you will need to eat about ten times a day.

Even with my lack of knowledge about some basic parenting skills, I still know that I am ready to be a dad because I just love you so much. I don't want you to think that I am completely unprepared because I know the important things such as your baby's needs come before your own and your baby needs to be loved and cherished. These classes are just helping me increase my knowledge so that I will be that much better. At one point, I whispered to your mom, "Did you already know all this stuff?" She said, "Yes, and that is why I am in charge." I couldn't agree more. When it comes to parenting, I think that your mom is going to have to tell me what to do on a lot of different occasions. I sure am glad that I married such an amazing woman.

The next class was very scary, but it was also extremely important. I told your mom that the one class that I definitely wanted to attend was called baby CPR. This class taught parents what to do in case their baby stopped breathing. I don't even like writing those words as it scares me too bad.

Dear Zoe || Love Dad

The instructor had little dolls not unlike the dolls that I am sure I will be buying you in the near future. These dolls helped us practice so that we would be ready in case we found ourselves in an emergency. I learned that if a baby ever stops breathing that I would need to blow into her mouth and press on her chest. We even got to practice so that we learned exactly what we would need to do. At first, the teacher said that I wasn't pushing down hard enough on the baby doll's chest. Babies are so small, of course I wasn't going to be pressing hard. I tried again. Still, she said that I needed to press down harder. It pained me to think about pressing down so hard, but I learned that it was necessary to perform CPR correctly. I prayed during class several times that neither I nor any of the other parents in the class would ever have to use this life-saving skill. Nothing could be worse than seeing your baby not breathing.

We also learned what to do if you were choking. Your mom and I don't have to worry about choking for at least a little while as you will be drinking milk for your first few months. (Actually, I don't know when you will start eating solid foods, but I bet your mom does. Don't worry you have at least one parent who knows what she is doing.) This part of the class terrified me too. The teacher said that all kids will choke at some point. When I heard this, I told your mom that I don't think that I ever want you eating solid foods then. You might have to go through life eating everything through a bottle if I don't learn how to keep my anxiety in check☺ Thankfully, you have a mother to maintain sanity in your life.

Our new class was a three part series specifically about the birthing process. I complained to your mom that I didn't really need to attend. It was exhausting spending all day at work only to head to the hospital for three hours of training with a group of strangers. We were going to be in the hospital for the birth, and I figured I could ask all my questions during the many hours of labor. At one point I even told your mom, "I am so tired from taking all these classes that I'm not sure I am going to be able to help out when Zoe arrives." I was kidding of course. I can't wait to take care of you morning, noon, night or even middle of the night☺

Everyone always described being at your child's birth as being beautiful. Based on some of the things I heard at the birthing class, beautiful is not a word that I would have chosen. The nurse passed around all different types of tools that could be used including forceps, a foli bulb, and a heart monitor that would screw into a baby's head. At one point, I felt that I had gone back to medieval times. Even your mom who is usually fairly fearless had a look of terror at points; her bulging eyes fixated on the instruments which were making their way around the room.

Dear Zoe || Love Dad

At one point during the class, your mom and I were supposed to go over breathing exercises and massages. I just couldn't take this part seriously. After seeing what I had just seen, I wasn't convinced that rhythmic breathing was going to do the trick. I thought that if the foli bulb was going to be used that the epidural should definitely be in place. I tried to keep my thoughts to myself as there was no use in causing your mom any more worry. When it was time to practice these breathing techniques, I just couldn't do it. I scanned the room looking at all the other future fathers gently massaging their wives backs, and I couldn't help but laugh. (Please don't read this and think that it is okay to not pay attention in class or to laugh at classmates. Your dad certainly didn't set a very good example for you on this particular night.) There was no way that rhythmic breathing and gentle massage were going to do the trick. God made doctors who made epidurals for a reason. Thankfully, your mom was having similar thoughts and she was therefore not upset by my immature behavior.

We were moving into our third hour of class when your mom started complaining about a headache. She often gets really bad headaches called migraines, but she said that this headache felt different. I wasn't very nervous; I was thinking that your mom was a pregnant woman who happened to have a headache. I wasn't thinking that the headache was being caused by her pregnant state. Nonetheless, I told her that we should call a nurse. As you know by now, calling the nurse after hours is not my favorite thing to do as we get transferred to a nurse about a thousand miles away. Regardless, I wasn't comfortable not calling; I would deal with the inconvenience to ensure your and mom's safety. We made the call and then waited in the lobby while our class was finishing up. We waited and waited. Finally after over an hour had passed, I called the number again only to find out that they were calling one of our "old" numbers. See, I had bought your mom a new phone for Christmas, and the on-call nurse was still using a number that she had from our IVF days. Was this really happening again, I thought to myself? How could such a great hospital and medical staff be associated with such a poor, inefficient on-call system?

Once I got a hold of someone, I firmly and rudely (I should not have been rude, and I don't want you to be rude when you are older. I was just so, so frustrated.) told the woman who answered the phone that I needed to speak with a nurse, NOW! What added to my frustration was that I was literally sitting in the Hershey Hospital parking lot while we were waiting to hear back from the on-call nurse in Alabama. Once again, why was this system implemented?

I told the woman that I would stay on hold until your mom could speak with a nurse. Your mom then took the phone from me and told the nurse her various symptoms. I listened intently trying to figure out what the nurse was saying, but it wasn't clear. Finally, your mom put down the phone and told me that the nurse said it was probably nothing. She did however request that your mommy call her doctor the following day.

NICU

Dear Zoe || Love Dad

Dear Baby Girl – July, 23-26

I went to work the next day and encouraged mommy to call the doctor to make sure that everything was fine. I needed to make sure that your mom was taking proper care of both her and you. The doctor said that he wanted your mom to go to the hospital. I was at work when I heard this news, and I immediately went to my desk picked up my keys and headed out the door. You still weren't due for another five weeks, and I was a little surprised that they wanted mommy to go to the hospital rather than his office. I figured that she just needed to get some tests, but I didn't want mommy to have to go through this process alone. We were a team and we will always be a team – even if mommy says that she is the captain and I am the mascot.

I raced home so that I could accompany your mom to the hospital. When I got home, mommy was very calm which made me feel much better. I might have become too relaxed because I decided that since I was home that I might as well go to the bathroom, get a drink, and eat a granola bar. Finally, mommy looked at me and said, "Remember we are supposed to be going to the hospital." With my mind clouded from the news that I had just heard, I had managed to forget the reason that I had come home in the first place. I needed to take mommy to the hospital. Mommy told me to go upstairs to get her bag because it was too heavy for her to carry. I grabbed her bag and went downstairs. Once downstairs, I grabbed my backpack and we finally headed to the Labor and Delivery Department.

The three of us stayed at the hospital all day long. Mommy got to relax in a nice bed whereas your dad only got a little chair. It was a weird day as we waited and waited not sure what was really happening. Your mom continued to not only have a headache but she had also become unusually hot. She had made me turn the air conditioner on full blast, and I sat in my little chair freezing hour after hour.

Because mommy still wasn't feeling 100%, the doctors said that they thought it would be best if she stayed in the hospital overnight. They wanted to make sure that mommy didn't have something called preeclampsia, a condition that could have been dangerous to mommy and you. Your mom and I decided that she should stay in the hospital to make sure that you were okay. When she found out she was staying, she asked me to get her some things from her bag. I went to look for it, and I realized that I had forgotten to bring it. I must have just placed it by the door when I retrieved it from upstairs. Mommy was really annoyed because I had not forgotten my backpack, but I did forget hers. She said, "I'm the one having the baby, and you forgot my bag." I couldn't stop laughing because I knew that I had made a mistake. I assured her that she would have her

Dear Zoe || Love Dad

bag, and I left to go pick it up. I was just looking for an excuse to get out of that freezing room.

We had learned a lot about preeclampsia during the last week because our friend, Kelly, was already in the hospital with this condition. Oh I forgot, Kelly is your friend Ava's mom. Remember when I wrote to you that our friends Brook and Jim were having a baby? Well, they decided to name her Ava. I bet the two of you are going to be best friends. Each week, the four of us would go out to dinner and talk about how excited we are were to welcome the new editions to our family. We used to even go shopping together at Babies R Us to pick out all the things that the two of you would need.

Anyways, Kelly had been in the hospital for the last seven days with preeclampsia. She had to lie in bed all day and all night. The doctors wanted her to rest so that Ava would be okay. When mommy went to the hospital, I was thinking that they would probably tell mommy that she needed to take it easy at home; I didn't think she would need to stay in the hospital such as Kelly.

Because there wasn't a bed for me to sleep in, I went back to our house and slept while mommy spent the night at the hospital. I called mommy in the morning, and she said that she thought she would be coming home soon. I was very happy to get this great news, and I told her that I was just getting dressed and that I would be picking her up soon.

I got ready and headed out the door about five minutes later. I had just turned out of our development when your mommy called. She said, "Where are you?" I told her that I was on my way. She then said, "You need to turn back; I have preeclampsia and they are inducing me tonight." Shocked, I said, "What? Were having the baby tonight? We aren't supposed to have the baby for over a month. I don't think she is ready."

Mommy had to explain the situation all over again. I heard the words she was saying, but I was struggling to comprehend. My heart started pounding in my chest. You weren't supposed to be here for another 5 weeks. I was anxious to meet you, but I was nervous about your and mommy's health. Had you had enough time to develop? Was mommy's preeclampsia going to make your birth dangerous?

I went to the house to gather all the things mommy had said she needed. She must have suspected that you might want to come early because she had just packed her "hospital bag" a few days prior. Mommies just have a sense of intuition that daddies don't.

Dear Zoe || Love Dad

Heading out the door, I saw one more thing that maybe I should get, the car seat. Mommy had told me to bring everything she could remember, but she had forgotten one of the most important things. Maybe your mommy really was going to need my help. I felt very happy knowing that even though I probably won't be as good as mommy and a lot of things, I am still very much needed.

On the way to the hospital, I called my mom, your Neeny, and told her that your mom was being induced tonight. Neeny was as shocked as I was to be receiving this news. She even asked the same questions that I had asked mommy. I assured Neeny that everything was going to be fine, but I wanted her to fly up to Pennsylvania so that she could welcome you into this world. Neeny had actually just arrived back in this country from a three week trip to Spain and Italy. Even though she might have been exhausted from all her recent travels, I knew that she would be in Hershey and at the hospital later that day. There was nothing in this world that was going to stop her from meeting her grandbaby as soon as physically possible. When I hung up the phone, Neeny said that she would be taking a shower and then immediately heading to the airport.

While I talked with Neeny, your mommy had called her mom, your Memom. Memom didn't even take the time to shower. She headed to the airport immediately. When she called and told mommy that she couldn't make that day because there were no flights, your mommy said, "Figure it out. I need you TODAY!" Mommy and Memom have a special relationship, the same way that you and mommy will. There was no way that mommy was about to have you without her mommy in the room.

Your mom and I spent the rest of the afternoon trying to wrap our heads around the fact that we were going to meet you. Seeing pictures of you in mommy's tummy had made me understand that you were really inside her, but I was still having trouble fathoming the fact that you would be in my arms soon. I was so excited to meet you that at times I even forgot all about the fact that mommy had preeclampsia and that you were coming early. Maybe you just wanted to see your dad? Maybe you were tired of being so cramped? Both of our lives were about to change dramatically.

Neeny arrived around 7:30 p.m. right when mommy was moved to the actual room where you were going to be born. Mommy and I were excited that Neeny had made it so that we could be assured she would be there to greet you as soon as you came out of mommy's tummy. Now, we just needed Memom to arrive. The nurses started to prepare mommy to have you. They gave her medicine that was supposed to help her with her preeclampsia. This medicine was called magnesium and it was pretty yucky. The doctors had told mommy that it would make her relaxed, but it wasn't very relaxing in actuality. What it did was make mommy really, really hot and very lethargic. She was so hot that we had to turn the air conditioning on so cold that the room was only 60 degrees. I was freezing! Thank God that I had remembered to bring my deluxe Snuggie or I might have needed to be admitted to the hospital to address a case of hypothermia.

Every couple of minutes, your mom would ask, "Is my mom here yet?" The magnesium was making your mommy not only cold and tired but also forgetful. She just seemed confused once the medicine really started to kick in. When Memom walked through the door, I had a huge sigh of relief as I knew that the final piece of the puzzle had finally arrived safely. It was going to be the four of us who would welcome you into this world with more love than you could even imagine. Now that everyone was here, the anxiety in the room turned to excitement and anticipation. Everyone was now ready for you. I leaned over to mommy's tummy and said, "Okay Zoe, you can come out now!"

Well, it turned out that just because we were ready to meet you didn't mean that you were ready to meet us just yet. As cramped as mommy's tummy had become, it was still the only place that you had ever known. You might have been confused as to why we wanted you to come out. Leaving the warm, sheltered womb for the freezing, sterile hospital room probably didn't seem like such a great idea.

The doctors decided that they needed to take some steps to "encourage" your exit. Mommy got a medicine called Pitocin, which was supposed to gently coax you out of her tummy. I learned about this medicine as well as some other techniques at one of the many classes your mom had made me attend. With the Pitocin started and your grandmothers in the room, the countdown to your arrival could officially begin.

You are my first baby, and I therefore didn't really know what to expect outside of what I had seen on TV and what I had learned in the birthing classes. For some reason, I had always thought that the process of having a baby was really fast. However, it quickly became apparent that this process known as "labor" was going to take awhile. Because I wanted to be awake and well-rested when you were born, I decided that I should try to sleep as much as possible during "labor." The real excitement was going to be when you came out and I could hold you and love on you. Anyways, your Memom was not going to sleep until you arrived as she wanted to be sure she could get your mommy anything that you needed. My staying up just didn't seem to make logical sense to me.

I closed my eyes, and the next thing that I knew it was the morning. I had slept for nine straight hours. What made this remarkable was the fact that doctors and nurses had been in and out of the room turning the lights on and off, doing procedures, and discussing mommy's care every hour that I was sleeping. I looked over at mommy and she seemed a little upset. I tried to explain my rationale for why I slept, but it wasn't a good decision to use a logical argument at this point in time. Neeny taught me a valuable lesson when I was a kid, she said, "It is often not what you say, but rather the mood of the person when they hear it that is the driving force behind their reaction." At this moment, mommy was definitely not in the mood for daddy to be argumentative.

When I woke up, mommy was in a lot of pain because the doctors continued to try to help her labor progress by the foli bulb. We had learned about this tool and technique in one of our classes, but I don't think that the teacher had been completely honest with the class. Using the foli bulb was very painful for your mom. Seeing your mom's reaction to this technique made me physically sick to my stomach. When I learned that this was the seventh time the doctors had tried to use this tool on mommy, I told them to stop. They weren't going to do this again. Part of being a husband is protecting your wife, and I wasn't going to let them continue to hurt mommy.

With mommy not seemingly getting any closer to having you, the doctors moved onto the next trick, breaking mommy's water. This procedure was much better than the foli bulb. It wasn't pleasant, but it was dramatically more tolerable than the foli bulb. I was excited because once this procedure was completed the doctors expected you to be here within 18 hours. I tried but I still couldn't believe it. I was going to be a daddy. Well, I considered myself a daddy as soon as the embryologists said your mom's eggs had fertilized, and I have loved you every second since. But, seeing you in person was something that would be totally new.

Finally, your Memom and Neeny were getting some rest. They had stayed up all night with your mom while I was sleeping. They both just sat in chairs right next to each other and stared at your mommy and all her monitors. It was about the cutest thing that you could ever want to see. These two women had been scared to sleep because they didn't want to miss anything. I was however concerned that they were wasting too much energy right now when they needed to be rested for when you arrived. Seeing Neeny's eyes finally close was a very welcomed sight.

The breaking of mommy's water had caused her to start having something called contractions. These "contractions" were uncomfortable for mommy. The pain of the contractions was more palatable than some of the other procedures because they were signs of progress. The contractions were your mom's way of getting

Dear Zoe || Love Dad

her body ready for your departure. As the contractions got stronger, I knew that mommy was getting closer to having you.

Having had a difficult labor up till this point, your mom decided that she should get an epidural sooner rather than later. During our "pain management" class, we had learned that the epidural was the best way to lessen mom's discomfort without having any negative impact on you, the baby.

You already know how I feel about blood and needles and you can therefore imagine the challenge I faced with mommy's epidural. As a part of getting epidural, she needed to have a big needle put in her back. Oh, the things mommies do for their babies. I held mommy's hands while the two doctors worked on getting the needle in the right place. I was really nervous, and I began to feel faint. My body was hot and I felt that I could fall down at any moment. I tried to sway back and forth to maintain consciousness, but each time I moved mommy said, "Stop moving." I wanted to be strong for mommy, and I therefore just stood still and prayed that I wouldn't collapse. With each passing second, I wondered whether I would become the second patient in the room. Watching the doctors continually struggle to insert the needle in the correct spot only made matters worse. Their seeming ineptitude coupled with my concerns about your mom's safety and my fear of needles made this experience quite unpleasant.

One of the doctors was new, and I was getting frustrated that she was taking so long. I was right about to tell her to step aside and let the more senior doctor take over when she said she was finished. I think that the stress of trying to decide whether to ask for a new doctor was also a major contributing factor to how I was feeling. With the epidural in place, mommy immediately started to feel better. Everything was looking up at this point.

For the next few hours, Memom and Neeny got some well-deserved rest. Not wanting to leave mommy alone by herself, I stayed up and watched all the monitors that were connected to her. I was able to tell what was happening inside mommy even while she was sleeping. I could even tell how fast your heart was beating because of a special device they placed on your mom's tummy. Watching the monitors was difficult for me because I wasn't always sure what all the various numbers meant. Was having your heart rate at 160 better than having it at 134? I am not a doctor, but I am pretty intelligent. I felt like I was in baby-knowledge limbo. I was able to understand the situation well enough to cause myself a lot of anxiety by noticing things that just weren't right, but not well enough to have a clear picture of what was happening.

Dear Zoe || Love Dad

The hours passed and my eyes stayed affixed to the various monitors. With everyone in the room asleep, I felt like we were the only two people in the room. It was a special time for your dad.

I would get so excited when I would see what I believed were signs of progress. When mommy started having contractions more often, I just knew you were getting ready to come see me. The doctors were outside of mommy's room watching the monitors, and they seemed generally pleased with your mom's progress as well. Being impatient, I went out to the island where all the nurses and doctors were stationed about 30 minutes after my initial visit. I wanted to see whether the prognosis had changed since we last spoke. They said that they were going to come into the room in about an hour to do another check.

Finally, the doctors came into the room after what seemed like way more than an hour. I crossed my fingers hoping that I would hear that mommy was ready to give birth. Unfortunately, the doctors said that she was still only 3cm dilated. At this level of dilation, it was clear that you were not coming out any time soon. I was disappointed. Your mom had been through so much of the last 12 months let alone the last 24 hours. I didn't want to see her suffer any longer. I just wanted the three of us to be together.

I tried to tell myself that I was lucky because you weren't supposed to come for another five weeks, but as I just told you, I am not a patient person. I was ready to hold you NOW! I was ready to see your mom with the biggest smile she has ever had. I wanted to see your Memom and Neeny with tears of joy running down their cheeks. But, this outcome would have to wait.

Mommy went back to sleep, and I gave Memom and Neeny the report once they woke up. The doctors said that they would come and check on mommy in about three more hours. I decided that this would be a good time for me to try and take a little nap because everything seemed calm. Mommy was doing well and so were you. Your heart rate was steady, and you were probably just relaxing not fully understanding what was about to happen.

The doctors returned in three hours as promised. Once again, they checked mommy to see whether she was any closer to letting you out of her tummy. You and mommy had grown so close while you were living in her tummy that I don't think either one of you was ready to make a change quite yet. The doctors did their check, and they once again said that mommy was 3cm dilated. This was not the news that anyone wanted because it meant that mommy's body just wasn't ready to let you out. Because you were coming so early, mommy's body hadn't been totally prepared for your arrival. Her body was still in the process of

Dear Zoe || Love Dad

helping you grow; her body still wanted to protect you by keeping you in her tummy.

Mommy and I talked with the doctors, and we asked what the plan was to make sure that both you and she would be safe. We both knew that the clock had started ticking once mommy's water had been broken. The doctor had originally said that you should be here by 5:30 a.m., and it was already 1:00 a.m. I knew that it was time to start thinking about a plan B.

The doctor told us that we might want to think about a procedure call a c-section where the doctors actually take you out of mommy rather than having mommy push you out. Your mommy and I told the doctors that we wanted what was best for our baby – bottom line. We came to the hospital to have a beautiful baby enter this world safely, and we didn't care how that happened. After listening to mommy and me, the doctors said that a c-section would be the best option.

The doctors wasted no time in getting mommy ready. As soon as the words "we would like a c-section" came out of my mouth, the doctors began to prepare the special room called the "OR" where the procedure would take place. It would be in this room that you would be born. Once the "OR" was ready, a nurse wheeled your mom out of the room for the last time with you in her stomach.

I couldn't believe that I was literally moments away from meeting you. I knew this day would eventually arrive, but I had never really let myself feel the emotions fully. Mommy and I had prayed so many nights for this day. You faced so many obstacles that I just could never let myself think about holding you in my arms for fear that I would never recover if something went wrong. I loved you already, and I knew from the moment I heard your mom yelling, "I'm pregnant" that my life would be forever changed. You would always be a part of my life.

Your mom and I knew there were many, many risks associated with having a baby and that no one was guaranteed a healthy, beautiful baby. We believed that God would give us the baby that He wanted us to have. But, we, like all couples, hoped He gave us a healthy child. With all these thoughts and emotions running through my head, I started to get in the sterile clothes provided to me by the nurses.

I pulled on the blue gown, the face mask, and the hair net. I was now ready (at least from a sterile clothing perspective). For the next 20 minutes, I waited with Neeny and Memom in the room your mom had just vacated. The doctors and nurses were going to get me once mommy was ready for her procedure. The 20 minutes lasted for what felt like an eternity. Your Memom looked very, very nervous, but your Neeny just seemed excited. If Neeny was nervous, she sure wasn't showing it. Neeny was being strong for your daddy.

It was so many months ago when your mom and I began this journey. It had started in Italy when we prayed at every church we visited. We had prayed for this exact day, the day we would be blessed with a child. My life was about to change forever. The gravity of the moment was not lost on me. I knew I was about to experience the greatest event of my life. I thought back to the pure, unadulterated joy I felt that morning when I heard your mom crying and yelling, "I'm pregnant." And, I knew seeing you live and in the flesh would be even more powerful.

I of course was nervous as I waited, but I was also excited. The reward of actually being able to hold you and kiss you served as a partial antidote to the anxiety which usually accompanied your mom's other medical procedures.

The nurse entered the room and said, "Ryan, we're ready for you." These words brought me back to reality. This was happening.

I walked across the hall and into the OR where mommy was already laying down on a new bed. The crowded room was a stark contrast to the calm environment I had just left. There were doctors everywhere. There were doctors who were monitoring you. There were doctors who were making sure mommy was breathing okay. There were doctors who were going to take you out of mommy's tummy. It once again hit me that your mom was having surgery. I tried not to look at the doctors or their tools because they made me too nervous. Any feelings of peace and excitement quickly turned to terror. I was petrified. My excitement was no longer capable of over-powering my fear. I was so nervous about my two girls. I felt faint as I made my way through the room, trying my best to not "see" too much.

I kept walking until I saw your mommy's face. I sat down right by her and took her hand. I told her that everything was going to be okay. I wanted to be strong for her even though I was more nervous than at any other moment of my life. Your mom was very, very tired from the medicine nurses had given her, and she was having a hard time staying awake. I hadn't pictured your arrival this way. Your mom was the leader; it was she who was supposed to be making the parenting decisions. The room was crowded, but I felt alone as it was I who had to protect you and your mom.

The doctor said that he was going to start the procedure, and I held mommy's hand and I said yet another prayer. I asked God to protect both mommy and you.

Dear Zoe || Love Dad

The doctors were working behind a screen that hid them from my view. I could hear them talking and everything seemed to be going very well. All of a sudden, I became hotter and hotter. With mommy looking very tired and my anxiety mounting, I had to do everything that I could to not pass out. I had never been so nervous before. I have never loved anyone the way that I love you and your mommy, and knowing that you were both in the middle of a surgery was tearing me apart.

The doctor sitting next to me said that they were getting ready to take you out of mommy's tummy. I was too scared to be excited by this point. I just wanted to hear you cry, a signal that you were able to breathe. The next ten seconds were the scariest moments of my life. I was still squeezing mommy's hand and saying my prayers as I waited to hear you. Your mom's body was moving as the doctors worked to release you from her stomach. I stayed focused on your mom to make sure that she was not in any pain as they continued to work on her. Her tired gaze didn't change.

All of a sudden the doctor said, "Here she comes." Still, I didn't hear you. I could hardly breathe. I just wanted to hear you cry. Then without warning, you let out a loud cry. You were alive and breathing. I WAS A FATHER!

I looked down at mommy and she was crying. Even though she was tired from all the medicine, there was nothing that could stop her from staying awake to hear and see her baby. The nurse brought you over so that I could see you. You were covered in all kinds of fluids, but you were still the most beautiful sight that I had ever seen. I took a picture of you so that I would always remember this moment.

Mommy was having a hard time seeing you because she had to stay on the bed. Once the nurses were able to make sure that you were breathing okay, they cleaned you off, measured you, and placed your footprints on your birth certificate. It was then that they brought you over to me so that I could hold you. You were so small that your weight was imperceptible in my arms. You were now swaddled in blankets, and you looked so cute and perfect. Mesmerized by you, your mom had to tell me to let her see you; I was just keeping you all to myself. I held you close to your mom, and tears poured from your mom's eyes. She kissed you and told you how much she loved you as she fought to stay awake.

I was holding you in my arms, and I distinctly remember seeing your nose flare as you breathed. It might sound odd, but I was so happy to watch your breathe through your nose because I can't due to something called a deviated septum. I was already hoping you would inherit my good not bad traits.

Dear Zoe || Love Dad

Holding you was an amazing feeling. I was nervous though because I had never held a newborn. I had always imagined mommy being the first person to hold you and her teaching me what to do. With mommy being sick and having to take medicine, I was called into action a little earlier than he had planned.

The nurses measured you and you were 6 pounds and 19 inches.

Dear Zoe – July, 26

You have only been alive for two hours, but I already love you more than I could have ever imagined. There is nothing that can prepare you for the emotions you feel when you hold your own child in your arms.

Right after you were born, your mom needed to get staples to finish the surgery. The doctor had actually asked me whether your mom wanted stitches or staples, a question your mom and I had failed to discuss. We never made it to the birthing class where c-sections were discussed because you decided to arrive after class 1 of 3. I chose staples after asking the doctor what he would do if it were his wife.

I went with you to the nursery while the doctors finished your mom's surgery. Your mom made it very clear to me that she wanted me with you; she said she would be fine. I walked with you to the nursery after briefly taking you into the room where your Neeny and Memom were anxiously waiting. They were both overwhelmed with emotion at th4e sight of you; a reaction that was completely expected yet still wonderfully touching. It was time for you to go to the nursery to get some additional medicines and tests. You were in a little bed called an isolate which I wheeled down to the nursery. There was not a bump on the smooth, hard floor of the hospital, but I still moved very slowly and deliberately so that I would not disturb you.

An interesting thing happened on the way to the nursery. Remember, how I have told you about Kelly and Jim and how Kelly was in the hospital with the same condition as your mom. Well, we were half way to the nursery when I saw my friend Jim standing in the hall. He was wearing the same blue, sterile gown as your dad. It turned out that his wife was now in the OR getting ready to give birth to their daughter. He was very happy to see you and to know that you were safely out of mommy's tummy. I felt slightly uncomfortable during our brief encounter however because you could see the fear and concern on his face. He was experiencing what I had just experienced only an hour previously; the fear that comes from having your wife prepped for a surgery that would impact both her and your baby. (You certainly assume you know this by now as I bet you

Dear Zoe || Love Dad

and Ava will be great friends, but I feel compelled to report that his daughter, Ava, was born without complication.) I wished him luck and we continued to the nursery.

You were in great hands in the nursery, and I decided to go and check on your mom. She had essentially commanded that I stay with you, but I needed to check on her. The last time I had seen her she was still in surgery.

The combination of having been taking various medications for the last 30 hours and having just undergone significant surgery had left your mom feeling quite crummy. Making an already challenging situation worse, the doctors and nurses had forgotten to give her additional medicine after the surgery. It was hard to see her like this. This moment, the moment she would welcome you into the world, had been on her mind since Italy. I knew she had not pictured this event as it was turning out. She was throwing up from the effects of the magnesium and the pain she was experiencing. Thankfully, she had her mom by her side comforting her and while gently stroking her head. Nothing however could stop her from focusing on you and your well being. She was constantly asking about you and making sure you were being cared for. She wanted nothing more than to see you and she implored me to bring you to her. I was able to convince the nurses to let me take you out of the nursery and back to our room so that mommy could see your cute little face if only for a few minutes.

Your mom was coming into and out of consciousness. By the time I arrived from the nursery, she had started to doze off. The nurses had given me a bottle, and I took this time to try and feed you. Both your Neeny and Memom watched as I gently raised the little bottle to your lips. We weren't having much success as all you wanted to do was sleep. I could understand because I was really tired too. The clock read 4:00 a.m. which was either really late at night or very early in the morning. Normally I would be asleep, but I was so excited to finally see you that there was no way I could rest now. I continued to hold you and wait for your mom to wake up. I knew that she desperately wanted to see you again.

You were so tired. I later learned that not only were you drowsy because it was so early in the morning, but you were also feeling the effects of the yucky medicine your mom had been taking over the last day and a half. Because your mom had been supplying you with all your nutrients and oxygen via the umbilical cord, you couldn't help but also get some of the medication. When the doctors first pulled you out of your mom's tummy, one of the doctors had performed a "startle test" where she lifted your arms and then let them go. At the time, I had been so overwhelmed with emotion and relief at the sight of you that I hadn't taken the time to question what was happening. I later learned that you were supposed to naturally react and move your arms to the side to protect yourself from falling. I remembered seeing your arms fall to the side succumbing to gravity without any resistance what so ever. The magnesium your mom had been taking was in your system too causing you to be very drowsy and to fail the test. The doctor must have not been overly concerned at the time as nothing was ever mentioned to me.

The failed "startle reflex" test was not a big deal in and of itself, it was confirmation that you were in fact impacted by the Magnesium. This medicine combined with the fact that you decided to come out of Mommy's tummy five weeks early was causing you to have some trouble breathing. I didn't recognize your breathing challenge right away. What happened was the following. When I was giving you your bottle, you started making a funny noise. You continued to look completely at peace, and I originally thought this noise might be an utterance all babies make. As it continued, there was something inside me that instinctively told me something might not be right. I walked over to a nurse and asked her to listen to you. She said that this noise was caused by you having to work too hard to get the oxygen you needed. I asked her what we needed to do, and she said it was best for you to return to the nursery. Your mom had awoken as I was discussing this situation with the nurse. I tried to explain to your mom that you needed to go back to get some additional assistance from the nurses. The medicines were still impacting your mom's judgment as she continued told me that "Zoe, needs to be with her family. She needs to be with her dad."

It was a difficult situation. Your mom was exhausted and confused. I had never thought that I would be the parent making decisions about what was best for you so quickly. Your mom was the captain of this team. I once again tried to explain to your mom that you needed help breathing and that you had to go to the nursery. I desperately wanted her advice and blessing. Nothing was working. Your mom wanted you to stay with the two of us. Finally, I said, "Zoe and I are going to the nursery. I will see you in a little bit. Try and get some rest. Everything is fine." I wanted to get you the assistance you needed right away, and I couldn't continue this debate. I knew what your mom truly wanted even if she was not able to say it; she wanted you to get the best care possible.

My instincts as a parent had already kicked in after only a few short hours. I knew that mommy wanted to see you, but I knew that I needed to do what was best for you even though it was hard for the two of us.

Dear Zoe – July, 26

I decided to get a little sleep when the nurses took you back to the nursery to monitor your oxygen. Exhaustion overwhelmed me. I had just experienced the greatest moment of my life. I couldn't believe that I had just met you. You were

Dear Zoe || Love Dad

so beautiful and perfect. I knew that I couldn't stay awake forever, and I wanted to get some energy while we had nurses watching over you.

Neeny was still in the room, and I asked her to wake me up in two hours. I didn't want to sleep for too long because I knew that I would be missing you. You were in good hands, but I wanted to check on both you and your mom. When I woke up, Neeny calmly said, "Zoe had to go to the Neonatal Intensive Care Unit (NICU). While you were asleep, Zoe had stopped breathing momentarily."

I immediately popped out of bed and said, "What do you mean?" My body was almost numb as it reacted to the news more quickly than my mind.

Neeny went on to explain that you had had an episode of apnea. I was petrified, and I knew nothing would make me feel better until I saw you and talked to your doctors. Immediately, I headed upstairs to find you. Before I ran out the door, Neeny told me that the NICU was on the seventh floor. Your mom would have wanted to come with me, but she had taken more medicine and she was still asleep. I decided that I wouldn't wake her; she had been so confused a few hours ago that I didn't think she would be able to understand what was happening. I needed to find out what was happening before I could explain the situation to her.

Before I could enter the NICU, I had to scrub my arms with an iodine solution to make sure that I was extra clean from germs. I scrubbed real hard to make sure that I would not get you or any of the other babies sick. The nurses told me you were at bed 13. I ran over to your bed to find you sleeping peacefully. You had a special mask on your face which was connected to a CPAP machine. I was so relieved to see you doing well that my heart stopped racing. I actually thought you looked so cute in your little CPAP machine. Your granddad, Papa Bear, wears a CPAP machine to help him sleep, and I knew that you were not in any pain.

I met your nurse, Alissa, and she was very sweet. She told me that you were getting a little bit of extra oxygen to help your breathing. I was so glad to see you that I didn't even notice all the different monitors that you were wearing. You had a machine to measure your blood oxygen saturation, a machine to measure your heart, and an IV to give you antibiotics. You were sleeping in a special bed as well. The bed had a heat lamp that would turn on to warm you when you body temperature got too low.

Dear Zoe || Love Dad

You looked beautiful. I was completely calm and at peace as I stood by your little bed; any fears or worries had been erased. I watched your chest move up and down with each breath mesmerized by how much I already loved you.

Some moms and dads get sad when they see their babies in the NICU, but I was happy that so many people were taking care of you. You had your nurses, Alissa and Heather, and your doctors, Doctor Michael and Doctor Doctor (no joke). Once I knew everyone was taking care of you, I went downstairs to tell Memom and Neeny that you were doing well.

God had not only blessed me with a beautiful baby, but he had also given me a new found confidence in my ability to be a parent. I had been tested and passed.

Dear Zoe – July, 26

I think I am making your nurse mad. Because you are hooked up to so many monitors, I am able to tell exactly how fast your heart is beating or how much oxygen is in your blood at any given moment. I have been watching the monitors like a hawk, and I always yell to Alissa whenever "your numbers" change. See, I am not going to let anything bad happen to you; Alissa keeps telling me to trust her judgment, but your daddy trusts himself more than anyone else☺

Your mommy is so sad that she can't come visit you today. She is in her bed, but she can't rest. Her stomach hurts from where the doctors had to take you out, but this pain is nothing compared to the pain she is feeling from not having you in her arms. She loves you so much that it is very hard for her to not be seeing you. She had been carrying you in her tummy for 8 months, and now you seem so far away. I try to tell her that it will be okay, but she just gets mad at your dad. There is nothing that can console a mom who wants to be with her baby.

Your mom is still taking a lot of medicine which has continued to make her tired and confused. There was an incident earlier in the day that was made me so sad. A doctor came to her room and asked her how her tummy was feeling? She opened her eyes ever so slightly and said, "I haven't felt the baby kick all day." I took her hand and told her that everything was okay. I told her that she had already had you and that you were upstairs resting in the NICU. It just about broke my heart.

There have been other times during the day when your mom has been much more lucid (a word meaning not confused). During these times, she has been trying to call her friends and family to let them know that you decided to come five weeks early. You will find out that mommy has a lot of friends and a huge family. The only problem has been that she still has lapses where she gets confused all over again. I had just come back from visiting you when I heard your mom tell one of her friends that the doctors wouldn't let her see you and they wouldn't let her have ice either. Although these statements were true, they were slightly misleading. I had to take the phone and let her friend know that your mom couldn't see you because you were in the NICU and your mom had to remain in bed. She couldn't have ice because she there was a small chance that she would need to have additional surgery. Her confusion about not feeling you kick made me sad, but her telling her friends that she couldn't have ice just made me laugh.

Your mom is so great. You are going to love her so much. Hopefully, she will get to see you tomorrow.

With mommy stuck downstairs in her room, I was able to spend a lot of time getting to know you today. I even changed your first diaper. I don't want to embarrass you, but it was pretty messy. I think I did okay, but I did let go of your legs at one point only to see them drop. I had been expecting you to keep them up in the air so that I could see what I was doing. What I forgot was that you were still under the effects of that icky magnesium medicine mommy had been taking before she gave birth to you. Shocked, I immediately asked the nurse if you were okay. You know you probably won't understand this until you have your own baby, but being a parent can be kind of scary. You see this little tiny baby and think she is so fragile and you don't want to make any mistakes. Thank God the nurse was there to tell me that everything was fine or I would have had a long day.

You are such a beautiful girl, and I was so happy that you made it out of mommy's stomach safely. You might have a lot of tubes attached to you, but I had never seen such a beautiful baby. I was so happy that my eyes started to water. When you cry, you usually are sad or frustrated, but when your mommy and I cry, it is because we are so happy.

Dear Zoe – July, 27

Your mom woke me up at five in the morning today. I was very, very tired after having a poor night's sleep. I had to stay on a little cot in mommy's room last night whereas your mom has a special bed. It even has a button which allows it go up or down. If you ever have to stay in the hospital again, I'll make sure that you get one of these special beds. And, I will happily sleep on a cot next to you so that you are not alone.

Dear Zoe || Love Dad

Daddy doesn't normally get up so early, and I tried to convince your mom to let me continue sleeping. Mommy's stomach hurts, but she had been told that she was finally allowed to leave the room. As soon as the doctor said she could leave the room, she woke me up so that I could take her to see you. I hadn't seen your mom so happy since she found out you were in her tummy. I was trying to get ready really fast, but I wasn't fast enough. Mommy couldn't wait any longer to see you. She kept saying, "Hurry up, Hurry up." Your mom was still in a lot of pain, but nothing was going to stop her from seeing you. She could hardly walk and I therefore had to push her in a wheelchair, a special seat that has wheels like a car.

We went to the room with the big sinks and scrubbed our arms to get rid of any germs before we headed to see you at Bed 13. I was so happy to have you and mommy together. Your mom was smiling so big when she finally got a chance to see you. She wanted to pick you right up and kiss you, but she knew she had to let you rest for a little while longer.

I wanted to show mommy how much I had learned on our first day together, and I volunteered to change your diaper. Everything started out well. I placed the new diaper underneath you and began to take off your dirty diaper. I took out the wipes and began to gently wash you off so that you would feel nice and fresh after your nap. Mommy could not believe how well I was doing. I was almost finished when all of a sudden I saw a little black balloon. The balloon was coming from YOUR bottom. It started small but quickly got bigger and bigger until it was the size of a softball. I was so surprised that I jumped and dropped your legs, AGAIN. It seemed that you had decided to play a little joke on daddy. I shouldn't have been surprised because I like to play jokes too. When babies are first born, they have a special kind of poo poo called meconium. I was about to be finished when you decided that you needed to go poo poo again. Meconium is very sticky which allowed you to make a poo poo balloon. I don't think I will ever forget this sight. My little, precious baby had just made a poo poo balloon. Your mom and I laughed and we knew this wouldn't be the last time that you surprised us.

It was time for you to get some more rest, and your mom headed back to her room. She sat back down in her special chair and I carefully pushed her trying to minimize any bumps just like I had with you one night earlier. We hadn't even made it out of the nursery before I could hear your mom sobbing. Our visit had gone great I thought to myself. Why was she so upset?

I stopped her chair and walked around so that I could see her. I asked her what was wrong. It turned out that she hadn't fully understood what being in the NICU meant. Even though she had known you were in the NICU she wasn't

Dear Zoe || Love Dad

fully ready to accept the sight of you with all the wires and tubes emanating from your little body. Her reaction to the NICU was completely different than mine. I had felt a great sense of relief when I saw all the special machinery attached to you; it made me feel better knowing you were constantly being monitored. Having heard your labored breathing and having learned about your apnea, I had been so scared that I appreciated the attention.

Your mom on the other hand had not experienced these incidents. She had been so sick over the last couple of days that I think our visit was the first time that she understood that you were sick. I know that she had pictured her first hours and days with you many times during her pregnancy. Neither of us ever really considered the fact that you would be born so early or that you would be in the NICU. Seeing you in your little isolate had made her so happy that she hated having to leave you. She wanted you in her arms not several floors away behind a locked door.

I tried to comfort her and tell her that you were getting great care. Even though she understood, she just wanted to be with you.

You don't need to worry about us though; both your mother and I will be fine. You just need to continue to grow knowing that we love you very much.

Dear Zoe – July, 28

Last night was my first night away from you. I needed to go back to work, and I therefore decided that I should stay at our house and get some rest. Living at the hospital had been pretty tiring. I thought I would sleep great in my big comfy bed, but I was wrong. I missed you and mommy. Since you were born, everything has just felt different. I care about you more than anything else, and you are always on my mind. I wonder what you are doing – feeding, eating, sleeping, opening your eyes, etc... Being a dad is such an amazing experience.

Even though I was not happy to be away from you, I was looking forward to going to work and telling all my friends and co-workers about you. Of all the things that have happened to me in my great life, nothing compares to having you in my arms. I never understood how people could hold babies for hours and hours. Didn't it get boring with their not talking? Well, it is not boring when it is your daughter.

The only problem I have when holding you is that it makes me very tired. Remember how I told you about my having something called OCD which makes me worry about things. I always thought it would get much worse when you arrived because I would want to make sure that I wasn't doing anything wrong.

Dear Zoe || Love Dad

What has actually happened is the opposite. I have never been as at peace as when I am holding you. I just love you so much; everything else fades away when you are in my arms. All I can feel is peace and happiness.

Work started out great because everyone was asking about you. I told them about how mommy was in labor for a very long time because you had liked it so much in her tummy that you didn't want to come out. I then shared how you were staying in the NICU so that you could get extra-special attention from all the nice doctors and nurses. To be honest, I wasn't getting much work done because everyone wanted to hear about you and see pictures of you. Finally, I decided that I really did need to do some work so that I could buy the house we are building just for you.

I was sitting at my desk when I got a call from you Neeny. The first thing she said to me was, "How is Zoe's heart, I heard that she had a heart problem."

Now, the heart is a very important part of the body. It is basically like an engine that keeps you going and gives you energy. It was your heart that I had been concerned about many months ago during one of your ultrasounds. I told Neeny that I didn't know what she was talking about. No one had told me about any problems with your heart. I couldn't understand how Neeny would know something about you that I didn't. I had just spoken with your mom a few hours prior. I was very confused; how would Neeny who was back in Florida know something about you that I didn't when I was only three minutes away from the NICU. She said that Aunt Alyssa had heard from Uncle Tait who had heard from Memom. I immediately got real worried and told Neeny that I had to get off the phone.

I called mommy and thankfully she answered the phone. She can't always answer the phone because there are no phones allowed in the NICU. I asked her what was wrong with your heart, and she told me that your heart had gone all the way up to 210 beats a minute. I then asked whether the doctor had said whether this rapid heart rate was a problem. Thankfully, the doctor had thought that it was probably nothing, but he would keep monitoring it.

Feeling slightly relieved, I asked mommy why he had to hear that his baby might have a problem from Neeny. Why didn't mommy call daddy? Daddy didn't think that he should have been the last to know about a potential problem with his own daughter. To tell you the truth ZoZo, I was really mad. I was so mad that I told mommy that I didn't want to talk to Memom because I probably didn't have anything nice to say.

Dear Zoe || Love Dad

Life lesson from your dad: It is okay to be mad; it is not okay to be mean or hurt other people because you are mad.

I know that Memom wasn't trying to do anything wrong, but it was frustrating. Also, Uncle Tait and Aunt Alyssa weren't trying to keep anything from me. Everyone was just trying to handle having someone they loved, you, in the hospital. I am however much more private that your mom's family, and I was hoping that having my sister married to your mom's brother wasn't going to always lead to situations such as this.

I guess now would be a good time to tell you about your family. You are going to have a lot of aunts and uncles because daddy has five brothers and sisters. You are also a very lucky girl because you have four grandparents who love you very much.

You already know Neeny, my mom. She was able to hold you about ten minutes after you left mommy's tummy. I never got to meet Neeny's mom (my Neeny) and it makes me very happy that you will have a grandmother. Neeny likes to pray for you and she will always be more than happy to take you to church or talk about God.

Papa Bear is my dad. Papa Bear loves you very much and he is always making sure that you have the best care in the world. When Papa Bear found out you were going to the NICU, he started going to mayoclinic.com and webmd.com to make sure that your doctors and nurses were taking extra special care of his little grandbaby. Papa Bear loves Italy, reading, and art. He may even give you a pretty painting for your room some day.

Memom is your mommy's mom. She has been waiting for you to get here since even before mommy and daddy decided to ask God for a baby. Memom is just filled with love. She sits at the side of your bed and just stares at you. Mommy said to Memom, "You know that Zoe is my baby, and Memom said, 'I know but I just love her so much that I can't leave her bedside.'" Memom has her own business in Texas, but she has decided to stay with mommy and daddy for over a month to make sure that you get everything you could possibly need. With Memom around, you will definitely have no shortage of love or attention.

Daddy Mack is mommy's dad. He is arriving at the hospital today to see you. Daddy Mack has a funny job. He is called a bounty hunter or bails bondsman which means that he helps the police put adults who act naughty in timeout. When adults go to timeout, they don't sit on a step or a special mat; they go to a place called jail. Most bail bondsman are tough, and Daddy Mack is no exception. He does however have a real soft spot for family. The minute he sees you, I know that he is just going to cry and cry. He cried through out mommy and daddy's wedding, and I am sure he will be even worse when he sees you.

Now that I have told you about your grandparents, I thought that I would tell you what I hope you learn from each of them. All of your grandparents are very special people, and I hope you inherit certain traits from each of them.

From Neeny, I hope that you inherit her strength, confidence, attitude, and faith. Neeny has many great qualities and you could learn a lot from her. Neeny is a very strong person who believes in doing the right thing. She is never intimidated by others because she believes in herself, and she has remarkable faith that God will always guide her to the right decision. When you get older, you will probably get nervous before a test in school, your first soccer game, or a big dance rehearsal. I want you to have the confidence in yourself that Neeny has in herself. (When daddy would get nervous about playing against good players in a soccer game, she would always say, "Those boys put their pants on one leg at a time just like you." It would always calm me down.) Finally, Neeny is very appreciative of all the blessings that God has bestowed on her and our family. I hope you find the peace and joy that comes from having faith in a higher power.

From Papa Bear, I want you to learn to be selfless and to put the needs of others before your own. I want you to learn to appreciate art, history, and literature. I want you to be kind to others and to offer them help without expecting anything in return. I want you to always keep life in perspective. Even though Papa Bear is very successful in business, he is much more proud of being a caring parent than his elevated status in his profession.

From Memom, I want you to learn to love, to be tough, and to be a hard worker. Memom just oozes love out of every pore in her body. You can tell she loves you by her words, by her hugs and kisses, and by her willingness to do anything to help someone out. Memom is also very tough. She runs a small business in West Texas where some customers don't always want to pay her the money she is owed. She may be a sweet and petite lady, but don't think she is weak. Finally, I want you to learn to be a hard worker. Memom works at least six days a week so that she can provide for her family. After work, she begins a second job of taking care of all the members of her family (kids, cousins, parents, grandparents, etc...) by cooking them dinner, taking them to the doctor, or just visiting them to lift their spirits.

From Daddy Mack, I want you to learn courage. Daddy Mack is a very courageous man. Sometimes the adults that he puts in time out get angry at him and try to hurt him, Daddy Mack tries his best to calm them down, but

Dear Zoe || Love Dad

sometimes they stay angry. Daddy Mack has a lot of courage to take these people to time out to get them the help they need.

Well, back to your heart. Like I had said, the doctors don't think it is anything to worry about, but I want to make sure that everything is okay. I am going to make sure that you get all the necessary tests to rule out any potential problems.

Dear Zoe – July, 29

I decided that I would come see you before I went to work. With you having the little problem with your heart, I wanted to make sure that you had had a good night. When I arrived at the hospital, guess who I saw? If you guessed your mom, you would be right. I definitely wasn't surprised. If mommy could, she would get inside your little crib and sleep next to you all night.

I was only there for a few minutes when the head nurse brought a bunch of nurses and doctors to explain to them who you were and why you were in the NICU. In medicine, they call these little conversations, "rounds." The nurse started out by saying that this was little baby, "Rice," who was two days old. She said that you were not on antibiotics and that you had not had any issues with breathing or your heart rate. Now, I was looking at mommy with a quizzical look on my face. Mommy started to laugh. What mommy and daddy found so funny if not infuriating was that everything the nurse said about you was WRONG. Your name is "Richardson" and you are three days old. You spent the first few days in the NICU on a C-Pap machine because you had trouble breathing and you just had a first bout of elevated heart rate the day prior. Finally, you were on day three of a ten day antibiotic treatment.

Your dad had two options. 1) He could get mad at the nurse. 2) He could find the nurse practitioner who has more responsibility over you and your case and tell her what had just happened. Now, my only concern was making sure that you would get the best possible care, and I therefore decided that getting mad at the nurse would not help you in any way. I decided to talk to Janelle, the nurse practitioner, and tell her that she would need to go and give a more accurate history of your case to the other doctors and nurses so that there would be no confusion.

Life Lesson from daddy: When deciding on a course of action, always keep your end goal in mind.

I had to go to work, but I gave you a kiss and told you that I would be back at lunch. I also asked mommy whether she could see whether your doctor, Dr. Michael, could meet with me at lunch to go over some questions that I had. It was already very clear you're your mom and I already viewed parenting in very different ways. Mommy was always holding you and talking to you. She was basically making sure that you got all the love a baby could handle. I shouldn't be surprised because as I already explained Memom and Neeny are the same exact way. Don't get me wrong, I would love on you as well, but I felt my main focus had to be making sure that you were safe and healthy. It was therefore important to me that I speak with the doctor and find out what was causing your heart rate to go so fast. The nice thing for you, Zo, is that your mom's and dad's respective parenting styles are perfectly complimentary and you are going to be a safe and loved young lady.

I had a hard time getting any work done today because I was anxious to meet with the doctor at lunch. My meetings seemed to drag on as I counted down the hours until I could get my questions answered. Finally, noon rolled around and I was able to go to the hospital. Dr. Michael was already at your bedside, and I was able to ask him some questions regarding your accelerated heart rate. Dr. Michael is a very kind and straight forward man. I am very glad that he is taking care of you this week.

I began by asking for an explanation as to why your heart rate suddenly jumped to over 210 beats a minute. Was it because you were born prematurely? Was there a problem with your heart? Did we need to do more tests? Dr. Michael calmly and confidently answered each of my questions. He said that it was most likely nothing. He explained that newborn babies and especially preemies will have some fluctuations in heart rate. He said that because you were already attached to a heart rate monitor that he did not believe any more tests were needed at this time.

I then told him that I have a condition called Supra Ventricular Tachycardia which makes my heart go fast just like yours had. Dr. Michael said that he didn't think that you had SVT because your heart rate would have gone much higher, but he was willing to do an EKG if I wanted. Of course I wanted him to do the test because I wanted to rule out any problems that you may have. Remember how I told you that I showed my love for you by ensuring you were getting the best care; well, you should consider each test I order as the equivalent to one of your mom's kisses☺ I think I learned this way of caring from my dad, papa bear.

Now, I don't want you to worry if you have SVT because your daddy has had it his whole life. I first realized that I had it when I wasn't that much older than you. I was planning on going swimming while on vacation, but I could feel my heart racing inside my chest. I told Neeny, and she promptly took me to the doctor. Eventually, I ended up in the hospital where doctors did tests on me and eventually discovered the issue. You don't need to worry about any of these tests. I have had tests on my heart my whole life and they don't hurt one bit. I wouldn't want these tests so badly if they were going to hurt you.

You also don't need to be afraid if you have SVT. I can show you how to make it go away. It is actually really funny what you do to make yourself feel better. You don't have to take a pill, get a shot, or have any medical intervention. All you need to do is stand on your head. That's it. Whenever my heart goes fast just like yours did, I just stand on my head and the change in blood flow causes my heart to go back to normal. There is another thing that you can do, but I don't like it. When I was first diagnosed, they told me to put my head in a bucket of ice water. This method worked, but it wasn't pleasant. Hopefully, Dr. Michael is right and your heart is perfectly normal and you won't have to worry about standing on your head or putting your face in ice water.

After having all my questions about your heart answered, I moved onto a different subject. I hadn't written anything to you about a test you had on your head a few days ago. I wanted to wait until I had more information. There was no use worrying you unnecessarily.

I was visiting you at lunch when a man who I had never seen previously came over to your little crib. The whole situation was kind of strange. He had a big machine with him and he said that he needed to take some pictures of your head. I wasn't sure whether he was a doctor, a nurse, or some type of technician. I also wasn't sure whether your mom or Memom had known he was coming for a visit or not. Given the inability to use cell phones in the NICU and my busy work schedule, there were times when I wasn't able to connect with your mom for hours. Anyways, he said that he needed images of your head and brain. It wasn't clear to me whether he was performing a routine test that every baby in the NICU would be given or whether the doctors had had some specific concern that they wanted to investigate.

I asked him whether he was able to answer some questions for me. Unfortunately, he explained that he was strictly a technician and any medical questions would need to be addressed to some other member of the NICU medical team. He gently moved the device along your skull being very careful not to hurt or disturb you. His patience and care were very much appreciated by me, a dad who just found out that his daughter might have an issue with her skull or brain. To make a long story short, the doctors wanted to see an image of your brain which is why this test was ordered.

I asked Dr. Michael about the results of this test as well. He said that the test showed a small part on your brain which was either a little cyst or a small bleed.

Dear Zoe || Love Dad

I was still trying to process this information when he said that he wasn't very concerned as this was a common finding. The plan was to continue to monitor the situation to make sure that it was not a bleed or cyst that was getting progressively worse. I continued to press Dr. Michael on whether he had concerns he was not expressing. He remained consistent, stating that he was not concerned as the results were not unexpected for a baby in your situation.

I felt differently today than I had months ago when Dr. Stein said he needed more images of your heart and brain. These words had sent me into a full-fledged panic. Today, my reaction was much more muted. God has really given me a sense of peace since the moment you were born; I have always believed that you would be able to overcome all the obstacles you are facing. You have only been alive for a few days, and you have already experienced so many challenges, apnea, possible sepsis, accelerated heart rates, and now a potential bleed or cyst in your brain. I have of course been worried, but my love for you is a more powerful emotion than fear. You and God have made me stronger than I knew I could be. I don't have time to worry; I only have time to love you and make sure you are getting the best care.

I love you so much, Zoe. You have already changed me so much. Stay strong and continue to fight.

Dear Zoe – July, 30

I knew that today was going to be a hard day for your mom. Some little girls dream of the day that they will get married. They play dress up and think about what their wedding will be like. Well, I think your mommy has always dreamt of the day that she would get to take her little baby home from the hospital. As soon as we learned we were having you, mommy started creating a special bedroom just for you. When we learned we were having a girl, she went out and bought the cutest clothes and hair bows she could find. Mommy's dream was coming true when she found out you were going to be joining our family.

The reason that today was going to be tough for mommy was because the doctors told her that she can't stay at the hospital any longer. When mommy had you, she had a surgery that takes a while from which to recover. While she was recovering, she was able to stay at the hospital only a few floors below where you were staying. Now that mommy was feeling better, which was a good thing, she had to go home, which was a bad thing. She didn't want to leave you at the hospital alone.

I knew that it might be a difficult night, and I was correct. Things started off poorly from the minute I got to the hospital. When I arrived mommy was having dinner, and Memom was holding you. I told Memom that a friend of mine at work had given me a book that we could read to you. Both your Memom and your mom love reading, and I was sure that you would too. Well, your nurse over heard our conversation and she said that we weren't allowed to read to you. Memom and I were kind of shocked because most doctors and child development experts say that parents can and should start reading to their babies even when they are still in their mommy's tummy. The nurse said that reading to you would be too much stimulation for you at a time when you needed to simply concentrate on growing. I was totally caught off guard because the buzzers, beepers, and other noises in the NICU seemed far more stimulating than Memom's tranquil voice would be.

I could tell that Memom might be upset because the nurse had made her feel as if she didn't know what was best for her grandbaby. Your Memom has been such an enormous help that I wasn't going to let her feel bad about herself for even a minute. She was doing an amazing job at being a grandma to you, a mother to your mom, and a mother-in-law to me. I decided that I needed to say something. I told the nurse that we want to do what is absolutely best for you, but we need to be told politely and in a non-condescending manner what "the best thing for you" is because we are new at this. Memom's face brightened as she appreciated that your daddy wasn't going to let a nurse intimidate her.

Life Lesson from daddy: Protect your family – be brave.

Even though Memom and daddy were off to a bad start, you were doing great. Your nurses had already taken off all of your breathing assistance machines, and the only thing you needed to learn was how to eat. Mommy came back for your seven o'clock feeding, and we met your new nurses. One of the nice things about the NICU is that you have a nurse watching after you 24 hours a day and 7 days a week. The only bad thing about this system is that you get new nurses and doctors every day. Right when your mom and I would get comfortable with the idea of a nurse taking care of our little baby, a new nurse would inevitably take over. Tonight you were going to have two nurses because one nurse was training.

Your mom and I talked for a while at your bedside while your nurses helped the little baby next to you. Mommy decided that she needed to go and make your food, an amazing gift that only mommies have. Your mom could make you food that came out of her skin? If you want my honest opinion, I think it is simultaneously amazing and gross. Anyways, I stayed at your bedside watching you and all your monitors. You were resting so peacefully in your crib that I didn't want to disturb you by picking you up. It took mommy awhile to get your food ready, and I was getting kind of frustrated because your nurses were not paying any attention to you. I love you so much that I was very sensitive to the fact that I didn't believe you were getting the attention you deserved. The baby next to you was very sick, and I knew that he needed a lot of attention, but I didn't like that the new nurses were ignoring you. As I sat, I got more and more angry. I watched the clock tick away without their even glancing in your direction. Finally, I couldn't take it any longer and I asked to speak to the nurse.

I walked up to the nurse and told her that I needed to speak to her. I wasn't going to be mean, but I planned on being assertive. I had to control my emotions as the comments from the previous nurse about "not reading to you" had already put me in a less than happy mood.

I said, "I have been hear over an hour and you have not checked on my baby or even glanced in her direction once. Now I understand that you have another baby to take care of, but I do not want you ignoring my baby." The nurse seemed shocked. I then went on to ask whether she would be giving you more attention if I were not at your bedside. She defensively said, "No, I am not going to sit and stare at your daughter. She is in the feed and grow stage." Her words only served to increase my anger and frustration. You were in the hospital for a reason, you needed constant care. I knew I had made my point, and I therefore remained calm and didn't let my emotions get the better of me. I told her that I would appreciate her keeping us informed if your care was going to change so that we knew that the different level of attention was intentional rather than due to a lack of interest.

When your mom came back, I told her what had happened. She was happy that I had stood up for you. Even though the nurses said that they did not need to pay as close attention to you now that you were doing so well, I did see an enormous change in their behavior after our little chat☺

Having just finished feeding you, mommy and daddy knew that it was time to go home. Mommy kissed you on the forehead and we slowly headed toward the door. Mommy had waited until you were sound asleep before leaving, but she was still struggling with the idea of being ten minutes away from you. No longer would she be at the hospital but rather she would now be at our townhouse. When hadn't made ten feet out of the NICU before mommy started crying. Your mom can be a very emotional person which is a characteristic that I really love about her. She is extremely empathetic and caring. Tonight, these characteristics were making her very sad.

I tried to reassure her and tell her that you would be fine, but no words could calm her. She had always dreamt of leaving the hospital with her baby in hand. Being separated you was never part of the plan. As I have told you before, there is nothing you can say to a mother who is sad about being separated from her child. I believe that the bond you will form with your mom will be the strongest bond you ever have. Your mom continued to cry as we walked through the hospital and into the parking lot. She was so sad that she kept saying things that didn't make sense. She was blaming herself for not being able to keep you in her tummy longer. She was saying that you should still be in her tummy and not the NICU. I continued to try to find the right words to lessen her pain, but there was nothing I could do. I had to just let her be sad. It was sad. Sometimes, you just need to be sad, and I think this might be one of those times.

I didn't like going home without you either, but I needed to be strong for your mom. I had already accepted the fact that you came early and needed to be in the NICU. My focus was already on taking care of you and your mom. Worrying about the past wasn't going to make anything better. I got to the point where I just looked at the positive side of things. I was glad that you decided to come when you did because you had stayed in mommy's tummy just long enough to be healthy. Once you were healthy, I wanted to see you, and I guess you wanted to see me too. I have never been accused of being patient, and it seems that you might be just like me.

I am sure you will have a good night. Get your rest, and I will see you in the morning.

Dear Zoe – July, 31

We couldn't wait to get to the hospital after having spent the night away from you in our townhouse. It was the first time that your mom was actually anxious to get out of bed in the morning☺ We couldn't scrub fast enough at the NICU sink, we just wanted to see you. When we went to your bedside, we saw a new nurse who we had not previously met. Just by the looks of her, I could tell that I was going to like her. Once we talked, I liked her even more. She had a lot of experience as both a nurse and a mother. She had a great sense of humor, and I was convinced that you would not be getting ignored today.

We asked how your night had gone hoping your night had been more peaceful than ours. Cindy, our new nurse, said that you had another episode of a rapid heart rate. I acted as if I wasn't too concerned in order to prevent your mom from worrying. I did however immediately tell Cindy that I would like to talk to your doctor, Dr. Michael. Dr. Michael came right over as he always does when I ask. When I told him that I would like to know the results of the EKG that had been completed a few days ago to see whether it provided any clues as to why your heart would decide to beat so fast some times, he told me that the results were not back. I looked at him and said, "Dr. Michael, you know this is the

Intensive Care Unit, correct? Waiting three days for the results of a test doesn't seem to be very intensive to me." He could tell that I was half-joking and half-serious.

Thirty minutes hadn't even passed when a man introduced himself as Dr. Chang. He was a neonatal cardiologist, and he was going to discuss your EKG with mommy and me. Dr. Chang spoke softly yet with a true sense of authority. He said that your EKG looked basically normal and that he was not positive as to what was causing your heart to beat so quickly. He asked our nurse for some graphs of when your heart was racing. He studied the charts closely and said that he thought that it was most likely not SVT. Daddy waited patiently as he explained the situation before I asked some questions. I said, "why did you say basically normal instead of normal? If it is not SVT, could it be more serious?" He immediately assuaged my fears by saying that he meant normal, but since you were not having an episode, it was tough to say it was completely normal. He also said that he was able to rule out more serious heart conditions that babies sometimes get. If you didn't have SVT, then you probably had something even more innocuous.

He said that he would continue to monitor you because it was interesting that you would have only these very short episodes of an accelerated heart rate. I looked at him and told him that as a father there was nothing "interesting" about this situation. He, as a doctor who studies the heart might wonder about the science causing the situation, but I, as a parent, just wanted a clear diagnosis. He said he understood with a smile, and I was pretty certain that you were going to be just fine.

Dear Zoe – August, 1

I think that I am going to write to you about the NICU; I could see it be a confusing place to start your life. When you get older, we can definitely talk about the NICU as I believe it will impact my life well after our time here is finished.

You have the best mommy in the whole NICU. Your mommy is always at your bedside kissing you, changing you, and whispering sweet messages in your ear. Some of the other babies are not nearly as lucky.

The NICU can be a sad place for many reasons. The most obvious reason is the fact that no one likes to be sick or see someone else sick. When the sick person is a little tiny baby, it is even more difficult to see. Some of the babies are so sick that God wants to take care of them Himself. He brings these little babies to

Dear Zoe || Love Dad

Heaven and makes them His angels. Since you have been in the NICU, God brought a couple of babies back to Him.

Another reason that the NICU can be sad is that not all the babies have such amazing mommies, the way that you do. There are some babies who don't ever have visitors. Some babies only get visits from their grandparents. Other babies only get periodic visits from their moms and no visits from their dads. Your mom and I pray for these babies; we want them to get the same amount of love and attention that you are getting.

When my friends at work, tell me to hang in there because they know that it is hard having a baby in the NICU, I tell them that we are lucky. I tell them to pray and think about the little babies who don't get visitors and whose parents don't have the money to buy them all the nice things that you are getting when you come home.

Mommy made a special friend while she has been taking care of you. Mommy saw a young girl who had just finished high school. Whenever mommy was visiting you, this young girl was visiting her baby. She would stay at her baby boy's bedside for 10-12 hours a day just like mommy. God gave this mommy a baby even though there was no daddy to help out.

Mommy started asking this young girl whether she had any family to help her, and she said that she lived at home with her mom and grandparents, but that she would be taking care of the baby by herself. She said that her mommy and grandparents smoked cigarettes and she didn't want her baby to have to smell this yucky substance. One day, this young mom told your mommy that she had been walking to the NICU from the Ronald McDonald House because the busses didn't run on the weekends. This young mom loved her baby so much that she was walking over half a mile many times a day to spend time with her little boy.

Thinking about how much this young girl loved her baby and how hard she was trying to be a good mom without any support made your daddy cry a little bit. Mommy told this young woman that we could take her home so that she didn't have to walk anymore. Memom also gave her some money so that she could get some food.

Life Lesson from Daddy: When you get older, I want you to know that there are many, many people who don't have all the wonderful things that you have. It is really important to help those who are less fortunate.

Dear Zoe || Love Dad

Daddy wanted to continue to help this girl, and he was able to find out how to send her some money and baby-supplies through the Ronald McDonald House. Daddy's friend at work also wants to help. I know you would be proud of mommy and daddy for helping out. See, you are already making daddy a better person.

Dear Zoe – August 2

You had a real tough day today Zoe, but you were very brave. You needed to have your IV changed this morning which led to a few problems. You arms are so little that the nurses had a hard time finding a vein for your medicine. They had to poke you with a needle about seven times which made your Memom very upset. At first she was sad, but when they continued, she got mad. She loves you so much that she hated seeing the nurses poking you even though she knew you needed your medicine. Finally, the nurses had to put the IV in your head because they were able to find a more easily accessible vein.

I came at lunch to see you like I always do. I love coming to see you; it always makes me forget about any of the problems or issues that I am having at work. Just being close to you puts a smile on my face. I explained to Memom and mommy that the nurses needed to give you the medicine, but I told them that I would speak with the head nurse to make sure you weren't going to be put through any additional trauma.

I had gone back to the office when Memom called to tell me that your heart rate had gone over 200 beats a minute for a third time (since you were born). Memom and mommy had been crying because they had hated seeing you get poked with the needle for the IV and they were now concerned about your heart. I was worried about you as well as Memom and your mom, and I left the office immediately to take care of the situation.

By the time I reached the hospital, I knew that I needed to speak to your nurse as well as the doctor. I told the doctor politely but assertively that they were not to continue to poke you with needles to get your IV. If they didn't have the skill to get an IV, then they weren't going to use you for practice. The nurses and doctors explained how hard it was to get an IV, but your daddy doesn't like excuses. I said, "You need to find someone in the hospital capable of giving my child her IV successfully. I don't care how hard it is; I don't want to have my daughter poked and prodded."

Lesson: I hope that you will always try your best at whatever you do. Never let yourself believe that you cannot improve or do better. If the nurses and doctors refused to accept the fact that missing veins was okay, I believe they could have possibly done better.

Dear Zoe || Love Dad

After addressing the IV situation, I turned my attention to what was a bigger concern, your elevated heart rate. There were many different doctors and nurses in the NICU which was definitely a good thing because there were a lot babies who needed attention. One problem however was that each doctor or nurse had his or her opinion about what was happening with your heart. The doctors and nurses have been telling your mom and me many different things about what was causing your heart to beat fast. First they thought it was SVT. We then heard it was EAT. Finally, they said it was just normal elevations because you are a preemie. I didn't know who or what to believe. I love you too much to accept "possible" explanations, and I told the cardiologist on-call that I wanted another test called an echo cardiogram. The doctor said that he would order the test because I had specifically asked for it.

Life Lesson from Daddy: I hope that you always have the confidence to demand answers to your questions. You should never been intimated by others' titles, age, experience, etc.... You should respect everyone, but you should not be deferential or intimidated because of someone's title, age, experience, etc...

For the rest of the night, you were very restless. Having been poked and prodded seemed to make you very upset. You had been sleeping so peacefully, but tonight you tossed and turned. I wish I could have made everything better, but there was nothing I could do. I wanted to take you out of the bassinet, but I knew you were tired and needed rest. It was hard leaving the hospital and I said a prayer that you would get rest and have a pleasant night.

Dear Zoe – August, 3

Because you had seemed so uncomfortable last night, I called the NICU early in the morning. When I found out that Alissa was going to be your nurse, I felt much better. Alissa is an awesome nurse who not only knows you and your needs but also cares a great deal about you. I called mommy and told her to get some sleep because I knew that Alissa would take good care of you until she got there. Between you and me, I was starting to get worried about mommy. She loves you so much that she hates not being with you for even a minute. A few days ago mommy and I went downstairs to the cafeteria in the hospital, and mommy said, "I hate this." I thought she was talking about her chicken fingers, but she was talking about being away from you. I said you have only been away for ten minutes and she is right upstairs. Mommy said, "I know but she is the favorite thing I have ever had." Daddy started laughing and said, "She is your baby not a thing." Mommy laughed too; she knew that she had accidentally said the wrong thing. Her laughter didn't last long however. She was really

Dear Zoe || Love Dad

struggling, and she seemed to be getting worse each day as pure exhaustion was setting in.

Dear Zoe – August, 3

You have had a great afternoon. The doctors gave you your echo cardiogram and you received a positive report. There were many different conditions that had been discussed when you heart had been racing, but most were proven to be inaccurate after this test. The cardiologist said that he did not see any issues of note on the images taken. The only lingering concern I had was due to the doctor telling me that you had a small, pin-size hole in your heart. Even after he explained that the little hole was to be expected given your age, it was hard digesting this information. I asked question after question regarding this hole to make sure that you were in fact as healthy as he had originally presented. Each of my questions was met with some variation of the following answer, "There is absolutely nothing wrong with your daughter's heart. The hole exists in ALL babies as it is critical for carrying oxygenated blood through the heart when the baby is in utero. It will most likely go away with age, but even if it doesn't, it shouldn't be an issue." Given all the different things I had been through with you since IVF, the delivery, and now the NICU, I had just grown accustomed to asking detailed and repeated questions hoping to ensure a complete understanding.

Having received a great report about your heart and having learned that the doctors would not be giving you any more IVs, I was in a great mood. You had overcome another hurdle. You were doing great, and I was now confident that you would be coming home soon.

With evidence that both your heart was healthy, I could focus on getting you home.

Your mom and I learned that you need to be able to do three things in order to leave the NICU. 1. Breathe on your own. 2. Regulate your own body temperature. 3. And, gain weight getting all your meals either from mommy or a bottle. You had already accomplished 1 and 2, and I was hopeful that 3 would be right around the corner.

Mommy wanted to feed you tonight, but I asked whether it would be okay if I tried. I told mommy that I didn't want you swaddled in your blankets when I was feeding you. I didn't want you to be uncomfortable per se, but I also didn't want you so content that you would immediately fall asleep. If we wanted to accomplish #3 on your NICU checklist, I figured you had to stay awake during our attempts at feeding you. Last time I fed you, you immediately went to sleep.

Dear Zoe || Love Dad

I started wondering what you were thinking. I figured it was something such as: "I'm so tired and relaxed in your arms daddy, I think I will just go to bed. Do you mind putting the rest of my food in the NG tube so that I don't have to stay awake anymore?"

I put the boppy (a special pillow used for feeding babies) on my lap and got ready. Mommy handed you over to me in your cute little pink outfit. I sat you up and looked into your pretty blue-grey eyes. I said, "Zoe, mommy and daddy want you to eat so that we can take you home. We made a really nice room for you that is much quieter than the NICU with all the buzzers and beepers." I held your head because your neck muscles weren't yet strong enough to hold yourself up. I took the bottle and slowly moved it toward your mouth. You started to open your mouth slightly which I took to mean that you wanted some milk. I slowly moved the nipple into your mouth and to my great delight you started sucking real hard. I was so excited and proud. We were doing it, I thought to myself. I could see the milk flowing through the bottle. You decided that you wanted to spit some out on your new outfit, but I didn't care. I was just so happy that you were sucking away because I knew you were learning.

I kept feeding you for about ten minutes, and you ended up eating 15ml. I was so thrilled that that you were learning how to take your bottle. You were already acting like a big girl even though you were still supposed to be in mommy's tummy. The doctors told us that learning to suck, swallow and breathe was difficult for babies, but I knew you could do it.

Dear Zoe – August, 4

I have been leaving work at lunch to come visit you in the hospital every day. I was sad this morning when I looked at my schedule to see that I had a meeting scheduled right when I normally come to see you. I decided that rather than be sad and miss you, I would just skip the meeting☺ Nothing could be as important as seeing my little girl.

Life Lesson from Daddy: In life, always try to remember what is truly important.

I was only able to visit a short time at lunch, but seeing you made my day. It is always hard leaving, but I feel better knowing your mommy is there with you. She literally spends all of her day either holding you or sitting by your bedside. I didn't even know that someone could love someone else as much as your mom loves you. You are very lucky to have a mom who is caring, loving, and really, really fun. You probably already sense that she is caring and loving, but trust me, you are going to have more fun as a kid that you could ever imagine.

Dear Zoe || Love Dad

When I came back to visit you after work, your mom and I needed to change you. As we stood by your bedside, we heard you go to the bathroom. I was thinking that we were lucky you were still wearing your diaper. Changing you is really hard these days because you love to move your arms and kick your legs. The minute we start to take off your diaper you begin moving like crazy. It is almost impossible to get your diaper on with your arms and legs flying all around. I wonder whether you will like to play sports like your mom and I. You know that I just want you to be happy. Maybe you will play sports and maybe you won't; it doesn't matter to me. I just ask that you always be a loving and caring person.

When we got your diaper off, you had left a big surprise. I don't know how a little girl like you could have so much poop when all you have been eating was milk. We started to change you, but I guess you weren't exactly finished. I got out the spray that helps make you extra clean and began to squirt your bottom. I guess you thought we were playing a game because you tried to squirt me back! You kept pooping and pooping for another minute. Every time we thought you were finished and would begin to put a clean diaper on you, you would start back up. Finally, you finished.

Your mom and I were talking by your bedside later, and mommy said, "I can't even imagine life without our baby." I wanted to be funny and so I said, "Does this mean you can't remember our wedding day?" Mommy said, "Yeah, I remember it, but it is no longer the happiest day of my life. Having Zoe was much, much better." I smiled and said, "I couldn't agree with you more."

Mommy and daddy were hungry and we decided to go downstairs to get something to eat. I was telling mommy about my day at work and she said, "I don't know how you can go to work." I said, "Well, you didn't know what it was like to go to work even before our baby was born." Mommy wanted to get mad at daddy, but she knew that I was just playing a joke. I told her that I of course missed my little girl, but I knew she was in good hands having such a great mom and grandmother keeping vigil.

We weren't downstairs for more then ten minutes when we heard the loud cracking of thunder and the bright flashes of lightning. Mommy immediately stood up and said we needed to go upstairs because our baby was scared. We left our food and went to check on you, and guess what? You were completely sound asleep. The NICU was always so loud and bright that you probably didn't even notice. Mommy and daddy stayed until around 11:00 when you finally settled down before heading back to the hotel. Mommy and I live about ten minutes from the hospital, but mommy said that was too far away from you. We therefore decided to get a room right across the street at the Hershey Lodge. Love you, Zoe.

Oh, I can't believe that I almost forget to tell you this. The most amazing thing happened today. When I picked you up and brought you to my chest tonight, your little arms wrapped around my neck for about two seconds. You chose daddy as the recipient of your very first hug. I can tell you right now that without question it was the best hug daddy had ever gotten. It might have been short in actual duration, but the memory of the feeling I got with your smooth, chubby arms wrapped around my neck will last forever.

One more thing, we are not going to tell mommy about the hug just yet. She would be way too jealous.

Dear Zoe – August, 5

You are having another great day. Mommy came over to the hospital early to give you your second bath. I always knew you were pretty, but you looked absolutely beautiful after your bath. Your hair was combed and your skin was so soft and smooth. Your mom then dressed you in one of the many cute outfits that we received after finding out we were having a little girl.

The NICU has been great because you are getting great care, but I really want you to come home soon. There are so many things that I want to be able to show you. We have been preparing for your arrival for quite some time, and I think you will be quite impressed. We found a book that rated all the products that a baby would need. Each of us then combed through the pages of this book looking for the best and safest products for you. Now, I don't want you to be spoiled, but it is really hard.

Lesson: My mother always told me that she would spoil me as long as I never acted spoiled. I plan on doing the same for you because I turned out pretty well.

I realized today that maybe you weren't taking your bottle (objective #3) because you liked all the attention you were getting at the hospital. Your mom was there all day long holding, feeding, and loving on you. When mommy went to the room to make your milk, you had nurses and doctors fussing over you because you are the prettiest baby in the whole hospital. Everyone that comes over to your crib can't help but smile when they see your face.

You might not get as much attention from strangers at our house, but your mom and Memom will probably give you even more attention (if that is possible). They might never let you out of their sight. Also, I think you are going to be shocked at how much more peaceful our house is than the NICU. At our home, you won't be exposed to all the beeps, cries, and rolling wheels that make you scrunch up your face in frustration.

Okay, I have made my plea for you to come home. Now, I will tell you about your day.

When I got to the hospital for my lunch break, mommy was already feeding you. She said that you looked hungry which was why she hadn't waited for daddy, but I think she just wanted to feed you herself. Like usual, you took about 10ml of milk before mommy decided it was time for you to burp. For some reason, you just don't like to burp. I know you would feel a lot better if you did, but it isn't an easy thing to explain to a baby. Your mom burps all the time and she might need to show you.

Mommy held you up to her shoulder and started to pat your back. Nothing. She decided to try and start feeding you again, and you drank another 10ml. I was so proud of you. I always knew you could do it. Unfortunately, you decided that 20ml was enough. Mommy once again tried to burp you in order to create more room in your little belly, but you decided that you would rather just take another nap. I started laughing because you are just so cute when you sleep. I really want you to come home, but I have to admit that there is something really funny about your desire to sleep during your feedings. Mommy continued to hold the bottle in your mouth, but you just lest it rest there while you closed your eyes and drifted off. I couldn't help but think of the day your mom fell asleep with the cracker in her mouth after her surgery.

I was exhausted today at work, and your mom and I decided that I should go and take a nap rather than come to the hospital. I went to the hotel to take a nap, but I decided that I wanted to write you this note instead. After I was writing for a while, I started to miss you and the next thing I knew I was in my car headed to see you.

When I got to the hospital, I couldn't find you. It turned out that you were doing so well that they moved you to the "crib room" which should be your last stop before coming home. Your mom and Memom must have gone downstairs to eat because you were alone which doesn't happen very often. You were sleeping and I decided that I shouldn't wake you. It was a tough decision to make because I wanted to hold you and see you stretch your arms and legs. Every time you begin to wake up, you spend a good five minutes stretching. You lift both your arms and your legs slowly and deliberately; it is the cutest thing I have ever seen. I had to settle for staring at you as you peacefully slept.

Dear Zoe || Love Dad

Mommy came back from dinner and I told her that I just couldn't stay away. I was still really tired, but I decided that I would go downstairs to get dinner and then join mommy back in the NICU for your last feeding of the day. Feeding time is always exciting because we love to see how you continue to progress. Because mommy had already fed you a couple of times during the day, I asked whether it would be okay if I took this final feeding.

Before I continue, I should tell you about something very sweet that happened. Today at daddy's work, one of his colleagues asked whether it would be okay whether she prayed for you. It was a very nice gesture given that she and I hardly know each other. (When someone says something nice about you or even asks about you, I immediately like them☺ It must be a parent thing.) I told her that of course it would be okay. Your mom and I believe that you should always say thanks to God for all the good things that you have such as your health and the food that you eat. We also believe that it is important to ask for His help when things are too tough to handle on your own. This was definitely one of those times.

About an hour passed when I received a letter on my computer from my co-worker. She had already sent along a prayer message to all of her friends. Maybe mommy and daddy were all wrong focusing on the doctors and the nurses for advice; maybe we should have been concentrating on asking the Big Guy Upstairs for more help.

Okay, now I can continue. Mommy had already changed you when I got back upstairs from my usual chicken tender dinner in the hospital cafeteria. I sat down in the rocking chair and prepared to feed you. Mommy lifted you out of your crib and handed you to me. I had a good feeling about this feeding because you have been making great progress. Mommy said that you had taken 26ml from the bottle earlier in the day, and I told her that I thought you and I could beat her record. The minute I lifted the bottle to your little lips, you began to suck away. I was cautiously optimistic because you hadn't started sucking so quickly in the past, but I knew that the real challenge was coordinating the sucking, swallowing, and breathing. If you wanted to get out of the NICU, you had to do all choreograph all three activities.

You started sucking and I could hear you swallowing. The monitors measuring your heart and respiratory rates also looked good. You were doing it; you were achieving the holy triumvirate of baby feeding, suck, swallow, and breathe. I gently moved the bottle's nipple in and out of your mouth when you would stop sucking to remind you why this big rubber thing was in your mouth. Each time I would pretend to pull the bottle away, you would re-latch and start sucking again. You were doing such an amazing job.

Dear Zoe || Love Dad

It was time to try to burp you, and I was very fearful that you would decide to go to sleep rather than burp. I lifted you up to my shoulder and prepared to coax a burp out of you. Your little arm was resting on my shoulder and you felt so comfortable. Mommy started crying because she said you looked so beautiful in my arms. Your mom had always told me that I would be a good daddy, but I think it was still nice for her to be proven correct. The image of my holding you tonight really sealed the deal. I patted you on the back gently trying to stir the gas loose from your tummy, but as usual, I was not successful. The nurses keep telling me that I need to pat your harder, but I just can't. You are so little and I am so big that I just get too nervous that I would hurt you. I would rather you stay gassy than have me upset you. I think you may already have me wrapped around your finger. I would keep this a secret from you, but by the time you read these words, I am sure you will have already figured this out.

Fortunately for me, you did not fall asleep and I was able to continue feeding you. When I reintroduced the bottle to you, you weren't as vigorous in your sucking but you did at least continue eating. You took the bottle for about five more minutes. When you were finally finished, you had eaten a 34ml, a NEW RECORD! We already make a great team.

Love you Zoe, and I will see you tomorrow.

Dear Zoe – August, 6

I didn't have a very good day today, and I think the reason is that I didn't get to see you until around 9:00 p.m. Rather than visit you at lunch, I had to go and see my doctor. Your doctors are very smart and they take great care of you, but daddy's doctor doesn't seem to be either very smart or caring. I wouldn't let you go to my doctor because you deserve the best. Do you want to hear what happened to me at my appointment?

Well, they always tell me to come to my appointment fifteen minutes early. This request has always driven me crazy; my time is valuable and I don't want to spend it waiting around in the lobby of a doctor's office trying to avoid getting. Now that you are here, my time is the most valuable as it has ever been. Any moment waiting is a moment I could have been spending with you. Basically, I was frustrated from the moment I walked through the entrance.

The doctor walked into the room and introduced me to Dr. Brandon who she said was a fourth year med student. Now your dad is pretty smart, and he knows that med students aren't actually doctors yet. Already in a bad mood, I told the

Dear Zoe || Love Dad

doctor that she should not introduce a student as a doctor as this was not actually true. She seemed surprised, but she nonetheless refused to respond.

I thought we could move onto the reason why I was there. The only reason that I went to the appointment was so that my doctor could refill my medicine (You don't need to worry; I was just getting my OCD medicine. I'm not sick.). When the doctor looked at my prescriptions, she said, "Do you need a prescription for this one? Isn't it over the counter?" Now, one thing you hope you get from a doctor is answers not questions. I informed her that I did in fact need a prescription which was why I was asking.

While she was writing out my prescriptions, she asked the student to talk to me about my weight. Your dad, not being in the mood to waste time, asked sarcastically, "Am I getting too skinny?" Remember how I said that I was pretty smart? Well, I am also what Papa Bear calls a smart aleck.

I don't always eat healthy foods like you do, and I know that I am getting a little heavy. But, was this really the time for this talk? Couldn't I just get my medicines and leave? The student was nervous and didn't really laugh at my joke. He then asked, "Why do you think you are gaining weight?" I said, "Is it because I am consuming more calories than I am burning?" Not knowing what to say, the student just kind of stood there.

Now, daddy wasn't being mean to the doctors, but I wasn't exactly being nice either. Please don't emulate my behavior on this day when you are older. I have much higher hopes for you. It was just hard to be chipper when I missed you so much.

Even before I went to the doctor, I knew that I should start losing weight. It is time for me to be start getting healthy. I want to be around for a long time so that I can see you go to college, get your first job, get married, and have kids. When mommy stares at you, she is able to focus on how beautiful you are and how lucky we are to have you. When I look at you I think about these things too, but I also can't help my mind from racing. Sometimes, I think about parenting questions. How will I teach you about the pros and cons of the internet? When is the right time to get you a cell phone? Other times, I get tangled up in very abstract questions. I wonder what you are thinking about. I try to figure out whether you can "think" given the fact that you can't talk. Doesn't one need words to formulate thoughts? Don't worry if you are a little confused right now, sometimes my mind goes so fast that it is even hard for me to follow.

Recently, I have been thinking about your childhood. Your Neeny gave me a great child hood, and I want to do the same for you. It is exciting to think about

Dear Zoe || Love Dad

your future because I know that you have such a loving family in your mom, grandparents, aunts, and uncles. For coming from such a big family, I feel pretty clueless about early childhood development. What will you be like when you are 1? Will you be walking? Just so you know, I don't care when you first crawl, walk, or talk. I will always just want you to be a happy, healthy, kind baby. That being said, I also want you to know that you can do anything you want; don't let anyone tell you otherwise.

Because the doctor had just told daddy that he was fat, I decided to go to the gym before coming to see you. I also took a nap because I have been really tired recently, and I wanted to make sure that I had energy when I saw you later in the day. Knowing your mommy and your daddy, I bet you will love to take naps too.

When I got to the hospital, your mom was ecstatic because she was able to give you 20ml of food not from a bottle but from her! She has always wanted to not only produce your food but also let you get the food directly from her skin. Some might say she has been a little obsessive about this unique ability that mom's have. Even before you arrived, she had read two books and went to various classes to teach her how to give you milk from her skin. So many things had not gone to plan thus far that I was thrilled knowing that you had been able to get your milk directly from her rather than the bottle. I knew how much it meant to your mom. Thank you for making your mom so happy.

Your mom was just finishing telling me about your last feeding, when you started to open your pretty, blue eyes. You weren't supposed to be getting up for another half hour, but I bet you could sense that daddy was there. You just couldn't wait any longer to see my smiling face☺

Your mom and I had to change you, weigh you, and take your temperature before we could give you your milk. You were not very happy that we were taking so long to get you dressed. You kept putting your hands in your mouth signaling to us that you were hungry. When we didn't give you your bottle, you started sucking on your pajamas, your blankets, and then daddy's hand trying to get some milk. I bet you didn't think mommy and daddy were very smart tonight – "How many signals do I need to give you before you feed me?" – Zoe. Well, we knew what you wanted, but we had to make sure that you were nice and clean first. Remember, we are still new at this. Things should get faster in the future.

You had taken 34ml from the bottle last night, and I was hopeful that you would take even more tonight. By the time I got you situated, you were wide awake which I took as a very positive sign. Sometimes you don't like to take the bottle

Dear Zoe || Love Dad

because you are so sleepy, and to be honest, I don't blame you. I know I wouldn't want to eat when I was trying to take a nap either. You felt great in my arms, and I was finally starting to get the hang of holding you in one arm while feeding you with the other. Usually it took a couple of seconds of my touching your cute, little lips with the bottle's nipple before you would open your mouth, but not today. As soon as the bottle got close to you, you closed on it like a bear trap and started sucking with all your might. Before I even knew it, you had taken 10ml's. I was sure that we were going to set a new record, but in the end, we tied our best effort at 34ml's.

Mommy went to go and make you some more food, and I held you in my arms for a little while longer before putting you in the crib. Mommy doesn't like to leave the NICU unless you are asleep, and I wanted to be able to leave when you mom was finished making your food. It wasn't that I wanted to leave you, but I think that your mom really needs to rest. All the time that your mom is spending at the hospital is taking a toll on her. One look at her is all you need to tell how tired and drained she has become. I decided that I should try to get you settled before she came back from making you your food. You would calm down for moments, but then you would stir again. You sure are a cuddle bug.

I just love feeding you. There is something about the process of holding you close and giving your nourishment that makes me feel that I am being a good dad. Each time that I feel that I do something right, I get a huge senses of relief and pride. All the doubts that I had over the last nine months (and more) about my abilities to be a father are slowly but surely fading away.

I always knew that your mom would be a great mom and she has definitely proved me right. I think God took some extra time when he made her so that she could be the perfect mommy. She just loves you so much. She knows how to feed you, change you, swaddle you, comfort you, etc.... If it involves you, mommy knows how to do it. You are really lucky to have her. Don't ever forget how much she loves you. Even when you are a teenager and the two of you disagree about whether you can go out with your friends, you should remember that she has never wanted anything but the absolute best for you. I know I won't ever forget the sight of your mom, exhausted and drained, keeping watch at your bedside; hopefully, this entry will at least help you appreciate her love for you.

Dear Zoe - August, 7

When your mom and I got to the hospital today at 10, you were still sleeping soundly. I think that you knew it was the weekend and therefore decided to take it easy. Today was the first time that I was able to give you your bath. Your bath was a lot different than mine. Your bath was very different than mine. I go to a special room called a shower where water essentially falls from the sky drenching my whole body. You on the other hand were able to take a bath while still lying in your crib. I bet you are getting pretty tired of your little crib at this point. Right now, your whole life takes place in this tiny plastic-walled bed. You eat in the crib, you go to the bathroom in the crib, you sleep in the crib, you play in the crib, and you even bathe in the crib. I am really looking forward to taking you home so that you can start to experience all the amazing things this world has to offer. Trust me; there is more to life than white ceiling tiles – the view from your isolate. With your continued progress feeding, you are going to find this out sooner than you know it.

Your mom took the lead while giving you a bath. My job was seemingly simple; I was to keep you dry by wiping you down. Mommy was wiping you down with a soapy wash cloth. Daddy, knowing his job was to dry you, started drying you immediately after mommy would wipe you down. After a little while, your mom realized that I was drying you before she had a chance to wash the soap off of you. Uh oh! I think I was just wanted to ensure you weren't getting cold, but leaving a soapy residue on you was certainly not the intent of this bath. I would love to tell you that this will be the last mistake that I will make with you, but I know it won't be. I will probably make mistakes for the rest of your life and I just ask for your understanding as they will never be due to a lack of love.

You seem to be really learning how to drink mommy's milk even without a bottle. Mommy was so happy today because you took 20ml of food directly from her.

You are doing so great baby that I am sure you will be home soon.

Because mommy has to make all your food, she needs to make sure that she is eating a lot. She never likes to leave your bedside and I always have to force her to go and eat so that she can continue to produce enough milk. After you did such a great job eating, I treated her to another great meal at the hospital cafeteria; we both got the usual, chicken tenders. It was nice seeing her in such a good mood. When we finished eating, your mom went to go and make your food while I sat by your bed. I wasn't supposed to get you out of bed because it is important for you to sleep in your crib and use all your energy to grow. I sat at your bedside watching you and you just didn't seem to be very relaxed. You were squirming, something that you love doing, and your heart rate was staying at an elevated rate. Even though I wasn't supposed to pick you up, I wasn't going to let you stay uncomfortable and I decided to get you out of your crib.

The minute I picked you up, you immediately started to calm down. Of all the time we have spent together, I have never been as happy as I was during the next hour with you in my arms. I realized that you felt very comfortable and safe in my arms. Your heart rate slowed, your body relaxed, and your face was peaceful as you lied in my arms. I knew at that moment that you would count on me for the rest of your life to be strong and comforting. You already needed me, and I want you to know now that I will be there for you. I have never felt as important as I did this morning. You already loved me and counted on me in a way that no one ever has. I won't let you down baby girl.

Mommy walked back in the room, but I didn't tell her about the moment that you and I had just shared. It was our moment, and I know that you have already had similar moments with her. I was nervous about being a dad because I wasn't sure that I would be good; this morning, you helped me realize that I was already great. You trusted me and loved me and that was all I needed. I know that you and I will get closer as the days, months, and years pass, but I will always remember this morning.

Mommy and daddy were talking and mommy said that she had just met someone while she was in the special room where she makes your food. She said that this woman also had a baby in the NICU and that she had gotten a bill for $700,000 from the hospital. Being the person responsible for making the money for our family, this news made me a little nervous. Too bad I had to hear this news right after our peaceful morning. Don't worry though sweetheart, everything will be okay.

Your mom stayed at the hospital all day today, and I continually told her that she needed to get some rest. Making your food saps a lot of energy from her as she has to not only make the food but also pump it out of her body every three hours regardless of whether it is morning noon or night. She hasn't really slept in weeks. Unfortunately, she is too stubborn to admit that she is tired. I could tell mommy was getting tired because she was starting to get a little fussy just like you were today. I think both the ladies in my life needed some rest today. Mommy asked me why I have never gotten sad with my baby, you, staying in the NICU. I think mommy was asking because she has had a very hard time with your being in the NICU. She cries everyday because she wants you at home so badly. I told her that I have not had one ounce of sadness since I heard your first cry seconds after you came out of her tummy. I asked God for a healthy baby, and he gave me you, the most precious girl in the world. How could I be sad when I just received such an amazing gift? To be honest, I was glad that you went to the NICU because I wanted you to get some special attention before you came home. I think mommy just wants to love on you 24 hours a day whereas I have always been focused on making sure you were happy and healthy. My mind has just been totally focused on the situation at hand; all my energy is being used to comfort you and your mom. I don't have time to be sad. I think the NICU is the best place for you now, and I know that you will be home soon.

Dear Zoe – August, 8

My life seems so much different since you were born. I see the world in a whole new way knowing that you are now a part of it. Do remember how I told you that mommy and daddy are staying in a hotel so that we can be closer to you and the hospital? Well, this hotel has a lot of kids in it, and I look at them and wonder what you will be like when you are 2, 5, 10, etc... I know you will be cute and sweet, but I wonder what your favorite colors will be. Will you be scared of roller coasters like your daddy or love them like your Aunt Alyssa. In some ways, I feel like a newborn myself because I feel that my life has just begun as well.

I used to lie in bed at night and worry about what I had to do at work or stress out about paying bills; since you arrived, I lay peacefully thinking about you and all the things I want to share with you. I want to show you my favorite movies and take you to get ice cream. I want to push you around in your stroller and let you explore the world. I can't believe how lucky I am to have you.

I woke up early this morning so that I could do your 7:00 a.m. feeding and so that mommy could sleep in. When I got to the hospital, you were sleeping very peacefully. You had been really gassy yesterday, and I took your slumber as a sign that this issue had resolved itself. After I wrote to you yesterday, I went back to the hospital for another visit. When I arrived, I learned that you had stayed awake for three straight hours. Now, I know that I shouldn't be happy about your not getting rest, but I do love holding you when you are awake. You stare up at me with your beautiful eyes and make the cutest faces. Sometimes, you even smile at your daddy which fills me with a feeling of happiness I have never known. I couldn't help but think that more of our time together would be spent with your staring up at me.

The nurse said that you had done very well feeding from the bottle over night. You had taken 30ml at each of your last two feedings, and I was starting to believe that you had really turned the corner with regards to feedings. I was crossing my fingers that you would take a lot of milk from me too when I got ready to feed you. Usually your mom is with me when I go to visit you, and she is the one who changes your diaper and your clothes. With mommy still at the hotel, I needed to do everything by myself. Thank God you are not a fussy baby because daddy didn't do too well. It took me about ten minutes just to get your outfit off. Then, I had to move onto the hard part which was changing your diaper. I am not sure whether changing all babies is difficult or whether it is just

Dear Zoe || Love Dad

hard changing you. As soon as your diaper comes off, you start kicking your legs and shaking your arms. I kept trying to move your legs, but each time I moved them down to position your diaper you would pull them right back up. Your little legs have gotten very strong from all the kicking you have been doing.

I tried and tried for about ten minutes, but finally, I called your nurse over to assist. I figure that I will get enough practice when we leave the hospital and are back at home. With a little help from the nurse, we were ready to start your feeding. I positioned you in my arms and began to offer you the bottle. Unlike the last few times that I fed you, you didn't seem very enthralled with the idea of eating. You let the bottle's nipple rest in your mouth, but you weren't sucking the way that you had in the past. In then end, you took 20ml which was a good effort for an early morning. I held you for another hour before heading downstairs for breakfast.

When I got to breakfast, mommy called and said that I needed to come and pick her up or she would just walk to the hospital. I told you she was stubborn☺ I tried my best to convince her that she needed more rest, but she just wanted to see her baby. She sure does love you, baby girl.

I decided to go back to the hotel and write this letter to you before heading back to the NICU around four. Memom and your Aunt Kim were going to the hospital to see you at one, and only 2 people are allowed to see you at any given time. (I think I forgot to tell you that your Aunt Kim was coming to visit you. She is your Memom's best friend and someone who already loves you so much that she flew all the way from Texas to see you.) I, being the logical man that I am, didn't think that going to the hospital to wait in the waiting room was a very good plan for the day. Aunt Kim got some bad news yesterday, and she was going to have to go home to Texas to get some tests. Aunt Kim is a very brave woman who has already survived an illness called cancer. Her doctors wanted her to come back to Texas because they thought her illness might be back. Because your daddy is never happier or more at peace than when he is holding you, I thought it would be a good idea to make sure that Aunt Kim got to hold you as much as possible today. There is no way she can be sad if you are in her arms.

You are having a much better day today than you did yesterday. You are not fussy at all, but I can't say the same for mommy. Your mom and I are two very different people who love each other very much. We do however sometimes disagree on things. Today, mommy thought that daddy should be spending more time at the hospital, but I calmly explained to her that there is only one of you. If Memom, mommy, Aunt Kim, and daddy are all at the hospital then only one person can hold you and only one other person would even be allowed in the room. Given how exhausted I am I thought it was a better use of resources if I stayed at the hotel to rest because I have to go to work tomorrow. Well, your mom is usually more emotional than daddy and my logical argument fell on deaf ears. In the end, your mom and I had to agree to disagree. If when you read this, you remember being upset with me on August, 8th, then I will admit that mommy was right.

Before I finish writing for the day, I did want to tell you one quick story. Something awesome happened today when I was feeding you.

You already know how much I enjoy feeding you. What you may not know is how these feedings have become even better as you have gotten older, bigger, and stronger. I love to just look in your eyes or play with your little fingers. As you have gotten older, I have already seen a huge change in your behavior. You are so much more alert and squirmy for that matter. With your increased size and level of energy, I have also noticed something very special. Today when I was holding you, you looked up at me and smiled. At first I wasn't sure whether to believe it or not, but just then, you did it again. I could definitely see you smile. I debated whether to tell mommy or not because I did not want to make her jealous that you were smiling at me and not her, but I decided that she would probably want to know. After all, I had finally told her about the hug you gave me and she seemed to handle it pretty well. She did get frustrated however when I started to tease her and tell her that you hugged me first because I was the person that took care of you the first day in the NICU when she was not allowed to leave her room. With your mom being so tired and drained, my teasing can quickly change from being humorous to annoying.

Your mom came back from getting your food ready, and I told her about how you smiled up at me after I had finished feeding you. As soon as I finished telling her the story, she started to laugh. I hadn't told a joke, and I was therefore very confused as to why mommy was laughing. She said, "I'm sorry daddy, but Zoe doesn't know how to smile yet. She is much too young." Now, you and I both know that mommy was mistaken. Your nurse was feeding another baby, but I called out to her to ask whether babies your age could smile. She said that babies can't really smile until they are two months old. She said that what I was seeing on your face was "gas pain." Basically, the nurse was telling me that his special moment with you was the result of you needing to burp or toot. Now ZoZo, I know what you look like when you need to burp or toot, and you were not making those faces. Mommy and the nurse may be right that *most* babies your age don't smile, but you must be advanced because YOU DID!

Dear Zoe || Love Dad

One more thing, you had your first temper tantrum today. I think you got mad at your nurse for disturbing you with various tests she has to perform every three hours. I watched as your heart rate climbed on the monitor and your face got redder and redder. You were just plain mad. I told your mom that you might look like me but you must have her personality. For the record (because she is writing this book), I should note that she vehemently disagreed on both accounts☺

Dear Zoe – August, 9

Today daddy began "Operation Get Mommy Some Rest." I know that you love being held in her arms, but I think you would agree with me that mommy needs to be doing a better job of taking care of herself. Since you arrived, she has been spending just as much time with you as when you were in her tummy☺

Last night, I went back to the hotel because I was tired. Actually, there is a little more to the story. Zoe can you keep a secret from mommy? Well, I trust you so here goes. I also really wanted to watch a soccer game, and I figured that you wouldn't mind my leaving because you were sleeping.

Well, I was waiting for mommy to call me to pick her up. It got later and later, and still I hadn't heard from her. Finally, I got nervous and called the NICU. The nurse said that your mom had just finished feeding you and she was preparing your next meal before she left for the night. Your mom had been at the hospital for the last 15 hours, and I was increasingly concerned that she wasn't getting enough rest or food. Your mom only worries about you, and she sometimes forgets that she needs to take care of herself as well. When your mom finally walked out to the car, I could tell that she was tired. As soon as your mom closed the door, she burst into tears. She said, "I want my baby home. I hate leaving her in the hospital."

Now Zoe, I am sure that you were sound asleep at this point and I am also sure that you know that mommy loves you with every fiber of her being. I tried to tell mommy how much you loved her because I know that you are still learning how to eat and that asking you to talk would be asking way too much. Mommy just couldn't stop crying. I rubbed her back and told her that everything would be okay. I became sad too because I hate seeing mommy cry the same way that I hate seeing you cry. Your mom said that you should still be in her tummy, and she was once again blaming herself for getting that sickness, preeclampsia. I told her that God wanted you to come early so that you could meet me, your dad, which is why He must have allowed her to get preeclampsia.

Dear Zoe || Love Dad

I tried to do everything thing I could think of to make her feel better, but sometimes mommy just needs to cry and let her emotions out. The only respite from my worrying about your mom was when my mind drifted back to you. I began to wonder whether you would be like mommy, a person who liked to cry and show her feelings, or like me, someone who kept his thoughts and feelings to himself. If I had to guess, I would bet you will be like mommy.

When we got to the hotel, mommy could hardly keep her eyes open she was so tired. I knew that she still needed to eat, and I went to the only restaurant that was open and got her a cheeseburger. Mommy ate the whole thing and quickly fell asleep. You know how I told you that I like to lie in bed at night thinking about you and the young lady you will become. Well, tonight I had to think about mommy. With mommy spending all her energy taking care of you, someone needed to take care of her.

I woke up this morning, and I decided to call Memom. I told Memom that she needed to talk to mommy and explain that she absolutely had to spend some time away from the hospital. Now Zoe, I don't want you to be mad at me for suggesting that your mom spend less time with you today. I only suggested your mom get some rest because I knew that Memom would be more than happy to hold you and love on you while mommy was sleeping. I never had a close relationship with my grandparents, and it is really important to me that you spend a lot of time with Memom and Neeny because they both love you so much. I am sure you will thank me for this because I know that both are going to spoil you.

I told Memom that if mommy didn't listen to her, then I would call your mom's doctor for help. Sometimes mommies get sad when their babies are born because they miss carrying them in their tummies and feeling them kick and move throughout the day. I didn't think mommy had this condition, but I wanted to make sure and keep on eye on it.

"Operation Get Mommy Some Rest" worked. Mommy spent a whole 2.5 hours away from the hospital this afternoon. I know it doesn't sound like a lot, but daddy was still proud of her.

I wasn't able to come and see you until 5:30 p.m. because I had some meetings at lunch. Daddy never liked having meetings at lunch, but he really doesn't like them now knowing that they are keeping him from seeing you. When I got to the hospital, Memom was just sitting in the rocking chair staring at you. You were sound asleep, but I knew it wouldn't last for long as you love staying awake at night. Even when you were in mommy's tummy, you seemed to want to stay up

Dear Zoe || Love Dad

from around 7:00 p.m. until midnight. I think this schedule is great because you are most alert when I get home from work.

You started stretching out your arms and legs around 6:30 p.m. which is what you do before you wake up. The doctors have told mommy that it is a very good sign that you wake yourself up for your feedings rather than having to be stirred by either one of us. Your mom came back to the hospital just as I was getting ready to feed you. I was happy to see her well-rested, but I also knew that her arrival might dampen my chances of getting to feed you. Both of us love feeding you, and we don't always like sharing this responsibility. Because I am such a nice person, I think I will let you mommy do all your feedings in the middle of the night when you come home and I will take your feedings in the early evening. Sounds fair right baby girl?

Your mom decided that it would be best if she fed you not from the bottle but from her own special milk producers. I understood that this was probably the best decision, but I was still a little disappointed. When mommy feeds you directly, we have to weigh you before and after you feed so that we can tell how much milk you drank. Mommy's milk producers don't have the lines that indicate how much milk you drank the way that your bottles do. We placed you on the scale, and I stood real close to make sure you wouldn't roll off. Babies your age aren't supposed to be able to roll, but I wasn't going to take any chances. You aren't supposed to be able to smile either but you did.

Mommy picked you up off the scale and held you close to start your feeding. You immediately started sucking and you even continued for the next 22 minutes. We were so proud of you. The progress you make every day is inspiring. It shouldn't be long before we can take you home. When you finally stopped sucking, it was time to put you back on the scale. Mommy and daddy were sure that you drank 20 or 30 ml. When daddy looked at the scale, you had drunk …. 8ml. Well, maybe it wasn't as much as we had thought, but I still couldn't be more proud. I was proud because you showed you were learning a new skill and because you made your mother so happy with your decision to take your milk directly from her.

I am really tired, and I am going to make a peanut butter and jelly sandwich and go to bed. I can't make any food for you now, that job is only for mommy, but I look forward to sharing my delicious peanut butter and jelly sandwiches with you in the future. See you tomorrow. Love you, Zoe.

Dear Zoe – August, 10

Dear Zoe || Love Dad

My day did not get off to a very good start this morning. I felt that someone was being rude and dishonest to me, and it made your daddy very mad. What made me the most upset was that I felt that someone was trying to take advantage of your daddy, your mom, and even you because he was trying to charge us more money for the house I am building you. When you were in mommy's tummy, I always liked to joke with mommy that he was going to be like the momma bear that protected her cubs against anything and anyone. Now that you are here, it turns out that daddy wasn't joking. I love you too much to let anyone treat you unfairly.

I am feeling kind of bad tonight because I don't think that I handled the situation as well as I could have. I got what I wanted, but getting what you want should come at the expense of being rude. You know how I tell you that I am proud of you for learning how to breathe on your own or learning how to drink from a bottle. Well, I really want you to be proud of me too. Nothing would make me happier then to know that not only do you love me but that you are also proud of the man that I am. I'm not sure you would have been proud of the way I spoke to the realtor today, and I know it would really upset me if I did anything that made you disappointed. My love for you just makes me want to be a better person.

Today might not have gotten off to a great start, but it sure did improve when your mom called. Guess who decided that she wanted to drink her whole bottle last night? Your mom called me at work and said that you had taken the whole bottle from your night nurse on two different occasions. The doctors had always said that some day a light bulb would just go off in your head, and you would decide it was time to take all your food. I guess the light bulb went off last night.

The news only got better as the day continued. The doctors were so happy and impressed by you that they decided to take out your NG tube which had been used to feed you when you were tired of drinking out of the bottle. Taking out the NG tube was great for three reasons. First, you know longer had to have a tube go all the way from your nose to your tummy. You have been so brave with all the treatments that you have had to undergo, but I know must be getting tired of all the tubes, wires, and monitors that you have been wearing. Second, you aren't allowed to go to mommy's and daddy's house with the tube; with the tube out, you are one step closer to coming home. And third, mommy and daddy can now see your beautiful face more clearly. Did you know that mommy had never seen your face without some sort of tube, tape, or bandage on it? You are 16 days old and your mother had not seen your beautiful unencumbered face until 1:00 p.m. today.

Dear Zoe || Love Dad

You were very brave when the nurse took out your tube. You only cried when the nurse had to peel off the tape that was holding the tube in place, and trust me, I don't blame you.

With the tube out, mommy was able to feed you 55ml of milk. Coordinating the suck, swallow, and breathe probably was a lot easier when you didn't have a tube stuck in your nose effectively blocking part of your airway. You are really getting close to coming home with your mom and dad, and I feel like it is the night before Christmas when you wait for Santa Claus to come and bring presents. I am just so excited. Seeing how big and strong you have gotten and knowing that the doctors have done all the tests they need, I am finally comfortable that being at home is the best place for you.

Mommy has always wanted you to be at home, but to be honest, I think I was more comfortable with you at the NICU originally. I had been really nervous when you were first born and were having trouble breathing. Your mom hadn't experienced this trauma, and don't think she understands how scary it was. I knew that you would be at home with us in the near future, but I wanted to have the doctors make sure that you were "A okay" before discharging you. With you in the NICU, I have been able to learn a lot of little tricks from the wonderful doctors and nurses. Now that I have the confidence that I can take care of you, I just want to hold you and love on you the way that mommy does. You will be home soon, and I can't wait to spend all day and night with you.

Dear Zoe – August, 11

You had a very busy day today little girl, but before I tell you all about it, I wanted to let you know what I was thinking about when I was driving home.

You were only born 2 and a half weeks ago, but I already feel closer to you than pretty much anyone else I have ever known. I tend to keep most of my real feelings to myself, and I often believe that people have a hard time understanding what I'm really like. As you will find out, daddy has a pretty BIG personality. I like to joke around and have a good time regardless of the situation. Because of this personality trait, people often assume that they know or understand me better than they actually do. They assign characteristics to me that aren't even close to being accurate. I guess I could correct them, but I never do. I sometimes get frustrated that I am not closer to more people. Sometimes I wish that people really understood how I viewed them and the world, but for some reason, I maintain this invisible wall around me.

There is no wall between us however, and let's make sure that there never is. Even though you don't know how to talk yet, I have the sense that you understand what I tell you. There is just something magical between us. I am not sure why I feel so confident that your understanding of me and my personality is so accurate, but I know it is true. Maybe it is because you bring out the "best self" I have. You are only a couple of weeks old and I am probably getting a little too philosophical right now, but I wanted to share my feelings with you. You already make me so happy.

I want you to think of me the way that I think of Papa Bear. I want you to always have a sense of comfort knowing that I will be there for you. I want you to know me better than I know myself. I want the unmistakable and nonreplicable bond that exists between a father and child.

Thank you for letting me tell you how I am feeling. Now, are you ready to hear about your day? It was another great day for you as you continue to get closer to coming home. I have become so used to spending time with you in the NICU and praying for you that I haven't really let myself even think about what it will be like once you come home. I didn't want to get my hopes up in case the doctors decided that they wanted you to stay for another week or so. I think the nurses and doctors like you so much that they don't want to let you go. I know I wouldn't if I were them.

Your day started in the middle of the night when you woke up on two separate occasions and took a full 60ml of milk at each feeding. Once that light bulb went off in your head, you have started to act just like daddy when it comes to eating – you eat until there is nothing left. Both mommy and Memom had a chance to feed you a bottle today, and you did a great job taking your bottle from them as well. You did such a great job that you were able to put on a little weight which for you is a good thing.

Because you are doing so well, the doctors have said that you might come home as early as two days from now. I would love for you to come home then because it is a Friday and I would be able to spend all weekend with you without ever having to go to work. My guess is that you will be coming home Saturday, but I hope I am wrong and that you come home earlier.

Before they will release you from the NICU, you have to take the car seat test. Basically, a nurse puts you in a car seat where you have to sit for 90 minutes. Mommy said that you passed, but she said you weren't exactly happy. Your mom has already spoiled you by holding you all day long. Not surprisingly, you are much happier being held in mommy's loving arms than you are being strapped in a plastic chair. Even though it might not be your favorite place, I was glad that you passed so that I know you will be safe when we are driving in the car. I can only image how nervous I will be when taking that first drive home

Dear Zoe || Love Dad

from the hospital. To overcome this anxiety, I think I am going to remind myself that your mom had made sure that the car seat was installed properly only a few days before she went into labor. She took the car and the car seat for a special inspection by a car seat installation expert. Mitigating my fear will also be the sheer excitement I have of finally being able to show you your new house!

Your day was busy enough having to do the car seat test, but your mom really wanted to get some professional pictures of you so that we can always remember how small and cute you were as a preemie. The photographer was very surprised by how big and healthy you were. Most people think the NICU is only for little, sick babies. They don't realize that there are many kids just like you who just need to "feed and grow" with a little bit of assistance. I couldn't make it to this photo shoot, but your mom has already planned another one in a couple of weeks. Your pictures are pretty expensive, but I think by the time that I need to pay for your college tuition that I will have had time to recover financially. As mommy likes to say, you are only a newborn once. Daddy pointed out to her that you will only be 7, 700, 7000, and 20,000 days old once too, but she didn't think I was funny. Now that I know the photos have been taken, I am very anxious to see them. I hope she is able to capture just how beautiful you really are. She should because it is pretty darn obvious☺

You were pretty tired after your big photo shoot, and I didn't get a chance to hold you because you were sound asleep when I arrived at the hospital after work. Not holding you today has made me a little sad, but I am just reminding myself that you will be home soon. When you come home, your mom, dad, and Memom are going to never let you touch your crib because we are all so anxious to have you in our arms. Well, I am pretty tired myself, and I think it is time for me to go to bed. Night, night baby girl.

Dear Zoe – August, 11

Some of the pictures that you took yesterday were already placed on the photographer's website. Now, I told you that it wasn't going to be hard for her to make you look amazing because you are so naturally beautiful, like your mommy, but WOW! I can't wait for you to see them. Your photographer loved them so much that she asked mommy and daddy whether she could put them on the front page of her website.

She was able to capture not only how beautiful you are but also how peaceful and relaxed you are when you are in mommy's arms. At first, I wasn't sure that we needed baby pictures because they are pretty expensive. Now that I have seen them, I want you to take them everyday so I won't ever forget how happy and content you were when you were first born.

Having passed your car seat test and having had your NG tube taken out, the only thing keeping you in the NICU is the little scale that the nurses use to weigh you. Just like your daddy, you aren't a big fan of getting on the scale. Unlike me however, you are having a hard time gaining weight. I asked the nurse, "How much weight is she really supposed to gain if all she is doing is drinking milk?" If I went on a liquid diet and gave up fried foods, pasta, and PB and Jelly sandwiches, I wouldn't be gaining weight either. The nurse laughed because she knew that I was only kidding, but I would have rather had her say, "You're right, Zoe can go home today."

You are continuing to do a great job feeding. At each of your meals, you have taken at least 50ml. It was only a few days ago when the idea of taking 50ml seemed like it would never happen. Now, if we can just convince you to stay awake during your feedings, then I think you will start drinking even more in the very near future.

Overall, you had a great day. The only disappointment is that I don't think you are coming home tomorrow. I tried to not get too excited about the possibility of your coming home on Friday, but I couldn't fool myself. I want you home so that I can see, hold and feed you whenever I want. I find some solace knowing that the doctors are keeping you a few extra days to make sure that you are in tip top shape when you leave. Staying at the NICU is the best thing for you, but it is still hard on me. Once I convinced myself that you were in fact healthy and that I was in fact a capable parent, I have started to want you at home nearly as much as your mother does. I say "nearly" because there is a very special bond between a mother and daughter; the strength of this bond is not something a dad will probably ever be able to understand.

Remember when I told you that I was starting to act like a momma bear that was willing protect her cubs at all cost? Well, today your mom was the momma bear. She is the tied for being the best mommy in the world with your Neeny and your Memom, which makes you a pretty lucky little girl. Mommy spends around 15 hours a day at the hospital which is more time than even the doctors and nurses. When they go home to see their families, your mom remains by your bed side. Keep this love and dedication to you in mind, when you process the story I am about to tell you.

Your mom arrived at the hospital around 9:00 a.m. for your feeding. I guess you had already gotten hungry, and the nurse had decided that she needed to start feeding you before your scheduled time. Your mom asked to take over the feeding as soon as she entered the crib room. The nurse was more than happy to oblige, and everything seemed to be going well. Your increased appetite how created a shortage of your mom's special food, and you were therefore taking formula at this feeding. Your mom noticed that you weren't eating as much as you had the last few feedings, and she began to wonder whether it was because you didn't like taking formula from her. See, mommy had been told by our favorite nurse, Alissa, that sometimes babies won't eat formula from their mommies.

Mommy wants you to be at home so badly that she asked the nurse whether she would take over and continue feeding you. Mommy figured that the nurse might have better luck feeding you your formula. The nurse looked at mommy and said, "You know that you are her mother." Mommy got sad because the nurse made her feel as if she isn't a good mother, which you and I both know is about as far from the truth as one can get. Your mom only wanted the nurse to help feed you so that you could gain the weight you needed to come home. Your mom didn't stay sad long. She got mad and having your mommy mad at you isn't a lot of fun. Mommy went and told the head nurse what had happened because your nurse was mean to your NICU friend Haley's mom too. Mommy wasn't going to be bullied.

Later in the day, your nurse "confronted" mommy and said that she had heard that she wasn't happy with her. Your mom told her that she didn't appreciate her attitude especially since she spends all her waking hours with you. I was really proud of mommy for standing up for herself, and I hope that you always stick up for yourself too. I had already told your mom that I would come to the hospital and address the issue with the nurse, but she said she wanted to try and handle it. There is probably a lesson for you in this story.

Life Lesson from Daddy: I hope that you learn to "fight your own battles" knowing that your daddy will always be right behind you waiting to assist if needed.

By the time I arrived, your mom had settled down. She had said what she needed to say and her focus could once again return solely to you, her daughter. I finally got to hold you tonight after a very long day. During your feeding, I was having a tough time getting you into a good, comfortable position. Your mom always laughs at me and says to you, "Daddy is as comfortable with holding you as your mommy." And, she is correct. You have gotten so strong that you are always moving your arms and pushing off my chest with your chubby, little legs. My struggle is that I see you as being so small and fragile that I don't want to hold you too tight for fear of hurting you. The nurses and mommy tell me that there is nothing I am going to do that is going to hurt you. It's just hard for a new dad I guess. Sometimes I get scared that you are going to fall right out of my arms because I am holding you so loosely and you are moving around so much. On the flipside, I am petrified to hold you too tight. I find myself in a real Catch-22. Your mom just watches me and laughs, but I am getting better.

Once I finally got you situated, you fell right asleep and had sweet dreams. You looked so peaceful. I always get filled with pride when I look down and see you peacefully resting in my arms. It is a wonderful feeling to take care of someone. Night, night Zo.

Dear Zoe – August, 13

Today is Friday, and I am happy because not only do I get off at noon today, but I also get the next two days off. I used to look forward to the weekends so that I could sleep and watch TV, but now, I love weekends because I get to spend a lot of time with you.

I was disappointed when the doctor told mommy that you weren't going to be able to come home today, but I am still really proud of you for all the progress that you have made. You keep eating more and more each day. You took 70ml twice last night from your nurse, Dee. Daddy told mommy that we might have to hire Dee to come over every night so that she could feed you; she sure does seem to have a magic touch.

When I arrived to see you a little after noon, your mom had just finished giving you your first real bath. You had been sponged off before, but this time, mommy put you in a little bucket of water. Some babies don't like the water, but you LOVED it. I think you might take after your Neeny who was a great swimmer as a young girl. She still loves swimming so much that to this day, she packs a bathing suit whenever she goes on a trip. All Neeny needs to be happy on a trip is a bathing suit and a Catholic church.

You were dressed in another one of your cute outfits, and you smelled just like what I have always thought a baby should smell like. For some reason, I had never realized that babies smell a like because their mommies use the same lotion on them. Babies don't smell like babies, they smell like Johnson and Johnson's baby lotion. I made a similar discovery in my late twenties when I smelled a bottle of perfume, Chanel No. 5. I had always thought that Neeny smelled a certain way, but what I didn't realize was that Neeny smelled like a fancy perfume. She never goes a day without it. I therefore guess that Neeny needs a bathing suit, a Catholic church, and a bottle of Chanel No. 5 to be happy.

Dear Zoe || Love Dad

The only problem post-bath was that mommy had run out of bibs, and your bib didn't smell nearly as sweet as you. Your bib had the smell of your formula; a smell I find quite gross. I might not like the smell of the formula, but I know that it has all the vitamins and nutrients you need. I will always give you what you need, but I am definitely looking forward to when you are finished with your formula and you starting eating the food that I like.

Your mom wanted to eat, and I was able to feed you. Once again, you did a great job. You took 60ml from me, and I was ecstatic because I knew that you would be coming home soon if you continued to eat so well. After feeding you, I once again got very sleepy. There is just something about you little lady that makes me so relaxed that I can hardly even keep my eyes open. Sometimes I get so tired that I need to put you back in your crib because it isn't safe to fall asleep with you in my arms. Mommy took a video of us sleeping, and we look just like twins (my opinion not anyone else's☺). I can't wait for you to be old enough to see it.

When I left the hospital, I called Neeny to give her an update. Neeny hates being so far away from you, but she had to go home to take care of your Papa Bear. Daddy showed mommy some of the letters that he has been writing you, and Neeny said that we had "simpatico." She then said that she wasn't surprised because she had simpatico with me when I was a little baby. Even though I consider myself to be a well-educated man, I had never heard the word simpatico before in my life. Neeny explained that the word is actually a Spanish word which explains why daddy hadn't heard it; I only know how to speak English. Neeny went on to say that simpatico is difficult to translate into English, but it means that you and I have a special connection. We understand each other in a way that no one else can. It made daddy feel really proud that Neeny thought I was a great dad and had a special relationship with you. I was so excited that I told mommy, and she got jealous. I started laughing. Mommy said, "No, I am serious. I want to have simpatico too. Did Neeny say that I had simpatico?"

I could not stop laughing. I tried to explain that Neeny had not said that daddy was the *only* one with a special relationship with you. I am sure that you have simpatico with mommy, but daddy decided to tease her a bit. Your mommy is the perfect mommy, and I am sure that you and she are going to be closer than close for the rest of your life. I can already picture the two of you snuggling up on the couch together watching TV or playing in the park. There was never any question that you were going to have a special relationship with mommy.

I said, "Maybe Zoe and I developed the special relationship on that first day when you didn't come and visit her. Remember, you were still tired from your medicine?" Mommy said, "No way. I couldn't help it and Zoe knows it." I didn't want to make her mad, and I therefore decided that I should stop teasing her. I didn't want to get confronted by your mom the way the nurse had.

I went home to take a long nap so that I would have plenty of energy when I came back to the hospital for what I hoped would be your last night at the NICU.

I turned on the TV to watch some shows, and I realized something. Since you were born, my frame of reference has changed completely. I now view all shows as a parent. I don't believe I am doing a great job of explaining what I mean, but let me give you an example. I was watching a show about teenagers who get bullied or picked on at school. Before you were born, I would watch this type of show and think back to when I was in high school. Now that I am a dad, I look forward not backward. Instead of thinking about my high school life, I immediately think about when you will be in high school. I don't want you to ever feel sad the way the students being interviewed on TV were. I even got nervous thinking about all the things that you will have to face in your life that I didn't. This might sound funny, but there were no cell phones and no internet when I was in middle or high school. Facebook and Google weren't even invented until daddy left college. There are so many things that will make your life complicated that I didn't have to handle. I know that you are only worried about eating, sleeping, and pooping now, but I know the day will come when you are going to be dealing with very complex situations and issues. You haven't even left the hospital, and I am already worried about your high school years. Know that I am always going to try my best to be a great dad. Of course I will fail at times, but know it is not from lack of effort.

I am sure that someday you will think that I just don't understand you. You will be right, but I want you to know now that I want to understand. When you read this in high school, know that I have been worrying about you and the pressures you will face in high school since the first weeks of your life. Please take it easy on me and try to help me take care of you. Please☺ Daddy is already scared.

When I went back to the hospital, I had the chance to feed you again. You did a great job. As usual, you gulped down the first 50ml in no time. I then tried to burp you, but I never seem to have any luck when it comes to burping you. The nurse once again told me to pat you harder; I wish they would understand that patting you harder is never going to happen. We need a plan B. You are too little and I am too big. Even though you hadn't burped, I decided that I should try to give you a little more milk because once mommy's milk is thawed it has to be eaten right away or it goes bad. Mommy's milk is like "liquid gold," and I didn't want to waste any. Also, I wanted to make sure that you were eating enough so

Dear Zoe || Love Dad

that you would pass your big weight test later tonight. You did a great job for me and ate another 15ml even though you don't seem very hungry. I think you might have just being doing me a favor because you know how badly I want you to pass your weight test so that you can come home.

Your mom and I went home as soon as you went to sleep. Mommy had moved out of the hotel, and she was finally going to spend the night at home. She was sad to leave you, but we both were saying a prayer that the next time we left the hospital that we would have YOU with us. You are going to love seeing the outside world, and I can't wait to show you it.

Good luck on the scale tonight. If you could, hold off going to the bathroom until after the nurse finishes weighing you☺

Dear Zoe || Love Dad

Home

Dear Zoe || Love Dad

Dear Zoe – August, 14

YOU DID IT! YOU ARE COMING HOME!

I woke up a little after 6:30 a.m., and the first thing I did was call the doctor to see whether you had passed your test. You passed; you gained 50 grams.

My elation was momentarily put on hold when the nurse said that you only took 30ml's and 50ml's at your two feedings. Your mom and I were apprehensive that the doctors would be disappointed with how much you ate and not release you. Because I knew that you liked to take your bottle from me, I jumped out of bed, put on shorts, and ran out the door so that I could be at your next feeding. I claim that I am the "feeding whisperer" and I wanted to make sure that nothing was going to get in the way of my taking you home today.

I felt that it was time for you to be at home. We had been very fortunate that such a wonderful hospital was located only minutes from our home because the NICU had enabled you to grow strong and healthy. You no longer looked like a preemie, but rather you simply looked like a beautiful newborn. It was time for you to leave the din of the NICU and relax in the quiet and serene environment or your home.

I got to the hospital just in time to take over the feeding from your nurse. You had already taken 40ml's by the time arrived, but the first 40ml is always easy. You needed your dad to take you to the finish line. I took you in my arms and you kept eating. I asked for the nurse to prepare more milk, and you took the extra milk as well. When all was said and done, you set a new feeding record with 74ml's. I took a sigh of relief as I knew the doctor would be happy with your morning feeding even if you had not hit your feeding goal last night. I was proud of you and me. I was confident that we had done enough for you to earn your release.

When the doctor came to see you, he said that he would give you a final check later this morning, but he said he expected you to be discharged this afternoon. I asked him the results of your cranial ultrasound. You may be wondering whether I had forgotten to mention that you had a cranial ultrasound last night. Well, I didn't want to say anything to you until I knew there was nothing about which to worry. Your results came back and there had been no change since you were two days old. The doctor said that he did not think that you had any bleeding, but rather he suspected that you had a little cyst that was completely harmless. He said your brain looked perfect – just like the rest of you (I added that part).

Dear Zoe || Love Dad

I held you in my arms and looked around the NICU knowing that I was finally going to be able to leave. I had appreciated all the care that you had received in the NICU from the doctors and nurses, but I had grown tired of the sterile and harsh environment of the hospital. You needed to be home with all the presents that mommy, daddy, and all your friends and family had gotten you.

I couldn't believe that today had finally arrived. Given all the prayers that mommy and I had had to say in order to have you enter this world, the moment of actually taking you to our house had seemed like it would never arrive. I remember driving through the snow to get to all of mommy's appointments. I remember seeing the flicker of your heartbeat on the monitor for the first time. All of the memories of the journey that mommy, you, and I had taken to get to this moment came rushing back. There were times when I was petrified such as the five minutes we had to wait after your first ultrasound for the doctor to come into the room and tell us the results. There were moments where I felt joy that I had never experienced such as the moment on Dec. 23rd when mommy received the call from the doctor telling us you were in her tummy. This journey has been absolutely amazing. My love for you has made me feel things that only a person who has been a parent can understand. The intensity of all emotions whether they be happy, sad, or nervous are much more extreme than what I had previously known.

Mommy arrived at the hospital and she was a ball of nervous energy. She immediately walked past you and I and started asking the nurse questions. "How much did Zoe eat last night? What was her weight in ounces? Did she eat enough? ....." Finally, I looked up at her and said, "Gina, calm down. I spoke with the doctor and she is going to be going home." You could see the relief and joy wash over her face. She might have been asking the nurse a lot of different questions, but the only thing that she really wanted to know was whether or not she was going to be able to take you home.

The doctor had told me that the only thing standing between you and the front door of the hospital was a physical evaluation that he needed to conduct in order to give you final clearance. Your mom and I went down to the cafeteria for hopefully our last time. Regardless of how good they are, there is only so many chicken tenders that I can eat.

Your doctor gave you your exam and you passed with flying colors. He had no concerns about your health and he said it was time for you to leave. You could not have wiped the smile off mommy's face if you tried. She hadn't been waiting for this day for 19 days or even 9 months; she had been waiting for this day her whole life. She kept saying that today was better than Christmas.

Dear Zoe || Love Dad

Our next step was to prepare you for your trip home. Mommy, Memom, and Neeny had already spent a lot of time finding the perfect "take-home" outfit. Finally, they had settled on two potential winners. One was a pink and one was white. I told mommy that I preferred the white even though anything would like nice on you because you are so cute. We decided to give you a bath so that you would leave the hospital fresh and clean. Your mom started washing your body as I washed your head. My attempt at helping was not very successful as your mom informed me that you always wash the head last so that you wouldn't get cold. Oh uh. Well, I am still pretty new at this.

Once we finished, we put you in one final outfit before changing you into the official "take-home" outfit. See, we wanted to feed you one more time and mommy was scared that you might spit up on your special outfit which necessitated an "interim" outfit. For someone who wanted you home very badly, mommy sure was taking a lot of time getting you ready to leave.

While mommy was feeding you, I began to pack the car in preparation for our departure. For being so young and small, you sure do have a lot of stuff. I was carrying three full bags of food, clothes, blankets, bottles, and diapers. When my hands were full, I had mommy put your special boppy pillow around my neck. I felt like a Sherpa, and I bet I must have looked pretty silly. I pulled the car around to the front of the hospital and went upstairs to get you and mommy.

We put you in your car seat and had the nurse check to make sure that you were nice and snug. It was really happening. I was taking you home with me.

The nurse said we were allowed to leave and just like that your mommy and I headed out the door with you, our precious baby girl. We hadn't even made it out of the NICU hallway when I stopped and asked mommy to take a picture of us. I wanted to capture this special moment. We walked down the hallway as a family for the first time. It was just the three of us.

Daddy put you in the car and made sure that you were secure. Mommy sat right next because she wanted you to enjoy your first ride in a car. I pulled slowly out of the parking lot, and hit the road. I had always thought that this drive would have been the scariest drive since the first time I had gotten behind the wheel of a car nearly 20 years previously. Never before had I been carrying such important cargo. In the end, it wasn't scary at all. You were sound asleep and mommy just sat there smiling. Every time I looked back in the rear view mirror, your mom was smiling at you. We had a peaceful, uneventful drive and were at home in fifteen minutes.

Dear Zoe || Love Dad

We walked in the door, and it was clear that you were going to like it. Mommy immediately sat down on the couch and held you. You both were the most relaxed that I had seen since you were born. Mommy had wanted to come home desperately, and I could now understand why. Things just felt different at home. We were surrounded by things that either we or our family and friends had bought you. There were two bassinets, a swing, a bouncy chair, a crib, and a playpen for you to enjoy. I wanted you to try your new stuff, but there was no way mommy was going to let you out of her arms.

Your mom finally put you in your play pen after your lunch, and I just sat next to you staring. Mommy said that I didn't have to constantly stare at you, but I couldn't help myself. You had grown so quickly while at the hospital that you didn't have much space in your hospital bassinet. I think you really enjoyed your playpen because you had room for your favorite pastime, stretching. With you lying peacefully and mommy and Memom relaxing, I went upstairs to take a nap. All the excitement had really wiped me out. You had the right idea with catching a little afternoon siesta.

As soon as I woke up, I headed downstairs to hold you. Life was a lot easier at home. Just yesterday, I would have had to drive 15 minutes to the hospital, found a parking spot, walked through the big hospital, taken the elevator up to the seventh floor, called the nurse to ask permission to enter the NICU, and finally scrubbed my arms for a couple minutes before I could hold you. Now, I simply walked downstairs.

I held you while Memom, mommy, and I watched Memom's favorite show on TV. Daddy usually likes to be in charge of what we watch, but Memom had been such an amazing help that I was glad to let her decide this time.

The couch and big chairs at our house are much more comfortable than the wooden rocker at the hospital. I sat there knowing that I could hold you forever. Having my very own family was what life is all about. I had never been happier than I was at this moment.

Even though I loved having you in my arms, I was excited to let you try out all of your various toys. First, we put you in your playpen which you seemed to enjoy very much. Next, I made the special bassinet that came with your stroller. Once again, you were very content. Finally, I brought down your bouncer from upstairs because it plays music and vibrates. You really loved this seat, and I think it will be the secret weapon when you are fussy and mommy and daddy have tried to calm you to no avail. It was hard to tell whether you were confused by the vibration or just simply relaxed. The look on your face was priceless.

Dear Zoe || Love Dad

You looked so cute staring at all the new scenery in our home from your little bouncer. Your eyes would look left then right then up then down. I think you wanted to make sure that you were going to like this new place.

I went upstairs and cleaned off the fan in mommy and daddy's room so that there was no more dust. We didn't want you to have to breathe any dirty air, and you were going to be staying with mommy and daddy tonight. Before you were born, mommy read many different books to help her prepare for your arrival. One of the books was about how to make your baby a sound sleeper. The main message was that your baby should go to her crib as soon as she comes home from the hospital. Your mom told me this was the plan, and I agreed because she knows much more about raising babies than I. You might therefore be wondering why you were staying in our room. Did we give your crib away? No, of course we didn't. What happened was, you were born and mommy got to see you. There was no way that she was going to let her little baby who had just spent 19 days in the NICU sleep in a room by herself down the hall. Papa Bear had told me that there is a big difference between what you plan on doing with a baby before she is born and what you actually do. As usual, Papa Bear was right.

I figured that you would be very ready to go to sleep because you had stayed up from 7:00 p.m. until midnight which was not usual behavior for a little baby. Mommy was worried because you weren't eating as much as you were in the hospital, but I think you might have been eating less at each feeding, but feeding more frequently. Regardless, mommy was already nervous by the time it came to put you to bed.

I had just finished feeding you after you had thrown a big temper tantrum. You were hungry and you wanted to eat right then and there. You didn't want to wait for you mom to heat up your milk and get your bottle ready. Because you had been so mad, I figured that you must have been starving. I was wrong as you only took 30ml's. Having finished eating, I took you upstairs to put you in your bassinet.

I placed you gently in your bassinet after I had changed your diaper and dressed you in a new onesie. Rather than go to bed, you started stretching your arms and legs and making your favorite grunting noises. Your mom and dad were ready for bed, but you must have still been excited. I held the pacifier in your mouth because you haven't completely mastered the art of sucking on it without it falling out. After 20 minutes, you were finally ready to go to bed for your first night in your new home.

Now, daddy hadn't been very nervous with you in the NICU because you were being monitored by all different types of machines all night long. Not only were

Dear Zoe || Love Dad

you hooked up to machines, but there was always someone in the medical field wide awake taking care of you. Tonight was going to be the first night when you would be in a room without anybody being awake. I knew that this day would come, but I was nervous. I kept asking mommy whether you were okay. Remember how we have "simpatico"? Well, I think you could sense that daddy was nervous, and whenever I got too worried, you would make one of your grunting noises to let me know you were just fine. Thanks Zoe.

You woke up at 1:30 ready for a feeding. I changed your diaper all by myself while mommy went downstairs to get your bottle. Good thing I put your diaper on correctly because you had the biggest poop of your life only ten minutes later. Between mommy and daddy you took 55ml's which was exactly what I had hoped for. I even got you to burp 3 times, a new record for me. I lifted you high on my chest so that your head could rest on my shoulder and gently patted your back until mommy finished preparing her next meal for you. She was very happy to see that you had eaten so much and that you were now sleeping.

You didn't wake up again until 4:00 a.m. I am confident that I helped mommy change and feed you, but I was so tired that I can't remember anything else that happened. I'm not sure whether I was the bottle preparer or the diaper changer. I had a sneaking feeling that this wouldn't be the last time I got confused by a middle of the night feeding.

When I woke up at 7:30, I walked around our bed to check on you. I peered in the bassinet and you were gone! Memom had gotten up early and she decided to take you downstairs so that mommy and daddy could get more rest. In all honesty, I think she was less concerned about mommy and daddy getting rest and more concerned about getting time to see you. You are really, really cute after all.

Dear Zoe – August, 14

I was lazy today and didn't "officially" get up until noon. I wasn't up long before I had the chance to once again prove that I am truly the "feeding whisperer." Mommy had been having trouble all morning giving you your bottles, and I told her to watch and learn. It didn't take more than ten minutes for you to suck down all 55ml's of your bottle and finish it off with a nice burp. Just like that, you were fed, relaxed, and ready to sleep once again.

Right before you went to bed however, mommy called Neeny to give her an update on how you were doing at home. While mommy was on the phone, I asked her to ask Neeny whether Neeny thought that you and mommy had "simpatico" the same way that you and I do. Mommy asked, and guess what

Dear Zoe || Love Dad

Neeny said? She said, "I will have to observe you in person." Daddy started laughing and laughing. When I looked down, you were laughing too. Some people will tell me that I was just seeing things because babies can't yet laugh, but I will go to my grave knowing that you laughed. Nobody can convince me otherwise. See, we really do have simpatico.

I put you down for a nap and went to Babies R Us to pick up some more presents for you. Your mom and I quickly learned that you do not like to be swaddled. You like to have your arms free so that you can rub your face or reach and grab onto things in your playpen. I needed to go to the store to pick up new sleep sacks that would fit you; you are smaller than we had anticipated. All the sleep sacks we had were too big; we never took into account the possibility that you could be a preemie. It is funny because you are still "supposed" to be in your mom's tummy. I am so glad that you aren't because I have never been happier than these last two weeks. I walked around Babies R Us picking out all the stuff that mommy had told me to get. I have always enjoyed shopping, but shopping for you is more fun than any of my previous shopping excursions. Before I picked anything out, I would study all the options trying to imagine what boppy cover you would want or whether you would prefer a cream or pink blanket. I'm sure you could care less, but it is fun pretending. Because I couldn't decide on the blankets, I just got both.

I think that I enjoy buying you things for two different reasons. First and foremost, I want you to have all the things that you want or need – without having you become spoiled of course. And secondly, I am proud of myself for being able to buy things for you and mommy. As you will learn, school can be boring at times and very challenging at others. By performing well in school, I was able to get a job that is both enjoyable and fairly lucrative. Now, I am not rich by any stretch of the imagination, but I do make enough to support your mommy and you. Knowing that I make enough money that mommy can stay home and take care of you makes me very proud because I know that you will be getting the best possible care. It is also nice knowing that I am allowing your mom to live the life she has always wanted. Hopefully some day, I will make enough money to help out other families who want the "best" for their children but can't currently afford it.

Now that I am thinking about it, work has been very different since you were born. I am a competitive person who believes in hard work, and I therefore have always tried hard at work to do my best. Since you have been born, I have approached work with a whole new vigor knowing that I am not only working for mommy and me, but rather I am now supporting you too. I miss you when I am at the office, but I know that what I am doing has a greater cause.

Dear Zoe || Love Dad

On the way home from Babies R Us, I stopped by Burger King to get your mommy an Icee because she has been working very hard to make sure you are being well taken care of. When I walked in the door, you and mommy were talking to Neeny and Papa Bear on the computer. Things sure are different then when I was a kid and the only reason to have a computer such as an Atari or Commodore 64 was to play video games. Now, your Neeny and Papa Bear were able to see you on their computer as if you were sitting next to them in Florida. Papa Bear was so happy. He just kept smiling and smiling. Papa Bear isn't always in such a great mood, and the fact that he was so happy means that you must be very special. Since you entered our lives, you have not only made my life better but you have also made the lives of many people including your grandparents, aunts and uncles, and nephews better. Mommy was able to get you to smile and Neeny said that you looked just like your daddy when you smiled. I hope you like your smile because mine is kind of crooked☺

You were getting tired, and mommy put you in your playpen. Rather than say good bye, I took the computer with Neeny and Papa Bear on it and placed it in your playpen right next to you. You kept staring at your grandparents as you fell asleep. Sometimes people say that technology makes things more impersonal, but I can't think of a more wonderful and personal use of a computer than what I saw today between you and your grandparents. Papa Bear is so happy that you are here that he even went on a diet so that he would be healthy and be able to see you for a long time.

I have to tell you a funny story now. I have already told you how your mom has been obsessed with nursing you since the time she found out you were in her tummy. Each day she has prayed for you to want to drink all your milk directly from her. Today, mommy went to feed you through her skin, which is how she does it, and you sucked real hard. Mommy jumped back and said, "No, Zoe!" She had been shocked by how hard you started sucking, and her reaction was to pull away. If that weren't funny enough, you were so hungry and determined to eat that you started sucking on mommy's finger hoping to draw out milk in whatever way possible. I was in the kitchen, and all I could hear were your mommy and Memom laughing. Mommy had been so worried that you wouldn't be able to get her milk and as soon as you started to really get the hang of it, she jumped away and told you "No."

Dear Zoe – August, 16

I just realized as I was staring at you wondering what I should record in your journal that your journal would be pretty long if I keep writing so much. I think I will try to shorten my entries or write less frequently, but it is hard because you change so much every day.

Dear Zoe || Love Dad

Today you went to the doctor for your first appointment, and you gained 7 ounces since you left the hospital two days ago. At this rate, you will be my size in a couple of years☺ Mommy was right, you must be much happier at home. I think you are enjoying the home, country cooking of Memom. No, I am not feeding you chicken fried steak yet, but I bet some of that fat and grease makes it all the way into mommy's milk because it was a heavy meal.

I found a new way to hold you tonight. It is great because I rest your head on the boppy and put your butt on my stomach. In this position, I can stare at your pretty face. The only bad thing about this position is that I could actually feel you going poop on my stomach; this was certainly a new sensation. Good thing I love you so much or I would have been pretty grossed out.

You are already so curious and observant. Your eyes dart from Memom, to a lamp, to your mom, to the couch, etc… all day long. I often try to put myself in your shoes and try to imagine what it must be like to be living in a world where everything is brand new. It wasn't long ago that you were immersed in a warm, dark pool of amniotic fluid. Now, you are breathing air and hearing, seeing, and smelling things completely foreign. Having a baby makes you look at the world in a whole new way. I am not sure what is going on in your head given the fact that you don't know any words. The one thing that I do know is that you never love daddy as much as when he is giving you a bottle. If getting you to love me and be content stays this easy, I will be a very happy man, but I imagine things are going to get a little bit harder in the future.

Okay, I can't help myself. I wanted to write one more thing. When you cry, it makes me really sad. Now, I know that you cry because you are hungry, but I hate the feeling of helplessness that I have. All I want is to always make sure that you are happy. It is so hard knowing that as you get older there will be times when you are sad or upset and there will be nothing that I can do. You will have friends who disappoint you. Teachers who fail to realize your potential. And bosses who are more interested in politics than fairness. I know that all of these things are natural and a part of life, but I already hate thinking about them. When you cry now and I can't fix things, I think about all these things. Know that daddy and more importantly God will always be on your side.

Dear Zoe – August, 18

You had an amazing day today Zoe. I can't wait to tell you about it. First thing this morning, a photographer came over to take your picture. She said that you were the most beautiful baby that she had ever photographed. Now, there are much more important things in life than being beautiful, but I have to admit that

Dear Zoe || Love Dad

I did like hearing how pretty she thought you were. Let me tell you about your big photo shoot.

The photographer wanted mommy and daddy to turn the heater on so that you would be comfortable. Even though you are gaining weight fast, you are still really skinny without much body fat to keep you warm. Daddy surely doesn't have this problem! The temperature outside is around 80 degrees, but I still turned the heater on to make sure you were comfortable. By the time the photographer arrived, you looked very comfortable. I, on the other hand, was beginning to sweat.

The first thing the photographer asked me was how hairy I was. Trust me baby girl, this is not a normal greeting. I said that I didn't think I was that hairy to which she said, "Let me see." I guess she thought that taking pictures of a baby with her shirtless dad would be very beautiful and artistic. After I lifted up my shirt, she quickly changed her point of view and told me to go upstairs to get a black shirt. I told mommy that all I wanted was some pictures of you, my baby girl. I didn't need someone critiquing my physique in the stifling heat of our townhome.

Next, she started moving your arms and legs to test your flexibility. I asked her to be gentle because I couldn't tell what she was doing. You are a baby not a mini-contortionist. Finally after telling me what to wear and putting you through a rather extensive stretching routine, we were ready to start shooting. She put us in all sort of funny poses. She would say look up, close your eyes, lower your shoulder, etc... I just kept thinking, "I hope she knows what she is doing." I was also sweating profusely at this point, and mommy had to keep toweling me down after each shot. After 30 minutes of posing and 2 minutes of photos, it was time for mommy to join us.

Mommy hadn't had you in her arms for more than five minutes when you decided to pee. You were naked, and pee got all over her. I started laughing while mommy just kept standing there. She didn't even flinch. Mommies just have something special in them that make them immune to things that would gross out a normal person. We took more pictures, and Memom said we looked great. I know two of us would, you and mommy. Hopefully, I didn't ruin them with my big, bald head.

I had to leave to go to work, but mommy said you had your picture taken for another five hours. She said you were very calm and well behaved – not like your daddy☺ Mommy showed me the prices of the photos, and I nearly fell over. I think I might have to decide whether I want to pay for your college or pay for 10 wallet sized photos of you. Of course I am going to pay for both. I won't ever forget these first few weeks with you, but I still want to have pictures in case my mind gets cloudy as I get older. I also want to have proof for when I tell you as a teenager, "I held you in my hands; now don't be afraid to tell me what is going on in your life."

When I got home from work, I was able to teach you something new. Changing you is not one of my strong suits. Today, I was having a particularly difficult time getting your outfit off. The buttons on babies' sleepers are impossible to get off. Why all your clothes don't have zippers is a mystery to me. Anyways, you were crying because you were hungry. I kept giving you your pacifier, but it would always fall out. You would try to roll to get it, but it was often too far away. What I decided to do was wrap your fingers around the outside of the pacifier until you were cupping it in your hand. You grabbed on tight, and then I raised it to your mouth. You started sucking, and I watched in amazement as you held your own pacifier in your mouth. You would even take it out momentarily and put it back in. Pretty amazing for someone who is still supposed to be in mommy's tummy.

As if you didn't already do enough today, you decided to have another "first" while your mom was holding you. Your head was resting against mommy with your right ear pressed against her. All of a sudden, you pulled your head back, looked at mommy's face, and then turned your head and rested your left ear against her chest. Before that moment, your little neck wasn't strong enough to hold up your head. It probably still isn't, but for that moment, you decided that you were going to do what you needed to do to become more comfortable. I like your independent spirit. At least, I like it for now.

Dear Zoe – August, 22

Aunt Jessica called to check on you and see how you were doing. We were talking for about five minutes when she asked daddy, "Are you all weird now that you have a baby?" I thought her question was funny, but once you get to know Aunt Jessica you won't be surprised. I told her that I didn't think so, but I could honestly say that my life would never be the same again. I didn't think about our conversation until a few days later when I prayed to God to help you take a poop. What used to make me excited was going to the store and buying shoes or watching my favorite shows on TV. Since you were born, what makes me happy is hearing you have a big burp or knowing you had a big bowel movement. Yes, becoming a parent makes you weird – especially to those who don't have kids.

While we are on the subject of things that are weird to talk about, I have to tell you that you have become a very gassy little girl. Whether it be burping or tooting, you always seem to be expelling some type of gas. There have been times when I un-swaddle you only to be met by a very unpleasant odor. For being such a cute little girl, your toots smell like those of a grown man. I want you to be just like mommy and daddy, but I was hoping that you wouldn't get this trait!

While we are on the subjects of traits that you have that I was hoping you wouldn't get, I have to tell you, baby girl, that you are very impatient. As soon as you wake up and want to eat, neither mommy nor daddy can get your bottle ready soon enough. You start squirming in our arms or you bassinet. Your next step is to put your hand to your mouth signaling that you are ready to eat. At this point, either mommy or I have gone to the kitchen to retrieve a bottle from the fridge. While we wait for your bottle to heat up, you start crying and crying. I have tried to explain to you that I am moving as fast as I can, but thawing a bottle just takes a little bit of time. You don't want to listen to daddy's excuses, and you continue to shake your head and swing your arms. Sometimes you even smack your daddy's face. With all your movement and screaming, I have often struggled to get the bottle in your mouth. But as soon as I do, you once again become the sweetest baby on the planet. Now that I know that you have inherited my gas and impatience and your mother's Texas temper, I sure hope that you inherit our good qualities such as our intelligence and kindness.

Your eyes are starting to change color. They started out an extremely dark blue-grey color. They were so dark in fact that it was hard to even see whether you had pupils. Now, they have started to lighten, and they are stunning. They are a deep blue color that I have never seen. Mommy and I don't think they will stay this way for long, but we are definitely enjoying them for now. Whatever shade they end up being, I am sure they will be just perfect.

Kelly, mommy's and daddy's friend, called today and she wants to bring your friend Ava over to meet you. The two of you used to have dinner together every weekend when you were still in mommy's tummy and she was in Kelly's tummy. I am very excited for you to see your old friend, and mommy is going to give you a bath for the special occasion. As mommy was getting ready to put you in the bath, you decided to toot again. I was glad you tooted before rather than after your bath because I wanted you to smell like a fresh baby, and right now you didn't smell so sweet. Mommy bathed you and I still didn't think you were clean, but what I smelled was the toot you had just had. Even though you were now clean, the air around the baby bath tub was still polluted by the smell of fully digested, soy-based formula. I don't think your formula smells good when it is freshly opened let alone after it has passed through your digestive tract. Once mommy took you to the play pen to change you, I could finally smell my sweet baby.

Dear Zoe || Love Dad

Just like you, Ava sure had grown since I last saw her. Your mom and Kelly took turns holding each other's babies. I was proud of you for being good for Kelly, Jim, and Jim's sister. You let them hold you without making a peep even though you were wide awake. Maybe you are going to be very social just like your mom. Now that I think of it, I am very scared of your being social like your mom. It might be hard for you to believe, but I didn't use the internet until I was a freshman in college and Facebook wasn't even invented until my late twenties. I think that Neeny and Papa Bear did an excellent job raising me, and I think that I will borrow a lot of their parenting principles. I have no idea what I am going to do about Facebook, IM, cell phones, and all the other gadgets that I am sure you are going to want. As much as everyone talks about how hard it is to take care of a newborn, I have a feeling that this is the easy part of raising a girl.

Dear Zoe – August, 27

You are already starting to help out your mommy and daddy even though you have only been home for a week. Mommy and daddy were told that we had to move out of our current townhouse and into a temporary apartment because our landlord wanted to sell where we are currently living. Now, moving is never very fun, and I hated the idea of having you move from the hospital to the townhouse to a temporary apartment and then to our new house all before you were five months old. If you think I hated it, mommy despised it. Because I will do anything for you, I called our landlord and explained to him that you had been in the NICU and said that it wasn't safe for you to have to keep moving. Now, daddy has a lot of pride, and before your arrival, there is no way that I would have asked this man for a favor. Knowing that I was doing something to help you, I was willing to swallow my pride and ask for his help. To my delight, he said that it would be okay. Now, I just needed to get out of the contract that I had signed with the temporary housing company. Once again, I decided to let them know about your stay in the NICU in order to garner sympathy. It worked. You are going to be able to stay in our current townhouse until your beautiful home is ready. I am so glad because you haven't even stayed in YOUR room yet. Mommy did an amazing job of decorating it, and she even commissioned a special painting from an artist to hang in your room. It is the picture of a little girl with a big tutu. Whether you like it or not, you will probably be in many tutus if I know your mother as well as I think I do.

You have had a very busy week. First, you had to say goodbye to your Memom who had to go back to Texas. I know that you will miss her, but I was actually much more worried about Memom than you. Memom just loves you with all her heart, and she was so sad having to leave to go back to run her business. She cried all night Monday knowing that she was going to have to say goodbye to

Dear Zoe || Love Dad

you. I was really happy that you had the opportunity to spend so much time with her because I know that you are going to love her with all your heart as you grow older. I didn't have a close relationship with any of my grandparents, and I definitely want something better for you. I will definitely do all that I can to insure you are able to develop a bond with these very important people. You are definitely off to a great start with your Memom.

Even though Memom had to go back home, you weren't going to be without a grandma at the house for long. Neeny came to see you on Tuesday, the same day that Memom had left. Neeny loves you just as much as Memom, and she was so excited that we asked her to come and stay at our house. Your mom and I have had friends who don't want grandparents at the house because they want to prove that they can do everything by themselves or because they want to make sure that they have a chance to create a more special bond than anyone else. I think these people are crazy! I am so happy that we have had so much help because you are getting spoiled. I don't even know why we bought a play pen or bouncer because you spend all your time in the loving arms of your mommy, daddy, or grandma. Of course, mommy and daddy could take care of you without help, but I don't know why we would want to. I am also not worried about someone else creating a special bond with you; in fact, I hope you create a special bond with me, your mom, your grandmas, your aunts, and all your family members. No one ever got hurt because they had too many people loving them. Remember, you and I have simpatico, and there is nothing that can ever take that away.

You are already such an important part of my life that I continue to think differently about all aspects of my life. I have had a very hard time at work this week as many people have made me frustrated. I just want to go to work to figure out problems and help the company make money. I don't really care about following the hierarchical protocols or worrying about who will get the next promotion. Life gets more complicated as you get older, and I have never understood this as clearly as when I am holding you in my arms. It seems that you have figured out the "right" way to live and be happy and you are only 1 month old. Most of the people my age think they know what makes them happy – work, status, money, etc… - but I think they have it all wrong. Happiness is pretty simple; it is holding your child in your arms.

When I get home from work, I can hold you and forget about the rest of my day. You are not only so at peace, but you are also so honest. Many people talk about how peaceful babies look when they are sleeping, and I can see why they say this. What I hadn't noticed until having you was how honest you are and how wonderfully uncomplicated you make life seem. If you are hungry, you cry and put your hand to your mouth. I know exactly what you want and what you need.

Dear Zoe || Love Dad

For some reason, this transparency of intentions gets eroded as you get older as you start to worry too much about what others might want or might think. By spending all your time guessing what others want, you often fail to spend time thinking about what it is you really want. I think that I should just act more like you rather than having you act more like me.

Your uncle Ryder and Aunt Joanna came to see you this week as well. It has been great having so many visitors since you were born. Everyone wants to see you and everyone says the same thing, "she is soooo beautiful" and "she is sooooooooo gassy." You might be changing every day, but the one constant has been your gas. You were tooting so much that your Uncle Ryder's eyes started to water and he had to ask Aunt JoJo to hold you. I guess that he assumed that because she is a doctor that she would be able to handle certain body odors.

Uncle Ryder and Aunt JoJo would argue about who would get to hold you. There is just something so special about holding you and feeling your heart beat and lungs expand. The sensation makes everyone smile. At one point, mommy had to ask whether she could finally get a chance to hold you because everyone was hogging you. You will certainly be seeing a lot of Uncle Ryder and Aunt JoJo in the future as your mommy and Aunt JoJo have become best friends and your Uncle Ryder is my brother. Hopefully, they will take you shopping because (1) they have a lot of money and (2) they like to buy nice things. Even if I didn't like them so much, I would still let them see you in the hopes of their sending you things☺

Every day is amazing with you being here with us, but there are times when life is even better than amazing. You and I had a very special moment yesterday when you were just smiling at me. For some reason, you love to smile at me more than anyone else. I think that you can sense how happy I am when you smile, and you want to bring the joy to me that only you can. What I learned is that if I smile real big when you are looking at me with your beautiful navy-gray eyes that you will smile back. First, the right upper corner of your mouth starts to pull up toward your eye, followed immediately by your cheek. Next, the left side begins to move until you have a full-fledged smile complete with a certain sparkle in your eyes. Each time that I see it is like the first time. It is just perfect. What makes it even more special is that you don't smile very much; when I get one, especially a big one, it is like no other feeling in the world. Mommy doesn't always believe me especially when I told her you started laughing, but you and I know. Your smile is kind of like a "shooting star" where as soon as you see it, you try to point it out to someone because of how impressive it is, but it is gone before they have a chance to react.

Dear Zoe – August, 29

Dear Zoe || Love Dad

Guess what? Today is your actual due date. I can't believe that you weren't supposed to be born until today; I feel as if I have been a father my whole life. Everything in my life has changed so dramatically (for the better) since July, 26th, your actual birth day.

Neeny told me that your aunts and uncles want to learn more about you, and they are wondering why your mommy and daddy haven't sent more pictures and videos of you. I assured mommy that we weren't trying to keep you all to ourselves, but rather we just didn't know that everyone wanted so many updates. I guess I should have known because everyone loves you so much because you are such a sweet girl. When I thought more about why I haven't been sending pictures or videos, I came to the following conclusion. There is no way that pictures or videos can do justice to actually spending time with you. Here are few examples. You don't smile all the time and therefore capturing a smile with a picture would be next to impossible. Even if I did get just the right picture, there is no way that the picture would accurately communicate the anticipation and hope that I feel while I am trying to coax you into a smile or the feeling of utter triumph and bliss associated with seeing your little lips curl. Given the fact that I could never actually achieve the capturing of the moment, I guess I just haven't bothered.

Here is another example. There is no way to effectively capture smells with current technology. Now, you might wonder why this is important. One of the things that I really want your aunts and uncles to experience is the absolutely noxious smell of your gas. Whew! You have a smelly, smelly bottom. I lack the verbal fluency to accurately record the experience of holding you on a particularly gassy day. I cannot believe how you can fill up an entire room with the smell of your gas. I want everyone to experience the real Zoe, and there is no way that they can understand you if they don't have the chance to walk into a cloud of your toots.

Neeny also mentioned that most parents are always bragging about their babies and that your mom and I don't seem to do this. As I thought more about Neeny's question of why I didn't want to brag about you to more people, I realized that there was more to this issue. She said, "Don't you want to brag about Zoe?" The short answer is, "No." When I am with you for the only couple of hours a day that I am not working or sleeping, all I want to do is look at you and hold you. For the first time in my life, I am just totally content. I don't need to brag or hear adulations from others. I don't need to hear someone tell me that you are beautiful or perfect. I KNOW. Nothing could possibly make my relationship with you any more special, and why would I want to make others potentially feel bad by bragging about how lucky I am?

Dear Zoe || Love Dad

Now, I do want to share the love and joy of having you with others, and I told Neeny that I would work to send out more pictures. It seems that everyone wants to hear about you so that they can get a little of the joy that mommy and daddy are feeling.

On a lighter note, you reached another milestone in the last two days. Congratulations, you now have baby acne. Don't worry sweetie, you still look absolutely beautiful. I often catch myself staring into your eyes because I have never seen anyone with such an amazing shade of blue; your eyes are literally navy. Hopefully, you are getting all of your acne out of the way now. If you have daddy's skin, then this probably won't be your last bout of acne, but your complexion seems to be more similar to mommy's which means you might be in luck.

To celebrate what should have been your birthday, mommy, daddy and Neeny took you on a little adventure. First, we went to go and see your friend Ava. You are both getting so big, and I can't wait for the two of you to realize you are actually in the same room together☺ Right now, you both just sort of do your own thing, but I am sure that in time you will be best of friends. Next, I took Neeny to see the house that mommy and I are building you. I am so excited to move into this house so that you have the nice, big room I want to give you. So much has happened since mommy and daddy bought the house (i.e. you were born) that I had forgotten what it even looked like. Walking through the model home, I was very pleased as I was convinced that mommy and I did a good job in picking out the perfect place to raise a baby girl. I already know which room I want you to have, the room right by me. I need to go to bed baby so that I can make some money at work tomorrow. Love you sweetie, Daddy.

Dear Zoe – September, 1

I decided baby girl that I would send my family some updates so that they would not stress mommy and I out anymore. Because they are about you, I thought that I should include them in my letters to you. Hopefully you approve of my joking ways. I think I'm funny, but you will have to let me know what you think.

Update 1:

Mom [Neeny] told me that all of you would like more updates on Zoe. I will therefore try to send more regular e-mails regarding her progress. In no way have I tried to exclude anyone, and I therefore offer the following explanations.

Dear Zoe || Love Dad

For those of you who have children, #'s 1 and 2 will probably make a lot of sense.

1. I am completely content. Having Zoe in my arms is such a great feeling that I don't feel the need to do anything else. Sometimes in life, you want to tell others about your accomplishments such as getting into a great school in order for others to enhance your mood by congratulating you. There is nothing that could enhance the experience of having Zoe. She is just Awesome.

2. Sending pictures or videos just doesn't seem to really effectively communicate what it is like to be around Zoe. I never have the camera when Zoe cracks a smile. The videos don't have a smell feature, and you guys can therefore not truly experience how bad she smells when she is having gas. Our entire townhouse smells like methane. You really need to be around her to experience her.

3. I have never e-mailed any of you on a regular basis. Now that I actually have a huge time commitment on my hands, I was surely not going to start.

4. After having her in the NICU, I got used to the idea of only providing "health-related" updates. There was always important news such as her head ultrasound found a slight bleed, but she is going to be fine. Or, she needs to have an EKG because she has had a few episodes of accelerated heart beat. Now that she is totally healthy, I did not think to send updates. Being in the NICU for so long sort of framed how I view updates.

5. I didn't know that anyone really wanted updates. If you want updates, just send me an e-mail.

I could go on, but you get the message.

Here is an update.

1. She is sleeping in around 3 hour intervals throughout the night.
2. She just started to get baby acne.
3. Her bottom smells worse than a porta potty that is sitting in the hot sun.
4. Her eyes are the most beautiful shade of blue. They are actually navy.
5. She has not said anything about missing any of you or wanting to meet you. Often I receive these messages from the parents of newborns, but I find them to be wholly inaccurate. She doesn't really know that any of you exist yet which is why I suggest your visiting her when you get the chance.
6. She continues to prefer bottle feeding because it is more efficient (she has made the logical choice), but she is beginning to give breast feeding a chance

Dear Zoe || Love Dad

Update 2:

- Zoe gave me a big kiss yesterday. Gina (my wife) claims that she is "rooting" on my face as she loves to talk about Zoe rooting, but I tend to disagree. The trick is to give her a kiss on the cheek (which currently is weird because you can actually feel the baby acne bumps on your lips) and then put your cheek to her mouth. She can't help but kiss you.

- We were able to look at the professional photos of Zoe yesterday. They are absolutely amazing. The only issue is that dad commissioning a painting from Europe is probably less expensive than a framed 16 x 20 picture of Zoe. That being said, she will only be a new born once. That being said, she will only be five years old and 17 days once too.

- The photographer was unable to convince me that I needed a poster size picture of me and Zoe. I asked her why she thought that I would want a picture of "a fat, bald man (wearing a glorified sausage casing for a shirt) cradling a precious baby in his hairy arm." She had no response and we therefore passed. You however may feel free to order this picture if you would like.

- Mom is either a liar or the feeding whisperer. Whenever I would ask mom how much Zoe had eaten during the night, she would say something such as, "100 ml of milk, 2 snack size puddings, and one turkey sandwich." Neither Gina nor I have ever been able to eclipse the 100 ml mark, but mom does have more experience. Mom also did this weird Mr. Miagi, Karate Kid thing to Zoe where she rubs her hands together and then holds Zoe in order to relax her. I will give her credit -- it did work.

Because I mentioned both in my update, I thought that I should tell you more about your kissing me on my cheek and your beautiful photos. First, let's talk about the first time you gave your daddy a big kiss. You don't always like me holding you in front of me with your body weight supported only by my hands and forearms. I am not sure whether you think that I might drop you – not a chance in this world – or whether you miss being close to my chest where you can hear my heartbeat. Nonetheless, I love holding you like this because I can I can see you much better than when you are pressed against me. Also, I am able to lean over and kiss you on the head or cheek and tell you how much I love you.

You were in such a great mood yesterday that you didn't even mind my holding you in front of me; you were smiling at me and making cute faces as leaned over and kissed you. I decided that maybe you would want to give me a kiss too. I leaned toward you and moved my cheek next to your mouth. To my surprise, you gave me a big kiss. I am not someone that likes kisses and Neeny used to get mad that I would never kiss her goodbye, but your kiss was so sweet. Like I have been telling you; everything has changed since you were born. Wondering whether I just got lucky, I decided to try it again. Success again!

Mommy was trying to claim that you were actually "rooting" on my face. She says that you were hungry and trying to get milk from my cheek. I think she is just jealous; remember how upset she got when she found out that you and I had simpatico? I think that you just love your daddy so much that you wanted to give him a kiss to let him know that you think he is the best dad in the whole world! I told mommy that someday you might want to give her a kiss too. I was joking, but mommy started saying, "she kisses me all the time when you are at work." Your mommy sure does get jealous easy when it comes to you.

Now, let's talk about your pictures. I knew that I was in trouble when I saw the first picture of you and you were the most beautiful person (man, woman, or child) that I had ever seen. Of course, I wanted your pictures to turn out well, but I was nervous that if they turned out too well that I would have no money by the end of the night. By the way, if you don't like school, maybe you should be a baby photographer because they seem to be making a lot of money based on what they charge. This is basically what happened. First picture – Zoe is beautiful. Second picture – Zoe is beautiful. Third picture – daddy is fat, Zoe is beautiful. Fourth picture – Mommy is beautiful, Zoe is beautiful. In all 35 pictures, you looked peaceful, beautiful, and angelic.

The photographer is actually going to take one of your pictures and use it in a store in order to try and get people to hire her to take pictures of their children. I hope that the people who hire her know that it is you and not the photographer that is causing the magnificence of the picture.

The photographer showed us your pictures and all the various books, prints, and murals we could purchase. She then asked what we would need for the walls in your nursery. It was clear to daddy that she was trying to sell us her high-priced items even though she was refusing to tell me the prices. Finally, she said that these pictures are priceless to which I said, I guess if they are free I will take them all. She didn't seem amused. She begrudgingly showed me the prices, and let me tell you, these pictures definitely had prices and they were "pricey" not "price-less."

In the end, mommy and I decided on five 8 x 11 prints and one large framed picture of you that we are going to hang in your room. Of course, I wanted them all, but I just couldn't afford them. I didn't want to have 35 beautiful pictures and no house to hang them in.

I can't wait for all of our pictures to arrive because I am going to love having all these images of you spread around the house. People may say that getting newborn pictures is silly, but the beauty of child truly is special. I will always love looking at these pictures and thinking back to all the emotions I was feeling during this first month of your life.

One more thing before I sign off for the night. I was driving home today, and I was just excited. I had the feeling you get when it is about to be your birthday or when you are heading to the airport to take a vacation. There is a feeling of anticipation knowing the next day is going to be very special. After thinking about how I was feeling, I realized that I have been having this feeling a lot lately. Actually, I have been having this feeling every day on my way home. What I was feeling was the anticipation of seeing you. Each day feels like my birthday because I am just so excited to be with you and to play with you. I obviously never forget that I have you in my life, but I don't always quickly connect the feelings of anticipation and joy that I am having with the fact that you are the sole cause. I wish I was able to do a better job of explaining this to you, but you should at least know that you make daddy very, very happy every single day.

Dear Zoe – September, 3

Today was my last half-day Friday until next summer, and I made sure to leave right at noon so that I could come home and be with you. Mommy has been doing such an amazing job taking care of you, and I wanted to let her take a nap and get some rest. I also figured that today would be a good day to spend some quality time with my daughter – just the two of us. You made me a father which will be the most important thing I will ever do in my life. I want to make sure that I am giving you all the love and attention that I can. I need to go to work to have money to buy you a house and food and clothes, but work will never have the same importance now that you are here. My heart and my focus are on you and mommy; everything else is secondary.

I got home and you were resting comfortably on mommy's chest. She really does spoil you; you are so lucky to have such a great mom. She is just so natural with you that I sometimes wish I was more at ease. She says that I am doing a good job, but I have been known to become quite flustered when I need to do more than one thing at a time. The only thing that I might do better than mommy is give you a bottle. She has been having some trouble as of late, and she was therefore very excited that I was going to be feeding you this afternoon. I think that you are so comfortable in mommy's arms that you get too relaxed which leads to your falling asleep without getting all the food you really need. You and I don't have this problem; you love eating when daddy is feeding you.

You drank 120ml; a new record for daddy. Now that you had a full belly, you were quite content to sleep in my arms. Unfortunately, I needed to answer a few calls and a couple of emails from work which led to my having to lay you down for about half an hour. When I went to check on you after I had finished my work, you were resting peacefully. I decided that I would still pick you up because I have missed you this week. I leave for work at around 6:45 a.m. and I don't get home until around 7:00 p.m. With both of our sleeping and eating needs, there isn't much time in the day for you and me to bond.

There was however one time this week after Neeny had left to go back to Florida where I felt the bond with you and mommy like never before. It was on the night that Neeny had left, and mommy and I were lying down in our bed while you rested nearby in your bassinet. You started to grunt and squirm and mommy picked you up and put you in between us. There we were – a family. We have been a family since the doctor told us that mommy had you in her tummy, but lying together on the bed really put everything in perspective. You have a huge family of grandparents, aunts, uncles, and cousins spread out across the country, but the three of us make up the core. I had my two girls next to me for the first time. It had been hard imagining the day when we would all be together and alone. From the prayers to have God put you in mommy's tummy to your long stay in the hospital, I often felt that this day would never happen. Now that it had finally arrived, I was so proud to have my very own family and to be able to call your mom my wife and you my daughter. I will always be there for you and put your needs ahead of my own. I am used to being a son and having Neeny and Papa Bear to lean on when I need help. For you, I will be that person who makes everything better. I want you to know that I am definitely ready for the challenge.

Let's get back to today. I decided that I would hold you even though you were perfectly content in your playpen. I just sat there and stared at you for the next two hours as mom got some well-deserved rest. As you slept, my mind wondered and I started to think about how you would be a big sister someday. Your mom and I knew that we wanted to ask God for more children even before you were born. After having you, I realize that I underestimated how amazing the feeling of being a father is. We will definitely be having more children as I have never felt more content or more alive than I have since you were born. The thought of you being the big sister when you are so small right now just made me laugh. I obviously know that you are my first baby, but I never thought of you as destined to being the oldest. Today, you are completely dependent on

Dear Zoe || Love Dad

mommy and me, but in time, you are going to be our little helper. I am sure you will be a great big sister when the time comes.

You slept for over three hours. When you finally awoke, there I was staring right at you. I hope you know that as you get older, you won't always have people staring at you when you wake up. You also won't have someone picking you up when you are trying to get some rest. There are a lot of great things about being a baby such as the constant attention, the presents, and the breakfast in bed, but there are definitely some things that I am sure you won't miss. I bet waking up to someone always staring at you will fall into the category of things you don't miss.

You woke up pretty grumpy. I tried to comfort you, but it was a challenge. You were crying with the occasional scream. It was clear you were hungry. Remember how I told you that I am not good at doing a lot of things at once. I couldn't figure out how to hold you and get your bottle ready. I put you in the playpen and then ran to the kitchen to get the hot water ready before you started yelling. I then filled a bottle with formula and dropped it in the hot water. I ran back to you to start changing your diaper. I tried giving you your pacifier, but you weren't interested. After changing your diaper, you started crying again, and I ran to retrieve the bottle. When I was carrying you to the couch to feed you, I noticed that you had something in your eye. Mommy told me to get a wash cloth. I tried to wet the wash cloth with you in my arms, but once again I was struggling at doing two things at once. I put you back in the playpen and started preparing the wash cloth. At this point, I took the wash cloth and picked you back up and walked to mommy. Mommy was laughing during this whole time because she would have held you while making the bottle with her left hand and cleaning your eye with her right in a bit of mommy magic. Her laughter didn't bother me, and I walked you over to her to get her help. She cleaned your eye, and we finally proceeded to the couch for your feeding.

Mommy had missed you so much during her nap that she asked whether she could feed you your dinner. I told her that I thought that would be nice. As usual, you fell asleep after eating only 60ml. Mommy did notice however that your bottom sure did feel hot as she was holding you. We decided to change you as your bottom, which never smells great, smelled very funky. Mommy and I had been hoping that you would go poop because you hadn't gone in over two days, and it was clear that you weren't very comfortable. Your face would often turn red as you grunted and forced gas out your bottom.

Mommy walked you to the playpen and started to undress you. She opened up your diaper to find the biggest poop of your life. Your fussiness was gone as you just sat there perfectly at peace now that your tummy was certainly feeling better. To give you a picture of what mommy and I were looking dealing with, you had poop on your bottom, your front, your legs, and your tummy. It was everywhere. Mommy even got flustered and put the diaper back on you so that she could take a moment to think about what she was going to do. She decided to take you into the kitchen in case we needed to bathe you. As she carried you to the kitchen, mommy thought she might have gotten some of your poop on her hand. If that weren't gross enough, she then promptly used that hand to wipe her face. Mommy started laughing as she asked me whether she had poop on her face which is not a question you ask every day. Fortunately for her, she didn't. We worked together to clean you up. We used two diapers, several wipes, and two wash cloths.

When we had finished, you were a new baby. You not only smelled a whole lot better, but you were also in a much better mood. You were no longer annoyed when I would give you little kisses on the cheek. Before your big poop, you had been pushing daddy's face away. Now, you were back to your sweet self.

Dear Zoe – August, 6

It is Labor Day Weekend, and I don't have to go into work today. Having three and half days with you has been great and EXHAUSTING. I don't know how your mom is able to do everything by herself when I am not here. For being such a little girl who sleeps most of the day, taking care of you this weekend has really wiped me out. Don't tell mommy this, but my job is a lot easier than hers. You should definitely thank her every day for the rest of your life for the amazing care she gives you. I'm not complaining because having you here is the greatest blessing that I have ever had; I am just letting you know so that you will feel indebted to mommy and me and do what we say when you are a teenager☺

There is not one thing in particular that makes taking care of you difficult; it is the cumulative effect of being tired and nervous that really drains me. Let me tell you about yesterday morning. You decided to get up at 5:00 a.m., and I wanted your mom to be able to get some rest. I therefore volunteered to feed you. Now that I was the designated feeder, the decisions and second-guessing could begin.

My first decision was how much of mommy's milk to heat up. Mommy hasn't been able to produce enough milk for all of your meals, and therefore her milk is considered to be liquid gold. Her milk gives you all the things that you need to grow big, strong and healthy. I want to make sure that I don't heat up too much milk because if you don't drink it at this feeding, then I have to throw it away. Being daddy's daughter, you might ask why I just don't heat up a little at a time which would be a logical solution. The answer is that you are Papa Bear's grandbaby, and you have inherited his lack of patience. There is no way that you would eat and then let me go heat up more milk after you finished a ¼ of your meal, then a ½ of your meal, etc… You would be screaming, mommy would wake up, and the whole plan would fall apart. I have told you over and over again that there is no need to yell and scream as I would never let you go hungry, but you just don't seem to believe me. Each second without your bottle is cause for severe frustration on your end.

The second decision is when to let you stop eating. The obvious answer is when you stop sucking on the bottle, but nothing is as easy as it sounds when you are talking about taking care of a baby at five in the morning. What makes this decision so challenging is that you don't eat the same amount every time you eat. There are times when you eat 120ml and there are others when you eat 40ml. I don't want to give you too much because this might hurt your tummy or make you spit up, and I don't want to give you too little because this will probably cause you to wake up in only an hour with hunger pangs. Because you don't talk yet, I try to follow your cues. This approach doesn't often work very well early in the morning because you sometimes fall asleep even though you are still hungry. If you happen to wake up, you start sucking on the bottle again. Do I wake you up or let you sleep? Who knows?

The third decision is deciding whether you have burped or not. Once again, this is seemingly easy. The challenging part comes from the fact that you love to make noises and sounds, especially when you are eating. You make a little purring sound like a kitten when you first get your bottle. This sound is your happy and relaxed noise. I don't remember ever being as content as you are when you first get your bottle. You don't have a care in the world – too bad this won't always be the case. As soon as I take the bottle out of your mouth to burp you (I guess deciding when to burp you would actually be the third decision.), you start making all kinds of grunting noises. Since I mentioned it, let me talk about deciding when to burp you.

It is vital that you burp so that A) you continue to eat and B) you don't spit up. Unfortunately, you are just not a great burper. I am sure that you will be talented at many things in your life, but burping is not going to be one of them. I think the best way to get you to burp is to feed you at least 50ml before taking the bottle away and patting your back. Mommy and Neeny think that I should be burping you sooner. What happens however is that if I try to burp you after 30ml and I don't succeed, you probably won't burp after the next 30ml either which means that you have now had 60ml without burping. See what I mean? It is really a fine science.

Dear Zoe || Love Dad

Now back to deciphering your grunts from your burps. I put you on my knee and lean you forward listening intently for that magical sound of air escaping from your belly. There are days when it is very clear as a loud burp will send reverberations throughout the room. On most occasions, the noises escaping you are much more subtle. Yesterday, you were grunting, growling, and hiccupping while I was trying to burp you. I thought that I might have heard a little burp, but I wasn't sure because it might have just been a growl. I continued to burp you, but you were getting tired and were ready to go back to sleep. Remember, how I already told you that I don't want you to fall asleep when I am feeding you because then you will wake up hungry.

It was too late; my indecision led to your going back to sleep which brings me to my 4th or 5th decision. How long should I hold you before putting you back in your bassinet? To make this decision, I take three things into account 1) how much did you eat 2) how many burps did you have and 3) what was the quality of those burps. In this situation, you had not eaten very much, but it was unclear whether you even had one burp. With this limited information, I decided to hold you in an upright position for about twenty minutes before taking you back to your bed.

The decisions don't end when I put in your bassinet. Even though you are sleeping, you still make all kinds of noises. With every noise that you make, I need to decide, "Do I need to get up and check on her or is she fine?" Yesterday, I think that your lacking of burping had made me especially nervous, and each peep you made caused an immediate response. My eyes would open, and my mind would start racing. Did she just spit up? Was that just a normal grunt? Should I get up and check on her? Many times, I decided that getting up to check on you was what I need to be doing. I was getting up so many times that I wasn't allowing either you or mommy to get rest. See, I like to put my hand on your chest to feel it rise and fall with each breath when I check on you. Many times, my worrying about whether you okay triggers my entering your room and disturbing your rest just enough for you to wake.

After getting out of bed and walking over to your bassinet several times, I just decided that I should pick you up and take you downstairs and hold you. There was no way that a light sleeper such as your mom was having any luck relaxing with me bouncing in and out of bed all morning. Now, do you see why it is tiring taking care of you?

Besides our morning together yesterday, you, mommy, and me did do other things this weekend. We went to go and see the house that mommy and daddy are building for you. Right now, the house is just a big hole in the ground, but soon it will be a big house where you will grow up. I was really excited to see many kids playing in their yards because I wanted to find a neighborhood that you would enjoy. Daddy didn't grow up around a lot of kids, and I want to make sure that you do.

You also went for two walks this weekend in your stroller. You loved being outside each time. I think that you find the gentle bumps from going over the cracks in the sidewalk relaxing. We had to cut our first walk short because I got nervous. We were walking when all of a sudden, I saw a dog approaching. I told mommy to take the stroller as I positioned myself in between you and the dog. I don't mean to sound overdramatic, but I was ready to tackle that dog if I needed to. Ultimately, no action was needed as the dog, a perfectly friendly golden retriever, turned around well before getting close to us. Mommy got a kick out of my willingness to take on this "family-friendly pet." Your daddy is really overprotective these days. Hopefully, I will loosen up for you sake☺

Dear Zoe – September, 7

You had a tough day today, baby girl. Today was the day that you started to get your immunizations. You had to get three shots in your legs. The thought of seeing you in pain made me sick to my stomach, and I asked mommy whether I could skip your appointment to attend a meeting at work. I thought this would be a great way to kill one bird with two stones. One of my fears of going to your appointment was that you would be mad at me for letting the nurse stick needles in your legs; how was I supposed to explain the immunization process to you when you are so little?

Mommy seemed very tired and stressed when I called her on the phone to see how you did. Mommy said that you cried and cried for over ten minutes which is not like you. Even when you were getting an IV put in your head in the NICU, you rarely cried. She then explained that you even got blood on your new outfit. It was hard for me having to hear that you and mommy had had such a difficult morning. Thankfully, you don't have to get immunizations very often.

Do you remember how I told you that you got baby acne? Well, it had continued to get worse over the last few days. You definitely have your mommy's sensitive skin which wasn't helping. Both your cheeks and chin were bright red except for the white flaky dry skin on top of them. All the books said that your baby acne would go away and that mommy and I shouldn't put anything on it. I knew that I shouldn't worry, but I hated seeing my beautiful baby covered in what looked like a dry-skin beard. Some mornings, I would walk around the house with you telling you that you should be happy that you weren't going to prom that night with your dry skin, nose boogers, and eye crusties. Your skin

Dear Zoe || Love Dad

had gotten so bad over the weekend that I would have taken you to the doctor if it weren't for your already scheduled doctor's appointment on Tuesday.

When I asked mommy what the doctor had said about your baby acne, mommy said that the dry skin on your face wasn't baby acne. What? The doctor told mommy that you had something called "cradle cap" which was causing your skin to peal. At this point, I felt like a bad daddy. Granted, you are my first baby and I have no medical training, but your face didn't really appear to have what I would consider acne. I should have gone with my gut and taken you to the hospital earlier. Fortunately, cradle cap goes away as you get older. You are such a beautiful girl that I wanted to make sure that you weren't going to have any scarring from the cradle cap; mommy calmed me down and told me that you would be just fine and that you would not have any permanent damage. (If it does, I think I will erase this part of the journal because I don't want you to hate me forever☺) The doctor said that we needed to put some baby moisturizer on the cradle cap to make it go away. I left work and went to get all the medicines that you would need during my lunch break so that I wouldn't have to cut into my "Zoe time" after work.

Now that mommy had updated me on the two things I had known the doctor would be addressing, your shots and your face, I asked what other things she learned. You are growing quietly nicely; you are up to 9 lbs. and you are now 21 inches long. The doctor said that you seemed to be a very healthy and happy baby. Mommy did mention one thing that made me a little nervous, but my nervousness probably says more about my personality than your health.

The doctor had told mommy that babies around your age start to smile and interact with their parents more. I know that I have told you that you have smiled at me or laughed when I said something funny to mommy, but these occurrences are more of the exceptions rather than the rules. In general, you don't always seem that interested in interacting with your mom and me. I know that you love us because you are comforted by our holding you and you always seem to stir when you hear one of our voices, but smiling and staring at doesn't often happen.

What made me a little nervous is that there is something called Autism that affects some babies, kids, and adults. Mommy and daddy know a lot about Autism because we both have master's degrees in education, and we have both read books about this subject. Anyways, some babies with Autism have a hard time understanding how others are feeling and sometimes they don't smile at their parents or friends. The doctor never mentioned anything to mommy about you and Autism at all, but daddy just worries too much some time. Neeny had also just told daddy a story about a little baby that she knows in Florida that has

Dear Zoe || Love Dad

Autism which probably caused daddy to immediately worry about you and this condition. You don't need to have any concerns because I don't care whether you have any conditions, sicknesses, or ailments; I will love you just the same, which is with all my heart.

One of the reasons that I was concerned about your not smiling is because I don't really know how old you are. No, daddy isn't stupid, but it is hard to know whether to use your actual birth date or your due date when looking at what you should be doing from a developmental stand point. You are either a 6 and a half weeks old or just a week and a half which is a big difference for a little baby. Depending on the doctor or the situation, mommy and I are told different answers. Who knows? I do know that I love you and that I need to go to bed.

Dear Zoe – September, 8

It is another day and another doctor's appointment. Today, you have to go to the cardiologist. Because mommy was so tired and drained from yesterday's appointment, I volunteered to go with her to meet your heart doctor. (Also, I knew you wouldn't be getting any shots☺) You had seen a few different heart doctors while you were in the NICU because of your accelerated heart rate. I was hoping that you would be seeing Dr. Chang today because he was really nice and he seemed very intelligent.

When the receptionist called your name, we went back to a special room where you were going to have an EKG. This test looks scary because there are a lot of wires that need to be connected to your chest, but although it looks scary, it is about the easiest test you will ever have. I know because I have a heart problem which has led to my having many different tests including this one. The nurse got you hooked up to all the wires and then hit the button on the computer to start the test. Ten seconds later, you were finished. The only thing that was interesting was that you kept tooting while you were in the exam room. It started to smell so bad that mommy got embarrassed and told the nurse that it was you and not her emitting all the gas.

Dr. Stone walked into the room, and I was a little disappointed that we would not be seeing Dr. Chang. Dr. Stone introduced himself to us and asked us to tell him a little bit about your history. I walked him through the episodes of accelerated heart rate in the NICU and told him about the various tests that you had had completed. He then asked what was seemingly a very simple question; "Why did you want to meet with me today?" I looked at mommy to see if she had an answer because I think she had been the person to schedule the appointment. When she didn't say anything, I knew that she in turn was expecting me to answer.

Dear Zoe || Love Dad

Finally, after a few awkward minutes, I looked at the doctor and said, I really don't know why we are here today. I then offered a possible explanation. I told him that I imagine we scheduled the appointment in the NICU when we were demanding actual rather than potential causes of your varying heart rates.

When you were in the NICU, mommy and I were very scared. We were new parents and we were not expecting to have our little baby hooked up to so many monitors and undergoing so many tests. Because we were so nervous, we had asked the doctors to explain all the things we had noticed such as your accelerated heart rate. Because I especially wanted so many answers, I think the doctors and nurses got used to ordering as many tests as possible in order to provide us with adequate, science-based explanations. Our appointment today was probably something that I had requested, but I just didn't remember. The time in the NICU was exhausting emotionally and physically, and my recollections of many of the days spent there are fuzzy at best. Some day, I will probably read this journal and be as surprised as you at all that went on during your first few weeks of life.

Since we were with him, I was happy to have him reassure mommy and me that your heart was function just right. He said that the EKG looked normal. He also said that after reviewing your file, he did not have any concerns about your heart. He did however suggest that you do a Holter monitor test for the next 24 hours. This test is basically a 24 hour EKG. Once again, your daddy has done this test twice in his life. Because I knew that it wouldn't hurt you and because I still wanted to be extra careful, I said that we would like to proceed with this test. Before he left, I asked him a few more questions about the slight hole that was in your heart when they had performed the echocardiogram. He said that it was probably still there as you were still too young to have it fully closed. Satisfied that you and your heart were in great shape, I told him thank you for his time and got you ready for the Holter.

The nurse walked into the room with the little box that contained the Holter monitor and all requisite patches and wires. I was expecting a special baby version, but your monitor looked just the same as the one that I had used as a full-grown man. By the time the nurse had finished putting the five stickers on your chest and stomach, none of your precious pink skin was even visible. You didn't mind the stickers or the wires at all; you just continued to lie comfortably on the exam table passing gas.

Mommy and I put you in your car seat, and mommy got mad at daddy because I told her that I thought she was doing it wrong. I wanted the straps to be even tighter. Mommy kindly reminded me that she puts you in your car seat everyday and that this was the first time that I had ever helped. What was really happening is that I had been nervous about your appointment which was causing me to worry about your car seat even when I knew your mom knew what she was doing. I ended up checking all the straps and buckles on the car seat before I was willing to let you leave on your journey back home. I kept checking the car seat over and over again. Thank God you are a healthy baby because your daddy gets nervous real easy. Love you baby.

Dear Zoe – September, 21

Writing in your journal is getting harder and harder because I am too busy – spending time with you. Every minute that I am writing to you means another minute without you in my arms or another minute without sleep. On the subject of sleep, you are sleeping longer and longer. You haven't hit four straight hours at night yet, but you have eclipsed the four hour mark during the day. Granted, the four hours in the day was in your mommy's arms. You sure do love sleeping on mommy.

I have a quick story to tell you about the first time mommy left the two of us alone. Your mom has not wanted to leave your side since you were born. She loves you so much that she won't even let me take care of you; she says she will just miss you too much. Finally, I was able to convince her to leave the house to go and get a flu shot without taking you with her. Your mom needs to feel confident that I can take care of you so that she can continue to do things such as see her friends or go out to dinner without being worried about you. (To be honest, I was nervous, but I didn't want to let mommy know.)

Mommy pulled out of the garage, and it was just you and me. Things started out okay. I was holding you in the crook of my arm while sitting on the couch. Then, you started crying. I got up and began walking around the house, and you settled down. This little trick worked for five minutes, but then you started crying again. Once again, I wasn't too worried, and I moved onto my next trick – taking you outside. We walked around outside and you enjoyed the cool breeze. Your eyes darted from side to side as you checked out plants, our neighbor's garage door, and the clouds in the sky. Uh oh, you started crying again. We went back inside and sat on the couch. You were squirming and just couldn't get comfortable. I put you in your little lamb seat which soothed you momentarily, but it certainly wasn't the complete fix I was hoping for.

Mommy had only been gone 20 minutes, and I was in real trouble. I didn't know what to do. I kept getting more and more nervous. I thought to myself, you and I just weren't ready to be without mommy. You were sad, and I was scared. You kept crying and I kept trying to make it better, but I had no success. By the time mommy arrived back home, you and I were waiting on the doorstep. You were in tears and I was in a panic.

Now, I tell you this story because it was a real turning point for me as a father. I realized after our misadventure that I was scared of you. Don't get me wrong, I wasn't scared that you were going to hurt me – although you did scratch me with one of your nails yesterday because you wanted your bottle so bad. But I was letting my fears get in the way of getting maximum enjoyment from our time together.

- I was scared you were going to wake up from your nap when I knew you needed your rest.
- I was scared you weren't pooping enough.
- I was scared that you were going to hurt you neck when you flung it backwards.
- I was scared you were going to spit up.
- I was scared you weren't learning how to smile.
- I was scared that you weren't in your car seat tight enough.

This list could go on and on. After spending that hour without mommy and being so worried, I realized that I just needed to accept that everything wasn't always going to be perfect. My worrying wasn't going to help you, and it was definitely not helping me. You needed me to be confident and calm, and I think you could sense that I was upset when you were upset.

If I was spending all of my time in fear, I was probably missing out on the pleasure of staring at your beautiful little face or feeling your lungs expand and contract against my chest. Everyone says that kids grow up so fast, and I knew that I needed to cherish all these moments rather than ruminate on what could go wrong. I know this is easier said than done, but I am going to try.

Inspired by my new mindset, I tried to really help your mom out over the three day holiday. Let me tell you, I don't know how mommy is able to take care of you all by herself when I go to work. Don't get me wrong, you are a very easy baby for which to care. You are still a little baby however, and you are in constant need of holding, feeding, or changing. The most obvious challenge is getting up in the middle of the night to take care of you. Sometimes waking up at 2:30 a.m. or 4:30 a.m. feels easy, but other times it is the hardest thing I will do all week. I think it must have to do with my REM cycle or something. During the week, mommy used to let me sleep because she wanted me to have enough rest for work. After helping her this weekend, I think that maybe I should be getting up in the middle of the night so that mommy has enough energy to take care of you! Don't tell her though because I like my rest.

Dear Zoe || Love Dad

I think that your mom appreciated my splitting night time duty. On Saturday, I even let mommy sleep in as I took the two early morning feedings. I think I have told you this before, but you are so easy going in the morning. You just want to snuggle with your mommy or daddy. On Sunday, I walked into mommy and daddy's room to see the cutest thing that I could ever imagine. You and mommy were taking a nap in bed together. You looked so comfortable in the crook of mommy's arm. Without daddy's snoring, the two of you were able to rest so peacefully. Well, I need to get ready for work; I love you baby girl. Thanks for making my life so wonderful.

Dear Zoe – September, 23

You had a lot of firsts this week – your first trip to Target and Babies R Us and your first dinner at a restaurant. With your two month birthday, the doctor said that we were allowed to let the rest of the world share in your beauty. Well, she didn't say exactly that, but she did say that you were finally off of house arrest. I will tell you about these trips in a little bit, but first, I need to tell you how you scared daddy.

Do you remember what I told you about the very first time that I went to sleep after you were born? Let me remind you. I woke up and Neeny told me that you had been taken to the NICU because you had stopped breathing for a moment. Ever since this time, and to be perfectly honest, even before this time, I have been fairly obsessed with your breathing. When mommy and I were picking out your baby furniture, I wanted to get the hardest mattress I could find because hard mattresses were supposed to help prevent SIDS which is a very scary thing. I think that I told mommy that I would make you a bed out of marble if that meant that you would be safer. I think you get the message; your daddy is very scared of you not breathing properly.

Well, this week we had another scare. At least, I was very scared. Mommy had to take care of you all day because I had a full day at work followed by a dinner meeting with some colleagues. I have never liked having to stay late at work because I would rather be home with your mom; now that you are here, staying at work late is even worse. I didn't get home until after 8:00 p.m. and you were getting ready to go to sleep. You were very fussy, and I wanted to give mommy a break so that she could shower and get ready for bed. In reality, I just wanted to be with you because I had missed not seeing you all day.

You kept crying and crying. I knew that you weren't hungry because mommy was just finishing up feeding you when I walked in the door. I decided that you were probably just really tired and "fighting your sleep" as mommy likes to say.

Dear Zoe || Love Dad

I walked you upstairs to your room and rocked you back and forth in the glider. Finally, you still decided to give in to your exhaustion and you feel asleep after forty five minutes. I very slowly stood up so that I didn't disturb you as we progressed to your bed. My ankles and knees made a lot of noise on our short walk to your bassinet, but you fortunately weren't disturbed.

I leaned over your bassinet to put you down and your breathing became irregular. It is very hard to describe exactly what I was seeing, but it seemed that you were trying to take several short little breaths on top of each other. You normally breathe through your nose which makes making an assessment as to what had really happened even more of a challenge. Regardless of what actually happened, the end result was a very scared daddy.

I called to mommy and had her turn the lights on so that I could make sure you were okay. When I looked down, you were completely fine. I don't know if my being tired or stressed contributed to my nervousness, but I hated going to bed that night. I was so worried about you.

Mommy said that she had noticed similar changes in your breathing when she was feeding you. I told her that I wanted her to call the doctor first thing in the morning. In my heart, I knew that you were going to be fine, but I was still in need of reassurance. Having gone through so many doctors appointments had not provided my hope of being less apprehensive, but rather it caused me to worry more. The highs and lows associated with these appointments were really starting to wear me down.

When I woke to feed you in the morning, I was just so happy to see that your breathing was not labored in any way. You peacefully took your bottle from me without ever opening your eyes. You could not have been more content as you sucked down your 100 ml of formula.

Your mom called the doctor, and she said that she wanted to see you the next morning. I was glad that the doctor was not concerned; something I could tell by her not demanding to see you right away. While your mom was calling the doctor and Memom, I called Neeny. Memom and Neeny agreed with the doctor that it was probably not something to really be worried about. I felt reassured by the three wise-women's advice, but I was still looking forward to your appointment where you would get a full assessment.

The next morning, mommy and I took you to the doctor. Your mom gave you a bath so that you would smell nice and look pretty for your outing. Your mom loves dressing you in your cute outfits whereas I just love putting your in your gowns or sleepers as they are the easiest to change your diaper in. I guess we have different priorities with regards to your appearance. The doctor examined you and said that she thought that you might have a little bit of acid reflux. I know acid sounds scary, but your mom has this condition and although it is uncomfortable, it is not too troublesome. The doctor said that she didn't think that you needed treatment at this time, but we could give you medicine in the future if things got worse. One of the reasons you would go on medicine for this condition would be if you were not eating; a problem you didn't have. You weighed over ten pounds at the doctor and you had started wearing your 3-6 months clothing. Losing weight and missing meals was not a problem daddy's daughter was going to have.

Mommy and I felt relieved that there was nothing serious going on with you. I asked whether you could just stop breathing because of this condition and the doctor said, "No." I also asked whether your spitting up was a real problem, and once again, she replied with a negative. I was so glad that heading into our big weekend, you got a clean bill of health.

Now that I have covered the not-so-pleasant part of your week, we can discuss your big adventures. Mommy had been waiting for weeks to take you out of the house to a target and other stores. Sitting around the house can get pretty boring for your mom; I bet you were tired of staring at the same two people all day too – even if they were your parents. The day had finally arrived for your big trip to Target. Mommy got you ready which always means putting you in a cute outfit and a head bow. I got your stroller ready and loaded in the car. I made sure you had formula and a bottle in mommy's diaper bag because your hunger could definitely derail our trip. After what seemed like thirty minutes, we were all ready to go. Mommy got all dressed up for her first trip to Target in weeks. Someone might have thought that we were getting ready for your baptism not a trip to get cleaning supplies.

Mommy put you in your car seat, and I carried you to the car. As soon as we got in the car, you started to cry. I was thinking that our trip might be over before it even started but mommy assured me that you would be fine as soon as the car started moving. As usual, she was right. She decided that we should stop at McDonald's to get a sweet tea. Your mom was really trying to make this the trip of a lifetime☺ I let mommy out so that she could go inside to retrieve her Tea while I continued to drive around the back roads of Harrisburg in order to prevent you from getting upset, something that happens when the car stops moving.

After our detour to the Golden Arches, we were once again on our way to your first adventure in retail. I took the stroller out of the car and snapped your car seat into place. We headed to the store, mommy, daddy and baby.

Dear Zoe || Love Dad

Mommy pushed the cart and took the lead on shopping. She was moving so slowly as she figured out which detergent or hand soap to get. Not that mommy is normally a speed demon, but her deliberateness was very much out of the ordinary. Having spent the last 8 weeks cooped up in our house had made mommy savor this outing like no trip to Target in the past. She examined the labels on all the detergents with such a high level of scrutiny and excitement that I had to remind her that you probably wouldn't stay relaxed forever. I would have thought that all the different sights, sounds, and smells would have been very stimulating, but you faded in and out of sleep for the entire thirty minute experience.

Your mom checked out and took our purchases to the car as you and I walked down to the Babies R Us. Before we got to Babies R Us however, I saw a new furniture store that I wanted to check out. I convinced mommy to make a pit stop; ultimately, this proved to be foolish as you started crying immediately. With one more stop to make, we quickly left the furniture store and proceeded to Babies R Us.

Mommy took you out of your stroller because neither one of us will just let you cry. With mommy carrying you in her arms, I took the empty stroller, the diaper bag, and the bag of goods that needed to be exchanged. I waited in line to make our exchanges while mommy took you around the store. We were trying to be fast, but the check out line was not nearly as efficient as I would have hoped for a store that caters to new moms with babies. Finally, I was able to get my refund of $7.00 which was probably not worth the wait given the circumstance.

I found your mom, and we tried to shop - quickly. I had to find the coupons in your mom's bag to insure I was getting the correct items. Not wanting to waste any time, I performed this search while pushing your empty stroller. Having secured the coupons, I picked up three large boxes of formula which I carried in one arm while balancing a waterproof bassinet lining in the other. Your mom was now in charge of the stroller and you, a combination that would have been easy if you had decided to actually stay in the stroller. We hustled through the store looking for the items on our list. In my haste, I managed to get some skin on my arm pinched between two of the boxes of formula resulting in a large bruise. I would have tried to put things down, but having a crying baby makes everything a race. I checked out and mommy took you outside.

Once outside, you mom put you back in your car seat as we prepared to go home. I carried our stuff to the car as mommy pushed you in your car seat which was now affixed to the stroller. We were both flustered by this point. As I loaded up the car, mommy started to unbuckle you from the car seat rather than

Dear Zoe || Love Dad

unbuckle the car seat from the stroller. (See, she only needed to pick up your car seat and put it in the car seat base found in the car.) Realizing the error in her ways, she stopped and we both started laughing.

Your mom had thought that today was going to be the first of many trips to the store. She envisioned a whole new world where the two of you or the three of us would go out on calm, peaceful excursions. No longer would the two of you be bound to the confines of our townhome. On the way home, our exhausted and stressed expressions told another story. Maybe taking a baby to the store is easy for some people, but those people were not in our car. I told your mom that I felt as if I had just gotten back from a two week trip to Europe. I hope you liked Target because you may not be going back for quite some time☺

Even though I was exhausted and just wanted to hold you in my arms and watch football, mommy and I promised that we would meet Kelly, Jim, and Ava for dinner. Your mom was so excited because she hadn't been out to eat, one of her favorite activities, since you were born. We decided on Dukes, a place that epitomizes the Central PA area. The portions are big just like your daddy.

You did a great job at dinner as you sat quietly in your car seat. I was nervous the whole time though because I didn't want anyone to bump into you. You have probably already come to this conclusion by now, but I can be hypersensitive when it comes to my baby girl. And I hope you know that you will always be my baby girl no matter how old you are. Mommy and I took some pictures of you and your friend Ava as we left the restaurant to commemorate this occasion. It is funny how everything seems so important when you are a parent for the first time. You probably won't really care to have a memento from your first trip to Dukes, but just in case, we have you covered.

Taking the photos was an interesting experience as only one of you wanted to smile. Your mom and Kelly hovered over each of you trying to coax a grin from your pretty faces. Ava was very willing to smile. You on the other hand, didn't make any expression let alone a smile. I assume that your lack of facial expression was due to the fact that you still don't smile often (you are only a week old biologically speaking), but I don't rule out the fact that you might have thought this exercise was pretty ridiculous☺ Anyways, it made taking the photos pretty easy as you never changed expression and therefore you were always ready for the shot to be taken.

Dear Zoe – October, 1

Dear Zoe || Love Dad

Guess what today is? It is your daddy's birthday. Thank you very much for getting me the new pair of shoes. I love them and I especially love that they came from you and your mom.

I think that today has been my best birthday ever because I got to share it with you. I know that I tell you this all the time, but my life is so much better since you were born. I have never been as happy as I am now. Birthdays are fun because everyone tries to make you feel special. This birthday was different because I felt more special than ever knowing that I was your dad. My mind knew that there was no way you understood it was my birthday, but my heart felt like you did.

You and mommy decided to come to visit me at work which was a great surprise. I met your mom in the parking lot so that I could help her get you into your stroller for our little adventure. I wanted all of my friends and colleagues at work to meet you because you are such a big part of my life. I knew that everyone was going to love you, but I was still surprised at how kind all of my co-workers were to both you and your mom. Each and everyone commented on how beautiful you were and how happy you looked. Knowing that it isn't always easy being a mommy, they also asked mommy how she was doing which meant a lot to me. I love you and your mom so much that it is important that everyone treat the two of you with love and kindness.

We walked around my office building for about a half an hour. I don't think a lot of work was getting done because everyone would come pouring out of their offices to see you when the caught a glimpse of your stroller. You were very well-behaved as a bunch of strangers touched your foot or made faces at you. I know that it has to be kind of weird having all these strange people invading your personal space, but people just can't help themselves when they are around you. You are just so darn cute.

We walked over to a restaurant and headed to our table. While we walked, I could hear a trail of "Ahs" as we passed table after table of customers who couldn't take their eyes off of you. You already know that you bring so much happiness to mommy and me, but you also bring smiles to just about everyone who sees you. There is definitely something special about babies, but there is something even more special about you, my baby. You affect people in such a positive way.

With lunch over, I had to head back to my cubicle. It was great seeing you at lunch, but it was hard saying goodbye. Being with you is a lot more fun than work.

Dear Zoe || Love Dad

Dear Zoe – October, 6

I am so glad to be home. I had to go to a big city called Chicago for a work trip which meant that I spent my first night away from you since you left the NICU. I have always missed your mom when I travel; now, I miss both of my girls. Thankfully, I don't have to travel too often with my job; I might be gone once or twice a month. If I did, I might need to find a new position as I don't like being away from you at all. Spending time with you is the best part of my day, and it was very challenging having to go to bed in a hotel all by myself. Yes, I did get a lot more rest without having to feed you, but I would have gladly traded zzz's for the chance to hold and kiss you like I normally do.

I hope to take you to Chicago someday so that you can see a big city. You don't know this, but where we leave now is what would be considered a small-town. Places like Chicago and New York are called big cities and they have a totally different energy about them. If you turn out like your mommy and daddy and like shopping and eating, then you will love big cities. Even writing to you about these trips makes me excited. This whole trip, I have been thinking about how you would be reacting to all the sights and sounds. As I write this, I am picturing you as a five year old holding my hand in New York as you point toward the sky to show me the skyscrapers in utter amazement. There are so many things that I can't wait to share with you, and a big city trip is definitely one of them.

When I got home from Chicago, I immediately picked you up from mommy and snuggled you close to my chest. I just couldn't stop giving you little kisses. What a great feeling to get home and have a loving baby to hold. Mommy could tell that I had missed you more than I had even expected. I just didn't want to let you down which was a good thing because your mom needed a rest. She is such an amazing mother that she definitely places all of your needs before her own. When I got home, she was sitting on the couch in her usual spot holding you. She hadn't even taken a shower yet even though it was around 8:00 at night. With your dad back in town, she could finally take a minute for herself.

I have many work trips planned and I am dreading them now that I know how much I miss you when I'm gone. When you get older, I will start bringing you little souvenirs when I go on trips; maybe then you will be happy that I have to go☺

I think I was still really emotional from my trip to Chicago when I happened to stumble across a TV show called, "If You Really Knew Me." I had seen this show in the past, but my experience watching it this time was very different. Basically, the show has high school kids tell their friends and classmates about themselves. Unfortunately, you will probably learn that not all kids are nice to

Dear Zoe || Love Dad

each other. What this show tries to do is to bring kids closer together by having them realize that they all have fears, problems, hopes, and dreams.

Life Lesson from Daddy: It's important Zoe to always treat everyone with respect and to be kind to all the kids at school even if you don't particularly like them.

On this particular episode, many kids had problems with their parents. One boy had a parent who always told him that he wasn't good enough. Another girl had a parent who ignored her and didn't show her any love. Now, I can't even tell you the last time that I cried. All of a sudden, I was just overwhelmed with sadness. I just couldn't understand what I was seeing and hearing. How could a parent not show his or her child love and attention? You are the greatest gift that I have ever received, and I have loved you with all my heart since Dec. 23rd 2009 – the day I found out you were in mommy's tummy.

Now, I know that there will be times when you are older – especially when you are a teenager – when you might not understand all the rules that your mommy and I have for you. Sometimes you may even become very mad at us, but I want you to always know that mommy and I love you. We will always love you. I am not perfect, mommy is not perfect, and we don't expect you to be perfect either. Please don't worry about disappointing us. There are times when mommy and I are going to be disappointed, but it will be because we just want you to be the happiest you could be. We will always be on your side.

I will let you know right now that I want you to be a happy kid and adult who loves life and tries her best to make the world a better place every day. I don't care whether you are an athlete. I don't care whether you have the best grades in your class. I don't care whether you are a creative genius. You're my baby, and I will always be proud of you. Don't believe me? Well, I am already proud of you when you finally have a big burp or poop. See, the bar is pretty low when you have a daddy who loves you as much as I do you☺

Dear Zoe – October, 7

Now I just told you that mommy and I will always be on your side. You may then be wondering why we have started leaving you in your crib (not your bassinet) and letting you cry without rushing to pick you up. I have to admit that I would expect such a complaint from a daughter of mine because I have been asking myself the same question too.

Dear Zoe || Love Dad

Well Zoe, being a parent is different than being a best friend. When you are a parent, you need to do what you think is best for your baby not necessarily what you want to do or what is most popular.

Answering the first part of your complaint is easy. It has to do with the fact that you are now a triple "B" – a big, beautiful, baby. You have grown so much that not only do you not look like you were ever a preemie, but you have also simply outgrown your bassinet. Just weeks ago, you fit so perfectly in your fancy, lace bassinet. Now, your size and your predilection (a big word that means something you enjoy doing) for rolling to your side made me think that staying in your bassinet might not a good idea any more. I was getting scared that you might have a hard time breathing if you rolled too close to the side of the bassinet.

Moving you to your crib meant moving you out of our room. I hate not hearing your cute noises throughout the night we reassure me that you are doing well, but like I said, I need to do what is best for you.

Now onto the second issue; why are we letting you cry? Mommy read a book called Baby Wise that teaches new parents such as your mom and me how to teach babies to sleep on their own. Having you learn to fall asleep while not being held by mommy or daddy is important so that you can do fun things when you are older such as go to sleep-over parties or move away to college.

The book teaches that you should let your child cry for about ten minutes before going into the room to soothe her (without picking her up). There is a big difference between reading the book and enacting its principles. When you read the book, it probably doesn't mention that heart-wrenching pain that comes from listening to your baby cry. Even if you know that what you are doing is in the best interest of your child, it is awful to hear your child cry knowing full well that you could stop the crying by picking her up.

Besides hearing you cry and knowing that you could stop it, the other awful thing about this new plan is the fact that I can't explain to you what we are doing. Well, I have explained to you what we are doing, but I don't think you quite understood. You certainly didn't say anything to me if you did.

Thankfully, mommy began this project when I was in Chicago, and I therefore got to miss a few days of hearing you cry. Now that I am back, I knew that I would unfortunately be forced to suffer along with her. Even though she was doing what the book said was best for you, mommy's tummy began to hurt as she listened to you be sad. By the time I got back from Chicago, mommy had completed two days of having you put yourself to bed. When I came home from

Dear Zoe || Love Dad

work the following day, mommy had just put you down. It didn't take long for you to start screaming. It was just awful hearing you be so sad. I couldn't help but wonder what was going through your mind. Did you understand that mommy and daddy were still downstairs? Did you think that we didn't love you anymore? With these thoughts racing in my head and my ears attuned to your yells, I told mommy that I just wasn't ready for this. I asked her permission to go upstairs and pick you up. I hadn't been able to spend a lot of time with you due to my trip and to my having been at work all day. I wanted to see you tonight. I missed you dearly, and I just couldn't justify leaving you in your crib crying when both of us wanted to be with each other. Mommy had been exhausted from trying this new technique, and I think she was secretly happy that I told her that you just weren't ready. She said I could go get you.

I ran upstairs as fast as I could and scooped you out of the crib. You still cried for a few minutes as you had become very worked up. It was so sad seeing the little tear trickle down from your right eye. I rocked you in my arms and told you that it was okay. I told you that I didn't like sleeping in my room by myself when I was a little boy and that I wasn't going to do that to you. As you grew comfortable in my arms, I told myself that I hope solving your problems will always be this easy.

Dear Zoe – October, 10

I have some good news; mommy found a book that teaches parents to help their babies sleep without using the "cry it out" method. Hopefully with the lessons in this new book and your recent discovery, your thumb, you will start sleeping by yourself without difficulty. Now, I know that letting you suck your thumb might not be a great decision given that it can lead to teeth problems, but there are things I like about your new finding. First, I can't think of anything cuter than seeing a baby suck her thumb. You attack your thumb with the same urgency as when you drink from your bottle. I always thought that you attacked the bottle for fear that mommy or I would take it away. I'm pretty sure you know that you won't take your own thumb away. I guess you just like to give everything you do 100% effort, a very good quality.

Second, having you self-soothe will help your mom and I out a lot. You have a habit of spitting out your pacifier. I can't tell you how many times your mom has had to pick up your pacie after you have ejected it from your mouth. If she didn't put it back in your mouth right away, you would start screaming. Now that you are in your own room, replacing your pacie is even less convenient than it had been. Having you suck your thumb might help us get more rest.

Dear Zoe || Love Dad

Papa Bear once told me that it is very easy to say what you are "going to do" with your baby before he or she arrives. He said let me know what you "actually do do" when your baby is screaming in the middle of the night and both you and your wife are exhausted. He may not have been very involved in taking care of his babies, but I think his words on this matter are pretty darn accurate.

Have a good night sweetie.

Dear Zoe – October, 17

Guess who loves smiling? You guessed it; you do. Work was pretty stressful today, and I wasn't very happy when I got home. Maybe you could sense I was upset or maybe you just really missed me because you greeted me with some big smiles and even a few laughs. Mommy has been telling me for the last week that you have been smiling in the mornings, but unfortunately for me, I have to go to work real early. Today, your smiles weren't reserved for only the morning hours.

Now, you might remember that I had told you that you smiled at me when you were in the hospital. I know the nurses said it was gas, but I still think they were smiles. You could tell that I was tired and stressed having you hooked up to all those machines. Your smiles kept me going and put me at ease. Just like today, you know what I need sometimes. I think that when we got home and became more comfortable, you decided that you would start acting like a "normal" baby and stop smiling for your first 10 weeks.

Yesterday was a very big day for you. Mommy and I dressed you in a beautiful white dress that Neeny has had for over fifty years. We took you to a huge, magnificent building with marble floors and solid gold decorations. Have you figured out what yesterday was yet? Well, here is another hint. There were candles and everyone was filled with joy. Did you go to a wedding reception at a fancy hotel? No, you were baptized.

Being baptized means that you are now an official member of the Catholic Church. God will always look after you and love you. Even when your mom and I are not around, you should feel safe because God and his Son Jesus are looking down from Heaven protecting you. In order to become a member of the church you go through a special ceremony where a priest pours water on your head and lights special candles. After he finished pouring water on your head, he made the sign of the cross in your hair with a special oil to celebrate. I know that this might sound kind of funny, but it really is a beautiful ceremony. You did a great job. You didn't cry at all. The only noise you made was a HUGE burp when the priest was saying one of the first prayers. It was really funny as all the families around us started laughing because they couldn't believe that such a cute little girl had made such a big noise.

Now, when you get baptized you are freed from all sins. Well, being your dad, I was pretty sure that you had never committed any sins. How could someone so sweet and beautiful as you be born with sin? Maybe God skipped you.

Because you were going to be baptized, you had a lot of people come to see you. Your Memom, MeMe, Daddy Mack, and Uncle Tait flew all the way from Texas to see you. Memom, MeMe, and Daddy Mack arrived late Wednesday night and they rushed through the door right passed mommy and me in order to see you. MeMe had never met you before, and she started crying as soon as she saw you because she was so happy. She took you from my arms and just stared at you as she cradled and rocked you in her arms.

Daddy Mack hadn't seen you since you were in the NICU. Remember how he would just cry and cry because he hated seeing you with all those needles and tubes in you? Well, he sure was happy seeing you now. You love your Daddy Mack; you just stare at his tired eyes. There is just something about him that makes you feel safe and comfortable. Maybe it is because he is a bounty hunter from Texas? Come to think of it, you should feel safe with him.

I am really happy having your mom's family in town because your mom needed a rest. She takes care of you every second of every day. She loves every moment, but I could tell that her mind and body were growing weary. With Memom in town, mommy knows that she can sleep all night and that you will still be getting all the love and attention that you need. Memom smothers you with pure love and joy. You can tell that when you are in her arms that nothing else in this world matters.

I am so glad that you are getting to meet so many new people who love you very much. The only thing that I don't like is that now I have to share you. Everyone wants to hold you and feed you; the only thing that everyone doesn't want to do is change you. It has been sad coming home from work and not getting to immediately pick you up and take care of you. It is important to me however that you have a chance to meet and spend time with your extended family so that you understand how many people love and cherish you. I guess I can make this sacrifice for a week.

After having the chance to spend time with your mom's family, you finally got a chance to meet your Papa Bear. I was really excited for you to meet him because he has helped daddy become the person that he is. Papa Bear is a big man who may seem a "little rough around the edges" but he has nothing but love in his heart. I have always been sure that you are going to love him and that he is going to love you. You already met my mom, you know, Neeny. She loves kids more than anyone, and I know that you are going to be excited to see her.

Neeny and Papa Bear came over early Saturday morning. They actually arrived when I was taking a shower. I came downstairs and you were in Neeny's arms. For a moment, I thought to myself, "Great, more people who want to hold my baby."

Neeny had put you on her knees and she was talking to you really softly and slowly. At first, I was kind of confused as I usually talk quickly and loudly at you. To my surprise, you started smiling real big at Neeny. How does she do it? You are my little baby, and you haven't started smiling at me consistently, but Neeny comes over and she has you smiling in less than ten minutes. I think grandmas just have some special tricks. Now that Neeny had had a chance to see you, Papa Bear got the courage to hold you. Like I said, he is a big guy with a confident personality, but I could tell he was scared of you. He asked Neeny to pass you to him.

Watching Papa Bear get ready to hold you was both funny and scary. I love Papa Bear, but he doesn't spend a lot of time around babies. I kept my eyes on you and him to make sure that he was supporting your head and holding you securely. He extended his arms and awkwardly brought you to his chest. You looked so small compared to him. Papa Bear was so happy. Even though you could tell he was still nervous, you still filled him with the joy that only a grandbaby can provide. He continued to reposition you as it was clear that he just couldn't get comfortable. Seeing him struggle reminded me of my first few weeks with you when everything was scary and challenging. He continued to look at you and talk to you for a few minutes, but when you made the slightest cry, he immediately asked Neeny to take you. I guess he only wants a happy baby in his arms.

With our families in town, mommy and I took everyone including you of course to our new house. The workers have been doing a great job because our new house already has floors, walls, windows, and a roof. I was so proud walking around the house because it makes me happy knowing that I am helping to provide you and mommy with a home where you can be safe and happy. There are three rooms upstairs that could be your room. Mommy picked one out that she thinks would be right for you, but I bet it is going to change before we move in. Why? The room that mommy picked for you is not closest to our room, and if I know mommy, there is no way that she is not going to have you as close to her as possible.

Dear Zoe || Love Dad

Well, the weekend was coming to a close and I was exhausted. You felt the same as you slept for over five hours after your baptism. Neeny said you were just happy and relaxed because you were now Catholic. Maybe she is right or maybe you were just tired from our keeping you up all day Saturday – passing you from relative to relative. I love having our families here, but I am looking forward to having you all to myself again.

It had been a long weekend. I was happy that people were leaving and that our lives would go back to "normal." Whether it was due to a virus, nerves, or exhaustion, your mom threw up last night. Now, you know how awful it is to be sick. You know what mommy said when she told me she had thrown up? The only thing she said was "do you think that Zoe is going to get sick?" Mommy didn't care at all that she wasn't feeling well; her only concern was you. She is such a special wife and mommy. You should kiss mommy when you read this and say thank you for all that she does for you. (I figure by the time you can read this that mommy won't be sick anymore.)

Love you, Daddy.

Dear Zoe – October, 27

I have been thinking a lot lately about how much your arrival has changed me. I think that the love I feel for you has made me want to treat everyone with love and respect. My new found love and respect for others can be attributed to a few things.

First, I want nothing more than for you to be proud of me. My dad is perfect in my eyes not because he has been successful in business or because he is funny but rather because he has such a kind heart. He worries so much about his family's happiness and well-being; he is always putting our needs and desires above his. When he is not helping us, he is reaching out to those individuals who are less fortunate. He helps those who others in this country have forgotten. He recently built a house and school in a country called Afghanistan for kids who need a special place to live and learn. I hope that someday you will be proud of me the way that I am proud of him.

Second, there are going to be many lessons that I want to teach you. These lessons will be my way of trying to help you live a life filled with happiness and pride. I figure that it isn't really fair for me to tell you to act a certain way if I am not willing to do the same. I hope that you are twice the person that I am when you are my age. People often say that they want to give their children more than they had as a kid. As Papa Bear pointed out to me (without any knowledge that it might be upsetting), I may not be able to provide all the same material things that I had, but nonetheless, I do want you to have more than I had. I want to give you more tools to live a life filled with accomplishments and happiness both as a child and as an adult than I had.

Third, you are so precious to me, and you have a whole life ahead of you. It might seem funny, but I never really walked around thinking about the fact that everyone was once a baby with parents who had hopes and dreams for them the same way that I have for you. Now, I can't help but look at people knowing that there are people out there who care for them the same way that I care for you. I can't even tell you how upset I would be if someone were mean to you, and I therefore don't want to be mean to anyone else knowing that they are someone's baby.

I am sorry baby if that was a little too deep or philosophical, but someday you will realize that there is more to life than formula and sea horses with bellies that light up and emit lullabies☺

Do you remember your stay in the NICU, the loud room with all the crying babies and loud alarms? Well, mommy and daddy finally got a bill from the hospital. You might think that it would be very cheap considering how non-luxurious the accommodations were. The truth is just the opposite; we had to pay extra for all the poking and prodding of you. All I have to say is that I am glad that I have good insurance because the bill came out to $78,000. In the end, we only have to pay $780 which is just 1% of the bill. We are very lucky to have such good health insurance because if we didn't, we wouldn't be able to buy the house we are building.

I am not sure whether you will be happy to hear this or not, but you have a lot of characteristics of your daddy. I think this is great because I am a pretty special guy, but I am not sure whether mommy thinks you are getting my best characteristics. First, you seem to need a lot of alone time. There are times when you are really fussy and your mom and I do anything and everything trying to make you happy. We rock you, we sing to you, we put you in your swing, we make faces at you and nothing calms you. Finally, we put you down in your crib, and you stop crying instantly. I think you just need some alone time like daddy to think about things without everyone in your space.

Second, you have started a very odd behavior. Recently, you always look over your right shoulder when mommy or daddy is holding you. At first, we thought you were straining to look at something, but we realized that you kept looking over your shoulder even as we would spin you around to give you the same perspective without the contortion. Now, I am not saying that your daddy likes to look over his right shoulder, but I am wondering whether you have just

Dear Zoe || Love Dad

become used to having your head rest on your shoulder the way that I did when I was a baby. Neeny used to do special head and neck exercises with me because I too always rested my head on my shoulder. Papa Bear says that it was because my head was too heavy for my little neck, but maybe I just thought it was comfortable like you. I think your new favorite position is cute, bizarre but cute. Mommy however is getting nervous, and she plans on calling the doctor. I think that will be a pretty funny conversation.

Finally, you have a crooked smile just like me. Not only is my smile crooked but my mouth is crooked even when I talk. To tell you the truth, I have always been a little self-conscious about this characteristic, but I am not anymore. Seeing that you smile like me makes me proud of my crooked smile. I think that I will always love having anything in common with my little baby.

One more thing before I quit writing. Your mom had the courage to leave the two of us alone this weekend for 2 whole hours. I love you little girl, but taking care of you sure is tiring. Mommy wasn't really gone very long, but I had you in your swing, in your lamb seat, in your crib, in my arms, and on my knees. I played you music, I read you a book, and I let you watch TV. When mommy got home, she started laughing as I was lying on the floor with my arm around you as you sat in your lamb seat. I was trying to get you to sleep, but it turns out that only one of us was exhausted.

Dear Zoe – October, 31

Tonight would normally be your first Halloween, but the town where we live celebrates Halloween on the last Thursday of October. You already got to experience your first Halloween party which took place at the office where I work. Your mom had been excited about this party since you were born. She got you an outfit from www.poshlittletutus.com; as you can probably imagine, your outfit was really darn cute. You wore a little shirt with a pumpkin on it and a great big orange tutu.

When you arrived at the office, everyone was gushing about how cute you looked. It was cold and mommy had put you in black tights as well, and you just looked perfect. It was great to see many of my co-workers kids too. There were a lot of little babies including your friends Ava and Taylor. You are so lucky to have so many friends with whom you can play.

Not all kids get to grow up in such a nice, safe town where people are usually friendly. I never really appreciated how amazing our town was until I knew that you were in mommy's tummy. There are so many activities for little kids that I bet you are going to have a great childhood playing with your friends and your mom every day. Not only are there a lot of kids, but there are also a lot of attractions designed especially for children. As soon as you get a little older, I am going to take you to a huge playground called Cocoa Castle. Doesn't that sound exciting?

The other nice thing about our town is that it isn't that expensive to live here which has two great side effects. First and most importantly, your mom doesn't need to work which means that she can stay home to take care of you. Secondly, we could afford to buy a nice new house for you to grow up in.

We already talked about Friday, but let me tell you about earlier in the week. I knew that you were going to come to my office on Friday for the Halloween party, but I didn't expect to see you on Thursday. Do you want to hear a funny story? Well, your mom and I had a friend named Connie Rey come visit us. Connie Rey deserves some credit for you being here because she was the person who first introduced your mommy and me. I had heard about your mommy, and I wanted to meet her, but mommy wasn't so sure at first. She would tell Connie Rey, "He went to Harvard; we are going to have nothing to talk about." Finally, mommy agreed to meet me and we have been together since that first meeting. I just knew that someday we would be married after I met her that night.

Now, let's get back to my story. I was coming out of a meeting when I got a text message from your mom. It simply read, "Were r u?" I knew that mommy had to take Connie Rey to the train station, and I was thinking that she might want to stop by and see me. I called her immediately. When she picked up, the first thing that I heard was you screaming in the back seat. Mommy said, "Zoe is screaming, I am crying, and I need your help. Meet me in the parking lot." You usually love the car and mommy almost never gets flustered, and I was therefore very surprised to be getting this call. I was however happy that I was going to get a chance to see you and mommy when I wasn't expecting it.

When I got downstairs, mommy already had you out of the car seat and she was feeding you. I told her that it was silly to stand outside, and we all went into my office. The three of us walked into the building and took the elevator up to my little cubicle. For the next hour you ate and ate and ate. Never before had you eaten more than 5 ounces of formula, but today you took over 7. It was great having you and mommy with me at work. I actually had some things that I needed to do, and I continued working as mommy fed you. I think you should come to work more often because it sure is nice having the company, and since you don't talk, you are not a distraction to anyone☺

I want to cover one final topic before I sign off for the night. I am trying something new where I really try and concentrate on what you are telling me.

Dear Zoe || Love Dad

What makes this challenging is that you don't talk, and I therefore have to try and interpret the pitch and volume of your cries along with the contortions of your face. Mommy thinks that I am kind of crazy, but I have decided that if I concentrate really hard that maybe I will better be able to understand what you are trying to tell me when you cry. It started when I was looking at you and realizing how frustrating it must be for you to not be able to tell us exactly what you need. I imagine your being upset and crying because you are in a wet diaper, and my deciding to feed you thinking you are hungry. I then picture you thinking, "I'M NOT HUGRY. I'M WET! CHANGE THIS DIAPER, NOW!" Not knowing this, I keep trying to feed you by moving the bottle in and out of your mouth only furthering your frustration.

I'd be lying to you and myself, if I told you that my concentration and focus have yielded truly positive results. There have however been small victories. You were crying and kicking your legs on Wednesday night, and I decided to really focus on what you were trying to tell me. Normally, I would just yell to mommy for help, but I wanted to prove to you and myself that I could be a soothing parent too. (Your favorite place to be is over mommy's shoulder; as soon as she slings you over her shoulder, you almost always calm down.) On this particular occasion, I stared into your eyes and softly spoke to you. "Zoe, what do you want?" Your face scrunched up again and you let out another scream. Again, I said, "Zoe, let me know what you need, and I will do it. I want to make you happy. Are you bored? Are you just tired? Are you sick of being held?" Of course you didn't answer me, but I think you appreciated my effort and you stopped crying. Soon after you stopped crying, you even started to smile and laugh as I had taken you up to mommy and daddy's room and placed you on our bed. I just talked to you for the next five minutes as you followed me with your eyes and laughed.

Dear Zoe – November, 5

I have a couple of new nicknames for you. The first one is "little heating pad" and the second is "little bobble head." Let me explain.

Mommy likes to make fun of me because she says that I will only be holding you for a few minutes when I say, "mommy can you take her; I'm sweating too much right now." Well, I think that she is exaggerating because I love holding you, and we spend a lot of time together. She is however telling the truth when I say that I get real hot when you are in my arms. Well, your heat source came in very handy this week.

The weather started to turn very cold, something mommy and I are not used to given that we both grew up in the South, and to make things worse our heater broke. Mommy and I woke up last weekend only to realize that the temperature in the house was 66 degrees. It was my turn to take the early morning feeding, and I brought you downstairs for some quality father daughter time while I gave you your bottle. I was freezing while I changed your diaper and prepared your bottle, but things changed when I put you in the crook of my arm and gave you your formula. You were still very warm having been in a fleece sleep sack all night. As I sat down with you and my Snuggie blanket, I quickly warmed up. You were my little heating pad. We watched TV and just snuggled; something you love to do already. Thanks, Little Heating Pad.

Your next nickname came from my desire to find an alternate to "tummy time" which you hate. I know that you need to continue to practice tummy time or you will go through life staring at ceilings which I imagine would get pretty boring, but I figure it might just take awhile with you. One of the reasons that tummy time is important is because it helps you develop your neck muscles. Unfortunately for you, you inherited daddy's head size which makes neck-muscle development an important task for you. I decided that if you didn't want to do "tummy time" that we needed to find an alternate way to accomplish the goal of neck muscle development. I have started to sit you up and force you to hold your own head in place, something that you can do but don't always like to do. We have been practicing this week, and I have to tell you that it is really cute seeing your little neck try to balance your ~~big~~ slightly above average sized head. You watch me with your eyes as your head just kind of wobbles back and forth. The uncontrollable and non-rhythmic movements make you look exactly like a bobble head doll. Of course, you are a very, very cute bobble head, but I think that goes without saying.

I am really glad that I am writing to you during this amazing time because it is really hard to remember all the cute, scary, and wonderful things that have taken place over the last year. Mommy and I were lying in bed last night talking about the first time that she was able to see you in the hospital. I hope that I wrote everything down even though I know that we won't ever forget that morning. Your mom was so happy to see you, but she wasn't prepared at all to see you hooked up to the monitors. She was telling me last night that seeing you in the NICU attached to all the machines was the hardest thing she has ever experienced. She just cried and cried that day because she was so upset that you couldn't be in her arms. Well, she is doing a pretty darn good job of making up for lost time as you are currently sleeping in mommy's bed with her as I write this.

On the subject of sleeping, mommy is trying to have you take naps in your crib. You however prefer to take naps with mommy in her bed. Mommy and I read parenting books that talk about the importance of having your child sleep in her crib in a room by herself. The books also talk about letting your baby "cry it out" if they become distraught. The more that I have thought about this issue, the more I think that YOU and not the books have the correct idea. You just love to be close to your mommy, and you probably like the smell of her bed as well because it makes you feel even closer to her.

I try to put myself in your shoes or socks because you don't wear shoes yet. If I were you and my parents left me in a little wooden cage in a room by myself, I would be scared and upset too. Because you don't talk yet, we can't tell you that we are watching you on a monitor. We can't tell you that we are still making sure that all of your needs are met and that you are perfectly safe. All you know is that you are now alone without the two people who are supposed to be taking care of you. As you know, I try to look to bears for parenting advice because they are not judgmental like many humans. Do momma bears leave their babies in an adjacent cave when they think their baby cubs need to rest? The answer is a definite, NO!

Don't get me wrong; we are still trying to have you learn to sleep in your crib during the day, but I certainly don't think that it is odd that you find it less appealing than mommy's bed. Ultimately, I don't care what the books say or what anyone says except for you. My goal as a parent is to have you love me and be proud of me; with your support, I don't need anyone else's approval. Before you get too excited and think that I will do whatever you like, I should point out that I want you to be the happiest, most successful adult you can be which means that I will always make decisions that I think are not only good for you in the short term but also in the long term. Part of being a successful adult is being able to sleep outside of your parents' bed which means that your crib is not going away any time soon☺

One more thing before I end this entry. I want the two of us to always be close. People at work always tell me to enjoy these times because it is really hard when your little girl is 12-18. Let's make a deal. You and I will always be close. I hope you know that I will always love you, and I will always try to do what is best for you. Personally, there is no good reason why your teenage years need to create distance in our relationship. Can we agree on this? I'm going to assume you agree unless you explicitly tell me otherwise☺

Dear Zoe – November, 15

Your Memom flew into town last night to see you and to help mommy take care of you this week. Unfortunately for me, I have to go on a business trip for the next four days, and I won't be able to see you. Knowing that your Memom is in town makes me feel better because I know that you and your mom will be getting just as much support and love as if I were still there. The trip will be hard on me, but it will probably be easy for you.

I always smile when mommy picks you up and puts you on her shoulder because you just look so happy. Your face gets smushed as your cheeks gets pressed upward towards your eyes as your chin rests comfortably on her shoulder. When you are on her shoulder, your eyes brighten and get bigger as you explore the room from your favorite position. Watching mommy take care of you makes me love mommy even more than I already did which I didn't even know was possible. I took a picture of the two of you sleeping in mommy's bed this week. My two girls sleeping peacefully – could there be a more precious picture?

Speaking of sleeping, you made some major progress in this department. Last weekend, I woke up around 7:30 to your crying on the monitor. I pretended to be asleep so that mommy would have to be the one to change your diaper. Don't get mad, I was really, really tired. My plan was working because I could hear mommy rolling out of bed to go and get you. Feeling guilty, I no longer pretended to be asleep and I said to mommy, "thank you for getting up with her twice last night." I had assumed that mommy had fed you at around 2:30 or 3:00 and was now feeding you for the second time. To my great shock, mommy said that she didn't feed you in the middle of the night. It was still very early in the morning, and I wasn't sure that I fully comprehended our conversation. I thought to myself, "What do you mean you didn't get up with her?" The idea of you sleeping through the night was so foreign to me that my first thought was that maybe I had gotten up with you in the middle of the night and simply forgot.

Well, it turned out that you had just decided to sleep eight and a half hours straight. You had never slept for more than four and a half hours at a given time which made this new development that much more shocking. I always figured that you would go from four to five to six to seven, etc.... You decided to surprise us, and we are very thankful. I would have been very nervous if I hadn't been woken by the sound of your crying because I was definitely not expecting this event. When I shared this story with my friends at work, they talked about how scary it is the first time their child sleeps through the night because you awake hoping that everything is okay with your baby.

Mommy was like a new woman the rest of that day as I had forgotten what my wife was like when she was fully rested. She said that she wanted to go shopping for new clothes before heading to the grocery store. I was happy that she wanted to do something for herself because she has really been very selfless since your arrival. All her energy and focus is on you. She deserves to spend at least a little time on herself as well.

Dear Zoe || Love Dad

Our shopping trip went very well as you took a long nap and we spent three hours away from the house. For the first time, we felt that being parents wasn't so hard after all. You make it very easy because you are such a good baby. Even your cries are very palatable as they are almost always for a specific reason – I'm hungry, change my diaper, stop messing with me and put me in my crib, etc…. We are so lucky to have such a precious little baby.

Mommy and I have not completely given up on tummy time even though we continue to investigate new and creative ways to build your neck strength that don't involve your being face down on your play mat. Let me describe to you what happens when we put you on your stomach. The first thing you do is rub your face back and forth on your mat. The best way to describe this behavior is to relate it to how a great white shark eats as it violently shakes its head back and forth trying to tear apart its prey. You don't use the same vigor, but you are not far from it. It is so hard not to laugh when you start this ritual. After a few moments of shaking your head, you may decide to lift your head slightly to see what is going on around you. Seeing you do this makes me realize that you are perfectly capable of lifting your head if you would like. We are now about twenty seconds into your tummy time at which point any novelty of being on your stomach is starting to wear off and you begin emitting grunts and groans that escalate with time. You aren't exactly crying, but you are making your displeasure clearly known to mommy and me. Finally, you start kicking your legs and moving your arms in complete frustration. Unfortunately for you, your movements only encourage and excite your mommy and me who think you are starting to crawl rather than expressing complete outrage. Rather than pick you up, we start cheering you on saying, "you can do it, Zo Zo! Keep going baby!" You are now annoyed by the fact that you are on your tummy and that your parents are so clueless.

It was during one of these tummy time experiences that mommy and I have decided that you crawled for the first time. Now, I am not exactly sure how to define crawling, but if it involves any movement, then you definitely accomplished this feat. Your feet and legs were doing most of the work as you moved them aggressively causing the slightest forward movement. Mommy and I were very proud of you; even if you were annoyed with us for not picking you up sooner. I can't yet tell whether I think you are going to enjoy crawling around the floor in a few months; you might just want to be held by mommy your whole life☺

Love you baby.

Dear Zoe – November, 22

Dear Zoe || Love Dad

You might find today's entry to be boring because it is more about me and your papa bear. I hope though that you read this after you have a baby some day because I think it will make a lot more sense to you then.

I was driving home from work today when I finally could truly comprehend something that Papa Bear had told me a few years ago. Let me explain.

When your mommy and I were getting married, we needed to select people to be in what is called our "wedding party." For daddy, I needed to pick someone called a "best man" who would stand next to me on the altar when the priest went through the most important part of the wedding ceremony. The best man is supposed to be someone who will always support you and be there for you. I wanted to choose someone who I not only loved and respected, but also someone who I would want to emulate throughout my life. To me, the choice was very easy. I knew from the day that I asked mommy to be my wife that Papa Bear would be my best man.

Papa Bear has always been there for me in every possible way. He has worked very hard in his life to make sure that I had everything I needed both in terms of opportunities and love to be a successful adult. Going through life, I always knew that I had a safety net. If I were to stumble, Papa Bear would be there. If I were to lose my job, Papa Bear would give me money for housing. If I was sick, he would find the best doctors.

Papa Bear doesn't just provide a safety net however. He has also shown me how to be a husband and a dad. He has never sacrificed the well being of his family for his career or any other pursuits. When I was little, he would go to all of my soccer games and school functions even if it meant him having to leave work early. He always expressed completely confidence in me – much more confidence than I had in myself. He was proud of me and he let me know it on a regular basis.

Driving home today, I started thinking about the day that I asked Papa Bear to be my best man. We were at our house in Charlotte celebrating Christmas, and I told him that I wanted to speak with him. I told him how much I have always appreciated his love and support and that there is no other person who I would want to be my best man. He was the only choice.

He smiled and said that he would be honored. We hugged and continued with the rest of our day.

Dear Zoe || Love Dad

Months later, it was actually time for mommy and me to get married. On the day of our wedding, he came up to me and told me that my asking him to be my best man was the proudest moment of his life. He said that it was the greatest honor that he had ever received. I was shocked by his comments, and I assumed that he was just being nice or that he was caught up in the emotion of the day.

Your Papa Bear has accomplished a great deal in his life. Let me share a little bit about his background. He grew up in a trailer park not a house. The first time that he ever left the state of Florida where he grew up was to go to Harvard Business School. Having graduated from Harvard Business School with Distinction, he wasn't even able to attend his graduation because he and Neeny already had two kids and he only had enough money to drive to Chicago to start his job. He eventually went on to become the CEO of his company. He has put all six of his kids through college without ever forcing any of them to take out a single loan. I could go on and on, but I hope you get the point that he certainly has a great deal to be proud of.

As I drove home tonight, I thought back to our conversation on my wedding day. I believed him. I really do think that having one of his children ask him to be the best man at their wedding was his proudest moment. It took my becoming a father to gain the perspective needed to digest his comment.

There is nothing that I will ever do that will be as important to me as having you love and respect me.

I want you to know that I truly mean what I just wrote, and I plan to live my life in a way that will make you proud of me. As I continued driving and thinking, I began to wonder whether this was God's plan all along. When He said, "Go forth and multiply," maybe He knew that having children would inspire all His sons and daughters to live better lives.

When I got home, you were sitting with mommy drinking your bottle. I smiled at you knowing how much you had just inspired me. I was waiting for you to realize the special connection that we have. You however just kept drinking your bottle and staring at the Christmas tree in the living room. Well, I guess I still have a lot of work to do.

Dear Zoe – November, 26

Yesterday was your first Thanksgiving, and it ended up being one of the most memorable Thanksgivings that either mommy or I had ever had. We went to Washington D.C., where the President lives, to see your Uncle Ryder, Aunt Jo, Aunt Jessica, Neeny, and Papa Bear. This was your first trip out of

Dear Zoe || Love Dad

Pennsylvania, and mommy and I were pretty nervous about taking you away from your home. Mommy had been so nervous that she started packing your suitcase over a week ago. By the time we were ready to leave yesterday morning, there was hardly any room in our SUV for me to sit.

I told mommy that I was sure that we were taking way too much stuff, but at the same time, I didn't know what we should leave behind. We needed your stroller, play pen, clothes, diapers, formula, etc.... When you added in my and mommy's clothes plus the air mattress, the SUV was completely packed.

Mommy had everything planned. I was to pack the car on the night before we left so that we could time our departure exactly with your schedule. Mommy would feed you your breakfast and then wait for you to relax before taking off on our 2 and a half hour drive to Uncle Ryder's apartment. We had a bottle prepared for you in case you got hungry, but we both were hoping it wouldn't be necessary.

In the end, you started to get hungry after about an hour and a half, and mommy and I were able to find a Starbucks where we could change and feed you. Everything was going great, and I started to think that travelling with a baby (by car) wasn't so hard after all. We packed you back in the car and called Uncle Ryder to tell him that we were just going to go to the hotel to see Neeny and Papa Bear rather than go to his apartment first.

When we arrived at the hotel, Papa Bear was waiting outside for his little grandbaby. We hadn't been parked for more than a minute before Neeny and Aunt Jessica arrived as well. Aunt Jessica had only seen pictures of you, and she was so excited to be meeting you for the first time. I went to hug Neeny, but she had already opened the door to get you out of the car seat. I guess a grandbaby is more exciting that a son☺ Before I knew it, Neeny had you out of the car and she and Aunt Jessica were taking you into the hotel.

Mommy and I finally caught up to you, and we all went to Papa Bear and Neeny's hotel room. Everyone was so excited to play with you, especially Papa Bear. He was right on the floor talking with you, and you just loved him. You kept smiling and making happy baby noises which made Papa Bear as happy as I had ever seen him. He even said that it was really smart to make him happy – what he meant was that he has a lot of money and he likes to buy things for those who are nice to him. How do you think we got the down payment for your house?

You were in such a good mood the whole day as Aunt Jo's family came to see you as well. You were truly the star of this Thanksgiving.

Dear Zoe || Love Dad

You were having so much fun that you didn't want to nap and follow your normal schedule. I figured that today was a special day and that your skipping of naps wasn't a big deal. We finally went to Uncle Ryder's apartment to get ready for a big Thanksgiving dinner. Mommy and I had picked out a pretty red, black, and white dress for this special occasion. You see, not all babies get to have Thanksgiving dinner at the Four Seasons. You looked so precious in your new outfit – then again, you look precious in all your outfits. Now that I think of it, you grow so fast that the sight of you in a new outfit is far from abnormal. Well, you looked especially beautiful today.

We put you in the stroller and walked to dinner. On the way there, I spotted a big Christmas tree with rows and rows of bright lights. I couldn't help but leave the group and take a slight detour with you because you love lights more than anything or anyone (except for your mommy. I know you love them more than me because I had been gone for four days in a row on a business trip and when I came rushing in the door to see my baby, you kept staring at the Christmas tree even as I plopped my face directly in front of you. I actually had to take you into another room before you would even acknowledge my presence.)

At the restaurant, you got to meet my best friend from college who I had not seen in nine whole years. It was great seeing him again and introducing him to the best thing that has ever happened to me, you. We went to a back room which was totally private. I parked the stroller and you began to cry. Mommy took you and walked you around the lobby, and you finally fell asleep.

Was skipping all your naps and changing your schedule such a good idea?

You weren't asleep for more than five minutes, when you started crying again. This time, Neeny took you and fed you your bottle which always calms you down. Correction; it has always calmed you down before tonight. With you still crying, mommy once again took you and walked around the restaurant. You returned resting peacefully in her arms.

Once again, you started crying the moment mommy sat down and stopped rocking you. This pattern continued throughout dinner until mommy finally looked at me and said, "Daddy, we need to go."

I had never seen mommy with such a nervous look. We had gone to many dinners with you, and you had been fussy before, but tonight felt different. For the first time, we weren't going back to our home. We were going to an apartment where no baby had ever been. There was no crib, swing, rocking chair, etc...

Dear Zoe || Love Dad

I said goodbye to my friend and grabbed my jacket as quick as humanly possible. Mommy and I then headed out into the night with our little crying baby. When we got to Uncle Ryder's apartment, you calmed down, but it was clear that mommy and I had made a big mistake by not following your schedule. You were exhausted.

Uncle Ryder and Aunt Jo showed up only a few minutes later. We all changed you and got you ready for bed. Your mom and I said good night, and we headed into our room for what would be a restless night on a pull-out couch.

Without warning, you started crying. Your crying quickly escalated to screaming. Panic came over me as I had never heard you cry for more than a few minutes let alone scream. You were absolutely inconsolable. Your mom tried all of her tricks; she rocked you, she gave you your paci, she rubbed your back, etc.... Nothing was working. With each minute, your screams became louder and louder. It was awful seeing you so upset. You were screaming so loud and hard that you would actually start to choke.

My stomach started to hurt as I was in physical pain seeing you with tears streaming down your face. Your mom continued to tell you that everything was going to be fine, but nothing was working. I called Memom to tell her what was happening, and she had no answers. She just got upset herself because she could hear you yelling in the background.

Finally, I told mommy that we should try to give you a bath because the water usually calmed you down. I ran into the bathroom and started the water. Miraculously, the sound of the splashing water seemed to calm you ever so slightly. Your screams were now reduced to cries and whimpers. Finally, a sign of hope, I thought to myself. Your mom continued to hold you in your favorite position, on top of her shoulder, as we both prayed that you were finished crying.

Thirty minutes had passed, but it had felt like much, much longer. There is no way to describe the feeling a parent gets when he sees his precious baby so upset. I would have done anything to make it better. Thankfully, I had stumbled upon something that seemed to be working. After letting the water run for about ten minutes, I decided that I needed to turn it off so that I didn't run up the water bill of Uncle Ryder. With the water turned off, you started crying once again.

I wasn't about to wait to see if you would stop, and I ran right back into the bathroom and turned it on. I figured that I would pay Uncle Ryder for any water that I used. I wasn't going to let money get in the way of your happiness. With the water back on, you once again settled. After you were asleep for thirty minutes, I turned on some white noise (via your mom's iPhone) and then turned off the water.

It was finally safe for mommy to go to bed. You were lying right next to her in only your diaper. Mommy had started to get you ready for your bath when the sound of the water calmed you down. We both decided that we didn't want to risk waking you up by putting your nightgown and sleep sack back on. Tonight, you were going to sleep in only a diaper until you woke up at which point, we would get you dressed more fully.

I looked at mommy and said, "We are leaving tomorrow. I can't see my baby like this." She was so happy because she was thinking the same thing. Yes, I wanted to see my family more, but you are my top priority.

Mommy and I went to sleep. I was on the floor so that you and your mom could have the bed to yourselves.

You slept through the night, but you weren't your normal self in the morning. Usually, it is hard to get you to eat in the morning because you just want to smile and play. This morning, there were no smiles coming from my little baby. It was so sad. I looked at mommy and said, "Did we ruin our baby? Will she ever be the same?"

Yes, I was being a little dramatic, but you had never been so upset. Now, you weren't acting like yourself. I had been traumatized, and I had just spent a very uncomfortable night on the floor praying that my little baby would stay asleep. Mommy assured me that everything would be okay.

After taking down your bottle with very little happiness, you went back to bed as mommy held you in her arms.

This morning nap lasted for another few hours, and I can not tell you how happy I was when you woke up smiling. MY BABY WAS BACK! I took you in my arms and hugged and kissed you.

I knew that our leaving was not going to be well-received by our family because everyone still wanted to see you. Still, I knew that what was best for you and mommy was for us to get home. I told everyone that we were leaving, and they all seemed frustrated. Their frustration didn't bother me one bit. I knew what I had to do for my family, and I packed up the car and prepared to make the drive back.

Dear Zoe || Love Dad

With the three of us alone in the car, we headed out of the city to our little townhouse. Mommy got sick on the way home because she gets sick in the car, but she couldn't stop talking about how glad she was to be headed home where we could reestablish your schedule.

New parents make mistakes, and I think that we made a mistake by taking you on a trip too early. Maybe some parents can do it, and I am happy for them. For me, I wasn't ready. I know that our leaving probably caused a lot of talk by the family members who remained in DC for the whole weekend. But, I don't need to be viewed as the best dad by anyone except you. You wanted to go home which is where we are now.

Dear Zoe – December, 5

I think that I needed you this weekend more than you needed me. Between the pressures of work and my buying you the new house, I was about as stressed out as I have ever been. On the drive home Friday night, I was completely overcome with worry and my OCD was raging out of control.

Mommy too had had a tough week because I was sick on Monday and Tuesday which meant that I couldn't be around you. We were nervous that you would catch what I had and we didn't want to take any chances. Now that I think of it, maybe my not spending time with you early in the week had contributed to my feelings of stress and worry. Anyways, mommy looked exhausted by the time I got home and opened the door. She was exhausted and I was exhausted and riddled with anxiety; who was going to take care of you I thought?

I told mommy that she needed to take a break and that I would feed you. I warmed your bottle and took you in my arm. As the sweet sound of you humming with satisfaction filled the air, my worries started to fade away. With each gulp, both you and I were happier and more content. You kept eating as I rocked you in your chair. It didn't take long for your eyes to gently close as you nodded off for the night. See usually, I try to put you right into your crib as soon as you fall asleep. Tonight however, I needed in you my arms. I needed your peacefulness/ calmness near me.

Mommy came into the room to check on us, and I think she was surprised that I was still holding you even though you were clearly asleep. She said that I needed to lie you down so that you would be asleep in your crib. Because she really does know best, I followed her advice and ever so softly lied you down. I didn't want to be away from you yet however, and I went back to the rocking chair. I sat there just thinking about how lucky I was to have you in my life.

Dear Zoe || Love Dad

You have already started to help me out. No medicines or doctors have ever been able to help me with my anxiety the way that you have in the short time you've been in my life. Thank you for being so amazing.

Well, I thought that I should tell you about a couple of new developments in your life. Both of these new behaviors are probably inherited from your good old dad.

First, you have seemingly discovered your voice. I called mommy to talk earlier this week, and I could hear you yelling in the background. At first, I was convinced that you were crying, but mommy told me that you weren't crying but rather you were simply yelling. I asked her if you were sad, mad, or upset, and she said, "No, she is just making noises." Maybe your screeches, gurgles, and shouts would annoy other parents, but they are music to my ears. See, I too like to make a lot of noises and I always have. Don't really know why I do it, but I guess it just helps me expel some of the trapped energy I have inside. Mommy thinks you are trying to talk, but I think you just like making various noises; whether you are actually trying to communicate is very much debatable in my mind.

Second, you have started a very odd habit. Do you remember that I said you started sucking your thumb? Well, you never really grew into a thumb sucker per se. There would be days when you would only suck on your paci and there would be days when you would suck on your thumb or maybe even a toy. Over the past week, you have moved on from sucking your paci, thumb, or toys. Now, you like to suck on your ENTIRE hand. I will look down at you, and you will be desperately trying to cram your entire fist into your mouth. Sometimes, you will actually succeed causing you to immediately start gagging until you spit up everywhere.

Mommy and I are nervous about this habit because we want to make sure that you don't choke yourself when you spit up. We don't really care that sucking your whole hand probably won't be good for your teeth when they arrive nor are we concerned about any accompanying social stigma that comes from being the parents of a whole-hand sucker. Our only concern is your safety. We always try to take your hand, but without fail you will simply put it back in as soon as we let go.

Last night, you proved once again that you were my baby – a child filled with weird quirks and a happy disposition. Your mom and I were frantically trying to get you to sleep. You were exhausted but as is the norm, you were fighting your sleep. As mommy rocked you, I noticed your hand take out your paci. You then took your other hand and proceeded to put it so far into your mouth that you spit up all over mommy. When mommy said, "No, Zoe! We do not choke ourselves," you raised your eyes and stared right at her. Seconds later you started giggling and laughing.

Immediately, I started laughing. Here I was the father of a 4.5 month old baby who not only choked herself to the point of throwing up, but also found it terribly funny when she was scolded by her mom. Neeny used to tell me that I would do such funny things that it was hard to discipline me. She said that it took every fiber of her being to not burst into laughter. I now know what she means. I of course chose to laugh right along with you rather than stifle my reaction. I guess I am a different parent than Neeny.

We had another wonderful day. It always makes me so proud and happy when you act like me – regardless of whether it is behavior one should be proud of. Because you look so much like your mom, I will take anything I can get.

Dear Zoe – December, 19

I haven't written to you in a long time because it is getting harder and harder to find the time. Your mom and I have been so busy with the new house we are building you; we need to go to the bank, pick out paint colors, find window treatments, etc… Also, writing to you isn't my top priority; playing with you is☺

We had so much fun together this morning. I decided to let mommy sleep late, and you and I spent the whole morning together. You were in a great mood having eaten, pooped, and burped – the holy trinity of baby happiness. The two of us just sat on the couch watching TV as you snuggled against my side. Never have I been so happy as I was this morning snuggling with my little baby watching Sportscenter.

You have changed so much since I last wrote to you. Two weeks ago you were just starting to develop enough strength in your neck to hold up your head, and you had finally found your voice. Now, your head is strong enough that you have actually started to embrace tummy time, something I thought might never happen. You laugh and smile more and more every day. Your laugh has gone from being just a giggle to a full fledge laugh with hiccups and gasps of air. Last night, you were laughing at your friend Ava like I had never heard. Usually, you just kind of ignore Ava, but last night, you would look at her and just start laughing. Something about her just made you smile. When Ava started crying, you thought she was even funnier. It was neat seeing you interact with another baby and your first friend. If you are anything like your mommy, you will be sure to have many, many more friends as you grow older.

Dear Zoe || Love Dad

After watching Sportscenter with your dad, you decided to take your midmorning nap. There I was, sitting on my couch with my precious baby. Being with you is so peaceful, but I will admit that I was glad when you finally decided to wake up. Because I didn't want to wake you, I kept my body very still in an unfortunate and contorted position. Even as I write this 15 hours later, I can still feel the pain in my side from where I must have been activating muscles I didn't even know I had. You woke up with a big smile on your face, and we just started playing. First, you played on your mat where you were constantly grabbing and hitting your toys. When mommy finally woke up, she wanted to show me how you have started eating rice cereal like a big girl.

She put you in your little lamb seat as she went to prepare your breakfast. It was in this chair that we really started playing. I must have given you 300 kisses in the ten minutes it took mommy to make your cereal. I would get my face in front of you and your eyes would get real big as you anticipated my descent. Next, I moved toward you preparing to give you little kisses and you would throw your arms out grabbing and scratching my face. As I got closer, your eyes would close and your mouth would open real big. Then, I would give you little kisses all over your cheeks and forehead as you smiled and laughed. It might not seem like a lot of fun, but we were having a great time. I don't think it will always be this easy to entertain you, and I know you won't always appreciate my little kisses this way which is why I figured I should make the most of the situation while it lasts.

Mommy came back with your cereal, and I was finally able to see you eat. We had gone to the doctor last week, a visit I will tell you about in a few minutes, and she had said that it was time for you to start eating rice cereal. Because I am at work early in the morning, I still hadn't seen you eat in person, but rather I had only seen you on my iPhone. (Even technophobes have to appreciate the advances in technology as they are able to quickly capture and subsequently relay information about loved ones. Without my iPhone, getting through the day would be much harder. Pictures and videos of you always bring smiles to my face while I am dealing with the stresses of work.)

Mommy took the cereal and put it on a long plastic spoon. You opened your mouth wide as if you had been doing this for years. As the spoon got closer, you mouth continued to open wider and wider until you could feel the plastic hit your lips at which point you instinctually flicked out your tongue like a lizard capturing his prey. Watching you eat was so funny because just as much cereal ended up on your face as ended up in your mouth. As your tongue reached out for the food, you would inevitably knock at least half the cereal off of the spoon and onto your chin. Your mom would then try to get this cereal back on the spoon as your head moved from side to side causing it to get all over both cheeks. You looked like a mess, but you were having a great time. I think you might have been getting some nutrients too, as long as a little bit of food was making its way into your belly.

Well I mentioned that I would tell you about your doctor's appointment, and I will even though it was very hard for your daddy. See, you know how I always tell you that I will always take care of you and protect you? Taking you to the doctor last week was in fact for your benefit, but it was for your long-time not short-time protection. What made the whole situation so awful for me was that I couldn't explain to you what was going to happen or why your mommy and I were going to make you get SHOTS!

It was time for your second round of immunization, and you needed to get two different shots. I had been fearing this appointment since your mommy made it. Yes, I knew that it was for your benefit and that not having you get your shots would be the absolute wrong thing to do. That being said, what really bothered me was that I wasn't able to explain this logic to you. You woke up last Friday as happy as could be. You were smiling and playing with mommy all morning. When I showed up at the doctor's appointment, I came over and kissed you on the forehead which led to your smiling back at me. I have always loved seeing you smile, but at this moment, it made me very uncomfortable. I felt like I was about to betray you and your love of me only made my sense of betrayal more difficult to handle.

You were smiling at me at least partially because you trust me. It probably hasn't taken long to appreciate the fact that your mom and I take care of your every need as best as we know how. You know that when you cry that mommy or I will be there for you to comfort you. Today, your protector was taking you to a sterile environment where a stranger would plunge two different needles into your little, chubby thighs. Even writing this to you a week later makes me upset.

The nurse called your name, and mommy and I took you back to the room where the doctor would eventually see you. The nurse weighed and measured you. To my great surprise, you were already bigger than most babies your birth age even though you had been born a full five weeks premature. Your weight was in the 75th percentile, your length was in the 80th, and your head circumference was in the 95th. I was so happy that you were growing so well and that you were so healthy. Next, the doctor came in the room and did her exam. She said that everything was great. The only noteworthy occurrence came when I asked a question about the size of your head. When I asked the doctor whether she had any concerns with the size or shape of your noggin, she looked at mommy and said, "No, it looks like her father has a big head. It is therefore probably genetic." Well, there you go; hopefully, you like your head because it comes from me☺

With the exam over, it was time for your shots. I wanted to leave because I did not want to see you in pain. I had already seen enough poking and prodding of my little baby in the NICU. Your mom told me that I had to stay. My nervousness started to cause me to get real hot as my body was reacting negatively to what I knew was about to happen. As I sat looking at you, I hated thinking about letting someone cause you pain while I was right there with you. I couldn't help but wonder what you were thinking? Were you going to be mad at me? Were you going to lose your trust in me? Were you still going to cry for me to help and protect you?

These questions and others continued swirling in my head as the nurse prepared your legs for the shots. I know that this all sounds terribly dramatic, but it really happened as described. Being a parent just makes you a different, more sensitive person.

Within a second, the nurse had managed to give you both your shots. Even though she did a great job, your screams started almost exactly when the second needle was removed from your left thigh. You screamed loud and hard, and I felt absolutely awful. I was so upset I was a little sick to my stomach. Mommy rocked you back and forth, but there was nothing that could be done at that moment. I wasn't sure whether you were crying because the needles had hurt, because the medicine hurt, or because you were shocked and disappointed that your parents lets this happen. It took a full five minutes for mommy to get you to settle down enough for us to put you in your car seat.

I put the car seat on top of the stroller and rolled you around the lobby as mommy paid the bill. Sometimes in life, the fear of an event is much worse than the actual event. In this case, seeing you cry was even worse than I had imagined. I kissed you and mommy good bye, and I went to work feeling down.

The doctor had said that the shots might make you fell a little "off" for the rest of the weekend. She turned out to be very correct. The next couple of days were some of the longest that mommy and I have had since we left the NICU. I have never figured out whether your legs hurt or whether the medicine in the shots caused you to feel discomfort, but you just weren't yourself. You cried easily throughout the weekend, and you never wanted to go to sleep. Mommy and I were so exhausted physically and mentally. Seeing you upset just breaks my heart. Not being able to take your pain and discomfort away was a terrible feeling. Your mom and I tried anything and everything to make you happy over those two days.

I wish that I had a video of your mommy and me consoling you. There were times when mommy was cradling you in her arms as she bounced up and down as if tracing a giant "M". Simultaneously, she was rocking you from side to side while I followed the two of you with a hair dryer. Other times, mommy would speed walk with you in her arms while I ran the vacuum cleaner over the same piece of rug for an hour. We were desperate, and we tried things that made sense and things that seemed totally ridiculous. Sometimes I would laugh as the three of us would lie in bed with you crying and us kissing and snuggling you. I laughingly told mommy, "What more can a little baby want?" I tried to keep the mood light because it was wearing on mommy. She was so tired on Sunday that she just started crying and wondering whether she had done something wrong that was making you not want to sleep in your crib. I told her that she did everything right and that a little baby can't have too much love. Well, I at least hope not because you would be in big trouble.

By Monday night, you were back to being yourself. It couldn't have come soon enough. We had a great week together as I tried to do a better job of helping out mommy. All my hard work must have been appreciated by you because as I said earlier, we had the best morning we have ever had. Well, at least I did. I really do think that you "love" me more on the days when I spend more time with you. Your love doesn't come without effort which is probably a very good quality to have.

I love you Zoe, and thank you for bringing so much happiness into my life. You have changed me in so many ways. I know that I say this too you often, but each week you help me more and more become the person I want to be. I therefore can't help but tell you over and over again.

Dear Zoe – December, 20

I was thinking about something today that I wanted to share with you. A few of my friends have recently made comments to me telling me how I've changed since you were born. Ava's dad said "You are so at peace and content. I wish I could always look for the best in people at work the way you do."

Now to be perfectly honest sweetie, I haven't always been someone who looked for others' best qualities in the work place. I used to believe that you needed to compete at work and be adversarial if necessary. These last few months however, I have just been happy and content all day. I think there are three main reasons.

Dear Zoe || Love Dad

First, since you arrived, I leave to work in the morning happy and fresh after seeing you and this feeling just carries me throughout the day until I get recharged at night when I see your smiling face again. Second, throughout the day, I try my best to be someone you would be proud to call "dad," and I don't think you would want a dad who was mean. Third, I try to exercise the same level of understanding with my co-workers that I have with you. See, you can't talk which means that I have to really try and understand what you need. I have to look past your actions to see what is truly bothering you. When you cry or scream, I need to understand what is causing this behavior. Now at work, someone might be screaming too, and I need to figure out why as well. It sounds funny, but it actually works. Try to fix the root cause rather than the symptom.

What I was really thinking about today however was whether I could some how help you get to the same level of peace and happiness as I have now before you became a parent. Since having you, I have not only been happier and more content, but I have also been a better all-around person. I think more about making money so that I can give it to charity rather than making money so that I can buy myself new things. Speaking of possessions, I now spend more time feeling saddened that there are so many needy people in the world rather than feeling jealous of all those people who have more. I'm telling you baby, you are the best thing to ever happen to me.

I'm not sure whether there is any way for someone to feel the love and sense of purpose that comes with being a parent unless you actually have a child, but if there is, I want to be able to explain it to you. There are going to be times in life when you might feel sad, frustrated, or lost. My goal is to try and make sure that you don't ever feel this way. Maybe if I set a good example for you, then you will learn to be a happy, motivated, caring, and passionate person. Maybe you can be filled with the love and purpose of a parent if we do charity work together throughout your life.

I don't know if I have the answer, but I really want you to be able to feel the way that I have felt since you came into my life well before you ever become a mommy. If I could do this, then I know I will have been a successful parent. It would be the greatest gift a dad could give a daughter.

Love you, baby.

Dear Zoe – December, 21

Today was a big day for you even though you probably didn't know it. Your mommy and I bought our first house today! At around 4:00, I gave a woman the

Dear Zoe || Love Dad

biggest check that I had ever written and in turn she handed over a set of keys to the house that mommy and I have been building for the last several months. When I got the keys in my hand today, it was the culmination of a very long process that began when we found out that mommy had you in her stomach. Before we knew whether IVF was going to work, mommy and I wanted to save as much money as possible so that we could go through as many cycles as we needed to bring you down from heaven. When the doctor told us that you were in mommy's tummy almost a year ago, we started thinking that it might be a good idea to buy a house so that you would grow up in a neighborhood with other kids. The extra space a house would provide would be an additional bonus.

Earlier in the day, I needed to go to the bank to get the money for the house. As I made the long drive, I reflected back upon the whole house buying process. You weren't even alive, but you played a major role in our decisions; so much so that maybe we should call the house casa de Zoe? We wanted a house in a safe neighborhood which fed into a quality school system. We wanted a house that had a guest room so that your grandparents, uncles, and cousins could come and visit. We wanted a big basement where you could roller skate, bike ride, or do other physical things during the winter months.

It took some time, but I think that mommy and I found just the perfect house. I am very confident that you are going to love growing up in the new house. Driving down the highway, I felt a real sense of pride. Knowing that all the years that I studied hard in school or worked hard at my jobs had allowed me to buy a house where you and your mom would be happy meant so much to me. I had never had a desire to own a home and I never saw home ownership as a major accomplishment. To be honest, I still don't. What I do view as an accomplishment is providing a safe and loving environment for you which I believe you will now have.

As I continued driving, I actually started to get sad. I was sad because I realized that many parents aren't able to give their babies all the new things that your mommy and I have been able to give you. Many parents aren't able to feel the pride and sense of accomplishment that I was feeling at this moment. My mind wandered to an e-mail I received earlier in the week from my friend Jeanne. Do you remember the mommy who was very young that your mommy and I met in the NICU? Well, Jeanne told me that she learned that the young woman had to take her little baby back to the hospital for heart surgery. Seeing you in the NICU had been so hard that I couldn't imagine how difficult it would be to take you back to the hospital. Jeanne also found out that the girl did not have enough money to buy her baby a crib. Your mommy and I had given her some money when she left the NICU so that she could get a pack and play, but she never found enough money for a crib. When we heard about this situation, we knew that we needed to help once again and we are going to be sending another check to her.

I want you to always understand that you have a lot of things that other little babies and kids don't have. It is important for you to be thankful and to never think that you are "better" than any kids because you might have more toys or a nicer house. Life isn't supposed to be about *getting* the nicest things but rather about *doing* the nicest things. When you are a little older, you, mommy, and I can do some projects to help others that are in need and you will have a better understanding of why I am writing this to you now. Just like I love you and want to give you every opportunity in life, many other parents feel the same way but don't have the necessary resources. It's important to help out these parents and kids whenever you can.

I feel so blessed today. Figuring out how to give others this feeling is something that I need to work on.

Dear Zoe – December, 22

I couldn't sleep last night as I mentally rearranged the furniture of your room in my head over and over again. When we move into the new house, I want your room to be just right. The other reason that I couldn't sleep was because I was very nervous about our big trip to Texas to see your Memom and Daddy Mac. After mommy and I bought the house, we had to come home and finish packing for the trip because we were leaving the next day, this morning, at 4:30. When our realtor had asked me yesterday whether I was nervous spending that amount of money, I told her that the only thing that I was nervous about was our impending trip. I just wasn't sure how you were going to do on the plane.

Your mom had packed A LOT of things for you. We knew that we were going to take your big stroller on the airplane so that we could push you through the Houston airport during a long layover. The stroller was not only heavy, but it was also very bulky. We had considered taking a smaller, umbrella stroller, but I didn't think it would be as comfortable or safe for you. Besides the stroller, mommy packed a bag with diapers, wipes, bottles, formula, fruit juice, toys, and clothes. As she arranged the items in the bag, I asked her why she was taking enough formula for three days. The trip was going to be nine hours not seventy-two. She said that she was concerned that we wouldn't have enough food if we were delayed which is not at all unlikely in today's world of air travel. She had an excellent point, but I still believed she was going a little overboard. Fortunately, I was able to convince her to leave two of the bottles at home as well as about 15 diapers and 20 wipes. I definitely wanted to have everything you would need, but I also knew that I was going to be the one carrying this bag, the stroller, my backpack and the diaper bag. Mommy on the other hand was going to have to carry only one thing – you!

It was 2:30 in the morning before I was able to fall asleep. In what felt like the blink of an eye, I heard the sound which I have grown to hate – the sound of my alarm. I was exhausted when mommy told me that I really needed to get up and pack the car. After only sleeping for two hours, packing the car in the freezing weather was not exactly something that I wanted to be doing. The cold weather did at least wake me up.

As I packed the car, mommy got you ready for the trip. I turned the car on and put on the heat so that it would be nice and toasty for your arrival. I finally went upstairs to see what was taking so long; mommy just looked at me and said, "She peed everywhere." Our trip was not starting out exactly as we planned, but a little pee was not a big problem.

I had been nervous for weeks in preparation for this trip. Some parents get nervous because they get embarrassed or anxious if their child cries in public, but I wasn't worried about what others might be thinking. My worry was that you would be upset by the loud noises or air pressure changes that accompany air travel. I get upset when I hear you cry; it just breaks my heart to know that you are sad. Being on an airplane wouldn't allow your mom and me the freedom to walk and rock you, our main weapon against your sadness. Once we were in Texas, I knew that you would have a great time with your grandparents and cousins. Unfortunately, it was going to take three airplanes to get there.

For the first time in your whole life, it was us and not you doing the waking up in the middle of the night. Besides having peed everywhere, you were off to a good start. I loaded you into the car, and we were off on our biggest adventure to date.

Having had to change and clean you had put us behind schedule, and we frantically made our way to the ticketing counter at the airport. You were in mommy's arms oblivious to the upcoming events. I had told you about the plan for the day, but I am confident you couldn't really grasp the concept of climbing in a metal tube that would fly hundreds of miles through the sky. Your mom and I had been to the airport many, many times, but this was our first time with a baby. The first change that we had to make was not taking the escalator as we just had too many things to safely make it down the moving staircase. Time was of the essence, and our detour to the elevators seemed to take forever. Once we got to ticketing, I checked the box for "Are you travelling with children under the age of 2" for the very first time. The machine pumped out tickets for both you and me. You are such a big girl.

Dear Zoe || Love Dad

With our load lessened by two suitcases, we made our way back up the elevator and up to security. Not needing to take your car seat with us, we were able to use a new seat for your stroller. This new seat allowed you to look forward rather than back at mommy and me, and your head moved from side to side as if you were watching a tennis match. No longer were you forced to stare back at your loving parents; the world was now open to you. There was so much to see and you seemed keen on not missing a thing. When it was time to go through security, mommy and I took off our shoes, belts, and watches, pulled out the computer, folded the stroller, removed all the formula, and handed over our bags while never putting you down. I was amazed at our efficiency as first-time parents. Maybe today wasn't going to be so hard after all.

We made it to the gate with about 30 minutes to spare. Before boarding, we changed you one final time. Mommy had to change you on the floor as there was no changing table in the bathroom. Don't worry; I served as a human shield to protect your privacy.

The flight attendant said that it was time to board, and we walked down the long hallway leading to the plane. I dropped off the folded stroller and one of our carry on bags at the end of the jet bridge before heading down more stairs leading to the tarmac. It was both freezing and loud outside. The propellers from the plan were whirling, and mommy had to cover your ears as you got startled. We found our seats and waited for the plane to take off. Your mom had hoped that you would make it to the plane before needing your breakfast. The doctor had told us that babies often do better flying when they eat during takeoff (it helps eliminate pressure that could otherwise build up in your ears). You were such a good baby and fully cooperated. With the plane getting ready to leave, I poured you a big glass of milk. Over the last two weeks, you have started to understand what your bottle looked like and a smile came across your face as I prepared this simple yet delicious breakfast. You started sucking away as we lifted off the ground. We were flying and you didn't seem to mind one bit. You were so happy the entire flight, and it was so much fun to spend time with my two girls.

We landed in Cleveland and had to quickly make our way to our next flight which would take us to Houston. I felt like a pack mule trekking through the airport with all of our stuff. I had two bags affixed to my body while I simultaneously pulled the empty stroller and a small suitcase. You were in the comfortable arms of your mom. She definitely got the better end of this deal.

You were talking away as we boarded the plan. Unfortunately, your happy noises turned to sad cries which then turned to mad yells. Mommy didn't want to start feeding you until we were about to take off, but I convinced her that it was time. It was clear that any further delays could result in a full-on meltdown. I prepared your bottle hoping that it would once again be the cure to your discomfort. I was right. With only a few minutes of yelling, you were back to your sweet self. Your mom was even able to have you take a nap for the most of the flight. Two down and only one to go, I thought to myself when we touched down in Houston.

The last flight was a breeze, and mommy rushed you to the baggage claim where Memom was anxiously awaiting your arrival. As soon as you saw her, you immediately recognized her which was a good thing because she snatched you away from mommy. Once again, I was left to get all the bags, load the car, and fix the car seat while your mommy and Memom got to play with you. Sometimes your dad gets the short end of the stick!

We made the long drive from the airport to Memom's house. The long day of travel was starting to catch up with you. You began rubbing your eyes which by now were very red and watery. I let Memom sit next to you in the backseat because she doesn't get to see you as much as your mommy and I do. We were about ten minutes away from the house when you started crying. The sound of you crying makes me want to cry as I feel so bad for you. Your cries got louder and louder with each passing mile until you were screaming so loud that you were choking yourself. I kept telling mommy to pull over so that I could get you out of the car seat and just hug you. Even if you wouldn't stop crying, I wanted you to know that was there for you. Mommy said that we just needed to get home. It was so painful as traffic seemed to move so slowly even though it was flowing at a rate well over the speed limit. The last five minutes of the trip were excruciating as your cries filled the car. My anxiety was through the roof. When I finally saw Memom's driveway, I took my seat belt off and grabbed the door handle. Mommy stopped the car, and I sprung out of the vehicle as if ejected from a cannon. I whipped open your door and kissed you on the forehead and told you it was going to be okay while quickly unbuckling you. With you in my arms, I rocked back and forth trying to calm you down. Mommy and Memom had run inside to prepare a bottle as well as get diapers and wipes to change you.

It didn't take long for you to calm down once I had you in my arms. You just love your daddy. With things having settled down and with mommy feeding you, I could finally relax after our long day. About thirty minutes after our arrival at Memom's, mommy asked me to go get something from the car. When I walked outside, I found your Memom's car in the driveway with every single door wide open. The three of us had been so concerned with making you happy that none of us had even bothered to shut our doors let alone lock them. On a day like today, I might argue that the earth doesn't really revolve around the sun.

Dear Zoe || Love Dad

All things considered, we had had a great day. Because I work everyday and because your mom and I often take turns caring for you, the three of us had never spent so much time together. Usually, I am feeding you while mommy is cleaning your bottles or I am napping while mommy is holding you. Today, we were a big family, and I just loved it. This day which had had me so worried actually turned out to be a real blessing.

Dear Zoe – December, 28

You celebrated your first Christmas a few days ago, and you must have been a very good girl because Santa brought you lots of presents. Not only was Santa feeling generous this year, but you received presents from Aunts, Uncles, cousins, 2nd cousins, neighbors, and pretty much anyone who learned of your birth. You are definitely a loved baby.

Even before Christmas arrived, you had already received more presents than most little girls receive for their birthdays and Christmas combined. In preparation for your arrival, Memom had spent a considerable amount of time and money preparing the house. When your mom and I finally settled down after our long day of travel, we walked around Memom's house to find more toys, clothes, and play things than you have at your own house! Memom's house had so many things that your mommy actually asked her whether you had had a second baby shower while we were back in Pennsylvania. You really are quite lucky.

It was very special having Christmas with you; I can definitely say it was my favorite Christmas of all. What made the day so much fun for me was to see how many people wanted to bring you a little something for this holiday. As a parent, there is nothing more special than seeing someone treat your child with kindness. Your mommy and I have a lot of thank you cards to write when we get back home.

I am always telling you how special you are and how much joy you bring to my life. I even remember writing to you about how you were able to bring days of happiness to Kim, Memom's friend who has cancer. What I have realized over the lat week is that your presence continues to have a positive impact on all those you meet. You just seemed to have an aurora that draws people to you. Over the last week, Memom's house has been flooded with people who want to meet you for the first time. Some of the guests at the house have been family members who have not always even got along. It seems that everyone is willing to put hard feelings aside for a chance to see the newest member of the family, you! Being witness to this outpouring of love makes me realize that everyone, at

Dear Zoe || Love Dad

their core, does hope for the best for you. I have told mommy that I should try to treat all people the way that I have seen people treat you.

Your greatest impact has been on your mommy's family. Last night, your mom, Memom, and Daddy Mac all sat down together to have dinner and then watch TV. It was only later that your mom told me that the three of them have not sat down and spent so much quality time together in over 10 years. She said that since your were born, her family has been much closer as everyone is so excited to be around you.

(I think it is important for me to point out the following after my last two paragraphs. Sometimes my love and belief in you might come across a little strong. Even though you were born of a virgin birth, you have visitors bringing your presents, and you have brought peace and love to this world, I DO NOT think you are the second coming of Jesus. Sorry, you are just my baby girl☺)

I realize honey that sometimes I might get a little too deep for a five month old, but hopefully this will all make sense to you someday. Because that day is still way off, I think I should at least write to you about some of the more mundane things that have happened this week.

My favorite experience that I have had with you this week took place during nap time. You still take all your naps in mommy's arms, but you are getting pretty big. At over 15 pounds, I am not sure how much longer mommy's little frame is going to be able to handle you. With this in mind, I tried to put you down in your crib for your afternoon siesta. I laid you down, and you seemed very happy to be alone. Remember you are my baby, and one trait of mine that you definitely inherited is my desire to be by myself from time to time. With all the visitors picking you up and smiling in your face all week, I think you were very ready for a little alone time this particular afternoon. For the next 25 minutes, I sat at your crib side and just watched you. As soon as I put you down, you rolled onto your side which has become your customary crib position. Today however, your side did not seem to be your final destination as you continued to swing your right leg over your left as you tried to roll. Over and over and over again, you would swing your leg and twist your head only to be inches from rolling onto your stomach. At first, you would swing your leg gently, but with each failed attempt you swung faster and harder. I was cheering you on in my mind, "You can do it. Tuck your shoulder. Come on, baby." You got so close so many times, but alas, it was just not your day. Finally, your grunts of effort turned to groans of frustration. Before frustration turned to anger, your mommy came in and picked you up. I guess I will have to wait until another day. (The day came the next morning when your cousin was taking your picture. With very little effort, you rolled from your tummy to your back. You utilized the weight of

Dear Zoe || Love Dad

your 95th percentile head by leaning it down and to your left. In no time, you were on your tummy smiling up at us.)

Before I sign off for the night, I should inform you that you might have chicken pox. This morning mommy received a phone call from her Aunt who told her that her daughter, who played with you all day Christmas, has broken out in a rash. Now, your cousin has already left town to go to a cheerleading camp in another city which makes diagnosing her a little challenging, but the cheerleading coach thinks it is chicken pox.

When I first heard, I was really nervous, but I have calmed down after talking to your Neeny. I told Neeny that I just never wanted you to get sick which I realize is not really rationale, but I hate absolutely hate seeing you upset. Just to make sure that I was doing everything that I could, I then called your doctor back home. She said there was nothing we could do but wait. Apparently, you could start getting symptoms anytime over the next two weeks. I guess it is going to be an anxious two weeks, but since IVF, I am actually kind of used to it.

(Update: Your uncle made your cousin go to the Emergency Room, and it turns out that there is a 90% chance that it is just a rash. We dodged a bullet.)

Dear Zoe – January, 10

Your mom keeps telling me that I can't write to you forever, but I am having a hard time stopping. I first thought that I would stop after you left the NICU, then I thought I would stop at Christmas, but there are always so many things that happen in your life. I don't want you to miss out on knowing about your earliest days. Each day with you seems so exciting that I hate to think that I will ever forget.

Last Friday is a perfect example. I woke up very early on Friday morning in order to make it to the airport in time to fly home to see you. I hadn't seen you in a whole week as I needed to go away for business, and it was starting to take its toll on me. You always bring such joy and stability to my life that going a week without holding you had left me feeling lost and stressed. When you add in a lingering cold, my week had been pretty miserable.

The lines at the airport were short and my flight was on time leading me to believe that today was going to be a very easy day. I sure was wrong. My plane left Las Vegas at around ten in the morning, and I was anxiously awaiting our reunion. As we landed in Detroit, I looked out the window to see what looked to me like a blizzard. The snow was falling from the sky in big chunks which normally would have been a beautiful sight, but all I could think about was a potential flight cancellation. I called your mom from the plane to let her know that I might have a delay due to the weather when she asked whether I had gotten her message. I said that I hadn't, and she then broke some bad news. She said that Memom, who had come back to Hershey with you and mom the previous day, was in the Emergency room. She was in excruciating pain due to a potential kidney stone. If your mom and Memom are in the Emergency room, then where were you?

I asked mom whether you were with them at the hospital, and she had said no. Fortunately, we have such good friends in Jim and Kelly that your mom was able to call Jim and have him come and get you from the hospital parking lot. Your mom didn't want to take you into the hospital and expose you to all the various germs floating through the air. Even though Jim had to leave work early, he didn't hesitate as he could certainly understand your mom's predicament given that he has his own baby your age.

As I let the information your mom was conveying register, I realized two things. First, I looked down and realized that my phone was about to run out of batteries at any moment. And second, my next flight was scheduled to take off in only twenty minutes. I began breathing rapidly as panic began to set in.

I deplaned and anxiously waited for my two other travel companions, Joe and Denise, to exit the jet-bridge. When I didn't see them after a few minutes, I made the decision that there was no way that I could miss my plane even if they did. You were definitely in very capable hands, but you needed a parent by your side. There was no way that your mom or Memom could have explained what was happening to you. First your dad leaves you and now your mom.

I strapped on my back pack as tight as it would go and began rapidly walking to my next gate. After about two hundred yards, I realized that my gate was not anywhere close and that I was not making very good time at my current pace. If I wanted to make it, I needed to run. There I was, a grown man running through the Detroit airport, in order to be reunited with his little girl. The jog was painful as I realized how out of shape I had become. My legs began to cramp and my lungs burned after only a few minutes. My asthma started to rear its ugly head as my breathing became more and more labored. There was an inhaler in my back pack, but I didn't want to waste any time getting it out until I made it to the gate. It was really a pathetic sight, one that you would have been mortified by if you were there and a teenager. I tried to push on, but I was just too out of breath.

When I saw a moving sidewalk, I gave myself permission to stop jogging. I jumped on the moving side walk and walked briskly making about as a good a time as I had been while running. It might sound ridiculous, but while I was rushing through the airport, I kept thinking of you. How could I let a little asthma keep me from my baby? I pressed forward until my gate was in sight.

I reached the gate just as they were finishing boarding. With the door open in front of me, I took the time to get out my inhaler and take two quick puffs. I took out my phone to try and call your mom while it still had a little bit of juice left, but I was unable to get a signal. I wasn't exactly sure what the plan was going to be when I landed because I did not have a car at the airport. You and your mom were supposed to be picking me up.

The speaker sounded, "Last call for Flight 26612 to Harrisburg." I looked back from whence I came hoping to see Joe and Denise, but they were no where in sight. I walked up to the entrance of the jet way to tell the woman at the gate that I had two colleagues who were en route. While I explained the situation, she scanned my boarding pass. As I stood at the entrance trying to stall so that Joe and Denise could make the flight, she said that I needed to board the plane. Normally, I would have done more to stall, but arguing with a TSA official is not a good idea. Plus, I couldn't risk not getting home to see you and to help your mom with Memom.

I walked onto the plane and immediately asked whether I was permitted to use the restroom before we took off. Thankfully, the flight attendant said, "Yes." I had planned to take a bathroom break in the terminal, but I simply didn't have time. I returned from the bathroom, and took my seat. There was still no sign of either Joe or Denise. They would both certainly understand why I left them when I had a chance to explain, but I really didn't want to have to have this conversation. Just when I thought all hope was lost, Denise boarded the plane quickly followed by Joe.

It had been a very hectic last twenty minutes, but things were seemingly working out. The snow continued to pour down from above, but there was no indication from anyone that it would prevent our taking off. Things were looking pretty positive with regards to my getting home. Settled in my seat, I was left wondering about what was going on back in Hershey. I decided that it was probably a long shot, but I tried your mom's cell phone once again hoping that we would have a better connection now that I was out of the terminal.

I was shocked when my call went through and I was able to get your mom on the line. I told her that I had made my flight and that I thought we were going to make it home. I relayed that my phone was about to die so that she would talk quickly. She explained that they thought your Memom did in fact have a kidney stone. Because she was going to be at the hospital, she asked whether Denise could take me to Jim's house where I would be reunited with you. We could then have Jim drive us back to our apartment. The plan was set. The day was definitely not turning out as expected, but I prayed that everything would turn out okay. Having such a good friend as Jim made me realize how fortunate I was. He and Kelly would certainly be taking great care of you.

Before long, we were off and headed back to Harrisburg. For a slight second, I thought to myself, "Who is going to help me take care of Zoe if mommy and Memom are both gone?" I hadn't seen you in so long that I had a momentary lack of confidence in my abilities. My parenting abilities were definitely up to par, but your mom was my security blanket. She helped me be a much better and calmer parent with her knowledge and skill.

Denise was willing to take me to Jim's house so that I could see you. Even though I was worried about your Memom, I couldn't help but feel some excitement on the drive to Jim's. The long week away had made me very anxious to see you. I walked through the door and immediately gave you a huge hug. You looked so different as I think both your body and hair grew substantially during my absence. Jim had been holding you knowing that you probably needed some extra attention which resulted in your having beautiful rosy cheeks.

I had been nervous that you might have forgotten me because I had been gone so long, but my worries proved to be without merit as you immediately smiled upon seeing me. I took you from Jim and gave you about twenty kisses as I hugged you tight. I knew that I had missed you, but I didn't know how much until you were back in my arms.

Jim and I put you in your car seat and loaded you into his car. Without the proper base for your car seat, we had to use the seat belt to hold your car seat. Jim, being the good friend that he his, had already read how to install your seat so that I wouldn't have to worry. You started crying on the way home, but I was able to soothe you with a little bit of milk. It wasn't long before we were home where you really perked up. I took you upstairs to change your diaper and put you to bed, and you could not stop smiling up at me. It felt amazing having you smile and laugh at me. Those first few minutes with you had been better than any moments I had had over the last week on my trip. Being away from you is already so hard, and it will probably only get harder as you get older.

I heard the downstairs door open. Your Memom had been released from the hospital and she and your mom were home. Your mom came upstairs to say hi to me and you, and she even helped finish changing your diaper. What had been a tough day was nearing its end. With all of my crazy travel, I hadn't eaten since

Dear Zoe || Love Dad

breakfast, but I waited in order to be able to feed you and put you to bed. I rocked you to sleep and everything seemed perfect. I love you little baby.

Note: I later learned from your Mom that you had quite the interesting reaction to your Memom's sickness. Your mom came downstairs to find your Memom groaning and moaning in pain on the floor. The pain had been so bad that sitting was no longer feasible. You were also on the ground as Memom had been playing with you. As your Memom moaned and groaned, you laughed and laughed. I hope that you thought she was playing; it would be pretty odd if you enjoyed seeing her in pain. Memom said that with each groan, you would just start dying laughing as if it were the funniest thing you had ever seen. She was in so much pain that even your beautiful laugh couldn't bring a smile to her face which is how she really knew she needed to go to the ER.

Dear Zoe – January, 13

I was lying in bed last night, and I was just overwhelmed with emotion. By the time you read this, you may still have never seen me cry because it doesn't happen often, but last night, a few tears definitely rolled down my cheeks.

We had just moved into our new house, and I could not believe how lucky and fortunate I was. I had a beautiful, healthy baby and a gorgeous and caring wife. My job was both challenging and relatively lucrative. The purchase of the new home was the final piece in the puzzle. The new home definitely brought me a lot of peace of mind. I was finally feeling settled. I had the greatest family that I could ever want to have and now I had a safe, healthy place for all of us to live.

Even though I was feeling very content last night, the last few days were anything but relaxing. I knew that the move was going to be painful for your mom and me, but I definitely underestimated how hard it would be on you. Knowing that it would be too difficult for your mom and I to handle on our own, I hired a moving company to pack up all our things and take them to the new house. Things seemingly started out well as they movers were able to pack up most of the townhouse on the first day. Without a crib or any other furniture, your mom, Memom, and you went to stay in a hotel. I wasn't invited because I snore too loud and your mom said she needed a good night's rest. My last night in the townhouse was spent alone, just me and a mattress.

I already told you about your trip to Washington D.C. (disaster), and I had some concern that you would have a similar reaction to the hotel. My fears were valid as your mom told me that you hated your stay in the hotel. When I saw the three of you the next afternoon, each of you looked exhausted (so much for getting a good night's sleep).

Dear Zoe || Love Dad

It turns out that the whole experience was less than pleasant. Things started bad from the beginning; apparently, you are scared of elevators. Your mom said that as soon as the doors closed, you started screaming. Once you made it to the room, you were less than thrilled with being forced to take a bath in the sink rather than your luxurious, plastic tub. Things only got worse throughout the night as you must have had a reaction to something in the room that ended up turning your face and body red. By the time the morning came around, your mom was thrilled to get you out of the hotel and into the new house.

I got home around 6:30 p.m., and it was very odd taking a new route home from work. When I walked through the door of the new house, I was expecting to see a lot more progress than what was laid out before me. The first thing I noticed was that there were no movers in the house. Things were going more slowly than expected and to make matters worse, we were in the midst of a snow storm. My main concern was you as you still didn't have your crib or all your formula. When the movers showed up an hour later, I told them that they really needed to find the box containing your formula before we had a screaming baby on our hands. With formula in hand, I then instructed them to assemble your crib ASAP as your bed time had already flown by.

By 9:30, your crib was ready to go and it was time for you to go to sleep. I thought that it might be a challenge because we had completely altered your schedule and you seemed generally unsettled by the new surroundings. Your eyes would dart back and forth from wall to wall trying to gain your bearings. You had just spent ten days in Texas only to come back and be forced to move from townhome to hotel to new house. I wish I could have explained to you that this was the final move because I could tell that you were frustrated with all the changes. In took awhile, but you finally went to sleep for the first time in your new home.

Dear Zoe – January, 16

People always say that babies change so fast. Having had you in my life now for over five months, I tend to agree even if my interpretation is slightly different from what others might be meaning. See, you do change every day, but I wouldn't call the changes progress. Rather, the changes are erratic and unpredictable behaviors that you seem to favor out of the blue. It is not as if you suddenly learn how to sit up, talk, or crawl. What does happen however is you start doing random things at an ever-increasing frequency. You have been so active these last couple of weeks that I thought I should tell you about some of your more recent behaviors.

Dear Zoe || Love Dad

Right around the day of the move, you started spitting. Now, I don't mean spitting like a grown up would on a baseball field; it is more similar to when you blow a raspberry on someone's stomach. Your Memom was the first to notice, and she pointed it out to me quickly as she probably imagined you would stop quickly and she thought it was pretty cute. Little did she know that for the next two days, you would be in a constant state of spitting. There was a constant hum emanating from you as you would stick your little tongue between your lips and blow out air and spit at all hours of the day. It didn't matter whether it was the morning and you were full of energy or whether it was late at night and you were preparing to go to bed. You spit before you ate and you spit in the bath tub. It was just the craziest if not funniest thing I had ever seen, felt, and heard.

The move into the new house seemed to jar you enough that spitting was no longer in your repertoire. Replacing spitting however was yet another quirky behavior. On the day after the move, you started grunting all the time. At first, I thought you were trying to have a bowel movement something that takes considerable effort on your part. When you continued grunting for an hour, I finally checked your diaper because I figured that if you had been going to the bathroom that whole time that your diaper was probably failing to keep your clothes protected. There was only so much that could be expected of disposable underwear. Much to my surprise, your diaper was completely clean. With your diaper back on, you once again started grunting away. The spitting was odd yet cute; grunting was just odd and I was looking forward to your moving on from this behavior.

Fortunately, the grunting stopped after only a day. It really was an odd sight seeing such a cute little baby scrunching up her face and grunting all day.

Even more recently, you have located your feet. It isn't clear to me whether you understand that your feet are connected to you as you have spent most of today trying to get them in your mouth. Not sure whether you would be more or less enamored with them if you knew they were connected to the rest of you. Given your inability to stand or walk, you are usually in one of two positions, lying on your back or sitting in mommy's arms. Your new obsession with your feet manifests itself in both situations as you will lie on your back and use your hands to pull your feet to your face forming a vertical circle – albeit a wobbly one. Or, you will fold you body in half at the waist desperately trying to reach your little, chubby feet. All day and all night, you try to get those little toes in your mouth without much success. The closest you have gotten is getting your sock in your mouth which I am not sure is very sanitary now that I write this. Not that I am comparing you to a puppy, but this quest to get your feet in your mouth reminds me of watching a dog try to get his tail.

Dear Zoe || Love Dad

Finally, you have discovered how easy it is to roll from your stomach to your back. Within seconds of being placed on your back, you immediately roll to the left (always the left) and onto your tummy. The only problem with this new behavior is that you don't enjoy being on your stomach. Given this lack of desire to be on your tummy, this behavior is quite peculiar. Here is what typically happens. I place you on your back, your roll left onto your tummy, you start yelling, I rescue you and put you back on your back, you immediately re-roll left onto your tummy, etc...... I try to talk to ask you why you intentionally put yourself in a position that you don't like, but you just look at me with your big, blue eyes and smile. During the day, going through this ritual is pretty tiring, but at night, it becomes exhausting. The last few days have reminded me of your newborn days when either your mom or I would have to get up with you every couple of hours. Last night, I wanted to have your mom get some rest because she does so much for you, and I took the monitor. Every couple hours like clockwork, I would hear your yelling, not crying, as you had managed to wake yourself up and roll to your stomach. I would lumber into your room and gently roll you back to your back or side, and you would immediately fall asleep. One time last night, your face was pressed up against the "breathable bumper" which helps make sure your legs don't get caught between the slats. You looked like a dolphin caught in a fish net. I just laughed and thought "what am I going to do with you." You of course know the answer; I am going to just keep loving you and laughing at your various antics.

Dear Zoe – January, 17

You were sick for the first time, and it was absolutely AWFUL! I guess that you and mommy caught the cold that I had when I was in Las Vegas because you both became extremely congested. With your light complexion, you looked absolutely pitiful with pink, watery eyes and a bright red nose. The only positive thing about your sickness was that you never had a fever which made me feel that as sad as it was seeing you sick, at least I didn't have to worry that you were in danger.

As I held you close to my chest, I could hear all the mucus and phlegm caught inside your sinuses. I tried to teach you how to blow your nose because I knew that getting rid of some of that junk would make you feel a million times better, but you, like all babies, just don't know how to blow their noses. Your mom and I got nose drops and a nasal aspirator to try and clear out some of the snot, but we knew we were making only minor improvements in your condition. It was a helpless feeling and a feeling that I hated. Simply waiting for the cold to past was not something that an impatient dad such as me handled well. In the NICU, there were at least doctors, nurses, and all types of medicines that could be deployed to help you. Now, we only had a nasal aspirator at our disposal. Please

Dear Zoe || Love Dad

know that your mom and I tried everything that we could think of to make you better.

You needed so much loving these last few days as it was clear you didn't feel well. Your smiles were less frequent and your laugh was non-existent. I held you whenever I was home and tried to tell you that it would be okay. If there were ever a time that I wish I could more clearly communicate with you it was during this sickness. I wished that I could explain why you were feeling so yucky. I wish I could tell you why I was jamming the rubber tube in your nose, an activity that you hated. (You hated it so much that when your Memom was here, she wouldn't do it because she didn't want you mad at her. I guess that is the difference between a mom and a Memom. A mom wants you to love her, but she will do what she has to do to improve your condition. A grandmother just wants love this time around; she has already done all the tough stuff with her own kids.) More importantly, I wished that I could tell you that this feeling would soon be over and you would be back to normal. Even with the severe congestion and general feeling of malaise, you were still such a good baby. You still didn't cry outside of when you were hungry or in need of a diaper change.

Because you were so sick, I could see and hear the fluids building in your head. For hours upon hours, you would sneeze and cough seemingly in vain. My wish was that these sneezes would bring with them at least some relief from the pressure in your sinuses and ears. These coughs and sneezes only served to annoy you rather than provide a momentary reprieve.

Your breathing also seemed slightly labored as your respiratory system was clearly impacted by the illness. When I talked to your mom, she had already called the doctor. Even though she too was sick, your mom was wonderful as usual. I don't know what I would do without her. She not only used the nose drops, but she had also gotten humidifiers for your room and any room in which you spent time. Ultimately, she had you sleep in her bed so that (1) you would feel the love that only a mother can provide and (2) you would have someone close in case you got worse.

After a few days, I could tell that you were finally on the mend as your big smile appeared more frequently and your eyes became less glassy. Thank God you are feeling better. I don't know how much more I could have taken☺

Dear Zoe – January, 18

I had figured that my days of being sick were over and that my role now was simply to help nurse you and your mom back to health. Last night however, I started to get a stomach ache as I was lying there next to you and mom trying to

Dear Zoe || Love Dad

go to sleep. You were still sick, and we decided that you should still be sleeping with your mom until breathing improved. At the old house, I would have never joined the two of you in bed. My fear (1) that I might roll over and bump you or (2) that you might off the bed would have been enough to keep me away. I had however solved this problem with what I thought was an ingenious solution. What I had done was slide the bed that you and mommy shared all the way against the wall so that you were safely nestled in between your mom and the wall. Moving created a problem as we no longer had a bed that abutted a wall, and I decided that it would be best if you slept between us until the guardrails I had ordered arrived.

You and your mom were taking up a lot of room in the bed, and I was forced to maneuver my 220 pound body into a very tight space. I was very uncomfortable lying there, but I didn't want to wake you or your mom because you were both finally able to rest after a long day of cold-induced misery. The minutes passed and my mind switched from the discomfort I was feeling from trying to remain still in such a confined space to a faint stomach ache. As time passed, the ache in my stomach magnified and turned to a feeling of nausea. Before long, it was abundantly clear that I was sick once again, and I ran out of the room and headed for the bathroom. Fifteen challenging minutes later, I was left hoping that my time spent next to you was not going to translate into your getting the flu which I had apparently caught. I spent the next 36 hours in bed sleeping and trying to maintain my fluids.

It wasn't until around noon the next day that I finally mustered the strength to go downstairs to get a bagel, a food that I thought would be good for my tortured stomach. As I turned the corner, I could see you in your bouncy seat staring back at me. You were so precious, and I wanted nothing more than do run over and give you a kiss as I do every time I see you. On this particular occasion however, there was no way that I was going to risk infecting you with my germs, and I kept a safe distance between the two of us.

I continued looking at you as I ate my bagel. You gave me a look which I had not ever seen previously. You looked at me very quizzically. I certainly couldn't read your mind, but if I were to guess, I would have to believe that you were trying to figure out why I wasn't rushing to pick you up and kiss you. My not coming over to you just didn't make any sense in your mind. It was so sad as I was clearly disappointing you. I tried to make the situation better by telling you that I loved you, but you continued to stare at me with wanting eyes. First, you were sick and now your dad was ignoring you! You were definitely having a very bad day. I continued to watch you even though it was painful being forced to stay clear from you, but I knew that you would thank me if you knew my reasoning.

Dear Zoe || Love Dad

I couldn't help but begin to walk over to you knowing that I would only go so far. First, your eyes lit up and then you started to smile and laugh. Next you started wildly flailing your arms as you aggressively jumped in your bouncy seat. It was such a great feeling, and only a feeling a parent could understand. You were just so excited to see me. I wanted to keep moving towards you and snatch you into my arms for a big hug, but my maturity prevented such a risky act. I might have felt really crummy for most of the day, but for those few moments, I couldn't have been better. There is nothing like having your child just love you for who you are and for what you do for them.

Dear Zoe – January, 20

I already told you some of the funny things that you do when I wrote you last week about the spitting and grunting. Well, I realized that there are a couple of other behaviors that are definitely worth recording.

Recently, I have noticed a specific behavior every time that I scoop you up into my arms. Within seconds of being close to me, you grab tightly onto my arm, shirt, or neck. Maybe you have always done this and maybe most babies have this tendency, but for me, it seems different as of late. I was thinking about this last night as you had my shirt in a vice-like grip as I walked you around the upstairs floor of the house showing you all the pictures of – YOU! As we walked, I told you that you didn't need to hold on so tight because I would never leave you. I would hold and protect for as long as I walk this earth. I continued walking with you when I started thinking about how you came into this world. I remember specifically praying to God that He help you hold onto mommy's tummy so that she would be pregnant and bring you into this world. I knew that you would need to be a fighter as clinging to mommy's tummy was not going to be easy. It seems like so long ago that your mom and I were going through IVF, but the experience has clearly impacted how we care for you as well as most other elements of our lives. Maybe IVF impacted you too. You came into this world holding on and fighting, and just maybe you were going to be holding on and fighting forever. Hopefully, you realize that your mom and I were fighting for you as well from the very beginning and that we will continue to do so. If you ever lose your grip, one of us will catch you.

It might sound funny or ridiculous, but your clinging to me brought back so many amazing memories of those days of constant prayer and worry. Your mom and I got so close to each other and to God during that first winter in PA when trying to bring you down from heaven was our only objective. Never will I forget how lucky we are to have you and never will I forget how much strength you showed to find a nice home in mommy's tummy when you were only six cells big.

Your other new behavior might also be telling me something about your future personality even though it is quite different. Your mom has started giving you not only cereal but also fruit and vegetable baby foods which you absolutely love. With the cereal, you always seem to create a mess, but you are much more careful with your baby bananas or baby peas as they are too good to waste. Rather than spit them out and smear them across your face, you carefully take bite after bite without letting any fall by the wayside. One byproduct of introducing new solid foods into your diet is that you no longer drink as much milk as you once had. Rather than drink 8 oz. on a regular occasion, you are much more likely to drink four as your little tummy can handle only so much.

One problem that I have is in knowing how much milk you are really going to want at any given feeding. Because you are less inclined to enjoy your rice cereal after the introduction of your baby food, it is often difficult for me to know just how full you are after a "cereal meal." For example, the last time that I fed you rice cereal might not have resulted in any actual rice cereal consumption as most of the mush ended up on your face, hands, bib or high chair.

Basically, it is very hard for me to know how full you are and therefore how hungry you will be for milk. Your mom has told me in the past that I "give up" too easily when feeding you. What she means is that sometimes you are still hungry when I decide that you have had enough. With this flaw in mind, I have tried to make a conscious effort to offer you the bottle even after I think you have finished. The last few nights, I have felt bad as you have seemingly choked. Immediately, I felt like a bad parent and apologized to you over and over again. Earlier today, I saw that you made the same noise when your mom was feeding you, and I noticed something. You were FAKING! As soon as the bottle touched your lips, you would pretend to choke. I couldn't help but laugh and be proud as you were able to figure out a way to more easily communicate to your dumb old dad that you were full. Your new method was quite effective I might add. If you are already this clever at 6 months old, you are definitely going to be a handful when you get older.

Dear Zoe – January, 25

God literally made you from your mom and me. A by product of this fact is that your appearance and personality are bound to be heavily influenced by ours. This fact of life is not something that usually crosses my mind.

Dear Zoe || Love Dad

I don't harbor any dreams of your following in my footsteps in any way. You are your own person, and you are already beautiful. Like I have written you from when you were first born, my only wish is that you lead a life filled with the joy and pride that comes from knowing you are making this world and the people in it better. I've lived my life; I want you to know that you should always live yours as you see fit. You don't need to go to my alma mater or pursue a career in business; those were choices that I made. You should make your own.

Even though I say that your resembling me is unimportant, I have to admit that I did feel a surge of happiness during a conversation I had with your mom while lying in bed yesterday. We were talking about all of the non-verbal cues that you tend to give us these days. You may not be able to speak, but you are very much capable of communicating. Recently, I have noticed just how expressive your eyebrows and forehead are. In an instant, your crinkled forehead lets me know that you are confused and trying to figure something out. Your eyebrows lifted skyward signal curiosity or happiness. I was telling your mom just how cute I find you when she said, "You know where she gets that from?"

I replied, "No."

Your mom seemed surprised by my ignorance, and she informed me that your facial expressions are just like mine. Without having much access to what I look like during most conversations, I had never really realized how expressive my face was. Your mom went on to tell me that you are just like me with your expressive forehead, crooked smile, and desire to have "alone time."

What your mom was saying made sense even if it was not something that I had ever really thought about. When I look at you, I see my baby and I am overwhelmed with a feeling of love that I had not known previously. But this love has nothing to do with your resembling me and everything to do with your being a beautiful, fun, and loving baby who chose to come down from heaven to be my daughter.

I tried to figure out what was causing me to be so happy knowing that you had some of my traits. As I said, I don't want you to feel pressure to be just like me or just like your mom. If I didn't particularly care if you took after me, then what was causing these feelings? It might have taken awhile, but I think I might have the answer which will probably seem odd to you.

There are things that babies, kids, and teenagers just can't understand. One of these things is the love a parent has for his baby. Nothing is as strong as this love and there is nothing more in this world that I want than to be close to you. Remember when I talked about having Simpatico with you? Well, seeing traits of mine in you makes me feel Simpatico. It helps me know that you and I have a bond that is stronger than any bond I will ever have with another human being. It is the closeness to you that made me so happy. Our shared traits only served to reinforce that we are inevitably linked, and there is no one else to whom I would rather be linked. You and I will always have a special bond, and I want you to know that you can count on me today and for forever (including high school☺)

Dear Zoe – February, 7

Every day I come home from work and get more and more excited as I approach the door. Why? Because on the other side of that locked door is my beautiful family – you and your mom. Without fail, I will look at you and you will stop whatever you are doing and smile at me. Seeing your genuine and complete excitement at the sight of me makes me happier than you could imagine. (Unfortunately for you, I don't think you will be able to feel these emotions until you have a baby of your own because it was completely foreign to me until you arrived.)

What I find really funny however is that you don't always stay excited after seeing me. Just this week, I had to work late and I didn't make it home until you and mom were almost finished with your bedtime routine. You were actually in the final phase which is supposed to result in your falling asleep. On this particular night, you were "fighting your sleep" as you were crying and trying to wriggle out of mom's arms with an arched back and flailing arms. Once I entered the room and you saw me, your mood immediately changed. My angry, tired baby completely altered her mood as a huge smile came over your face. I leaned over and kissed you good night, but my posture hadn't even gotten back to completely upright before you were crying and yelling again. I would have thought that you would have been excited that I was home for at least a few minutes, but I guess my powers are limited to only the first, fleeting moments.

There are so many things that I love about you; seeing your big, happy face is just one that always stands out. I love your laugh which sounds somewhat akin to a sheep's "bah bah" if she were making the noise into a fan as the cadence is amazingly quick. I love the fact that looking at yourself in the mirror will always make you stop dead in your tracks as you stare and admire the beautiful baby in front of you. I love that you consistently reach up and try to rip off my nose, lips, eyes, and necklace with what is quickly becoming a fairly strong grip. I love that you are so stubborn that you refuse to roll from your stomach to your back even though you know how; preferring to yell for my or mom's assistance. I love walking into your bedroom in the morning and having absolutely no idea where or in what position I will find you within your crib. I love watching you jump in your jump-a-roo as never has the expression "pure-joy" been more

Dear Zoe || Love Dad

appropriate. I love that you will spit up and then laugh as if it was the funniest thing. I love that you will take a nap for about ten minutes and wake up smiling as if you had slept for hours (you didn't and your mom and I are still exhausted☺) I love that you need so much attention that you can completely exhaust two, what I had previously believed were capable, adults. I love that I just read this part of the book to you and you were entranced because it was about your favorite subject, YOU! I love that you may never learn to crawl because I have the sneaking suspicion that you enjoy being carried on my shoulder. I love holding you in my arms listening to the same lullaby night after night waiting for you to fall asleep in my arms as you gaze at the fake constellations on the ceiling. I could go on and on, but I hope you understand that I just love everything about being your dad.

Now that I think about it; there is one thing about being your dad that I don't love – seeing you upset. I'm not sure what I am going to do because it is getting harder not easier as you get older. It is just an awful feeling seeing you get so sad; your little lip starts to quiver and your eyes start to squint. Within moments, the air is filled with your cries which start out fairly modest but can quickly turn into room-filling screams. It is just terrible seeing you this way, and it actually physically causes my stomach to ache as I get so flustered and anxious. Even though I often know that there is nothing really hurting you, there is just something about seeing your baby cry that really torments a loving parent.

Knowing how much your displeasure upsets me and remembering my note to you after your last doctor's appointment, you can probably imagine that I was not looking forward to your next visit. That visit unfortunately took place this past Friday. I wasn't sure whether you would actually be getting another round of shots, and I held out hope that your visit would involve nothing more unpleasant than getting placed on a cold scale while naked. It was therefore very unsettling when I ran into Jim the day of your appointment at which time he let me know that your friend Ava had just gone to her six month appointment and gotten more shots.

My anxiety immediately spiked as I pictured your smiling face in my mind. You had no idea that you were about to be driven to the doctor for more shots. At the time I was receiving this news, you were probably happy as could be bouncing in your bouncer or playing with mommy. I couldn't help but begin to feel once again that I was betraying the person I love most; aren't dads supposed to protect their babies from pain? I wanted to call home and tell you, "I'm sorry sweetie."

I went back to my desk and checked my calendar hoping to find an important meeting that corresponded with the time of your appointment. Basically, I was hoping that I could find an excuse to not go to this visit as I wasn't sure I could stomach seeing you get poked in the thighs again. I guess my co-workers weren't planning on working very hard this Friday afternoon as my schedule was completely clear. It looked like I would be accompanying your mom to this dreaded event.

We met with the nurse initially, and she took all your measurements. You continue to grow at a well-above average rate outpacing most non-preemies let alone those born early. You were over the 60th percentile in weight, 70th in length, and 97th in head circumference (sorry; probably not going to change any time soon). It was now time for the doctor to come into the room and answer the questions that your mom and I had.

You had a new doctor whom I had not previously met because she was taking some time off from work due to the fact that she just had a little baby of her own. She was exceptionally nice, and I could tell she was smart because she couldn't stop saying how beautiful you were. You really are a beautiful little girl with a wonderful smile and disposition to match. She answered all the questions that your mom and I had. Basically, you are a very healthy little girl. All the scares of the NICU are fading away.

The biggest issue that you are currently having revolves around your sleeping habits. Your mom continues to think that she somehow did something wrong when you were little because you refuse to sleep in your crib during naps. You simply prefer to be held. I have tried to tell your mom that I don't think that there is anything wrong with her holding you. I say, "You can't 'ruin' a baby by loving her too much.'" There is going to come a time when you will be too big to hold at nap time, and I am sure that when that day comes, your mom will look back longingly at these months when you fell asleep in her arms.

The other issue that your mom had with your sleeping patterns is that you have to be rocked to sleep at night. Once asleep, you do a great job of sleeping through the night. The problem however is that you are completely unwilling to "put yourself to sleep." Rather, your mom and I need to go through an elaborate and often physically demanding routine each night. I have told her and anyone else who will listen that I just don't think it is natural to leave a baby alone in a crib and expect her to not cry out for her parents. I wouldn't like it if someone just up and left me without telling me where they were going. It would be even worse if this someone was the person I depended on for all my needs. Humans have wondered the earth for 200,000 years, and only in the last thirty have we decided that babies need to put themselves to sleep in their cribs. I'm just not buying into this belief.

Dear Zoe || Love Dad

I made this argument to the doctor, and she said that there was nothing wrong with what we were doing. She did however warn us that you were now getting to the age where you would be "getting used" to this routine and therefore breaking this habit would only get harder and harder. I told her that I just love you too much to let you cry. We went back and forth, and she was very respectful of my beliefs. She did however explain how we could try to wean you from this habit of needing to be rocked to sleep.

Here is the method. First, we would put you into your crib before you were fully asleep. Then, we would let you cry for five minutes before going back into your room. Once we entered the room, we would pat you on the back and speak softly and reassuringly to you without taking you out of your crib. Once settled, we would leave the room again. If you cried again, we would repeat what we had just finished doing. It wasn't until the third time that we were supposed to get you out of your crib. Now, I tell you this because I think you should know what kind of advice I was getting. Don't worry though; there is no way I am going to let you cry for five straight minutes. I didn't pray to God so hard to have you so that I could let you cry in your crib for no good reason. I say "no good reason" because no one, doctors included, has successfully convinced me that letting you cry is good for YOU. The typical rationale revolves around the need of your mom and me to get our rest. Well, I will sacrifice my rest for as long as I can if it saves you from crying, alone in your room.

Without anymore questions to be answered, your doctor said goodbye and said that the nurse would come back in to give you your shots. You were going to be getting three shots, and I was a nervous wreck. Two shots were bad enough, but at least they could be administered quickly by a coordinated nurse willing to use both hands at once. What was going to happen with three? Your mom and I could do nothing but wait. My schedule was fairly wide-open on this afternoon as I stated earlier. There was however one meeting that I "needed" to attend. Our appointment was taking much longer than I had expected, and I was getting to the point where I would be late if I didn't leave soon. Your mom could sense that I wanted to leave as I continually stared down at my watch. I explained the situation, but I am not sure that she really believed me.

Minutes passed, and there was still no sign of the nurse. Finally, I told your mom that I really needed to go. I did have a meeting, but the truth is that I just couldn't do it. I could not see you get your shots again. I know I sound like a broken-record, but I really do HATE seeing you cry. I had been DREADING this appointment all day knowing how upset you had been after your last visit. When I saw a valid reason for leaving, I took it. Yeah, I was a wimp, but I knew you were in good hands with your mom. Later that night, your mom told me that you cried and screamed just like last time. Even hearing the story made me sad and uncomfortable.

Now, I want you to know that I wouldn't have left if I felt you needed me, but I knew that your mom could handle the situation. It was love and affection you needed after shots, and no one would be able to console you as effectively as your mom. Things had been different in the NICU. In the NICU, I stayed with you when you were having procedures because you needed me to make sure you were getting the proper treatment. There was no need for me to oversee the administration of the shots. I just didn't feel that my presence would make you feel any better. Why make us both suffer?

I drove back to the office trying my best to not think about what you were going through. Maybe the shots wouldn't bother you this time? Of course, I was only trying to fool myself, but I thought that it was at least worth a shot. Thankfully, my meeting helped me take my mind off of things. By the time my meeting was over, I was sure that you were back to your happy go lucky self. Knowing that the worst had to have been over, I called your mom to see how you did. She said that you just cried and cried for about five minutes until she got you out into the waiting room where you stopped crying so that you could stare at the other children and parents in the room.

Your mom and I really need to get you out of the house more often if the sight of strangers is so appealing that it allows you to overcome physical pain. We do have an excuse though. Having been raised in Florida and Texas, we don't even know whether it is safe to take you out in freezing weather. Living in a small town without a mall only complicates this matter further. How many times do you really want to go to Wal-Mart?

You were quite happy the rest of the weekend which was definitely a pleasant surprise considering your reaction to the last round of shots. Because you had been so happy seeing people at the doctor's office, we did take you out on a little adventure on Saturday. We took you to ... Wal-Mart. You loved it, and I can only hope that you continue to love Wal-Mart as you get older because the prices there are definitely budget-friendly. Your mom used to buy clothes at Nordstrom's when we lived in North Carolina, but with no Nordstrom's within a hundred miles, she has had to settle for the Target's and Wal-Mart's of the world.

The weekend had come and almost gone, and I started to get sad because I love spending all day with you and your mom. The three of us have so much fun together just being in the same room. I think that maybe there is another reason, besides the cold weather and lack of options, that have led to our staying home

Dear Zoe || Love Dad

more often; we just enjoy being around each other. Who needs outside entertainment when we have you, a clever and ever-changing little baby around? This weekend, you finally decided to roll not only from back to front but also from front to back. You then used this knowledge to roll around the living room with reckless abandon.

It was Sunday night, and your mom volunteered to put you to bed so that I could watch the Superbowl. The Superbowl is the biggest sporting event of the whole year, and your mom knew that I wanted to watch it. You too love football, but it was definitely passed your bedtime. I told her that I could help put you to bed because I would rather hold you as you fell asleep than watch the big game, but she insisted.

I sat back in my chair and put my feet up. I was excited for the game and you were obviously in very capable hands, those of your mom. I watched the first ten minutes of the game, but I was interrupted by your yelling. It was surprising because you had been going to bed fairly easily these last couple of weeks. I continued watching the game figuring that your mom must be trying to burp you causing you to get frustrated. When you continued to cry with more and more frustration, I ran upstairs to see what was happening. I entered the room, and you were in your crib screaming. Your mom was standing next to the crib telling you that it was going to be okay. What? Clearly, it wasn't okay or you wouldn't be screaming.

I looked at your mom and asked her what she was doing. She then told me that she was doing what the doctor had told her. She was going to let you cry for five minutes and then she was going to try and soothe you. What? I thought we had decided that this method of teaching you to fall asleep was not something we were going to do. I was so confused and I increasingly upset as your cries continued.

I moved forward to pick you up out of your crib, and your mom said, "Don't. It hasn't been five minutes." Your mom is always trying to do the right thing, and she is the best mommy a little baby could have. She was trying to do what she thought was best for you and she had the strength to listen to your screams if it ultimately was in your best interest. I, on the other hand, am much weaker. Even if I thought this was what was best for you, which I don't, there is no way that I can be in the same house as you and listen to you cry for even one minute. Remember, I left the doctor's appointment early because I was so stressed out.

I told your mom that I didn't want to do the "cry it out" method for all the reasons I had mentioned to the doctor. In my head, I was thinking, "how could your mom and I have communicated to each other so poorly in this situation that she thought I was okay with this." Your mom was exhausted both physically and emotionally. You could hear it in her voice. She said that she couldn't keep holding you for all of your naps as well as every time you woke up in the middle of the night. I am not sure whether she really meant this or whether she was just having a moment of complete exhaustion. She never gets a break. I go to work five days a week, and I come home refreshed and excited to see you. Your mom never gets this chance. Don't get me wrong, she absolutely loves staying home with you, but it is hard. Tonight, I could sense that she was struggling. She was struggling to take care of herself. She was struggling to find the confidence in herself that she was in fact doing the right thing by holding you when you went to sleep.

She had read in several books that you shouldn't be holding your baby at naps. She desperately wants to do everything just right, but she doesn't realize that she already is doing everything perfectly. Being a parent is both very hard and very simple. What is hard is having to figure out how to make sense of all the "parenting advice" you get from doctors, the internet, other parents, family members, strangers, and just about anyone else that you might meet. I am sure that most people give advice that comes from a very good place, but what I am learning is that there are many, many ways to raise a baby. There is not one correct way to put a baby to sleep, to schedule a day, and to teach new skills. The more I think about being a successful parent, the more I have realized that giving your baby all your love is really the only thing needed. Babies thrive on love not on whether they take exactly a 45 minute nap at 9:30 a.m. every day. And, no one gives more love to their baby than your mom.

I couldn't explain this all to your mom right at this moment because you were still terribly unhappy. I simply told her that I could not listen to you scream and that I would be responsible for putting you to bed from now on. I leaned over and picked you up, but you were so upset that my embrace didn't immediately resolve the issue. I put you on my shoulder in your favorite position, but still, you kept crying. I couldn't tell whether you were mad at us for letting you cry or whether you had become so worked up that it was hard to immediately calm down. Regardless, you continued crying. Your mom never left the room because she too loves you too much to see you upset. Now that we had decided to "break doctor's orders" I knew that she would be begging to take you from me knowing that she usually held the key to your calming down.

I handed you over to her and you started to slowly relax. Your cries turned to whimpers, and it was just that saddest sound a father could hear. I sat down on the floor as your mom rocked you in her arms. She held you close to her chest and tried to let the warmth of her body soothe you in a way that only a mother can. It was terrible listening to you catch your breath in the same rhythmic way that you had previously been crying. You had been crying so hard that your body couldn't quickly revert back to normal breathing. With each reassuring pat from your mother, you became less and less agitated.

I knew that I had made the right decision in going to pick you up. You need to not only be loved, but also need to have confidence that your parents will be there for you. There will certainly come a day that you will be mad at us and think that we aren't treating you right, but in the back of your mind, you will always know that we will do anything for you. Giving you this confidence in us is extremely important, and I don't think that you could possibly have this security at your tender age. Right now, I will always error on the side of loving you too much and overly instilling this confidence.

People may say that we are "babying" you too much. Guess what I say. She is a baby and more importantly she is MY baby. Love you, dad.

Dear Zoe – February, 15

I have always thought that Valentine's Day was a silly holiday; in my life, it had created awkward situations, disappointing situations, and unnecessarily expensive situations. My views however changed this year because I now have a beautiful little baby girl in my life. You have just made me a big pile of mush and sentimentality. I was hoping to take you and your mom out for a nice lunch, but it turned out that I had a meeting at lunch that couldn't be missed. It was disappointing thinking that I wasn't going to be able to see you during the middle of my day, but then I thought that maybe I could convince your mom to have a family lunch in the small, unimpressive cafeteria at work. She said yes, and my day was made.

I love having you at work because everyone makes such a commotion over you. You don't have to worry about becoming a star athlete, a straight "A" student, or piano prodigy to make me proud; you already have. Your mom also likes coming up to work because she is very social and a proud parent too. She likes everyone fussing over you just as much as I do.

Someone made a very truthful observation while I was walking with you on the third floor where I sit. He said, "You should bring your daughter here more often; she IS pure joy." I said thank you and continued to move forward with your stroller. He then said, "I'm serious; you can't help but be happy when you see her." His words were so kind, and I knew that he truly meant them. The man who made these comments is a very special person who had undergone a tragedy in his life. See, he has four kids, but he used to have five. One of his children had to go back to heaven very unexpectedly which meant that this man would not be able to hold and kiss his youngest child anymore.

Every single time that I talk to this friend of mine at work, I can't help but think about this horrible tragedy. When he said those beautiful words about you, it really touched me because I couldn't imagine how hard it was for him to send one of his babies back to heaven. Not only has my friend been able to continue to appreciate how special children are without any bitterness or sadness, but I know that he has also been able to sustain a great love for God. He is definitely someone that I can learn a lot from.

After what was a great day, I was ready to put you to sleep as is our routine. These last few nights have been such a breeze because you have been exhausted by the time I laid you down in your crib. For some reason, last night was different. When you were real little, I would get so nervous when you weren't going to sleep quickly. You could probably feel my tension, which only caused you to become more agitated. Over the last few months however, I have really found my stride as a dad. I've been changing diapers in record time (for me at least) and coaxing you to sleep with great confidence. Even though you didn't go to sleep right away, I knew it wouldn't be long.

You finished your bottle and looked up at me as if to say, "I'm not ready to sleep just yet." I took your cues, and we just kind of stared at each other for about five minutes. The constant advice of "cherish these moments because they go by so fast" has finally started to resonate with me. With this in mind, I was in no hurry for you to fall asleep. You make the cutest little cooing noise when you are tired and have a full belly. I looked down at you and we just cooed at each other for about five minutes before I decided that if I didn't try to get you to sleep soon then my window of opportunity might pass for good.

I got up from the chair and started to gently sway back and forth with you cradled in my arms. For the longest time, you would immediately start screaming when in this position as if to say, "I know you are trying to make me go to bed, but I AM NOT READY!" With my new calm, confident demeanor, your resistance has waned to a large degree these last weeks. I rocked you back and forth gently. You closed your eyes and seemed to totally relax – except for your left arm/ hand. It was as if your left hand had a mind of its own as you reached up to slap and grab my neck with great ferocity. You then gripped my face and pulled with all your might. Each of my gentle rocks was accompanied by the thrashing, grabbing, squeezing, or scratching of your left hand. It was shocking to me how strong the hand of a 17 pound baby could be. When you had my lips clutched in your vice-like grip, I was in legitimate pain.

Dear Zoe || Love Dad

I looked down thinking that you must be agitated, but I was completely wrong. Your face was completely serene. It didn't make sense to me how one of your appendages could be exerting so much force while the rest of you was completely composed. It was so shocking that I just started laughing. As I laughed, the situation became funnier and funnier to me as I desperately tried to not disrupt the majority of your body which was rapidly falling asleep. Stifling the audible portion of my laugh only served to intensify the physical elements of my laugh. My body was shaking and vibrating in a way that I was hoping would mimic your little vibrating lamb seat which you seem to enjoy. Maybe I was going to stumble on a new method for calming you. With each slap of my face or grab of my nose, I laughed harder and harder. My attempt to completely stifle myself from emitting any noise came to an abrupt and loud ending as I let out a huge laugh which promptly awakened you. I just couldn't help it; you were so funny.

You were far from thrilled that I had awoken you, and you started to cry. I tried my best to get you back to sleep because I knew that your mom was tired, but there was nothing I could do. I bounced, I rocked, I offered you the paci, but nothing worked. Sometimes I really just think you need to feel the love that only a mother can provide. Your mom heard your cries and her footsteps on the stairs meant that you were going to get what you wanted.

I must admit that I get an enormous sense of accomplishment when I am able to put you to bed by myself because it makes me feel that I am being a great dad – something I always wanted to be but wasn't sure would happen. But, I also love when you want your mom and not me. It is somewhat hard to explain because as you know, we have simpatico, but I love that you and your mom are so close. I know how much your mom loves you and I know how special you make her feel by giving her love and attention. Even before you were born, it was very easy to envision the two of you as best friends. I would close my eyes at night when she was pregnant, and picture her walking hand and hand with you in the mall or park. I could see you crying to her when your friends made you mad. I could see you sleeping in the same bed even when you were adult. The relationship you have and will have with her will be the most special you ever have. You are lucky to have her in your life and she is lucky to have you.

With you in mommy's good hands, I went downstairs to watch TV. Your mom showed up about two minutes later. You must have just really needed that special touch from your mom because it sure didn't take long to get you to sleep.

I think that you had a pretty good first Valentine's Day. When your mom came downstairs, she told me that she thought you and I should do something special every Valentine's in the future. What a great idea. I think that I have come up with a great plan. One thing you will learn when you get older is that your dad loves shoes, and I bet you will follow in my footsteps☺ (When I put a pair of shoes on you recently, you jumped so hard in your bouncer that I could tell these new additions were very much appreciated.) Your mom says that my closet looks like a Sneaker Store. Well, how about I take you to get a new pair of shoes every Valentine's Day? It will be our tradition.

It is now time for me to go to bed and say my prayers. One more thing before I go that I wanted to tell you. Every single night since you were born, I go to bed thinking about how lucky I am to have you and your mom in my life. It doesn't matter whether I am at home or on the road or in a good or bad mood, my last thoughts of the day are always about my family. Thinking about you makes me so happy and relaxed that I have started to sleep better and better every week – especially since you started sleeping through the night. Well, I think that I am sleeping better because I am so happy and relaxed during these last few waking moments, but maybe it is because I am exhausted from taking care of YOU! I guess it doesn't really matter why because it has been a wonderful change in my life.

Dear Zoe – February, 19

Another week has passed, and I am spending a great Sunday with you. The whole family woke up early this morning and your mom and I decided to take you to breakfast. Okay, your breakfast was at home, but I do think you appreciated leaving the house. We found a great little restaurant that I am sure will quickly become a family staple as it is close, quiet, and quaint – at least at 7:00 a.m.

I can remember as a little boy wondering whether I would be a good dad. I would say to my mom, your Neeny, "You are so lucky that I am such a sweet kid. I hope that I have kids who are just like me and my brothers and sisters and not like (fill in the blank of many former classmates)." She would laugh and say that I didn't need to worry; she was sure that my kids would be great. I guess I was squarely in the nature camp as opposed to the nurture camp during my pre-adolescent years.

As I got older, Neeny would tell me that she would like to think that "my being a good kid" had a lot to do with her parenting. She said that I needed more work than any of her children. Hard to imagine, but at least it gave me hope that I would be able to play a significant role in how my kids turned out even if there was nothing I could do to alter the genetic makeup I would be passing along.

Dear Zoe || Love Dad

When your mom and I were getting ready to have you, I would think back to these conversations. If I was going to play such an important role in my kids' development, was I sure that I knew what to do? I was really nervous. Once you arrived however, all these worries went away. Parenting really wasn't that hard I thought; actually, it is really simple.

This week has caused me to get a little nervous again because I realized that in the near future, I would have to start correcting your behavior. Of course, I would still be loving you with everything I had, but I would be upsetting you at times for sure. Being a parent means that I have to prepare you to live a full and successful life; I have to decide whether there are times when short term disappointment is needed for long-term gains. Even though I knew this day would come, I was hoping that it was well into the future as I really like the stage we are at now. What has been happening that got me started thinking about this?

First, there was recently a book published about a woman who said she was a "Tiger Mom." Basically, this mom would always demand perfection and maximum effort from her kids because she believed it was the best way to prepare them to be happy, capable, and confident adults. My parenting philosophy is quite different from hers; I am more like the "Pussycat Dad." My philosophy is that you just love your child with all your heart and things will turn out okay in the end. I will always encourage you to do your best, but never will I let this advice overshadow the love that I have for you. Anyways, wouldn't trying your best every moment of everyday be really exhausting? I haven't read the book, but I think it is probably very thought provoking, but don't worry, I am not convinced that I should start pressuring you to not make sure no food gets on your clothes when you are devouring "baby bananas."

Second, the weather finally got a little warmer and your mom enthusiastically took you out for your first walk in the new neighborhood. She had been waiting months for this day as you had really enjoyed these strolls last summer and fall. Maybe you were having a bad morning, but you didn't particularly enjoy this experience the first time she took you out. Not to be deterred, your mom decided to take you out for another walk later in the day after you had taken your afternoon nap. Apparently, our $800, top of the line stroller wasn't providing you the ride you wanted and you began to cry and cry. You kept yelling until, your mom picked you up and carried you. When your mom told me the story, I immediately envisioned how silly your mom must have looked walking through the neighborhood with you on her hip while pushing an empty stroller. There is certainly nothing wrong with your desire to be held and loved on by your mom, but Zoe, come on, isn't this a little ridiculous?

Dear Zoe || Love Dad

I love that you want our attention, and up until this point, I hadn't ever seen an issue with this desire. This incident however did cause me to think about whether we were giving into your whims too much. I thought, "At what age can you spoil a child?" Was it time for me to start telling you "no." I decided that I could justify mom's picking you up because it would be a problem that would resolve itself. Certainly, you would hit an age when it wouldn't be "cool" to be hanging with your parents. Granted, I was overlooking the bigger issue which was that you had us wrapped around your little chubby fingers, but this is going to be hard for me.

Third, you don't "play" very gently. I'm a 220 pound man, and there have been times when you are close to making my eyes water. I already told you that you have a tendency to slap, grab, squeeze, and hit me with surprising strength when you are going to bed; well, what I didn't mention is that this behavior is not limited to your bedtime routine. If I get too close to your head, I am libel to get scratched in the face or have an ear pulled. Recently, you have only increased your arsenal with the addition of teeth. These two, little weapons can inflict a lot of damage on anything that makes its way into your mouth. Your hitting and biting are definitely not malicious in any way, but you are getting too strong to let this behavior continue. I certainly don't want to get a call from your kindergarten teacher saying that you bit two kids and slapped another. What am I supposed to do? You are just playing and it really doesn't bother me. To be completely honest, I am the one who usually initiates it. Your intent is good – playing with dad or relieving the pain of getting new teeth. Are you able to understand that I can correct your behavior or say "no" without implying that you are doing something wrong? I think this is a little complicated for you; you aren't even seven months.

Finally, you made two babies cry yesterday. For the record, you did nothing wrong. You however, like your good old day, just seem to be misunderstood. I don't really know why the first baby started crying, but I think you did trigger the reaction of baby number two. You love babies so much. Whenever you see another baby, your eyes get real big and your arms start flapping as if you are a bird getting ready to take off. Both your parents have big, loud personalities, and I think that with you, the apple has not fallen far from the tree. We were meeting two of your friends for lunch. When Taylor's mom got her out of the car seat so that she could see you, you stood up real tall and just started yelling in excitement. Moments later, Taylor's lip started to quiver and tears began running down her face. Before you knew it, your friend was being walked around the restaurant in her mother's arms. It happens. When Ava showed up a little later, you once again became very enthused. Ava's mom was holding her and Ava's dad was holding you. The two of you were having a good time. Ava reached out and pulled on your bib which got no reaction from you – way to be

Dear Zoe || Love Dad

strong☺ I guess you thought that Ava wanted to play and you reached out and squeezed her hand. Uh oh! Ava started crying, and you were once again left standing there with no baby to play with. I think you might be a little too strong for your own good.

Once again, you did nothing wrong even if the end result was that you caused three babies to cry in less than a half hour.

Is it time for me to start correcting you and not catering to your every whim? Well, I don't want to be a Tiger dad because there is more to life than becoming a world-class musician or rocket scientist. There really isn't anything wrong with wanting to be held by your mom. If you can't tell that biting my hand hurts me, but you know that it helps you, then isn't using me as a teether pretty rationale? Can you help if other babies misinterpret your behavior?

The day to discipline you will come, but it isn't coming today. Do I make excuses for your behavior; Absolutely, I'm your dad☺

Dear Zoe – February, 25

I have felt extremely blessed since the day that I learned you were in mommy's tummy because I knew that you would bring me and your mom so much joy. At the time however, I did not know how becoming a father would force me to reexamine just how fortunate I really am. I just appreciate things more now that I have you.

I have told you on many occasions how lucky and proud I felt to be able to buy you a new house where you and mommy could play and be safe. Knowing that not all parents have this ability, I certainly felt fortunate when I was signing the papers that led to our getting the house. What I have come to realize however is that the house is just the most obvious sign of my good fortune.

What makes me feel so fortunate is all of the positive things in your life.

See, very few babies in this world have two loving parents, four loving grandparents, a new house, plenty of food to eat, top-notch health care, toys, and limitless opportunity. As I rock you to bed most nights, tears roll down my cheeks as I think about how lucky both you and I are. Never have I been so emotional.

Watching the news is no longer simply an intellectual exercise, but rather it is now an emotional one. These last few weeks have highlighted many Arab countries overthrowing their governments, and these stories have a new meaning to me now that I am a father.

I can't help but think of how different my life would be if I were in these brave people's shoes. Would I have been able to become a father? Would you and mommy be okay due to your premature birth? Would I even have the chance to be writing this book? I just happen to be living in a country where there are great doctors who can help people like your mom and I not only have a baby but keep that baby healthy when she is born prematurely. Going through IVF was stressful, but it was a gift. Having you in the NICU was tiring and worrisome, but it was also the most special weeks of my life.

I guess that I just want you to know that I am so thankful that you came down from heaven to be my daughter. I love you more than I thought possible and you have changed my whole life. You have made the world a better place, and I now feel a responsibility to make the world better too. I hope when you get older, you will want to help those who weren't given what you and I have been given.

Dear Zoe – March, 1

A few weeks ago, I remember telling you how there is no better feeling than walking in the door after a long day at work and seeing your face light up. Your smile makes me feel as if I am the most important person in the world. You can therefore probably imagine how sad I was yesterday when I jumped in the back of the car (you and mommy were picking me up for lunch) only to cause you to start crying. It was awful; I was so sad. Thankfully, the restaurant was only three minutes away, and I was able to get you out of your car seat and hug and kiss you while telling you everything was okay.

I think that I had just scared you because you had been almost asleep and when you awoke from your dream, you just saw a man with a hat. You didn't see your daddy. There have been a few other times this last week when my arrival didn't seen to bring the same amount of joy to your face as it has in the past. These experiences have really made me think. How will our relationship change and evolve as you grow older?

I knew that the day would obviously come when the sight of me wouldn't result in utter euphoria, but I thought and hoped that this day would be well into the future. I figured that there are many reasons why you almost have to love me right now. I have every advantage in the world. First, you really only know two people which means that I am not having to compete with girl friends, boyfriends, employers, or anyone else for your affection. Second, you are dependent on me for just about everything. If you want to go to a new room, eat,

Dear Zoe || Love Dad

or sit in a clean diaper, you need either me or your mom. Who wouldn't have at least a certain level of admiration for this person? Finally, I cater to your every whim and desire. There will be a time for discipline as I have explained, but we are not at that point. You want to scratch or bite me? "Go ahead; you are probably just teething or trying to communicate," I tell myself.

Your occasional, apathetic responses to my arrival have led to my contemplating one question. Do I have to accept that I will play a smaller and less significant role in your life as you grow older and develop into a young, independent woman? The more I thought about this the more I realized that I believe the answer is "No." Our relationship will definitely change but I am committed to maintaining our closeness and therefore the significance of our bond. There will probably be times when I will have to do the heavy-lifting in our relationship as your natural development will cause you to seek to distance yourself from your "dad," but I am going to fight as hard as I can to make sure that you always feel close to me even if you don't show it.

Why I am telling this to you, my little baby? The simple answer is because you and your mom are the most important people or things in my life. Rather than spend time worrying about my future career or retirement plans, it makes more sense to me to think about our future as a family. Nothing is more important to me now and nothing will be more important to me ever.

I want you to know that even though I spend most of my days at work and away from you, you are always close to my heart. I enjoyed my work a lot more before you arrived because now, I miss you while I'm gone all day. Also, satisfaction from a job well done at work pales in comparison to the feeling I get from doing my best as a dad.

On days when I am not feeling motivated to go to work, I remind myself that I, your mom and you still need to have our own lives. We can't just sit around all day telling each other how much we love each other. The love we have for each other should hopefully allow us to go out and have fuller, happier existences. If I hadn't have met and married your mother, I wouldn't have gone back to business school and eventually ended up having a great job. Making your family the most important thing in your life shouldn't mean that you forget about everything and everyone else. Coming to this conclusion was actually quite hard for me because I think I could be happy just staying home and playing with you all day every day, but I don't think that is what God would want from me. He wants us to enjoy this amazing world that He created for all of us.

Dear Zoe – March, 3

Dear Zoe || Love Dad

We have an amazing woman in our lives, and I thought I should take some time to record what a wonderful wife and mother she is. Even though I am the one writing to you, I hope I have done a good job of expressing how much your mother loves you as well. You can see in the way she looks at you that you mean everything to her.

Your mom likes to say that "A mother's work is never done." Even though she says this jokingly, I think that it really does express how your mom feels. Your mom has really lived this belief since the day that she found out you were in her tummy. Her life has changed even more than mine. Her connection to you was immediate, and she quickly decided to do anything and everything that she could to make sure you were healthy and getting proper care. To this day, she continues to always think of your needs first. It is not uncommon for her to hand you to me when I get home from work because she needs to use the bathroom. I will sometimes later learn that she tried several times to use the restroom only to stop as you grew fussy every time she attempted to put you down. She REALLY does put your needs above her own at all times.

One of your mom's cousins says that she fell in love with her husband all over again when they had kids. I have always loved your mom, but I can better understand what this cousin meant after observing your mom this last year. There is nothing more special than witnessing the connection between the two of you. The two of you just embody what I think God had in mind when he decided to create this world. Between the two of you exists a love and closeness that I have never seen. Witnessing this connection first hand and on a daily basis is so special, and I feel so fortunate.

Describing your connection to your mom is challenging because there are not many things in this world that just go together as well as the two of you. When you are on her hip staring out at me, you look happy, content, and confident. It is weird to say, but I often just view the two of you as one entity. You fit together like puzzle pieces and your connection is so natural that I can't help but believe that her hips were designed with your little body in mind. Sometimes I will call you "Joey" and not Zoe; because I think that you get confused and think you are a little kangaroo who should be in your mother's pouch.

I realized recently how much your mom has helped me be a good parent to you. Because your mom is such a loving and capable parent, my relationship with you has been enhanced. Your mom is definitely in charge when it comes to you. She is the person who knows how to give you a bath, how much food you should be eating, how often you should go to the bathroom, etc.... She is also the person who is able to comfort you when you seem inconsolable; she is the one who can get you to sleep when your exhaustion is preventing you from relaxing. For someone like me who tends to be worry, her abilities have allowed me to simply love you with all my heart without having my emotions wasted on nervous or anxious thoughts. Without your mom, I know that I would not be the father that I am today. Everything I know about how to care for you has come from her. And when you consider that being your father is and always will be my greatest achievement, you can understand why I am so indebted to your mom. She has enabled me to experience the greatest joy of my life – being a father to you.

I don't know if you realize this, but your mom has never been away from you for more than an hour and a half since you were born (except for one time when you were with your Memom for a few hours). She never has any time to herself. She is your life, and you are hers. Taking care of you and meeting your needs always outweigh any other plans that she would otherwise entertain. Some days I wish that I was more capable as a parent so that she could take some time to herself and not have to worry about whether you were alright. I want her to not be stressed about whether you are taking a long enough nap and to just take some time and reflect on what an amazing child you are and on what an amazing mother she has become. Maybe some day this will happen.

Her constant focus on you doesn't allow her enough time to reflect on what an amazing woman she is. Maybe her reading this entry will help stimulate this realization.

Onto some more mundane things that I at least wanted you to know. Your mom has started taking you to the library for "babies and books" as well as to a music class called "kindermusik." You absolutely love these classes and it isn't because of the books or the music. You just love other people. Your legs start kicking and your arms start flailing whenever you see babies or mommy's friends. I sometimes wonder what it is about other people that make you so excited. Regardless of the cause, I'm proud of you because I think that a genuine care and interest in others is a tremendous quality. The world would be a better place if more people cared about people the way that you do.

You are so special and I know that you will always bring joy and happiness to whomever is in your life.

Dear Zoe – March, 10

Today's entry is going to be short, but I wanted to tell you something that I was thinking about today. You have a supreme confidence about you, and you expect others to treat you well at all times. It is funny because I never think of you as being spoiled, but rather I am impressed with your self-assured nature and your healthy sense of self. If you are hungry, you cry until you are fed. When you drop a toy, you look at it and stare until it is retrieved.

Interpreting this behavior had me thinking all day. What I ended up concluding is that I and many others could learn a lot from your current worldview. (I say "your" worldview, but I also suspect this belief system is fairly consistent amongst babies your age." Why shouldn't you have your needs met, especially when you are currently unable to meet them on your own accord? There is something very honest about your approach to life. You believe that you should get what you want and you are not afraid to ask for it. Why settle?

As you grow older, I hope that you maintain this belief system. It will certainly need to be amended slightly in order to prevent you from being wholly self-centered. But, a fundamental expectation that others treat you well is not something that ever needs to change. In turn, you should treat all your friends, family members and even strangers in a similar manner. Treat others with respect and help them succeed because everyone deserves the best in life.

It is kind of amazing to me how much watching and observing you stimulates "big questions" in my mind. Often, you seem to have figured out a better way to live than I or other adults have.

Dear Zoe – March, 19

I was late to work this morning because my new alarm clock didn't go off in time. If you are wondering why I am telling you this, it is because YOU are my alarm clock. It seems that you decided to sleep in this morning.

A few weeks ago I decided that getting up to your gentle cries and smiling face was much more appealing than a loud, harsh beeping cell phone. You are so happy and loving in the morning that you have made what used to be the worst part of my day quite enjoyable. When I start to hear you move around or send out what I like to think of as "early warning cries" (they seem to simply be your way of indicating to us that you are awake rather than cries of sadness), I slowly pull myself out of bed and get your bottle ready. I am still in somewhat of a tired daze when I fix your bottle, but I am totally awakened when I enter your room to see your head lifted off the mat and looking up at me. I love you so much, and I feel this love so strongly in the morning as we are reunited after (hopefully) a long night's rest.

As you know, I often try to put myself in your place. Why are you so happy in the morning? Do you know you are going to get your diaper changed? Are ready for your bottle? Did you miss me? Is it the thought of finally escaping from your wooden cage located in a dark room? Maybe it is simply because you are well-rested. I am not sure, and I don't think you will ever be capable of telling me, but I do know that I love it. As happy as you are to see me, there is no way that you are feeling the pure joy that I am feeling at that exact moment. To feel this happiness, you will need to have a baby of your own☺

Your mom was telling me today that she has decided to teach you how to do sign language. We had already purchased a DVD called "Baby Signing Time", but we originally got it because you love watching babies. It seems that your mom has decided to use it for its intended function as well. To supplement this DVD education, she took you to a class where could practice these signs with others. You loved it of course because you were surrounded by two of your favorite things babies and moms. As your mom was telling me about the class, she mentioned that the teacher said that teaching your child sign language has been shown to increase their IQ by 8 points. I figured this was a good thing.

A couple of hours passed before I really thought about this comment. All of a sudden, I turned to your mom and said, "Are we teaching Zoe enough stuff?" She looked surprised and a little mad. Because she is the person who spends all her time with you, I think she thought that I was implying that her parenting skills were lacking in some way. You know by now that I certainly don't believe that to be the case. I continued, "I just love Zoe. I want her to be happy and I have no interest in living my life through her. Some parents want to brag that their kids walked early or talked early, but I just don't care. I am so happy with her that I will never feel any need for her to be more than what she is. She will always be perfect to me."

Even as I expressed this sentiment to your mom, I was worried. Had my focus on "not-pressuring" you gone too far in the opposite direction? I never want to pressure you and there is nothing you could do to make me more proud of you or to love you more, but I want to make sure that I am giving you all the tools you need to live a full, happy life. When I thought about giving you more IQ points by teaching you sign language, I started to wonder whether there were other activities that we should be doing. Should I try to be building you into a super-baby?

Your mom just looked over at me like I was crazy. Did I really just suggest that we try to build a super-baby? I guess she was thinking, "No."

Thinking about whether I was teaching you enough made me think about the challenges of being a parent for the first time in a long while. You are so much fun to be around and your mom knows so much about how to take care of you that I have been able to simply focus on "fun stuff." All the hours of worrying

Dear Zoe || Love Dad

that I did when you were still in your mom's tummy had begun to seem unnecessary. I had been confident that I was doing a really good job, but I guess there will always be a little doubt when you care so much about the result.

Your mom and I talked about this issue for a little while longer, and I tried to reiterate to her that I thought she was doing an amazing job raising you. You definitely have no shortage of love or interaction. I am not sure whether we will change anything moving forward, but I just wanted to let you know that I am always on the look out for how I can help you.

As your dad, I will always love you and try to help. Sometimes, I won't know exactly what to do or say to help you, but I want you to know that since you were a little tiny baby that I have tried.

Have a great night, and I look forward to seeing you tomorrow morning.

Dear Zoe – March, 28

It has been eight months since your entered this world, and I am not sure who has changed more – your or me. The easy and obvious answer is you. You started out as a six pound baby incapable of breathing or eating without assistance. The last eight months have seen you change daily. It wasn't long before your C-pap machine came off and you were guzzling down your formula. More time passed, and you learned how to smile at your ever-doting parents and make sweet noises that melt our hearts. Just this week, you started crawling by pulling with your arms and sliding your fully covered body across the wood floor.

Given all these changes, you might think that there is no way that your 34 year old dad could keep pace. I certainly haven't gotten any taller, and I hope that I haven't matched your 13 pound weight gain although I am admittedly worried. On the surface, most people might see very little change in me, but my mind and heart are different.

The instant you were born, my life changed forever. Feelings that I had previously been unable to access flooded my heart and mind. It sounds odd, but I felt like a completely different person because the world and my identity had magically changed with your first cries.

Never before had I felt so much love and satisfaction. Never before had I been so at peace. Never before had I been so alive. It was as if I walked through a secret passage that led to a whole new world where everything was just better.

Dear Zoe || Love Dad

These feelings have never left me. Being a dad is the greatest gift one could ever receive. Not only are you given a child, but you are unable to unlock a better "you." Being a good dad means being a better person.

In the beginning, it wasn't always easy trying to make the changes that I thought I needed to make. I want nothing more than for you to love and respect me. I also want to set a positive example for you, and I know that you are always watching. "How can I lead a life that is worth emulating," I have asked myself many times.

I realized that a good rule of thumb was to always try and make the lives of the people you meet just a little bit better. The beauty of this mindset is that it places your happiness back in your own hands, something very attractive to a person such as your dad, who likes to be in control. No longer am I compelled to address every slight or unfair judgment that comes my way because *getting* credit isn't as important as *giving* credit. No comments or rewards handed out at the office will ever be important as a simple hug from you. Work is just another situation where I am able to make you proud by my actions towards others. Your arrival has just put everything in a much better perspective. Don't get me wrong; there are still times when I feel forced to confront unfair treatment. Helping others' reach their personal and professional goals doesn't mean that I or you should be taken advantage of. These moments feel different than they did a few months ago when I was protecting my ego and career. Now, my assertions are to protect my career and ability to provide for you.

Sorry if that got kind of boring. Hopefully, it will be helpful when you are much, much older. You don't have to worry about anyone taking advantage of your good works as long as your mom and I are always by your side☺

Dear Zoe – March, 30

I am pretty sad today because it is going to be two whole weeks until I see you again. I had to go on a trip for work, and your mom decided that she didn't want to stay at home by herself. Because your Memom misses you desperately, you and your mom have headed to Texas to see her. These two weeks are going to be very hard for me, but my pain is eased knowing how much fun you are going to have with Memom. She loves you so much that you can't help but be overjoyed around her. She blankets you in love and attention from the minute you ~~step off~~ get carried off the plane. At the time that I am writing this, you have only been gone for a day, and I already hate it. I miss you and your mom so much.

Dear Zoe || Love Dad

Without our normal night time routine last night, I was lost. I ended up going to bed way later than normal because the house just didn't feel right without you and mom around. I love our time together each night. On many nights I hold and feed you with tears in my eyes as I am just overwhelmed with emotion. As we rock back and forth, I thank God for you and your mother. I just can't believe I am so blessed. It almost feels disconcerting being so happy for someone like me who has battled with OCD and anxiety my whole life.

Knowing that you were leaving, I cherished our night time routine even more than usual this past week. A few nights ago, I had really missed your during the day. I get home from work so late that there are often times when our only interactions are during our morning or night feedings. Well, I just wasn't really ready to have you go to bed after I had given you your bottle. There are some days when you finish your bottle, and immediately roll to your side and start sucking your thumb. (I know that having you suck your thumb is allowing a bad habit, but there is nothing and I mean nothing cuter than seeing you suck your thumb and twirl your hair as you go to bed.) On other nights, you finish your bottle and look up at me with a very satisfied grin. Because I am supposed to be "putting you to bed" and following "your routine," your mom doesn't like me to play with you or talk to you at these times. She says that I just need to rock you to sleep and not lead you to believe it is play time.

On this particular night, I was thrilled when you finished your bottle and looked up at me with your big, beautiful eyes. The combination of missing you so much that day and knowing that you were leaving for a couple of weeks gave me the confidence to disobey your mother's wishes. I looked down at you and smiled; a gesture you returned in kind. You then took your hand and started to grab my face – something you love doing. I continued staring down at you and smiling. It was such a nice moment because only when you are really tired do you remain calm in my arms. During the day, you are always squirming, trying to get loose.

Before I continue, I need to let you know about how we have started to communicate with each other. We have this special noise that we make to each other. I am not really sure how to describe it; I guess it is like a crackling hissing sound. You only make this sound for me which only furthers my belief that we have our own special, unique bond. Whenever you make it, I think that you are saying, "I love you" in your own, unique language. Your mom is getting concerned that I am teaching you a sound that is not actually a recognized language. She claims it could stunt your development, but I think she is just upset that this sound is reserved for your dad and not her.

Now we can get back to the story. I decided that maybe I needed to burp you, and I was about to get up from the chair when you made our special sound. It warmed my heart, and I know that I will never forget moments like this for the rest of my life. I hissed back which only led to more hissing from you. We went back and forth like this for a few minutes. Our actions certainly would have looked odd to an outside observer. Here we were a dad and his little girl, communicating back in forth in a language all their own. It is moments like this one that I never knew came with being a dad. Pure happiness and joy enveloped me as everything else in my life faded into the background.

Minutes passed, and I knew that I still needed to burp you. I lifted you up and put you on my shoulder. I rubbed your back, but nothing was coming out. I carried you around your room just enjoying the feeling of having my baby in my arms. Not knowing whether you were asleep due to your being on my shoulder, I moved you so that I could see your face. As I adjusted you so that you face was no longer looking over my shoulder but rather staring at me, I was greeted with about as big a smile as you have ever made. It was a great surprise. For some reason, I just started laughing. I had thought you were tired and potentially asleep, but you had decided that it was play time. I loved it, but I knew that my laugh was probably going to alert your mom to what was happening.

It didn't take but a few seconds before I could hear her coming up the stairs. We were busted! She walked in the door and said, "I can hear you up here. I know that you have been making your special noise and playing with her this whole time." I tried to use the excuse that I was trying to burp you, but she knows me better than that. She knew that I was getting sad about having you leave, and she let me slide this time without getting frustrated or annoyed. She took you out of my arms because there was no way that you were going to go to bed with me at this point. I said good night went downstairs as happy as a dad could be.

Dear Zoe – March, 31

I'm in Houston, TX for a work trip, and I miss you very much. It was so sad this morning. After not being able to connect yesterday, I finally got the chance to talk with you. Your mom put her phone on speaker, and you started crying when you heard me make our special "I love you" noise. You don't understand why I am not there, and I hate thinking that you are feeling abandoned by me. Maybe I am being a little too overdramatic, but you will learn that being overdramatic is what happens when you love your baby so much. We stayed on the phone together for a short while as I told you about my day in Houston. My eyes continued to fill with tears as I told mom that I just needed to get off of the phone or I would be too upset.

Thankfully, I don't have a job that causes me to travel very much. It has been terrible not being around my family these last couple of days. I have just felt out of balance without your calming influence on me. It does however make me very happy that you are getting to spend so much time with your grandparents, great grandparents, aunts, uncles, and cousins. Growing up, I only had two grandparents and my relationship with them was not as loving as the relationship you have with all four of your grandparents. Seeing videos of you playing with your Papaw or cousins makes me know that my loss is at least someone else's gain. I want to keep you all to myself, but you bring so much joy and happiness to everyone you meet that it is important that I share you with the friends and family.

Today was not only difficult because it was yet another day without you and your mom, but also because I had to visit a children's hospital for work. Don't get me wrong, I volunteered to go on this trip because I want to give back to the sick kids and try to brighten their days just a little. But, seeing young kids in pain or in difficult circumstances has always broken my heart art and it is definitely worse now that I am a parent. Thank God that you are a healthy and strong baby.

The kids were so brave and strong as they dealt with their respective, challenging situations. There was one boy whose story really upset me. I wasn't able to meet him, but my co-worker shared the following with me. He just learned that he had cancer, the same disease that Aunt Kim has, and he has been in the hospital for three weeks. During that whole time, his mother has never visited him. It not only made me sad for him, but also extremely mad. As a parent, I don't even know how this is possible. I love you with every fiber of my being, and there is nothing I would not do to make your feel better. If you are ever in the hospital again, your mother and I will be right by your side. When I think of this young boy's story, I am not sure which is more painful to him – his medical condition or the way he is being treated by his own flesh and blood. There are going to be times in your life when you will face challenges be they medical, personal, social, or professional, and I want you to know that you never do anything alone. You will always have your mother and me supporting you as best as we possibly can. It doesn't matter whether you are 12 or 54, we will always be your parents.

I actually have "never alone" etched into my wedding ring because I know that I face nothing without the love and support of your mom. When you get older, I think that I will get you a ring, bracelet, or charm with this same saying because you will never be alone. You will always have me by your side whether I am here on earth or in heaven with all the angels.

Today was not only special to me because I got to be around some amazing kids, but I also helped celebrate your mom's birthday from afar. Since you entered our lives, neither your mom nor I seem to really want the material things for which we used to long. Something happens when you experience the true happiness that comes from having a child that makes new, material presents seem very unimportant. Because of this situation, I was struggling figuring out what I should get your mom for her birthday. Finally, the perfect present came to me. Your mom loves you more than anything in the world, and I therefore decided to get her something to remind her of you. I wanted to surprise your mom, and I therefore didn't wrap a present or even mention what I was planning. I called your Memom and told her to take your mom to her favorite jewelry store and pick out a new ring which would include both your birth stones, diamonds for mom and rubies for you. It was a great feeling when your mom called me a few hours later to let me know that she found the perfect ring. You will learn as you get older that there are few things that bring as much happiness to you as making someone you love feel special and important.

Every time your mom looks down and sees her beautiful ring, she will be reminded of how much she loves you. Right now, she doesn't really need a reminder of you because every time she looks down she actually sees *you*. You have been attached to her since you left the NICU. There will be a time when you will be off to school or visiting your Memom and the sight of the ring will just bring a smile to her face. I know this because I have a watch from Papa Bear that serves as a constant reminder of how special he is to me. Hopefully, mommy will give you the ring I bought her today when you are older and you will wear it and think of her.

Dear Zoe – April, 2

There are so many reasons why I have chosen to write this book to you, and one of those reasons is so that you know me better. Having lived through so many experiences, I hope that maybe you will read this book when you are older and realize not only how much I have always loved you, but also what I find to be important in this world. Part of being a parent is taking responsibility to provide information that catalyzes thought and growth. My goal is not for you to become a clone of me, but rather I simply want to pass down wisdom I have attained that you may or may not find useful.

I was in two situations today that made me think that this entry was worth writing. First, I attended a special brunch with college All-Star basketball players because my company sponsored an event at the NCAA Final Four. The lunch was honoring these athletes because of their physical abilities to play a game at the highest level. What I found interesting however was that after the students left, the only topic of conversation was about how nice and humble they were. The crowd came because we were fans of their talents on the court, but we

Dear Zoe || Love Dad

left being fans of their work ethic, love of family, and humble nature. Television and media celebrate certain types of people who have excelled in athletics, politics, business, music, etc... to a much greater extent than those who have excelled in being "good people." Growing up, you will most likely look up to and idolize people for external talents, but I want you to know that people still really value what type of heart you have. You might think that being an honest and loyal friend is unimportant because the end of the year awards at school focus on academic and athletic achievements rather the personal characteristics. You should know that I will always care more about how you treat others and the fabric of your character than your grades or athletic accomplishments.

Second, I also had the chance to attend a concert this afternoon featuring what I felt was a very talented band. I don't normally go to concerts even though I enjoy music very much. As I stood there, it was such a nice experience as the music engaged me in a very real way connecting with me physically (I could feel each drum beat in my chest), mentally (I thought through the lyrics and their meaning), and emotionally (I experienced a wash of feeling as I pictured you and mom). I am not sure what the future holds, but unfortunately, classes such as music and art are often the first to get cut from school programming during challenging fiscal times. For some reason, these subjects are deemed much less important than science and math. During the concert, I couldn't help but think about how important art and music are to this world. The people of the world will continue to be moved and have their lives enhanced by great artists such as Leonard DaVinci, Michelangelo, John Lennon, Aretha Franklin, and May Angelou hundreds of years after their death. There is real value in the arts as they are able to connect with individuals in very important ways.

What I hope you will take away from the first part of this entry is that making the world a better place and enhancing the lives of others may not always be celebrated. Please don't let this lack of public acknowledgement discourage you. There will be a time and a place where your character will matter to people more than anything else you have accomplished. From the second half of this entry, I hope that you place great value in the arts even if politicians and school administrators don't. Math and Science are important to any society and can bring a tremendous amount of good to civilization, but art can be truly transformative.

Dear Zoe – April, 29

I am really starting to wonder whether I will ever stop writing in this book. Every time I try to stop, there is a thought or feeling that I desperately want to capture before it escapes. Your arrival has allowed me to feel so much more deeply than ever before. The only way that I can think to describe what I am experiencing is to use an analogy. I never really thought that I had bad eyesight – see, I never knew any different. I was even surprised the day that the doctor suggested that I would benefit from wearing glasses. When I finally slipped on a pair of glasses, I could not believe how different the world looked. It was so much bigger and grandiose now that I could see more than ten feet away. Having you is like putting on a pair of special glasses. My mind and heart are now simply more capable of experiencing than they had been previously. Each day I want to write to you, about you, or some combination of the two because I am experiencing life in a new way. I have the insatiable urge to write because I can't help but believe that my daily life is really amazing and worth recording now that you have opened my eyes to a whole new world.

I just looked back at my last entry, and I think it deserves somewhat of an explanation. One thing that you may not know about your dad is that I am pretty scared of flying. I completely understand that it is the safest method of transportation, but I still have a hard time comprehending how a giant steel tube can fly through the air and bounce around in turbulence without falling to the ground☺ One of the many reasons that I write to you is so that you would be able to understand what I wanted for you in case something ever happened to me. I hated even writing that last sentence because I always want to be there for you to make sure you are healthy and happy. Life is unpredictable however, and I decided when your mom and I started this journey that I would write to you in case something happened to me. When I was in Houston on my trip, the combination of my missing you so much and my OCD definitely caused me a lot of anxiety. One way that I could at least make myself feel better was to write in your book – something which always makes me feel close to you. Like I said, I meant what I wrote, but I could see if you thought it was a little abstract for a nine month old.

The day before you arrived back home, I felt like I was ten years old on the day before Christmas. I tried to distract myself with little chores around the house because I was just so anxious to see you. It had been a full two weeks since I got to hold and hug you, and seeing you on the computer really paled in comparison to having you in my arms. It isn't a lot of fun having a big house if there is not a wife and baby to share it with. Even watching soccer, my favorite activity, couldn't cheer me up. Fortunately, I had a little project that I needed to complete on this evening, the last before you come home, which provided a welcomed distraction. Your mom had told me that you had taught yourself how to "pull up" which meant that I needed to lower the mattress in your crib. Now, lowering the mattress should have been a very simple task as no tools were even required. Unfortunately, your dad is not exactly the most "handy" and it took me over an hour to get your crib into its new position. I was sweating profusely as I bent over the side of the rails crazily trying to get the four wing nuts loose so that the mattress could be re-positioned. The rails of the bed were pressing against my rib cage causing a great amount of pain. My head hurt as all the blood from my waist up seemed to be pooling in my skull due to my being bent over. It really was my love for you that made me not abandon the project midway. I accomplished the task knowing failure was not really an option. My fear however is that the future of any bike, fort, or bunk beds you may want will be in jeopardy unless your mom has a knack for engineering.

I was so excited as I drove to the airport to pick you up. I was a little nervous too because I knew that it would make me really sad if you didn't know who I was. I took solace however in the fact that you are so friendly and lovable that you would probably smile and go to me even if you didn't remember I was your dad. (For safety reasons, we will definitely need to work on this trait as you get older.) I was expecting your mom to call when you landed in our hometown, but she decided to surprise me and just walk out of the airport to greet me without warning. As soon as I saw you, I jumped out of the car, ran, and scooped you into my arms for a big hug. I kept hugging and kissing you; I even forgot to say hello to your mom, my wife. She didn't care because we both know that you are the real star of this family now.

Your mom decided to leave you with me while she went inside to get the luggage. I just kept hugging and squeezing you, trying to make up for the lost time over the past two weeks. I might have squeezed you too tight because you spit up all over me☺

The two week hiatus from being a hands-on-parent had left me feeling as helpless as the first day you came home from the hospital. I didn't know what to do when you spit up. I was so flustered looking for a rag or something to clean both you and I off that I finally concluded that I my only recourse was to go inside and find your mom. It wasn't long before an announcement came over the speaker in the airport terminal that a white Chevy Equinox was going to be towed unless the driver returned immediately. I had been so focused on you that I had just abandoned the car, which was still running, in an illegal area. I told your mom that I needed help. She looked back at me incredulously. Had I really left the car parked illegally to come and get help with a little spit up? In a word, yes! Her patience with me ran out. She took you back to the car and explained my inadequacies to the security guard. He just laughed as I assume he could relate. Dads don't always know what they are doing which is one reason why God made mommies.

I rode in the backseat with you as we headed home; you were even more beautiful and precious than I remembered. Your eyes were a prettier shade of

Dear Zoe || Love Dad

blue and your smile was even more perfect. It was such a relaxing ride home knowing that my family was together safe and sound.

You had definitely changed a lot since you left, and I was sad that I missed these last two weeks. Your teeth were more pronounced, your pronunciation of "dada" and "momma" were clearer, and your crawling was much improved. Why did I ever agree to this two week trip? How could I miss all these changes? I realized however that I wasn't always going to bear witness to all the amazing things that you do. You will grow up and change, and there is nothing that I can do to slow down the process or witness every milestone. Never before had I been sentimental until you arrived. Then again I have never cared about anything or anyone as much as I care about you. Now, I look back longingly at all the milestones that have already come and gone. Thankfully this book is keeping a fairly accurate record.

Your mom told me that you hadn't been sleeping very well in Texas. She was surprised because you had been doing great prior to this trip. At first, we thought that it was just taking you awhile to get used to a new crib and a new house. Only later did your mom discover that your Memom, like all good grandmothers, was taking you out of your crib at the first sound you made. She was so sensitive to your "needs" that she would pick you up and feed you in the middle of night even if you weren't crying. Having spent months perfecting your night time schedule, your mom was none too thrilled with this discovery. She was so upset that she actually made your Memom sleep with her in a different room so that she could keep an eye on her. I wanted to tell you this story because it says a lot about your Memom who just loves you with every fiber of her being; she will always do anything to make you happy. And, your mom who wants the best for you and is confident that she knows what "best for you" is. She is right too and that is yet another reason why I think God put her on this earth specifically to be a mom.

I also wanted to give you some background before I tell you about your first night back home. I wasn't exactly sure what to expect given the changes that your Memom had introduced to your sleep schedule. When it came time for you to go to bed, I was so excited to be able restore our night time routine. Feeding you your last bottle before you drift off to sleep is my favorite time of the day. I am so relaxed looking down at your sweet face as your eyelids become heavy and you gently drift off to sleep. Even on the nights when you fight your sleep, I cherish this time knowing full well that these moments won't last forever. Our bond will always be strong, but I know that it will change as your bottles are replaced with sippy cups and your crib is transformed into a toddler bed. Tired from all the travel, you went to bed with ease. As soon as the bottle came out of your mouth, your thumb was popped in and you were out.

Dear Zoe || Love Dad

I walked down stairs to spend time with your mom whom I hadn't seen in two weeks. Now that you were asleep, it was time for me to spend time with the other love of my life. You might not have been in the room, but your presence was still felt. Every story your mom and Memom shared revolved around you. She would tell me about your reactions to all your extended family. Even though your mom and I have our own relationship with each other, we often spend our time together talking about you and not each other. You are the most important person or thing in both our lives; it is only natural that you are the main topic of conversation.

It had only been about an hour when I heard you start crying on the monitor. I never like hearing you cry, but tonight was absolutely heart wrenching. Babies cry as their method to gain attention and you are certainly no exception. There was however something different about this cry. It wasn't the sweet, soft cry you had when you were in the NICU. It wasn't the loud cry you normally use to alert your mom and me that you are ready to wake up, eat, or change activities. It wasn't the coughing cry you use when you are just plumb mad. It wasn't the aggressive cry that signals your frustration at not being able to accomplish a task. It wasn't even the pathetic whine of "Momma, momma, …." which expresses disappointment and confusion over your parents' inexplicable refusal to comfort you (i.e. why won't your mom take you out of your car seat when she is sitting right next to you.) Simply, it was different. I had never heard you sound this way. The only thing I knew was that it saddened me in a way that no previous cry ever had.

I ran up the stairs trying to figure out what you were trying to communicate. You didn't sound hurt or sick which at least provided some comfort. I remained unsure about what I was hearing until I scooped you up out of your crib. Your crying stopped as you wrapped your arms around my neck; a response you usually reserved only for your mom. It hit me. You were just sad and afraid.

You hadn't been back in your old crib for over two weeks. Waking up in this unfamiliar surrounding must have made you so scared. Where were my parents? Where was Memom?

I held you tight and told you that everything was okay. I told you that I loved you and that I would always be there to protect you. We rocked back and forth until you were calmed down. As we swayed, my mind went back to all the times when I had snuck into my parents' room as a little boy after waking up in the middle of the night with bad dreams. I distinctly remember wondering where I would go when I was the dad? Who would protect me? Feeling scared is such a terrible experience; I hated knowing you had to even go through a minute of feeling this way.

Having you in my arms is always special. This night was different than usual however. I felt more needed by you than I had ever been needed by anyone. The importance of the role that I play and will play in your life was made crystal clear. I was your dad, the man who would protect and comfort you.

I might know my limitations. I might know that only God is able to protect you from all the problems of the world. But on this night and at this moment, you thought of me as the person that I always wanted to be. To you, I was strong, compassionate, dependable, and caring.

Dear Zoe – May, 3

There is something about putting you to bed at night that just makes me cry. Early in the week, you were fussy and I decided to sing you a little song. The song turned out to be quite long as I told you the story of how you came to be. I started with meeting your mom and took you through all the stages of IVF, gestation, and delivery. By the time I was finished, you were asleep and my cheeks were drenched in tears. Thinking back to all the things that your mom and I went through to have you just made me appreciate your being in my arms so much. You had overcome so many obstacles. I just cried and prayed to God thanking Him for making this exact moment possible.

Putting you to bed each night gives me at least an hour a day when I am relaxed and completely focused on you. I think that I am doing an excellent job of taking the time to appreciate all the little changes that you go through on a weekly if not daily basis. I know that I won't ever be able to recapture these early months of your life and that I therefore need to be really "present" and appreciative of this time. That being said, there is nothing that I can do to prevent myself from being saddened by the fact that you are growing up. There are so many things that I already miss. I miss the sense of accomplishment that I felt when I got you to take your bottle in the NICU. I miss your enormous burps after every couple of ounces of formula. I miss your newborn laugh that sounded like a sheep saying "bah-bah." Most of all, I miss you making our special noise that always made me feel that you were telling me that you loved me.

I remember asking my mom when she enjoyed being a mother the most. Did she like it when we were babies? When we were in elementary school? High school? She would always say that she loved every age. I take solace in this answer because it is sometimes hard to imagine that I could enjoy being your dad as much in the future as I do now.

Dear Zoe || Love Dad

Fortunately, I have you to help me when I get nostalgic for the times we shared when you were even younger than you are now. I may miss things that you have stopped doing, but you are constantly making me feel better by doing even more precious things. Just a few days ago, you pulled the bottle out of your mouth when you were finished after your morning feeding. This behavior is not new. What happened next however was surprising. You took the bottle, lifted it up, and offered it to me with a big smile on your face. When I pretended to take a sip, your face lit up with laughter. Our special noise might be a thing of the past (you haven't made it since you got back from Texas), but you still love me very much.

Sharing your food has continued to be a bonding experience between the two of us. Just tonight, you decided to share your bananas with me. The softness of a banana combined with your vice-like grip and lack of fine motor skills led to your basically smushing banana on my mouth. I might have gotten messy, but I did appreciate the gesture.

There is one fear or at least concern that I have about your growing up. As you have probably figured out by now, there are sometimes when I talk to you as if you are a little baby. There are other entries that you would only be able to understand if you were much older. Some entries you probably won't be able to truly comprehend until you have a baby of your own. What makes me scared is not having our nightly chats. These talks allow me to tell you how much I appreciate you and how much I love you. I take the time to explain how scared I was when your mom was in labor. I share all my feelings with you as I hold you in my arms. There is something special about these times when I know that you don't comprehend my words yet somehow fully understand me.

Your mom recently wanted me to stop holding you for so long after you fall asleep at night. She said that you needed to learn how to "put yourself to bed." I told her that this time is not just for you, but it is also for me. I then tried to explain to her that I believe you will always remember these nights. My words might be incomprehensible to you, but the sound of my affected voice and the tears on my face do the communicating for me. It all goes back to the Simpatico we have. We can communicate without words.

In my heart, I know that these nightly feedings mean a lot to you now and will mean a lot to you forever. What makes me nervous is the fact that sometime in the near future, our nighttime routine will have to change. You will be too big to get comfortable in my arms. You will understand human emotion well enough to question why I am crying yet struggle to comprehend my answer of "because

Dear Zoe || Love Dad

I am happy." Our relationship will change; I just pray that I continue to make it better and better☺

Dear Zoe – May, 10

Tonight, as I watched you play, I couldn't help but think about how you already have all the qualities and characteristics needed to be a successful adult. I had been interviewing for a new job at work which meant that I would need to go through many rounds of interviews. Watching you tonight, I saw the determination, curiosity, drive, and courage that you have. These are the same traits that I was trying to convince my interviewer that I had.

You still don't know how to walk and your crawling is limited, but your sense of adventure is great. I had come from work and immediately greeted you on the floor. We played with your toys for only a few moments before you got bored and started moving onto the next thing. Today, you wanted to climb.

You crawled over to the couch and continually tried to pull yourself up to a standing position. You tried and tried, but success was not coming. I sat watching your focus and determination with amazement. Since I have become an adult, I am not sure the last time that I took on a task that I had never previously completed with such grit and drive. You would pull up and fall down only to start over again. I started thinking about the new position for which I was interviewing. There were times throughout the process when I wondered whether I was making the right decision. Was leaving Marketing for Sales the right career move? I had never done Sales; would I be any good? The questions in my head weren't in yours. You were wholly focused on the task at hand; a task that you had never attempted. I thought to myself that if my nine month old daughter can tackle new challenges everyday without fear, then her dad should be able to do the same.

As I sat there watching you, I started to think about other things I could learn from you. Is there a lesson in your tendency to ignore me and your mom when we tell you to "Stop doing something?" I think the answer is probably, "yes." There are going to be many times in your life when people tell you that you shouldn't do something. Often, you should take this advice. But, there are going to be times when you need to have the confidence in yourself to decide to keep pushing forward. Great leaders can't always follow the rules or no progress would be made. I hope that you don't lose your stubborn streak as you get older because a strong belief in yourself is vital to your being a happy, successful adult.

Dear Zoe || Love Dad

I started thinking about my interviews and the questions that had been asked of me. It was funny because I started thinking about how I could have answered if I were you. I decided that you probably would have gotten the job over me☺ What would you bring to this position? You could say something such as "I will bring a fresh set of eyes, a thorough attention to detail, and an unbiased point of view." When asked for examples, you could describe how you use all senses when investigating a new toy. I only see that it is a pink dog. You however use all your senses in determining its value. First, you see it with your eyes and decide whether you want to get any closer. Second, having decided it is worth your time, you move closer and pat it with your hand to see how it feels. Third, you listen as your patting stimulates the dog to make various noises. Fourth, you put the stuffed animal in your mouth to see whether it makes a good teether or not. Having used four out of your five senses, I would say that you have a much better and more rigorous understanding of this toy than I.

You really are special, Zoe. My hope is that you will read this entry at some point in your life and know that God gave you all the "stuff" you would need to be successful in this world. You had all the qualities as a nine month old baby. Life has a way of making situations much more complicated or daunting than they need to be. Trust yourself and know that I have always believed in you.

Dear Zoe – May, 16

Changing your diaper is getting to be nearly impossible. The days of your sitting still and patiently waiting for your mom or I to clean up your mess have officially ended. As soon as the second adhesive is removed from your dirty diaper, you are ready to escape. You immediately start rolling in a manner that reminds me of alligators on the National Geographic Channel in some primal death spiral. Having only two hands to control your legs and body, slide a new diaper beneath you, clean you off, and discard the soiled diaper is tremendously daunting when you are not cooperating. Let me tell you about what happened today.

I might love you with all my heart, but I must admit that changing your diaper is not one of my favorite activities. Your mom was upstairs taking a very well-deserved nap. It was clear from the smell in the room that your diaper needed changing. Knowing your lack of interest in staying still these days, I gave you a toy which I hoped would occupy your attention and mitigate your flight response when you diaper came off. I got a fresh diaper and slid it under your old diaper as I always do.

When your diaper came off, I was pleasantly surprised. You had definitely pooped, but the affected area seemed to be fairly contained. I lifted up your legs only to find some more "matter" heading up your back. Nonetheless, I was confident that I could accomplish the mission.

I was holding your legs when you tucked your left shoulder and rolled. It was so fast that there was nothing I could do but hold on for dear life. Not wanting to hurt your legs, I didn't try to roll you back into a better position, but rather I simply followed your movement. Asking you to roll onto your back didn't work. I decided that I just needed to wait a moment until you were willing to turn back around.

While I waited, I moved the dirty diaper out of the way so that I wouldn't put you back into the dirty diaper. I continued holding your legs while I picked up the old diaper. Unfortunately, your poop rolled out of the diaper and onto the carpet during this exchange. There wasn't much that I could do about it at this point, and I just left it there.

Finally, you rolled back toward me, and I was able to place you down on the clean diaper. What I had failed to do however was clean you off. Placing a dirty behind on a clean diaper isn't exactly the smartest thing that I have ever done. The clean diaper quickly became a second soiled diaper. I was so flustered. Your mom was upstairs sleeping, but she seemed very far away. I kept thinking that this really can't be as hard as I was making it.

Frozen with my thoughts, you once again tried to roll away. I was able to maintain control of your legs which prevented even more soiling of the carpet. We waited for a few minutes before I essentially conceded victory to you. There was no way that I was going to be able to clean you off and get you into a new diaper.

I am not sure why I decided on my next course of action. It seemed logical to me at the time. If there was no way that I could wipe you off and hold both your legs simultaneously, I would need a different way to clean you up than wet ones. I picked you up in my arms and carried your half-naked body up stairs to your bathroom. I filled you little tub and sat you down in the water. (It was kind of like a bidet – very sophisticated I thought.)

Your butt hit the water and you started laughing. You always enjoy baths, but this reaction was more pronounced than your normal enthusiasm. You definitely knew that you were using the bathtub in a whole new manner. When you shirt got wet, the whole situation became that much more amusing to you.

It had been a long time since I had felt so overwhelmed and so incapable. I was exhausted at this point, and I called for help. Your mom came to my aid. Not being someone who likes waking up abruptly, I wasn't sure what reaction I would be receiving. She stood in the doorway and just joined in the laughing.

I wanted to tell you this story because I just get a kick out of every aspect of being your dad. I sometimes worry about not knowing what to do in certain situations. Times like today however make me realize that not knowing can lead to a lot of fun. You don't expect me to do everything just right – in fact, you seem to like my mistakes. I hope you know that I don't expect you to do everything just right either. How about we both just continue to try our best because it seems to be creating a lot of happy moments in our lives thus far!

Dear Zoe – May, 25

Your Papa Bear's birthday was last week, and I wanted to tell you what we got him because I think you would very much approve. Buying presents for him has always been a real challenge, but I knew exactly what I thought we should get him this year. My becoming a dad really helped me select what I think was the perfect present, a donation to his favorite charity. The charity, ACEFCO, he supports helps build and run orphanages in a country called Afghanistan which is very poor. Many children in this country don't have parents because their parents give them up due to an inability to provide even the most basic of a child's needs such as food to eat and water to drink. Knowing how much I love you and how much you love me in turn makes me so sad for both these parents and these children. I have know how important this charity is to Papa Bear for many years, but having you in my life has truly enriched my appreciation of his dedication to this cause.

Your Papa Bear is a wonderful man who has always placed the needs of his own children before his own. Now that all of his children, your aunts and uncles, are out of the house and living on their own, he has turned his attention to supporting children throughout the world who are in desperate need of assistance.

I wanted to take some time to explain the three reasons why I decided to make the donation to ACEFCO in your Papa Bear's honor. First, I have never been more focused on being a person of whom you could truly be proud. I have told you this many times in this journal, but it is so important to me that I don't mind repeating it. How I defined success completely changed on July 26th. I have tried to change my thinking from how I can "better than others" to how can I "make others better." This change in mindset has definitely been a challenge for someone who has always been a competitive athlete and who now works in corporate America. But, I know I am closer to the person God wants me to be

Dear Zoe || Love Dad

for changing my thinking. This first change in mindset led me to consider making a charitable donation.

Second, I kiss, hug, and tell you I love you many, many times every single day. And, you provide just as much love back to me. It absolutely breaks my heart for both the children and the parents who don't have the opportunity to share the special moments you and I share on a daily basis. Never have I been as happy or more at peace than when you smile up at me and say "Da Da." I have been so blessed to be your dad, and I like to think that you have been blessed to be my daughter. I believe that it is important that you and I always try to help those who were not so fortunate. How can we spread the special love we share as a parent and child to others? Every child should feel loved and every parent should feel that he or she has given their child hope and opportunity. It was this thinking that made me think that I should find a charity which focuses on orphanages.

Finally, I tried to think of what you could give me that would make me the happiest. Now that I was a father, I am much more capable of putting myself in my dad's shoes. It dawned on me that what I would want from you would be a present which showed that you had embraced some of the values and beliefs that I had spent my life trying to teach you. I have already told you that I don't want you to be a mini-me, but I do hope that you will respect some of the life lessons that your mother and I will bestow upon you. Being a parent is the greatest gift that I have ever received. It is also the greatest responsibility that I have ever been given. I take this responsibility extremely seriously as I know Papa Bear has. Nothing would make me more proud than for you to grow up and tell me that the lessons that your mother and I taught you have made you proud of the woman you have become.

Making that donation to ACEFCO allowed me to express that sentiment to my dad.

Dear Zoe – May, 31

Your Aunt Jessica came to visit you this weekend. She had such a great time just hanging around the house chasing after you. It was really great for me to see a side of my baby sister that I did not know existed.

Your Aunt Jessica is a very special person to me because I believe that she "gets" me in a way that many people don't. She understands when I am joking and when I am serious. She appreciates my mind and my heart. She enjoys my outward persona but never lets it overshadow my true self. Because our relationship is so strong, I was very excited for her visit. What I was not expecting however was her to be overly affectionate towards you. She has been around many babies in her life, but she has never proven to be the "mothering" type. I don't doubt that she can or will be a great mother, but this part of her personality has never been on display in front of me.

I knew that she loved you, but I had previously thought that she would be much more interested in spending time with you when you were older and able to go shopping, her area of expertise. I was definitely wrong. She hugged you, kissed you, changed you, bathed you, and loved on you as if you were her own. It was really quite amazing. You just have this special ability to bring out the best in people. I can't tell you how many smiles you elicit when we walk through a restaurant or the local Wal-Mart. There is just something in your face, your smile, and your laughter that attracts others two you and triggers positive feelings. It is really impossible to be around you and not be happy; your aurora just won't allow that to happen.

Aunt Jessica returned safely to her house in Florida, but I was happy to receive an e-mail from her thanking me for allowing her to visit. She wrote that it was great to be around such a loving and positive family for the weekend. Fatherhood has changed me more than I could imagine. Reading this note made me realize that maybe the greatest change is that I have gone from being a fairly anxious and pessimistic person to someone who is truly positive. When you combine my feeling so blessed to have you in my life with the sheer joy you bring to me with each smile, there is no way that I could allow pessimistic thoughts to overwhelm me. Being a dad is such a wonderful gift that I really feel thankful every single day. In you, I see what is beautiful and meaningful in this world. I see hope, happiness, courage, love, and peace in your daily actions. What I hadn't known however was that your Aunt Jessica was now able to see some of these same things in me.

Dear Zoe – June, 6

Last night, you unexpectedly woke up at around 11:00 pm. Your mom picked you up and cradled you in her loving arms, but you just cried and cried. Watching you cry is so upsetting to me that I always want you in my arms so that I can at least feel like I am doing all I can to make you feel better. When your mom reluctantly handed you over, you screamed even louder. This reaction made me realize that you must not be feeling very well as you really prefer the loving touch of your mom when you are sick. Between the arrival of some new teeth and a runny nose, you must have been feeling pretty miserable.

We tried to figure out what we could do besides just rock you and whisper softly that everything would be okay. We did everything that we could think of; we changed you, gave you some ibuprofen, rocked you, and fed you. The bottle seemed to do the trick as you sucked down a full six ounces. Now that you had calmed down to some degree, I once again asked your mom to let me hold you.

It might seem silly, but I concentrated really hard on comforting you with my embrace. I tried to communicate that everything would be fine and that you could always count on me through the hug that I was giving you. I closed my eyes and focused on the strong emotions I was feeling. Without the ability to tell you that I loved you and that I was sorry you didn't feel well through words, I was left to communicate through osmosis. It didn't seem to work completely, and as crazy as it sounds, I was surprised. There was just something in me that told me that if I concentrated real hard that I could somehow make you "feel" better even without the use of words. Months ago I had feared being left alone with you and now I thought I could communicate complete thoughts and messages through a hug alone. I had definitely come along way with regards to my parenting self-confidence.

You didn't relax until I gave you back to your mom. You snuggled up against her as if you could never get too close. You are so lucky to have a mom who loves you so very much. I sat down on the floor and waited for you to calm down. It was definitely time for me to go to sleep, but I couldn't relax until I knew that you were feeling better.

Remaining in the room would also allow me to support your mom. I know that your mom sometimes gets stressed when you are up in the middle of the night. Sitting on the floor next to your rocker would hopefully quell some of her anxiety. Her mind isn't unlike mine at these times as fears and worries take center stage. She starts to worry that maybe you will stop sleeping well and that we are headed back to the sleepless nights that served as the backdrop to your first few months with us. What I believe is really happening is that seeing you upset really bothers her too; she worries as a way to take her mind off the feelings of sadness that she is experiencing at that moment. I, on the other hand, remain surprisingly calm in these situations. Seeing you upset and your mom anxious makes me focus on what I need to do to help each of you. It isn't unlike how I felt in the NICU. My restless mind is temporarily quieted as my irrational OCD obsessions are supplanted by a greater concern – the well-being of my family.

I continued sitting at the foot of the glider in your room until you became restless once again. I reached out to pick you up, and you quickly relaxed in my arms. I told your mom to go to bed as you could see the fatigue in her expression. It only took a few minutes before your muscles stopped twitching and contorting and you succumbed to exhaustion. Seeing a peaceful look return to your face temporarily erased the exhaustion in my body and mind.

With you sleeping serenely in your crib, I returned to my room. My mind drifted off to one of the parenting classes that I took before you were born where the teacher had said that it was very normal to need a break from your baby if he or she was crying or screaming. The teacher said that it was fine to put the baby in a safe place and take a few moments to collect one's emotions. I have found the complete opposite to be true for me. There is nothing that I want more than to be with you when you are crying. At these moments, I feel that you need me most. Never do I think you cries are in vain, but rather I know that you cry because you are in need. My assumption is that you would much rather be smiling than crying. It is during these moments when you need me the most, and I relish the opportunity to bring you even a little bit of solace. When I am able to bring you some consolation, I feel more important than at any other moment in my life.

The advice of the teacher was correct, and I definitely think that some parents need to take heed of its tenet. I just feel very blessed that for some reason God gave me the strength to want to respond to your cries with calmness and compassion. I think it is also easier for me than most parents because I have an amazing support system in your mother who spends all day and night with you. My "tank" is full when I am with you as I have been at the office all day dealing with the complaints of people who are not nearly as cute as you☺ What I am trying to say is that your mom and God deserve almost all of the credit for times when I am able to be the dad that I want to be.

Dear Zoe – June, 13

Today's entry is going to have two parts. First, I am going to tell you about my hopes for your future. Admittedly, the first part is going to sound a little preachy. You will have to just bear with me and understand that you are always on my mind and that everything I do from reading to watching TV triggers my thoughts about how to be the best parent I can be. There is no longer a me that exists outside of my identity as a "dad." Second, I will tell you about your weekend because I am beginning to notice a particular trait that might need some correcting.

There are a few things that I have been thinking about over the last couple of days that I wanted to share with you. You are still a little or at least pretty little baby, but I am constantly thinking about what I will need to do in the future to be a good dad. I suspect that the challenges that I faced going through IVF and then the NICU might be easy when compared to your teenage and young adult years. The world changes so fast that I know you will be faced with difficult

Dear Zoe || Love Dad

situations that neither your mom nor I ever had to handle. It makes me sad thinking about all the pressures that young kids feel in today's world. There are so many different reasons for children to be happy and thankful, but I don't think that all children feel this way.

Tonight, I watched a show on bullying. I wish I never had to explain what the word bullying meant, but I know this is not possible. Bullying is when a person or a group of people try to make someone else feel bad about himself or herself. I know that this probably doesn't make a lot of sense to you. Why would someone want to make someone else feel badly about himself? Unfortunately, it is true. Bullying has become a real problem and it only seems to be getting worse as there are more and more outlets from which to tease or ridicule others.

I wanted to share a story with you. When I was a young boy, in the third grade, there was a young boy named Chris Kepler. (There are very few students whose names I remember at this point in my life, but I remember him.) He was different from the rest of the kids; he had a hard time sitting still and he often liked to make funny noises. Some days, he would get up from his seat and just run out of the classroom. As you can probably imagine, he didn't have all that many friends because he was just so different. Not only was Chris different, but he was also a very, very bad athlete. He was always picked last for all the teams in our P.E. class. I was a very athletic kid, and I was also extremely competitive. I wanted to win at everything, and it wasn't uncommon for me to throw a fit when I lost. During one particular day at P.E., my teacher made me a captain which meant that I would get to choose the teams. The sport was soccer, which was my favorite. I am not sure what caused me to do what I did next, but it has brought me a great sense of pride my whole life. With my first pick, I chose Chris Kepler. I think that I understood that it must be really awful being picked last all the time. I figured that he would feel really special if he was actually picked first for a change. When I said his name, he, the other kids, and even the teacher seemed shocked. I on the other hand felt so happy. I don't think that I could tell you a single thing that I learned during third grade with regards to spelling, math, social studies, or science. I can't tell you about a single goal I scored in any of my soccer games. The only thing that I can remember from this year of my life with certainty was my choosing Chris to be on my team.

I hope that you know that doing the right thing and making others feel positive about themselves will make you feel better than any other thing you will do. You will accomplish a lot in your life, but I think that you will find the most happiness in the achievements that enhance the lives of others. Watching that show on bullying made me realize that it was important that I teach you from an early age that bullying is never okay. You may have bad grades, you may play poorly in sports, you may even break our rules, but there are few things that would make me more disappointed than finding out that you were bullying other kids.

I know that this entry might seem a little dramatic given that you are only 10 months old, but I think it is important for you to know what I want for you. Standing up for what is right is sometimes tremendously difficult to do. Maybe this entry and these words will give you the confidence that otherwise you might lack.

The other thing that I wanted to share with you is something that I recently read. You are going to have a childhood that is completely different than mine. For example, I never sent an email until I was a freshman in college. And, my first cell phone wasn't until I was in my mid-twenties. Social media sites such as Facebook didn't enter my life until after thirty. All of these technologies will be at your fingertips as a kid, and it makes me very scared. Usually, I can look back on my life as a point of reference for what you will be doing or experiencing, but society has changed so fast that I am just going to try my best to advise and parent you about situations I never knew.

What I wanted to share with you is that I think it is still very important to take time to yourself to think and write to friends and family in a way other than short-hand texts or status updates. (By the time you read this, you will know what I mean.) I don't want you to sit down and write a book like the one I am writing you, but I do think that you should learn to communicate in more than robust way than offered by various social media platforms. It seems that kids are using less and less words/ letters to communicate with each other. Of course, I am sounding really old right now, but I think that I should at least express my wishes to you. I read an article about the lost art of letter writing, and it led me to want to tell you my thoughts on this subject. It wasn't the article alone however, but also my experience of being your dad.

When I put you to bed each night, I really allow myself time to contemplate the awesomeness of being your dad. Sitting there with you in my arms for ten, thirty, sixty minutes, allows me to think more deeply about my role in your life and your role in mine. It is during these times that I am often compelled to fire up my computer and write to you. Thoughts which I didn't know existed come to light during these times when I allow my full range of emotions and the full power of my intellect to work harmoniously together. It is only when I actually begin the process of writing however that the full depth of my thoughts and feelings coalesce. Even if you were to never read a word of this book (which I really hope is not the case), the writing of it has been a very meaningful journey for me. These letters to you have allowed me to understand fatherhood in a way that I am convinced would have otherwise remained hidden.

Dear Zoe || Love Dad

I don't expect you to write long letters to your friends instead of text messages, but I still hope that you do take time every once in a while to stop and really think about what you want to communicate. Thoughts and feelings are often too complex to be accurately conveyed in just a few words.

If you are like me, you will probably find the beginning portion of this entry very thought-provoking and useful. If you are like your mom, you might have already skipped to the next entry hoping for something better. We are just two very different people, and at the present time, it is impossible to tell which one of us you will resemble most.

Moving onto your present day, I think that you are really starting to develop a temper. All babies are easily frustrated given their inability to communicate or control their own destinies, and I have been thinking that your little outbursts could be simply attributed to your age. Now, I am really beginning to wonder. These last few weeks have seen your biting, pinching, and yelling become more frequent occurrences.

There are many examples including your nightly screaming fits when you get out of the bath tub or the bites you use to get our attention. You get very mad when you don't get what you want. At first, I was a little concerned as disciplining you will not be something that I will ever enjoy. It only dawned on me today that a little bit of a temper is probably a good thing. Your temper seems to stem from your belief that you should get what you want and be treated as you wish. In many ways, it is sad that adults often lose this belief system and settle for sub-par treatment from friends, family members, and co-workers. Having a temper and throwing fits might not be the most appropriate reaction, but a reaction of some kind is definitely warranted.

As I continued thinking about this issue, what I decided was that I would rather have you have this strong sense of self-worth, then have you be willing to accept not getting what you want or being mistreated. Your mom and I will have to work with you so that you want the "right" things and the "right" treatment. We will also have to work on your reaction to the apparent slights that trigger such explosive reactions. If however we can harness your temper so that you remain unwilling to settle for anything less than the best for you and others, then we will have done an excellent job as parents. I am not exactly sure what this process looks like, but I do believe it can be done.

Love you, Zoe.

Dear Zoe – June, 19

Dear Zoe || Love Dad

Today is a really special day, and it is all because of you. What makes today so special is that it is my first Father's Day. Your mom has been asking me what I wanted to do for weeks; my response was always something to the effect of "It isn't a really big deal. We should just do what we always do on a Sunday." In my mind, I should be thanking you for making me a father rather than you and your mom thanking me. Being a father is a blessing that I cherish every day; I don't need recognition for being blessed with this gift.

It wasn't until this morning when you and your mom surprised me with donuts and a new pair of shoes that I began to appreciate the importance of today. What has made the day so special however was not the shoes, donuts or calls from my family, but rather the recognition by everyone family, friends, and strangers that being a father is an important job. Everywhere I turned from our walk in the neighborhood to the shows on TV, people were celebrating the relationship that a dad has with his children. So many days are filled with stories of sadness, misfortune, or superficial pursuits that it has been very edifying to have the focus of so many people be on something that is truly valuable.

With all the focus on my being a dad, I decided that it was a good time to focus on whether I am doing a good job or not. Your mom says that I am doing great which I value tremendously as I have immense respect for her parenting skills. I remember being so scared when you were in your mom's tummy because I hadn't spent a lot of time caring for babies. My fears only got worse when I went to the parenting classes with your mom and realized that I didn't know the first thing about how often a baby eats, sleeps, or goes to the bathroom. When you arrived, I quickly realized though that loving you with all my heart would guide me in the right direction. Caring for you is both very complicated and very simple. It is complicated because I have to try and interpret your signals to guess at what you want or need. Simple because you only want very few things – milk, food, and a clean diaper. Mostly though, you just want love and attention and those are two things I know I will always give you.

So, do you want to know what you have been doing this last week? Let me just give you some of the highlights. The first story is an example of how much I love you and how much fatherhood has fundamentally changed me. I don't get to spend as much time with you as I would like because I have to go to work Monday through Friday. By the time I come home, I can't wait to see and spend time with you. You have gotten to the point where my carrying you around is not always your first choice of activities. You are simply to busy preferring to be crawling and climbing than being held. On Friday, we were playing on the ground together as we normally do. I was lying on my back looking up at you as you tried to climb onto the couch to see what your mom was doing. After a long

Dear Zoe || Love Dad

week at work and a half hour of chasing you around the living room, I closed my eyes momentarily. It wasn't more than a few moments until I felt something hit my face. Without even opening my eyes, I said, "Mommy, did Zoe just throw up on my face?" When I heard her laughing, I knew the answer. I kept my eyes closed and shut my mouth for fear that your spit up would spread to these areas. Your mom got some paper towels and cleaned me off. This is going to sound crazy, but it was a nice moment between father and daughter.

Let me explain. The idea of having someone spit up all over me, let alone my face, absolutely horrifies me. My OCD is still bad enough that the sight of any body fluids is liable to cause me to be paralyzed with anxiety. Here I was having throw up all over me, and I wasn't the least bit concerned. This is actually kind of gross, but I didn't even wash my face with soap being satisfied with only the moist wash cloth supplied by your mom. It might have been a bizarre way to prove the point, but I think it shows that I am just a different, healthier person when I am with you. You bring out the best in me. My love for you inspires me to be better than I thought I could be. Now that I have proven my love for you, I would appreciate your making this the last incident involving your throw up and my face☺

I was not only the only one reaching new heights this week. You, my little baby, literally reached new heights when you climbed all the stairs in our house. It was a proud and terrifying moment for me. Proud to see you figure out what you needed to do to get your little body up these enormous steps. Proud that after multiple tries over multiple days, you were so stubborn that you accomplished what I had thought impossible for someone your size. Terrified that you were fearless enough to cause yourself great harm if not under constant supervision. And finally, proud that you would constantly look behind you to make sure that I was there in case you needed me. Knowing that I have instilled this confidence in you means that I must be doing something write as a dad.

I hear you crying upstairs…. this entry is going to have to wait.

Dear Zoe – June, 20

Last night was so sad. You just wouldn't stop crying. There was nothing that I, your mom, or your Memom could do to comfort you. We tried everything. We gave you medicine for pain, we gave you a Popsicle to soothe your gums, we took you outside for fresh air, etc… No matter what we did, we simply couldn't figure out what was bothering you.

You are not a fussy baby at all which makes times like last night so confusing, frightening, and sad. The hours of crying started to wear on me just as they had when we took you to D.C. for thanksgiving. I tried to stay calm as I could see the anxiety in your mom's face. She and your Memom have always struggled in these situations ever since you were a little baby in the NICU. Don't get me wrong, these times are very tough for me as well. I simply feel that it is my responsibility to look after all three of you. Any strength I have in these situations comes from this desire to project a sense of quiet confidence to the three of you.

Time after time, I picked you up in my arms hoping that my embrace would calm you down. I tried as I always do to communicate just how much I love you through my hugs, kisses, and words. Each time, you screamed louder and louder. Being away from your mom is never what you want in times of distress. It was very hard however for me to "not be doing something" when you were crying. I needed to be "helping" in some way.

You seemed to be quieting down at around 9:00 when I took a shower and got ready to go to bed. Your mom was rocking you to sleep in your room. I was therefore shocked when I came downstairs after my shower only to see you, your mom, and your Memom sitting on the couch watching TV. Tonight was going to be a very long night.

I didn't tell your mom, but I was very close to taking you to the hospital. I was getting very nervous as nothing seemed to make you feel any better. You might not have had a fever or any obvious symptoms, but something was clearly upsetting you. You never stayed up this late.

Finally, your mom gave you a bottle and you settled down at around 11:00. When I woke up this morning, it was such a wonderful sight to see you smiling back at me. The problems of last night were gone as you welcomed me with your soft chant of "Da Da, Da Da, Da Da." I told your Memom that I still wanted your mom to call the doctor because I wasn't ready to have a night like we did last night again. I would be happy never to have a night like last night again.

I am happy to report that the doctor did a thorough exam of you today, and you are very healthy. He said that he was able to see some spots on your throat which were probably causing you some pain. With the virus of last week still in your system, you might continue to feel a little discomfort, but he was confident you were well on your way to feeling healthy again.

Now, that I have told you why I had to stop writing last night, I want to finish what I was planning on telling you.

Dear Zoe || Love Dad

I had just finished telling you about your climb up the stairs. It wasn't more than fifteen minutes after this feat that I went about installing the gate which would prevent such trips in the future. Unfortunately, this project was more challenging than initially expected and it took hours and not minutes. Because your safety was at stake, I concentrated hard and overcame my engineering inadequacies to complete the task.

It felt somewhat like watching Shark Week when I waited for you to approach this new gate. You were the great white and I was the scientist testing a new cage. Would it withstand your onslaught? It didn't take long for you to crawl over to the stairs. Within moments, you discovered a flaw in my assembly. The gate was too far forward on the first step which allowed you to hold on the gate and place the edge of your feet on the first step. You were precariously balancing your whole body weight on your toes as you clung to the first step. It was a disaster waiting to happen. Remember how I was telling you that Father's Day was a day for me to evaluate my performance as a dad? Well, at this moment, I felt like a failure.

I told your Memom that she would need to take you away so that I could make some modifications. Twenty minutes later, I was ready for you to test it out again. You approached this new obstacle with a sense of curiosity. It wasn't long before you had grabbed the gate with both hands and started shaking. You don't have much muscle, but I could see your biceps tighten as you tried with all your might to pull the gate open. You continued shaking the gate while clinching your teeth and grunting. The juxtaposition of your grunting, scrunched face with your cute dress and big bow was really a sight to see.

With the gate not budging, you started investigating other ways to get to the stairs. You tried to squeeze your 97th percentile head through the bars which I immediately knew just wasn't going to happen. You tried to climb up the side of the stairs therefore bypassing the gate altogether, a clever yet futile strategy. It took ten minutes for you to concede round one to the gate, but I don't believe this battle is over☺

The other big news of the week is that you renamed your Memom. She is now your Nana. Your mom had noticed you saying something new since your Memom arrived. It wasn't until a few days ago that she realized that this new word "Nana" was actually being used to describe Memom. Although Nana is a common nickname for grandmothers, neither your mom nor I had ever even spoken this word in your presence. How you decided to call your Memom Nana is a complete mystery. Once we realized it however, you made your Nana cry the first time you said it to her after our realization that it was your new name for her.

Dear Zoe || Love Dad

There is one more thing that I wanted to share with you before I stop writing. It is actually about your mom and your Nana. These past weeks have allowed me to see the tremendous relationship that continues to exist between your Mom and your Nana, and I want nothing more than for you and your mom than to have the same bond. I was walking past your Nana's room the other day, and she and your mom were just lying in bed reading their own individual books. They were so content to simply be in each other's presence. It was as magnificent a sight as I had ever seen. It conjured up as great a sense of grandeur as the Sistine chapel had on my trip to Italy because it showed the beauty of the mother daughter relationship. You will have your own life with your own friends, but I want you to always remember that your mom and I will always love you more than you can imagine.

Dear Zoe – June, 21

Last night, I once again went to sleep with tears of joy on my face. I started thinking about the times when you have trouble sleeping and you cry out for me or your mom. Picking you up, holding you close, and ending your tears brings me indescribable joy. I know I have told you this already, but I can't help but tell you again. I want you to know just how much you mean to me. You have to understand that you have brought me more contentment than anything ever has. Never before has a simple hug from me been able to bring complete comfort to someone else. No one has ever appreciated my embrace more than you. No one has ever been as comforted by me as you. Being your dad is simply the best thing that has ever happened to me; I am so happy that you love me as much as you do. It is such an awesome responsibility, and I hope that I am always able to comfort you as I do now. Remember, you are never alone.

Hopefully my shortcomings as of writer have not overly interfered with the successful conveying of this message. Since I was a little boy, I have always felt that I wasn't doing "enough." I could be better at sports. I need to get into a great college. I should be advancing faster in my career. Never was I at peace. Your smile and embrace has made me accept myself in a way that had previously eluded me. Loving you and being kind to others is the key to happiness which I had always been seeking.

Thank you for letting me digress. I will once again return my focus to you.

I was worried about you today because one of your favorite people, Nana, left this afternoon. I hated that Nana had to go back to Texas today, but she has a business to run back home. She is such a wonderful person, and you love her so much. She smothers you with affection which is exactly what a grandmother should do.

If there is one thing I would change about my life right now, it would be the fact that your mom and I live so far away from all our family members. It was so sad tonight when you crawled over to the stairwell, looked up and said, "Nana, Nana." You definitely miss her. I don't know how much of your day was spent wondering where she had gone. Your mental capacity remains an unsolvable puzzle. My hope is that you were too focused on exploring the world, which still presents new wonders every day, to stay sustain any sadness. You should know that your Nana would come and live with you if it were at all possible. I also know that she would be on the first plane out to PA if I ever called and told her that we needed her help.

Uh, oh; I need to go check on you.

I just returned from your room, and I think I should tell you what happened. As I was finishing that last paragraph, you started to move around your crib trying to get comfortable. Unable to settle, you started crying. I ran upstairs knowing that I was going to make everything better. Writing to you always makes me emotional, and it was this mindset that accompanied me as I scaled the stairs. I couldn't get to you fast enough as your cries became louder and louder.

You were standing in your crib when I crossed the threshold into your room. Moments later you were in my arms. When you started crying even louder, it just broke my heart. It When I had just written that I always hoped I would be able to comfort you, I never thought that my ability would end within the next hour. Of course, you still love me and need me, but it is hard for me to think that I won't always be your panacea.

Fortunately, your mom was able to get you to relax. Ultimately, I just want you to be happy regardless of whether the soothing source is your mom, your Nana, I. Being the answer to your problem is not as important to me as making sure your problem is solved. I know you love me.

I hope you have sweet baby dreams tonight.

Dear Zoe – June, 25

"I am always going to be there for you. Even if I am not in the room, I hope you know you can count on me. I am your dad, and dads protect their babies. There is no reason to be scared."

Dear Zoe || Love Dad

I have said these words to you many times over the last three days. You have had so much trouble sleeping recently. It is just breaking my heart to awaken to your cries hour after hour.

It all began about four days ago when your Nana left and you were getting over your sickness. Over the last three nights you have actually gotten up 21 times; a number that is even greater than when you were a little newborn. Your mom and I have tried everything to figure out what is causing your discomfort. We have taken you to the doctor, researched sleeping problems on the web, given you medicines, yet nothing seems to be working. My best guess is that it is a combination of a few things. First, I think you have forgotten how to put yourself back to sleep when you wake up. When your Nana was here, any peep from you immediately led to her going into the room to comfort you. Although I appreciated her giving you so much love and attention, I think it might have contributed to this issue. (Your mom should have banned her from this action like she had in Texas.) Second, I think you might be getting old enough to have anxiety when you are not around your mom or me. Finally, I think that you are sad that your Nana has gone and you are subconsciously afraid that you might have your mom or I leave as well.

I of course don't know whether any of these reasons are the actual cause, but they seem pretty logical to me. Seeing you so sad has made me once again think back to when I was a little boy. I remember having a really hard time sleeping some nights too. My mom was always so sweet to me because she knew I didn't like going to bed by myself. She would come into my room and sit at the foot of my bed until I fell asleep. You need to know that I will do the same for you. It doesn't matter how many times you wake up. Your mom and I might be exhausted, but we will help you get back to your old pattern.

Last night, we put you to bed at your normal bed time and hoped for the best. Unfortunately, you had awoken three times before midnight. Finally, I had to get some rest myself. It must have only been twenty minutes after I finally fell asleep when I heard you crying again. I could hardly move because I was so tired from being up so many times the previous night and then having had to go to work. I dragged myself to your room. I put my hand on your back and told you it was going to be fine. Just like my mom had been there for me, I was there for you. I lay down on the ground and told you I would stay there with you; you didn't need to be scared.

It was therefore a great shock when I woke up with your mom standing over me and you in her arms. Exhaustion had overcome me. Even though I was directly next to your crib, I had failed to stir when you got up a few hours later. Your

Dear Zoe || Love Dad

mom had come to the rescue. She told me I needed to go back to bed and that she would take over.

Your mom and I were so tired today as we both tried to function after a night of many interruptions. I am not sure how I was able to get up so many times when you were a little baby and still go to work. God must give new parents extra strength.

I hope you know that your mom and I are not upset at you at all. Some times parents complain about their babies getting up in the middle of the night and this complaining really annoys me. See, you only get up because you are scared, hungry, wet, sad, etc… Why would I be mad with you when you are the one who is upset? Do I wish you would sleep through the night? Yes, of course. But if you don't, I know it is not your fault. I feel bad for you as well because I it must be really draining to cry hour after hour.

Remember, how I was telling you about your temper? This last week has seen an increased frequency of "fits" where you scream, cry, and throw your head back. I feel the exact same way about your temper tantrums as I do about your getting up in the middle of the night. I wish you wouldn't get so frustrated, but I don't blame you. Seeing you cry or scream will always make me upset regardless of the reason. I don't really think that my picking you up so that you don't hurt yourself on the stairs is a truly valid reason for you to scream, cry, and yell, but it hurts my heart nonetheless. I think there is a life lesson here. When you get older, I hope that you always feel compassion for those who are sad or upset. It is easy to play judge and reserve sympathy for only those whose feelings you believe are warranted. Since becoming your dad, I have decided that this isn't really how people should be treated. No one would choose crying over laughter. How often do we really understand the person's predicament? Therefore, it is only human to be empathetic to everyone's tears.

The other epiphany that I have had this week about your temper is that you are actually communicating quite effectively. As someone who loves efficient, concise communication, your tantrums are actually worthy of praise. Because we can't communicate through words, throwing your head back or biting is actually a pretty good way to get my attention and express your aggravation. If you keep biting when you are old enough to communicate more clearly, then we will have a problem. Until then, I am just going to have to deal with a few teeth marks on my skin each week.

On a brighter note, we did have a lot of fun together today. Your mom woke up with a migraine, which is a really bad headache. I therefore took care of you all morning and afternoon so that she could get some very well-deserved rest. I am

Dear Zoe || Love Dad

going to end this entry by telling you how far I have come with regards to having confidence in my parenting ability. You might disagree however based on our walk☺

We both love taking long walks – me walking and you riding. Given your mom's need for a rest, we went for a full hour today. It was great. We talked the whole time which probably looked weird to the neighbors who would have seen a grown many carrying on a long conversation with a baby. I care about you not them though so it doesn't matter. I told you how much I love you and how lucky I was that God sent you down from heaven to be with me. I reiterated that you were welcome to sleep through the night if you so chose. (I was willing to try everything but letting you "cry it out" at this point.) I pointed out various things that we saw on our jaunt – a motorcycle, bunny rabbit, landscaping, and an airplane. It was just perfect. You weren't talking a whole lot, but you did do a little singing intermixed with some "Da-Da's" which was nice.

I must admit that I thought I was being a great dad and husband today. It wasn't until I got home and took you out of your seat that I began to question my status as #1 dad. See, you were sopping wet when I got you out of the stroller. Being the conscientious parent, I filled up a sippy cup with plenty of water so that you wouldn't get thirsty. Being the parent who is better at working outside the home than in it, I didn't screw the cap on properly which led to it leaking all of you. You had spent the last hour thirsty yet drenched.

You were very sweet to not make a big deal about it☺ I think I did a better job with your lunch. I gave you all your favorites, yogurt, blueberries, bananas, and grapes. To top it all off, we shared a frozen ice together. I have decided that the best time of my day is no longer bed time but rather any time when I share food with you. It is a great bonding experience between us. I introduced you to frozen, flavored ice when I thought you were teething. Let's just say, I might have made a mistake because you absolutely loved it. You started climbing all over me to get more. It was quite painful for your dad as you decided that my chest hair was perfect for grabbing when pulling up to reach for more. Regardless of the pain that now often accompanies our sharing of flavored ice, I love these moments. Life doesn't get any better than sharing a frozen treat with your baby girl.

I said that I was going to end by telling you that I think I am growing as a parent. What made me really feel this way was how I have been handling your trouble sleeping. I am not scared or worried at all. Before you were born, I would have wanted to spend hours reading the internet or calling other parents looking for answers. These days, I have a quiet confidence in myself and my abilities to be a parent. Your mom is still the boss when it comes to most things,

Dear Zoe || Love Dad

but I feel that I am now more of an equal partner. She had to do all the "heavy-lifting" during those early months. She just always knew what the right thing to do was. Now, I think that I know what is right. I have decided that being a parent is actually quite simple. Love your baby, listen to your baby, try and understand your baby and things will turn out just fine. Please know that I am trying my best.

Dear Zoe – July, 2

This might sound odd, but it always makes me happy when you fall asleep either with me or on me. I see falling asleep as something that only occurs when you are both physically tired and mentally at ease.

Earlier today, we were out on one of our daily walks. As usual, I was talking non-stop telling you about a wide range of topics including puppies, air travel, and the importance of being nice to people. Usually, you respond with grunts or yells during these father-daughter talks. When a few minutes passed with the only noises coming from me, I walked around to the front of the stroller only to find you sleeping peacefully. Given your tendency to fight off naps with all your might, it was reassuring to see your willingness to take a little siesta during our stroll. Of course, there was two ways for me to interpret your sleeping. First, I thought that maybe you were just tired of hearing me talk incessantly about things that your mom claims make no sense to a baby who only has three words in her vocabulary. Or second, you were happy, relaxed, and confident that your dad would take great care of you, conscious or not. I certainly hope that the second interpretation is right, but I could understand #1 as well.

We walked in the door, and your mom was so proud. I still am not sure with whom she was more pleased. Regardless, it was a really great way to spend the middle of the day.

There are so many things that happen on a given day let alone a week that I often have a hard time picking out what is most important to tell you. Should I tell you about my call to the poison control center yesterday because you might have consumed a teeny, tiny amount of laundry detergent? (They said you were absolutely fine. Your parents weren't as we beat ourselves up, but you were.) Should I tell you about your 1st birthday invitations which made you smile and laugh uncontrollably because you saw a pretty little girl on them (you)? (You are not alone in this reaction; the little baby in the picture has that same affect on everyone she meets☺) Should I tell you about how your mom got me out of the shower this afternoon to ask me to examine your poop because she thought it looked weird? (I gladly did without hesitation showing how much a man can change in a mere eleven months. My diagnosis was that you didn't chew your mandarin oranges as well as you could have, but that there was nothing to worry about.) Or, should I update you on your biting? Yes, your biting is definitely a worthy topic as it has led to my left arm looking as if it was in a street fight.

I have really mixed emotions about your biting. To be honest, there is a part of me that likes it. I see the biting as a natural extension of your personality which I absolutely love and wouldn't change for the world. It can be described in many, many ways. You are fun-loving, energetic, fearless, confident, rational, curious, happy, aggressive, sweet, and many other things. Your biting is probably most attributable to your rational, fun-loving, and confident side. Usually, you bite because your mom or I are restraining your from doing what you want. You therefore make the rational decision to let either of us know your displeasure because you are confident that you will be set free to pursue an activity that is more fun.

There are other times when you bite seemingly out of boredom. I told your mom that you put everything you see in your mouth; it only makes sense that you put other people's limbs and digits in your mouth as well. You do know however that you will need to stop biting soon, right? It does really hurt and I don't want you to hurt anyone else with your mouth – this includes words (future) or actions (now)☺ Last week, you made me very nervous as we were playing with your friend Ava when I could see a look in your eyes that made me feel Ava was in danger. To be frank, it looked like a scene that could have been filmed on the African Sahara by a team from National Geographic. Here is what happened. Ava started crawling away from you when you all of a sudden took off after her. You caught up to her and put your arms on her back. Moments later you opened your mouth ready to chomp down on your unsuspecting friend. Timed seemed to slow down as I could foresee the awful outcome that was about to happen. Thankfully, I was right there to ward off the attack. A few more seconds and I would have been forced to have a very uncomfortable conversation with our friends Jim and Kelly. We still have time to correct this issue due to your not being in school or daycare; hopefully this is just a phase.

Now that I think about it, biting isn't your only aggressive tendency. One odd yet probably good thing is that your aggression is usually reserved for me, your dear old dad. Your mom was shocked yesterday when you were slapping, hitting, scratching and squeezing the various features on my face. I, having become used to such behavior, thought nothing of it. I told her that if you thought that was bad, you should watch when I put you to bed.

Many times over the last week, I have been completely unable to stop myself from laughing as you stared up at me after your pre-bed bottle and played with every feature of my face. You can clearly tell that you are exhausted by the glazed-over look in your eyes and flat affect. Nonetheless, you use your hands to explore my face as if it was the most interesting toy in the world. Without question, your hands and fingers will be in my mouth scratching my teeth and gums. You have also started to try to rip my ear off of my head – which I hear doesn't actually require that much strength. (I have actually been quite nervous on a few occasions.) You have also taken a keen interest in my nose. Given the small circumference of your little fingers, I think you were close to touching my brain a few days ago by way of my left nostril. I should film these nightly facial investigations because it is so funny how your facial expression does not change as you pull, squeeze, prod, and manipulate all areas of my head and neck. It sometimes appears that your hands are not even connected to your body because your face is sending one message – I am so tired – while your hands are sending a completely different one – this is very interesting. Between your biting and your nightly attacks, I have become one tough dad.

I am not exactly sure how to let you know that your biting, scratching, and pulling actually cause pain to whomever is on the receiving end. My plan is simply to wait until you can talk to have all of these discussions with you. Waiting for a dialogue certainly sounds better to me than some of the other suggestions that I have been given – the most common being to bite you back. (No thanks.)

If you haven't figured it out by now, I am banking on a lot of things occurring when you start talking. You are not a dog that I feel compelled to train via classical conditioning principles by rewarding positive behavior with a treat. You are my little, baby human. I think I can wait another year to verbally explain to you that you don't need to be scared at night because I am in the room next door. I can tell you that biting hurts which is why I don't want you to do it. I can teach you that falling can hurt a baby rather than let you learn via experience. Some people might think that this parenting viewpoint is ridiculous; I however don't care because I think it is right for you. And with each passing day, I am more and more convinced that I know what you need.

I have told you a lot about what has been going on in your life this week, but I also wanted to tell you about what a positive impact you have had on me this week.

Seeing you every night literally calms and inspires me. I must tell you thirty times a day that I love you, but I sometimes feel that the English language doesn't have the "right" words to really help me convey how I feel. I feel more than love. I feel appreciation. I feel peace. I feel satisfaction. I feel confidence. I feel clarity. And, I feel inspiration. If you take all of these feelings and added love to the mix – you would have how I feel about you. Maybe we just need to make up a word so that I can more accurately describe to you how I feel because the word "love" just doesn't suffice.

Now that I think of it; you might understand exactly how I feel. I know that I wrote earlier that I think your attaining language fluency will help me communicate better with you. It wasn't until just this moment that I realized your language attainment could actually be a burden to our communication. Coming into your room and cradling you in my arms when you are crying is so much more powerful than simply saying "I love you." Maybe the real challenge for me as a dad will be making sure that you know how I feel about you when you learn how to speak. I don't think that words would ever be able to make you understand how I feel about you as much as my actions toward you. Right now, to borrow an expression from your mother, I am "your whole world." As I write this, I am anxiously convincing myself that this is going to be the easiest time to communicate my feelings to you. Your lack of verbal fluency and your inability to care for yourself, forces me to attentively cater to you and your needs and very intentionally express my feelings toward you. I think I should make a mental note to always concentrate on making you "feel" my love as words will never suffice.

You will have to bear with me as I actually got kind of sidetracked during that last paragraph although I believe it might be one of the more important epiphanies of my life. Sometimes I get wrapped up in my own mind which doesn't always function in a very linear manner.

What I had originally intended on telling you was how you helped me with a problem I was having at work. Holding you at night helps me interpret the events of my day with great clarity. Anger and frustration – emotions that can cloud judgment – just don't exist when I am holding you. Each night as I revisit the different issues I am facing, I try to think about how I would explain my day to you, a little baby. Would I be proud to share my thoughts and actions to the person whose love I want most? Other times, I try to think about what I would tell you if you were asking my opinion on how to handle situations you were facing? Would I tell you that you should confront your friend in order to not show weakness on a play date? If not, why do I get to play by a different set of rules?

Of course there are some things that are appropriate for adults that are not appropriate for little babies such as you, but I think this rational can be a convenient crutch in many cases. The situations that adults face are different than those of children, but the principles of being fair, nice, kind, empathetic, etc… are always going to be the same. Maybe adults just make their own lives too complicated under the guise of sophistication.

Dear Zoe || Love Dad

The bible has a passage about the importance of teaching your children the right things to do. Never has this passage made as much sense to me as it does now that I am a dad. I think what makes me come to better conclusions with regards to the handling of various situations at work is that by trying to pretend that you are coming to me for advice, I am able to tap into my "ideal" self. I feel a great sense of responsibility for helping you become a happy, caring person. I believe in God and I believe in heaven. I want to raise a child in God's image using His son Jesus as a guide. There are many people who believe different things about God and heaven, but I think that all parents have some sense of wanting their children to be better than they are. Channeling my issues through you helps me find a "better" me.

Dear Zoe – July, 6

There are very few noises that are capable of waking me up as I am a very deep sleeper. Fortunately for you, one of these sounds is your crying. When I rushed into your room last night, your mom was standing over your crib as you just cried and cried. I could tell your mom was very conflicted because she of course wanted to pick you up and comfort you, but she also desperately wants you to get back on your old schedule that had you sleeping through the night. Before I was able to do anything, she told me "Do not pick her up" in what she used to call her "mean teacher voice."

See, my picking you up would mean that letting you cry for the last ten minutes was completely in vain. Your mom was already sad as your tears bring nothing but pain and anguish to your two parents who love you so much.

I was however pleased when your mom let me reach into the crib and pat you on the back. You calmed down immediately for me. Like I always tell you, I try to treasure these moments when a simple embrace from me cures all your problems. I unfortunately know that you will face problems in your life that I can't quickly solve.

I stopped rubbing your back at your mom's request. There was no way I was leaving however until I knew that you were back asleep and at peace. I continued leaning over the crib with my right arm dangling over the wooden rail. Something very funny was about to happen. You once again began to stir and quickly rose to your feet. You weren't crying however. I looked down only to see your head resting against my arm as you continued to suck your thumb. Your eyes were closed and you were as calm as could be. You had actually fallen asleep while standing up and resting your head against my arm.

Dear Zoe || Love Dad

It was the cutest and most precious thing that I had ever seen. Even though I am usually exhausted, you make waking up in the middle night very rewarding. I may be physically tired, but I will never tire of your showing of affection.

I just love you so much.

Oh, one more thing. Don't worry; I am never going to allow the "cry it out" method regardless of how many people tell me it is the answer. How could I ever let you be upset when all you want is to hug me or your mom? I am just going to enjoy these days because I know they won't last forever.

Dear Zoe – July, 15

We have had a very tough couple of weeks; every night you are waking up between 3 to 10 times. Everyone in the house, you, me, and your mom, is exhausted. I feel an enormous amount of pressure mounting as I am the only person who still feels very strongly about not letting you cry yourself to sleep. Family members, co-workers, doctors, nurses, and everyone in between tells me that you should be crying yourself to sleep so that you learn to go to bed on your own. My resolve is still unwavering. There is simply something inside me that tells me that I am doing what is best for you by getting up and consoling you. Our relationship has led me to believe that only your mom or I can know what is best for you because there is no way that someone else can love you as much as we do. It is this love that gives me the confidence I need.

You are almost a year old, and I have noticed such a big change in me over that time. Today, I don't lack any confidence about my abilities as a parent. Never would I have imagined my disagreeing with your mom about what is best for you, but there are now times that I do. (Just so you know, she wants only what is best for you too. We just sometimes have a different opinion which is a good thing because it challenges each of us to figure out what really is best for you.) See, you make me feel like I am the best parent in the world when you hug me or rest your head on me. When you smile and laugh, I just feel the bond that we have. Without these reassuring acts, I wouldn't be the parent I am today.

You and I are a team, and I know that we will get through this sleeping issue together. It is definitely going to be hard, but you have always been a fighter. You began life having to latch onto your mom's tummy which you did during the implantation step of IVF. You were then born earlier than expected and had to go to the NICU to learn to breathe and eat on your own. There is nothing that you have not been able to do, and I know you will overcome this challenge as well. As always, I will be by your side.

Dear Zoe || Love Dad

The only reason I would change my stance is if someone told me that you would be better off if we tried a new "method" at night. If I have to go to work exhausted every day to make sure you know that I will always be there for you, then I will. I see being a parent as doing what is best for your child or children, not what is easiest. Getting up is very tough on me at times, but if it helps you get a better night sleep then I will continue to do it. If letting your cry for a few minutes will help you learn to put yourself to sleep which will be better for you, then I will consider it. I just refuse to allow you to be upset to make my life easier. I didn't ever pray to God for a baby who slept through the night. I prayed for a baby, and I will be thankful for all that having a baby entails for the rest of my life. You are strong and so am I.

Now, we do need to talk about your biting. Do you know that it hurts a lot to be bit by you? With eight teeth and the jaw strength of a Rottweiler, you have done some serious damage to me since I last wrote you. My left arm has red marks and dark bruises all over it. Your biting has gotten to be such a habit that you actually bit me twice over the last three days when you were asleep!! I was holding you up to my chest as I always do when I am putting you to bed when I suddenly felt the searing pain that can only mean that I have become a victim of a sweet little girl who just loves to bite anything and ANYONE.

Unlikely your sleeping troubles, this behavior is something that needs to be addressed even if it leads to your crying. I need to help you understand that this behavior is not acceptable. What I have been doing is putting you in your playpen for 30 seconds and calmly telling you "No biting." Someone told me that I need to use a stern voice, but I am not going to use a stern voice with my precious little baby. I am not mad at or frustrated with you, I simply need to teach you better ways to communicate. (However, this method certainly gets your mom and my attention. Your mom is so scared of experiencing the sharp pain that follows a bite that she gets "jumpy" every time you come close to her. She is literally scared of you every time you pull up on the couch because her legs are potential targets.) It is hard watching you cry, but the short duration makes it at least palatable.

Dear Zoe – July, 24

We did it. I am so proud of you. To be honest, I am really proud of myself as well. You have had such a great week of sleeping. Many nights you go to bed and don't wake up until the morning. Other nights, you may choose to get up once, but you always go right back to sleep with a few reassuring pats from your dad.

Dear Zoe || Love Dad

I am so happy that I did what I thought was best for you; there is definitely a lesson here for you. You should always believe in yourself. You are a very special little girl who I am sure will grow up to be an exceptional woman. Life is sometimes not as complicated as people will try to make it. There are probably hundreds of books and thousands of articles written about "getting your baby to sleep," but I just didn't think the issue was too complicated. You cried because you missed being around your mom or dad – a totally normal response in my opinion given the fact that you literally rely on the two of us for ALL of your needs. I would cry too if I was in your little crib by myself. I am so glad that I trusted myself and my own ability to understand the situation rather than immediately defer to "experts." You are my baby, and no one cares as much about you as your mom and I.

I haven't mentioned it in a while, but we still have "simpatico." There is a special bond between us that I know will never go away. You also have special bonds with your mom and you're Nana, but our relationship will always be different which makes me so happy. (I didn't say "better" because if I did your mom and Nana would be very mad at me. I just said different.) I just knew in my heart that you were going to start sleeping better if I worked with you and talked to you. You would start sleeping better if I was able to show you somehow that I would always be in the next room waiting to come to your aid. There have been many accomplishments in my life athletically, academically, and professionally, but few if any have made me as proud of my work in getting you back on a sleep schedule that works for you and us.

Moving to a new subject, I am actually on an airplane right now. Unfortunately, I am going to miss your first birthday due to a conference for work. Because you are still a little baby, I don't think you will notice that we are celebrating your birthday a few days late. Don't worry I won't keep letting this happen throughout your life. You are way more important to me than any work engagement.

It has been such an amazing year. There is no way that I could have imagined how my life would have changed with your arrival. My world has changed so dramatically that I feel like a newborn in some odd way. My understanding of the world has been radically altered due to the new perspective you have forced upon me. My heart is filled with so much love that I see my role on this earth as being one of helping others not simply myself. Success will never again be measured by money or professional goals – success will be measured on whether I am a dad you can be proud of.

The year has gone by fast, but it has also gone by slow. Of course it is sad when I look back at pictures of you when you were first born knowing that I will never

Dear Zoe || Love Dad

be able to hold your little 6lb body again. You have grown up fast. The only thing that makes my feelings of nostalgia better is the fact that I know I have cherished every single moment with you. I loved going to all your appointments when you were in your mom's tummy. I was so thrilled the day that the nurses took out your NG tube so that I could just gaze at your beautiful, unencumbered face. And I have so many fond memories of our night time routine. I really tried to appreciate all the special moments that we shared as I knew they would be fleeting. Writing to you has also been a wonderful experience as it was yet another way for me to connect with you.

With my leaving for a conference, your mom let me break our rule of "not holding you when you nap." I just sat there snuggling with you like we have always done. You would occasionally wake up, look at me, and then plop your head back down again after verifying that I was still there. I hope you know that I will always be "right there" for you and I hope you always feel comforted by my presence.

As I was reflecting on this last year, I couldn't help but think about how you came into this world. It was very shocking getting a call from your mom saying that she was going to have you even though you weren't due for five more weeks. At the time, I was very nervous because I wanted to make sure that both you and your mom would be okay. Now that a year has passed, I am so glad that you came early. The way I look at it now is that I just happened to be given 5 extra weeks with you. I actually thanked God for bringing you to me early because you mean so much to me.

I love you so much little girl. I am going to miss you while I am at my conference, but I know you will be having fun with your mom and Nana.

Dear Zoe – July, 24 (Part II)

I didn't realize that I would be writing to you again tonight, but I also wasn't expecting to receive the call I just got from your mom. I received some sad news as your mommy's cousin just had a baby who died suddenly after only one day. Being a parent, I just don't know how one handles a situation like this. Your dad is really sad right now. I loved you since the moment the nurse walked you into the "implantation" room carrying you in the little metal box. My love just grew and grew so that by the time you were born, I was more in love with you than with anyone who has ever walked this earth.

I think you know how much I love you and how lucky I feel to be your dad. Hearing news like this however can't help but make me be even more thankful that God blessed me with you. There were so many obstacles that you had to handle, and you have always been so strong.

I think what is making this situation so hard for me is that we found out yesterday that the little baby needed to go to the NICU just like you did because she was having trouble breathing. The whole situation has just hit very close to home. I had always been concerned about your health, but deep in my heart, I knew things would be okay. I bet most parents feel this way. I don't want to write anything to make you scared, but I am just really emotional right now. I wish I were home with you instead of on this plan headed to Phoenix, AZ. Know that I am thinking about you and wishing I could give you a big hug.

I know that the little baby has just decided to go back to heaven to be with God, but it is still sad.

Even though I haven't written to you about the other little baby that was implanted in your mom along side you, I still do think about this baby that God wanted to come back to heaven. I love this baby and I know that he/she will always look after you, your mom, and I. Hopefully tonight, she will look after your mom's cousin's little baby too.

I love you sweetie, and I thank God every day that He allowed you to come down from heaven to be my baby.

Reflections on Year 1: Dear Zoe – September, 1

You might be wondering why I haven't written to you in such a long time. The answer is quite simple – I didn't want to write this entry. I told myself that at some point, I would need to stop writing this book to you. I never want my words to be more of a burden to you than a source of happiness. There will be a time when you should capture your life from your and not my perspective.

The date of my final entry continued to be pushed back. At first, I thought that I would stop when we found out whether you decided to come down from heaven to be in your mom's tummy or go back to join God and all the other angels. Then, I thought that I would stop when you were born. Your early arrival and NICU stay made me want to record these moments and the last entry was postponed again. Certainly, I would stop writing after we got you home. I would be too tired from the sleepless nights. Wouldn't I? The answer was clearly "No" as each day with you seemed worthy of commemorating. I finally decided that this book would end with your first birthday. It would be a milestone for you and for me. Your first birthday would represent the end to the absolute best year of my life.

Dear Zoe || Love Dad

What I hadn't understood when I first started writing to you was how this exercise would affect me. Taking the time to think and reflect on how radically my life was changing each day with you in it only enhanced the experience of being your dad. Writing became a way for me to get closer and closer to you even when you were not in my presence. Each entry provided an opportunity for me to comprehend how much I love you, how much I love your mom, and how much I love God. It has really been a transformative experience for me.

My hesitance over writing this last entry however is not simply due to my not wanting to give up these moments of emotional awakening and clarity. What has bothered me the most knows that you are growing up? At some point, you will understand this sentiment. I certainly could never understand the reticence parents had about the natural occurrence of aging. Only your arrival provided insight to what so many parents have expressed to me over my 34 years. Holding your 5 pound body in the NICU was scary and beautiful. It was a feeling I will never forget, but yet a feeling that I know I won't ever have again. I already wrote to you telling you how much I already miss certain things about your babyhood such as the special sound you used to make only for me. Preparing to write this entry, it made me so sad knowing that our nightly ritual of my rocking you to sleep after giving you a bottle is becoming a thing of the past.

I have done a very good job of cherishing every day with you. Going through IVF and then the NICU certainly helped me understand how lucky I am to have such a beautiful little baby. That being said, there is still a certain amount of sadness knowing that you are getting older. I don't look back on this first year with any regrets, but it still is hard to let go of these amazing times.

I of course know that our lives together are just beginning. New experiences, emotions, and memories await us, and I am anxious to experience the future. It is just really hard to see your baby grow up. There really is something special about a baby. With each passing day, you get closer to a time when your life won't be so simple. The days of wanting nothing more than attention from your mom and dad, a clean diaper, and a full stomach of milk will be over in the next few years. You will move onto school where I won't always be able to make sure that everything is okay. I have liked having the ability to shield you from the negativity that sometimes exists in this world, but I understand that those days are numbered.

Like I said, I am sure that you wouldn't really be able to understand what I am writing even if you could talk and understand language☺ You might have to wait until you are a parent of a one year old before you truly can understand what I am trying to say.

We have had an amazing year. I wanted to thank you for making my life more special and meaningful than I knew possible. You have changed my life forever. You brought clarity which led to a calmness I had not known. Even as I struggled at times with my OCD given the challenging combination of stress and exhaustion, I can honestly say that I have never been more at peace than I have this last year. Life is pretty simple when you have a baby girl. You realize that all people should be treated with love and respect. You realize that you would never want anyone to do anything to your child that could cause them to be upset and you therefore realize that you shouldn't do anything to anyone's "child" (which would include anyone who has ever walked this earth) that would make him or her upset. Life isn't amount competition or one-upping anyone. Life is about making everyone's life a little better, and I never understood this until I had you.

Life has been really great since you showed up. I have been really pleased with all the changes that have taken place in my life. It feels really good to try and live up to a standard that I believe you would be proud of. Whether it is at work or at home, I am inspired to be more than what I thought I could be. I have been freed from the shackles of "success" in the traditional sense because "success" has been redefined. Success is utilizing your talents for the greater good. I feel content and inspired for the first time in my adult life. My life isn't just about me; it is really about everyone else. And, living for others is much simpler and rewarding than a life spent chasing personal pleasure. I attribute this new belief to your birth; I only wish I could provide this mindset to you when you are still young.

I guess I am also lucky that God has enabled me to embrace being a parent in the way I have. It is probably a myopic, selfish thought, but I sometimes wonder whether becoming a parent has just had a more profound impact on me than many others. If the answer is yes, then I wonder why?

After becoming your dad, I struggle to understand how the world has so many problems. Your birth immediately made me a kinder, gentler person. Holding a little baby just fundamentally changes you. It is almost like making scrambled eggs; the eggs literally change in form never to return to their former shape or consistency. There is no way that I could erase my new outlook on life nor would I want to. I'm just lucky, I guess.

Your being so special certainly enabled this change. When I look at you, I literally have a visceral reaction. I can feel pure love coursing through my veins.

Dear Zoe || Love Dad

It makes me enormously proud to be your dad. It also makes me proud that I am able to love you as much as I do. The last sentence probably sounds a little ridiculous, but I do mean it. Loving you and being a good dad to you (on the days when I really excel) makes me more proud than anything I have ever accomplished. I wanted to let you know this because there are many things that I have accomplished athletically, academically, and professionally. Maybe some day you will be stressed out preparing to take your SAT's and you will remember this paragraph. You will know that I graduated from Harvard with honors, but this accomplishment pales in comparison to helping you sleep through the night. I already hate all the "pressure" that is cast upon babies let alone kids. When I hear parents bragging about talking, walking, eating, potty training, etc…, it saddens me. Why can't we just relax and appreciate people for who they are; why is there a need for competition. You should know that I will always be proud of you because you a true blessing.

Given how blessed I feel to be your dad, I couldn't simply let go of the question of "Why had I changed so much? What made my becoming a parent different than others'?" What I realize is that my change was enabled by many things and most importantly many people. Growing up with two parents who always loved and protected me taught me how important the role of a parent is. Observing a loving mother for the first 34 years of my life taught me what a dedicated parent looks like. Having a father who believes in me and my abilities eventually led to my believing in myself. Earning a good income allowed me to worry about being a great dad rather than on finding the money to meet this month's mortgage. Sharing your care with your Nana who does nothing but love you has given me the only rest I have needed. And finally, marrying a woman who is filled with love, strength, kindness and compassion gave me the perfect partner in raising a child. To these people, I will be forever indebted.

I may be preparing to stop writing to you with such frequency, but I will never stop loving and spending time with you. Given that you can't read, there will be no perceptible change to your life. We will continue to develop our bond. There will be new games and adventures that will enhance our relationship. I have already told you that I am committed to always being close to you, and I continue to stand behind this assertion. You are my number one priority and no birthday will be able to change that.

I have probably written long enough about how challenging it has been for me to actually commit to writing this last entry. It is now time to talk about something exciting – your birthday.

I promise that I won't make this a habit, but I actually had to be out of town for work on the actual day of your birthday. Because you are still so young, I knew that you wouldn't be any more upset that I was gone on your birthday than you would be with my simply being gone. It was definitely harder on me than it was on you. I was so excited on your birthday that I couldn't even sleep through the night. I was acting like you when you were a newborn.

It was an important milestone. Given all you had gone through, it was a day for me to really thank God for blessing me with such a beautiful wife and such a healthy baby. Being alone gave me plenty of time to miss you and reflect on how special you are to me. Of course, thinking about what you mean to me is already a daily occurrence, but I was extra pensive on this day.

We talked on the phone as soon as I was sure you would be awake. One thing that I have definitely learned during this first year is that you don't ever want to wake a sleeping baby. Waking a sleeping baby when you aren't available to help get that baby back to bed would be even worse because then you would have an upset baby and a REALLY upset mommy.

I wished you a happy birthday and told you that I loved you, but you didn't seem too interested according to your mom. One thing that I love about you is that you already have high expectations for how you should be treated. You are also extremely loyal to those who treat you well. Each time that I go away for a work trip, you ignore me for some period of time upon my return. I try to explain that I have to go away so that I can afford to buy the house, clothes, and food that you and mommy need, but you just can't understand this rationale at this point in your life. You just seem to think that I left you for no good reason. I hate any moment when you don't seem interested in me. It just breaks my heart. Your love for me is the most important love that I could ever want and any expression of love for me from you radically changes my mood. Everything seems a little better after a hug or kiss from my sweet baby. I will say however that as hard as these times are for me, I am proud of you for already having such lofty standards. Part of the reason I believe that you are so close with your mom is that she never leaves your side. You can always count on her to love and care for you. Unlike your dad, she doesn't leave for work every day or go on long trips. You appreciate this about her, and I want you to know that I appreciate that about her as well.

Maybe this is a good time to talk about your mom for a little bit. Because this is the last entry, I want to make sure that I write a few things about her so that you will be able to look back at this book and understand how much she has always loved you. I believe that I have done a good job of detailing her strength and courage through the many entries about the IVF and birthing process. She showed strength that only a mother could have during these physically demanding times.

Dear Zoe || Love Dad

It was very clear to me from the first week that I met her that she would some day be a tremendous mom. She had and has all the qualities that a mom should possess. She is loving, caring, strong, funny, playful, firm, and kind. Through out your life I will surely give you many presents, but the greatest thing I will ever have done from you is picking out the best mom in the world.

I have tried to include all the wonderful things that your mom does for you throughout the book. I know however that I have certainly failed as fully detailing her contributions would have added a thousand pages to this already growing tome. Even if I never wrote a word about her, I know that you will always appreciate what she has and will do for you. The way you look at her or call her name is so precious. Being a parent can be difficult both physically and emotionally; being a mom is even harder. See, your mom really is the captain of the family. She is your primary care taker and the one who ensures you are getting everything you want and need. My ability to be a good dad is very much predicated on having a tremendous partner in your mom.

I have definitely grown during this last year. It seems like a very long time ago that I was standing outside waiting for your mom to come home after she had left us together for the first time. My abilities have increased through repetition and my confidence has grown through the overcoming of obstacles and the sheer repetition of many acts such as changing your diaper. Never was there a better example of my confidence than my refusal to let anyone convince me that that you should simply "cry it out." There are still times however when my nerves, my anxiety, or my OCD simply get the best of me. The weight of trying to be the best dad I can be to you becomes too much. It is in these times that I lean on your mom for support the same way you will lean on her throughout your life. These moments of personal self-doubt or weakness are definitely few and far between, but knowing that your mom is always there for me and you is a tremendous luxury that I never take for granted.

She never gets an hour off let alone a day off. Her role is to ALWAYS be your number one provider. It is an awesome responsibility and one that she has embraced with every fiber of her being.

Knowing that being the best father than I can be is more important to me than anything I have or ever will do, I feel so blessed to have your mom helping and inspiring me on this journey. The pages of this book focus on my thoughts and my feelings towards you and our bond. What I don't often say is that your mom, my wife, has played a critical role in making me the father that I am. Rocking you to sleep with tears in my eyes would not have been possible without your mom's support. My confidence in her abilities allowed me to think not strictly of

Dear Zoe || Love Dad

the mundane – please God let my baby fall asleep. I knew that I would never be alone, and I therefore had the chance to really contemplate the meaning of being a parent, a luxury not always possible for other parents. Your mom took care of all the hard, thankless elements of being a parent to a newborn. She made sure you were fed, clothed, rested, etc.... leaving me with ample time to really focus on the emotional elements of parenting. When you would see me cry, there were tears of joy. When you saw your mom cry, they were often tears borne out of anxiety and exhaustion.

I know there will be many disagreements between you and your mom as you get older. What I want to tell you now is that you should always trust that any decision she makes, she will be making because she loves you and wants the best for you.

[I had just written about how I was not sure why being a parent had such a profound impact on me while not necessarily having the same effect on others. It just struck me when I was writing the paragraph above. I had the support system to focus on the meaning of being a parent. I have a great job, a new house, a beautiful wife, and loving family and friends. When I look at you, I don't worry about how I am going to feed you. When I look at you, I don't worry about future medical expenses. Instead, I see a father and daughter playing catch, riding bikes, and other enjoyable yet clichéd activities.

Maybe this realization will inspire me to start giving more money or time to charity. I can think of no better gift than to give other parents the feeling of pure joy that comes from helping your child. I know that I have been lucky, but even I have been underestimating just how fortunate I really am. Hopefully, you will always appreciate what you have while trying to make the plight of others just a little bit better.]

If you can't tell, I love your mom very, very much. Now, I can get back to you.

With my work trip finished, I headed to TX where you and your mom had flown to celebrate your birthday. Your mom really wanted the opportunity to see her family and to share you with all the people in her life that mean so much to her. I was so excited to see you. You on the other hand seemed slightly annoyed that I had been gone for the four days. Your mom and Nana seemed to get all your love and attention. They deserved it as they both have always done such a great job of caring for you, but I think I deserve a little too. Like I said, you are fiercely loyal to those who do the best job of showing you love and attention, and I had certainly failed by going away for nearly a week.

Dear Zoe || Love Dad

You have such an amazing ability to bring joy to anyone in your presence. For the entire week of our stay, the house was always buzzing with people wanting to come and see you. Regardless of whether they were a young child or an elderly adult, everyone just smiles when they see any one of your cute expressions. (This impact you have on people has led to one of my favorite yet silly games. Often, I tell you how much I love you, but the love for you goes beyond just your parents and family. Many times over the last couple of months I have told you things such as "Daddy loves, Mommy loves you, Canadians love you, dog-owners love you, mail carriers love you, etc… With the many people you meet gushing about you, I figured that you should know.) You adore the attention because you are your mother's daughter, a true sycophant. I get exhausted with all the people in and out of the house. Some times I just want to spend some time with my daughter without having a crowd clamoring for your attention and affection. I shouldn't be so selfish, but I am the one after all who paid for you☺ (Another one of my favorite sayings when I am explaining to your mom why you and I have a special bond.)

On the day of your party, your mom went to pick up your cake. I walked in the door and saw the most magnificent cake. It was huge. It was ridiculous. And, it was the greatest cake I had ever seen. Your mom had decided to have your whole party have a color scheme that would match your birthday outfit. The colors of aqua, hot pink, and zebra (not a color, but you will understand later) made for a wild yet great looking cake. I had been somewhat hesitant to spend $140 on a cake for a one year old birthday party, but once I saw it, I couldn't think of a better way to spend $140 (outside of charity of course). What made the cake even more special was that the woman who made your cake had also made your mom's first birthday cake. Your mom said that your cake was much nicer than hers had been. I sarcastically said, "Well, she has had thirty years to practice. I sure hope it is nicer."

I tried to sneak a nap before the guests arrived. I knew the party was going to be big because everyone in your mom's hometown seems to claim some type of kinship to your mom and Nana. My wish was for a small intimate crowd. I wanted those closest to you to have ample time playing with you and enjoying your company. By the time the last guest had arrived, there were 47 people at your Nana's house. You don't even talk, and your birthday was bigger than any party I had ever had by a multiple of at least three. You should feel very lucky that nearly 50 people wanted to come and wish you well on this special day. Even though this large number was not what I would have wanted, I was very glad to see the huge smiles on the faces of both your mom and your Nana. They loved every single second and they deserved all the well wishes after the trials and tribulations they had been through from IVF to the NICU to now.

Dear Zoe || Love Dad

I am sure that I would have been able to remember this party for the rest of my life, but a certain incident absolutely guaranteed that I wouldn't forget. It happened as you were opening presents. It is still hard for me to believe this really happened. I was sitting on the ground with you, your mom, and your two young cousins, Michael and Evan. You were helping your mom open the presents one by one. Near the end of this somewhat embarrassing opening spree (you had 30 or so presents), your mom began helping you with one of your final presents. She pulled out a cute dress from the pretty bag, a bag that was still garnering your attention as your mom showed the guests the outfit. As she held the dress in the air showing the rest of the guests, Michael said, "Scorpion. Scorpion." Knowing that 90% of your clothing has some sort of animal, flower, or insect, his comment didn't seem terribly important. My assumption was that he wanted us to see the embroidered scorpion on your dress. Your mom continued showing the dress, you continued playing with the bag, and Michael continued to say, "Scorpion." His voice inflection had however changed which made me think twice. I took a closer look at this beautiful dress only to see an actual SCORPION. I was terrified.

I think that I am a pretty good dad, but I have never thought I would be good at doing some of the "manly" things that dad's are supposed to do. I have already told you that I have grave concerns about my ability to assemble a bike for you when you are older let alone something such as a play house. One other area where I have always known I would be lacking is in protecting you from insects, rodents, snakes, and other animals. When I woke up that morning knowing we were having your party, I never imagined that I would be tested by the presence of a potentially lethal insect. Overcome with love for you and your mom, I reacted quickly and without hesitation. I grabbed the dress from your mom which was serving as the temporary playground for the scorpion and swiftly yet calmly walked the dress and the scorpion outside. Fortunately, we all escaped without being stung. I triumphantly walked back into the house proclaiming to your mother that I had saved her and your life. She was both thankful and annoyed knowing that this would be far from my last proclamation. All kidding aside, it did make me feel proud knowing that my love for you and your mom is so strong that it could help me overcome my fears. I always write to you that I would do anything for you; I am glad I passed the first test.

After a great birthday week in Texas, it was time to go back to our house and begin year 2. Your mom was very nervous about our trip home because it was going to be an extremely long day. We would be leaving Texas at 10:00 in the morning, but we would not be reaching our house until nearly midnight.

The day certainly started out inauspiciously. By the time we finished checking our baggage at the airport, we learned that our first flight had been delayed. I knew that it was going to be really hard on your mom, your Nana, and Daddy Mac to say goodbye. My only hope was that we could make this farewell swift in order to potentially dull some of the pain. The flight delay meant that our goodbye would now be lasting an additional hour. My fears were realized as everyone except for you and I sat staring at each other on the verge of tears for the entire delay.

Finally, we were able to board the plane and start the voyage home to our new house. It was the first time that I had flown with you since you were a little baby. You are so big and energetic now that it quickly became apparent to me that this was going to be a very long day. You were in constant motion; you would jump from my lap to your mom's lap constantly. When you weren't hopping between the two of us, you were standing up looking at anyone and everyone on that aircraft. You just love people – a trait you picked up from your mom, not me. Fortunately, everyone around us was excited to try and entertain you. You are so cute and have such a wonderful personality that everyone just likes to be nice to you. I already knew that you could "light up" a room with your smile and laugh; now, I know that you can "light up" an entire plane as well. You are only one, but it is already very clear that you are always going to bring so much happiness to those around you. Your mom is the same way. There is just something very special about the two of you. You each have the ability to bring out the best in other people with your kind, genuine demeanor.

We landed in Dallas and had to rush to our next flight. There was no time to waste as the hour delay had eaten away any cushion in our schedule. We were still 12 hours from our final destination, and I was exhausted. You were wearing me out. The exhaustion was welcomed however as I had missed you so much over the last two weeks. With your mom and Nana getting so much of your love and attention over the last couple of weeks, it was great to have so much father/daughter bonding.

You were just exhausted by the time we arrived in Chicago. The lack of space to roam combined with your not taking a nap had caught up to you. It was so sad as you just cried and screamed when we tried to get something to eat in the Chicago airport. We still had another flight to take. There was nothing that your mom and I could do except hold, hug, and love you. Your exhaustion was only matched by ours. The three of us looked as if we had been travelling for weeks not hours. Your mom had been right to fear this long day of travel. Due to our tired state, your mom and I were much more lax in our parenting than we would have normally been. When you wanted to crawl around on the dirty airport floor, we obliged not thinking there was any other way to keep you calm. Some experts say that exposing your children to germs is an effective way to build up their immune system (something that helps you fight infection and disease). If this is true, you might never get sick. You were licking and biting the dirty leather seats what had problem been unchanged in the last thirty years given their appearance. Who knows how many butts have rested on these faux leather seats? I couldn't believe I was letting you do this especially as someone who suffers from OCD.

We made it home and we didn't even try to put you to sleep in your own bed. The trip to Texas had completely eradicated all of the sleep training that I had done with you. Your mom and Nana had started sleeping in the same room as your crib in Texas, and you were more than happy to take advantage of this situation by waking up many, many times each night. It might not have been the right thing to put you in bed with us since we were back in our home and hoping to repeat your old schedule, but neither your mom nor I had the strength to stand at our bedside on this night. The three of us had a good night sleep, and it made me miss those early days when your bassinet was right next to our bed. It just felt perfect having my two girls, the two people I love the most, right by my side.

It was now time to start year two. It was definitely sad saying goodbye to year one as it had been so amazing, but I knew year two would be just as meaningful. If year one was about not only loving you but also about my adjusting to all the changes that came with being a first time parent, then maybe year two would be even more about you. Yeah, I will try to look at it this way.

My fear that the Texas trip had once again altered your sleep schedule was proved accurate as you continued to get up several times each night following this trip. Your mom always gets much more stressed about your sleeping than I. Her stress quickly turns into frustration and second guessing. We were only a few days into year two when she proclaimed that she should have been putting you to sleep when you were drowsy rather than letting you fall asleep in our arms. (She has made this assertion every month of your life; it always occurs when you have had a particularly challenging night.) I told her that she simply needed to give you time. I knew that you would return to your old ways; I just needed her to wait. Don't worry, I reaffirmed that letting you "cry it out" was still not an option.

I tried to explain to her the following. The trip to Texas had derailed your sleep schedule and it was going to take some time for you to re-adjust. I then told her that it was really important for you to go to Texas so that you could have a relationship with her family who loved and cared about you so very much. These next weeks might be tough, but the relationships you were building with her family made it completely worth it. She agreed and managed to calm down, at least a little.

Dear Zoe || Love Dad

I went on to explain that holding you while you went to sleep was the best part of my day. The night time ritual that you and I shared was always a very special time for me and I hope you. I didn't regret my holding you when you went to bed even if it meant my having to get up in the middle of the night. I am turning 35 in a month, and I had never experienced a situation as emotional and meaningful as any of the times I got to hold my baby and rock her to sleep. No way, would I have been willing to give those times up.

These two arguments worked and she has stopped worrying about your sleeping at night. The fact that you have once again started to sleep through the night hasn't hurt either☺

Now that you understand how much I love our night time ritual, you can probably have a least a little better understanding of how sad the following is to me. Your mom has banned me from giving you a bottle at your nighttime feeding. I thought that your turning one only meant that you were going to have a party and everyone was going to celebrate your life. I was already sad knowing that you were hitting a milestone, but I didn't realize that your one year check up would come with various recommendations on how to parent. Apparently, you need to stop using a bottle around your first birthday. I tried my best to preserve your night time bottle, but there was nothing I could do. Your mom's mind was made up. I even went so far as to bring up the fact that you were really only 11 months old due to your being born prematurely, but she was resolute in her beliefs.

Not giving you your bottle was very distressing to me. This was our special time. It was sacred. For the first few nights after your mom's decision, I continued to bring your milk in a bottle and claim I "forgot." This trick only lasted a few days before your mom caught on to what I was doing.

Giving you your milk via a sippy cup just wasn't the same. You weren't relaxed, and you didn't fall asleep in my arms. After only a few sips, you squirmed and fought. You simply would not go to sleep in my arms. I wasn't ready to change. I would literally go to work each day and wonder whether you would ever love me as much as you had during year one. There was just a black cloud over my head. It might sound silly, but you have to understand that your love for me means more to me than anything in the world. The thought of you loving me even the slightest bit less is completely devastating.

After a week of not being able to get you to sleep and having to call your mom in for re-enforcements, I decided I had to take a stand. I prayed to God and asked Him to help me put you to sleep on my own. I needed to know that our bond was still strong. That night, you once again fell asleep on my chest. My prayers had been answered. We had done it again. You did still love me. I went to work the next day completely content and rejuvenated which led to my have an extremely productive day. The black cloud had been lifted; everything just seemed a little brighter.

I hate to stop writing to you for so many different reasons. First, I always want you to have a record of how much I have always loved you. Regardless of what you grow up to do and "accomplish," I want you to know that you have already had a greater impact on my life than anyone I have ever known. Second, I think that someday you will want to know what you were like when you were "little." This book will hopefully provide a least a glimpse into these early days. Third, writing to you has really helped me process all the changes that are taking place in my life. Becoming a parent can be scary and overwhelming at times. Taking the time to write to you has really helped me make sense of all these changes and brought great comfort to me. Finally, I will miss all the feelings/ emotions that I experience with each journal entry. Writing to you allows me to feel the full range of emotions that God imbued within me. Never have I felt more alive than during this last year and through the exercise of writing I am able to truly embrace these emotions. It isn't always easy for me to express my feelings, but I never mind expressing feelings to you. I want you to truly understand me without pre-tense. Writing to you helps me understand not only who I am but also who I strive to be.

Although this is supposed to be my last entry (maybe I will just start book 2), please know that I will continue to love you every day for the rest of my life. The words and thoughts that had been recorded in this book will continue in my mind and in my heart. There is simply no possible way that I will ever stop loving you and caring for you.

Zoe, I love you. Thank you for fighting so hard to become my beautiful, healthy child. My hope for you is that you live a happy, fulfilling life. Your life will always have challenges, but please remember that you have been blessed with many things. What I have learned through becoming your dad is that the biggest and only real challenge each of us faces is how we can make the world and the lives of others better.

Bonus: Dear Zoe – December, 28

I have spent the last few months going through the many pages of this book trying to find all my spelling and grammatical errors. Editing a text would not be one of my favorite activities, but this exercise was quite different. Reading entry after entry, I was able to relive the greatest two years of my life. My decision to record my thoughts and feelings over this seminal time in my life was one of the best decisions that I have ever made. Not only will this book hopefully be something you will cherish, but it has also helped me become closer to your mom and the rest of my family. Each person who reads the book expresses how little they knew about what was going on in my head as I tried to be the best husband and father I could be. The book has definitely greased the wheels for my communicating with those whom I love and cherish the most. Once again, you are having a positive impact on my life and the lives of others.

Because I have an excuse to write to you one last time, you probably know that I am going to take it. The good news is that our relationship has continued to evolve and deepen every single day. Any fears that I once had that stopping my daily or weekly reflections would somehow create a distance between us were not warranted. There have been many times when I have been tempted to write so that I ensure that your latest development or behavior will live into perpetuity, but I have managed to fight off these urges. I had to balance my desire to record your life with letting you live your life. Ultimately, the recording of the past will never be as important as the possibilities of the future.

There have been many changes to your life and many interesting occurrences and I am therefore trying to cull them down into those which I think you will find most interesting later in life. I think I have a few.

First, your night time routine has definitely changed since I last wrote to you. You still get rocked to sleep, an activity which has become increasingly challenging given your size. The biggest difference is that it is now your mother and not I that does the rocking. You were sick for about a month (all of October) after coming home from one of your many trips to Texas. You just couldn't seem to get healthy as you had the roto virus, a cold, and finally croup. I desperately wanted to continue our nighttime routine, but there is no substitute for your mom when you are not feeling well. Giving up this special time was hard on me, but I knew that I would need to adapt. After all, I had managed to overcome giving up your nighttime bottle. What I decided to do was to bring you upstairs for about a half hour to hour right before your bath so that the two of us could just enjoy each other's company after our respective long days. This proved to be a great decision as the two of us have a lot of fun together playing, running, and laughing while your mom gets some well-deserved "alone time." Now, I smile and laugh every night rather than shed tears as I once had when I held your sleeping body in my arms.

Second, I think that I should tell you about your episode with croup. Thankfully, both your mom and I had croup when we were kids and we therefore did not fear this odd ailment which made you sound like a barking seal. You had been congested for days. You cough was frequent but loose, and it was exceptionally painful having to listen to you get worse and worse knowing that simply expelling this mucus would have made you feel so much better. In vain, I tried to teach you how to spit, but there was nothing I could do but hope and pray. Your cough started to change as the looseness was replaced by a distinctive barking sound. Your mom and I both knew the reality and we called the 24 hour nurse to get advice. She told us that we should take you into the bathroom and expose you to steam in order to keep your throat moist. We did as instructed. You looked so confused and upset when at 3:00 in the morning you were trying to sleep in the hot, steamy bathroom being temporarily inhabited by you, your mom, and your dad. The three of us stayed in that bathroom for an hour. By the time I turned on the lights in order for us to better be able to exit, all surfaces in the room had standing water from the extreme humidity.

You woke up early sounding worse than you had at 4:00 when we returned you to your crib. I called the doctor's office and attempted to schedule you an appointment. I explained the situation to the nurse who seemed reluctant to schedule an appointment when turned your dad back into the assertive, aggressive man I had been while you were in the NICU. When she said, "Please put the phone up to your daughter so that I can listen to her breathing." I simply said, "I can do better than that. You can listen to her in person as I am bringing her into the office right now. She is sick and she needs to see someone." I had been pleasant for the first ten minutes of the call, but I was not wasting any more time. The doctor hadn't even sat down on the stool to begin examining you when she said, "Your daughter has croup. I could hear it when I first walked into the room." My decision to demand an appointment had been vindicated and you started to feel immediately better as the doctor prescribed medicine. I tell you this story because I want to make sure that you know that even though I cry all the time now thinking about how much I love you; I still haven't gone soft☺

Thirdly, you made your television debut just last week on NBC! You know that I believe you are definitely worthy of national exposure, but this opportunity is not common in case you are wondering. The Today Show came to our hometown to film a segment about the company for which I work. The woman who is in charge of our PR department asked me whether I wanted to bring you and mom to the taping of the show. The show was about the Holiday season and was to feature the house built out of candy which resides at our company store. The timing was perfect as your Nana and Meme had already scheduled a trip to be at our house during the taping. Your Meme was so excited. She had told all of her friends about the appearance as soon as she learned about it. When the day of the taping finally arrived, your mom dressed you in one of your many cute outfits. You looked especially precious on this particular morning.

Dear Zoe || Love Dad

When the host, Sarah, and Santa arrived, my friend in PR made sure that you were right in the front row. You were ready for the spotlight. Sarah was wearing a very festive holiday outfit when she approached you with a big smile. She reached out and took you in her arms which led to your bursting into tears. The smile on Sarah's face turned into a sympathetic frown as it was clear she genuinely felt bad about causing your distress. Your mom immediately took you back from Sarah and told you everything would be okay. Your mom and I should have known better because Sarah was wearing a Santa hat, and you hate seeing people in hats. (Oddly enough, you don't mind people in masks as no one at Halloween scared you even as you were fighting off your episode of croup.) It took a few minutes, but you once again calmed down. Your fair skin bore the evidence of your crying as the skin under your eyes remained pink. Sarah's future attempts to interact with you resulted in more crying, and we left believing that your debut would have to wait. Last week, the show aired and you, your mom, Nana, and Meme made the final cut. The camera caught mostly the side of your face and the back of your head as you were seeking comfort in the arms of your mother. Nonetheless, you can definitely tell people that you were on the Today Show.

Finally, I wanted to tell you about your cousin Tia whom we just had the pleasure of meeting over the Christmas holiday. Many entries have detailed how much you have inspired me to be a better person. Loving you has allowed me to better understand how to love. Having spent the last two years as your dad (in utero and in the world), my capacity to care for not only you but for all people has grown tremendously. Never was this as evident as during Tia's visit.

My sister Amy lives very far away in a city clear across the country. The physical distance between us has certainly led to a certain amount of remoteness in our relationship. She left to go to college when I was still in middle school and she hasn't returned since. Over the years, we have continued to speak infrequently and our connection has continued to erode. I was therefore extremely pleased to note that our bond is as strong today as it has been in the last 25 years and you deserve much of the credit.

As you know, Amy and her husband David adopted a little girl named Tia from a country called Ethiopia. You and Tia are only two weeks apart in age, and I was so excited for the two of you to meet. I had not anticipated what transpired which I believe was ultimately a blessing in disguise.

Being 16 months, the two of you were more than happy to ignore each other on most occasions. Every once in a while you would interact briefly when YOU would steal her toys. Your assertive, dominant personality remains and I can't wait for my first call from your pre-school teacher in a few years.

Dear Zoe || Love Dad

I wanted to write to you about Tia not because of the interaction between the two of you however. I wanted to share how **I** was able to connect with Tia. No, I am not trying to toot my own horn, but rather I wanted to let you know how being your dad has helped me become a much better husband, son, brother, and uncle.

Tia is such a beautiful and affectionate little girl. I am not exactly sure why but she and I have a special connection that is very similar to the connection that you have with your Nana; it simply defies rational explanation. Whenever I would enter a room, Tia would walk over, stare at me with her dark brown eyes, and slowly extend her two arms skyward in an effort to get me to pick her up. Without fail, this routine occurred every single time the two of us were in the same room. Many explanations were offered by the various members of my family for why she took such a liking to me ranging from the fact that she prefers men to women to the suggestion that my rounded features and bald head make me look like a giant baby. I however have a different explanation. It might sound crazy, but I think she could tell I was a loving father who would know how to take care of her. She was able to see in me all the changes that I had made since you arrived. She knew that there was nothing I deem more important than caring about you and she knew she would be safe in my arms as well. I know this sounds crazy, but I think it is as plausible as the "big baby" argument espoused by others.

Tia was only able to stay for a few days because she became very sick. She was more congested than you have ever been and her deteriorating health became scarier and scarier. My sister was physically and mentally exhausted from having to care for Tia without the help of her husband who had to remain in Seattle. Tia had only slept for about 9 hours over a three day period and the wear and tear on both she and my sister was clearly evident.

My sister brought Tia into my room at around 5:00 a.m. on the third day of the visit and told me that your grandma, Neeny, thought that she should take Tia to the hospital. My sister's mind was clouded by the exhaustion of the trip and her concern for Tia. She said that she didn't think it was necessary, but I felt that she wanted my opinion. Never in my life did I picture this scenario. My older sister was seeking my counsel on her sick child. I looked at Tia and listened to her chest. It was clear to me that Tia needed to go to the hospital to be checked out. My sister agreed, and the three of us headed out into the early morning searching for a hospital in a city in which neither of us lived.

Even though Tia was sick and feeling crummy, she continued to love being held by me. I felt tremendously proud of myself. I was being a better brother and

Dear Zoe || Love Dad

uncle than I had ever been, and I know that it was all because of you. Tia was so comfortable with me that I had to tell all the doctors and nurses that I wasn't her dad but rather her uncle. (She doesn't exactly look like either my sister or I, which only added to the confusion for the staff☺) We were able to leave the hospital knowing that Tia had a virus which she was well on the way of beating. The doctors were able to rule out any serious problems which left all of us feeling much better, especially knowing that you had been potentially exposed.

Spending time with you and Tia made me realize just how lucky our family is to have the two of you in our lives. I saw in Tia what I often see in you, the miracle of your existence. I often look at you and picture the small metal box which contained your 8-cell body on the day of your implantation. Seeing your vivacious self now, I am humbled by God's decision to grant me a child through this spectacular process. (I personally believe that God would have no issues with IVF or any other fertility treatments. As the creator of man and all things, he provided the intellect that ultimately resulted in the fertility advancements that my wife and I were able to utilize.) I just heard today that the first IVF baby will turn 30 this year. I am so lucky that I happen to be living at a time and place in history where this amazing procedure was accessible.

When I would look at Tia, I am amazed at how she became my niece. Her beginnings were never far from my mind during our many interactions during this trip. In her big brown eyes, I could see the sadness that engulfs the people of Africa who live their lives in fear and poverty in way too many instances. Her default expression was much more reserved than yours, and I couldn't help but think of how much different her first months on this planet had been when compared to yours. It was only when you engaged with her that you saw the pure joy and happiness that should define the existence of all children. I am so thankful to Tia's birth mom and my sister and her family for facilitating Tia's journey to the U.S. where she will have many opportunities.

I think that I really am going to stop writing (at least this book) after this entry. You should know that I anxiously await each and every day that we spend together. I love you so much. Every day with you is the greatest blessing of my life.

I will love you always.

Dad

Dear Zoe || Love Dad

Part II: Reflections

Dear Zoe || Love Dad

Reflections: Introduction

I wrote this book for my daughter and for my wife so that they would know how deeply I love them. Communicating my feelings has always been somewhat easier for me in written rather than spoken word. Each entry expresses my thoughts, feelings, and emotions at that given time. There were some days when I was writing at Zoe's bedside in the NICU and others that I was writing on a plane 15,000 ft in the air. Some days I was scared and others I was overcome with joy. In re-reading some of my work, I realize that my voice often changes. When Zoe was not yet conceived, my image of my baby was more abstract and I wrote to him or her as a child angel who could easily understand the words and thoughts of an adult. The sight of my sweet little baby changed everything, and I wrote to MY baby who was now in front of me. I wrote and I wrote to help bring me closer to Zoe. I wanted her to know how much I loved her even when my words meant nothing and my gestures meant everything. Some days I wrote to Zoe knowing that one day she would be a teenager or adult and have only this book to understand and remember her first year. The inconsistencies can be understood as a father's attempt to relate to his daughter in the present and future. There were even some days that I wrote to better understand how I was feeling.

Months have passed since I first started writing, and I have begun to think that there might be value in making the book I have written to my daughter and wife available to couples who are considering the IVF process or couples who have had a child in the NICU. In the age of the internet, finding technical information about the IVF process is not hard. One too can learn about the NICU and its impact on parents and families. I however believe that there is a big difference between understanding IVF or the NICU and living and feeling the IVF process or the NICU.

I have been so blessed by God to have a beautiful healthy baby who was the product of IVF and who spent her first three weeks in the NICU that I wanted to share our story. I wanted to take other couples on the stressful journey in a way that only an autobiographical account can. This book does not necessarily contain the typical or normal range of emotions felt by a parent going through these processes, but rather it contains MY ACTUAL thoughts and feelings. It is my hope that my words bring comfort and hope.

Dear Zoe || Love Dad

Reflections on IVF: Round 1

Having had OCD my whole life, I was never very confident that I could handle the responsibilities and pressures that come with being a parent. There were times in my life that I was washing my hands hundreds of times a day because they "felt" unclean. For years, I have stayed as far away from blood as possible for fearing of catching some disease. With my level of OCD, how would I possibly be able to handle having a child? I continued thinking this way for most of my adult life, and it wasn't until I met my wife that I really had to stop and truly think about this issue. We hadn't been dating more than a week when she expressed that she would definitely want to be a mother. Considering that I thought I would marry her after our first date, I figured it was time to really think this parenthood thing through. I told my wife that I wanted to have kids too whenever the subject arose, but there was a difference in wanting kids and believing that I could really handle having kids. Months turned into years, and I wanted to propose. She was and is the love of my life, and I knew that she was who I would want to spend the rest of my life with. Was I really going to be okay with this whole being a parent thing? I knew that it wasn't fair to propose unless I was ready to have children with her. In thinking about this issue, I took solace in the statement that no one is ever ready to be a parent. In some weird way, this logic suggested that my lack of preparedness was actually a sign that I was ready.

Like I have already written, the issue was not whether I wanted kids because I did. The issue was my fear that I would not be able to handle the stress that comes with bringing a perfect, living being into an imperfect world. I thought about the issue for months, and it became clear to me that the woman I wanted to marry was strong enough to help me be the parent I wanted to be. My wife was born to be a mother just as her mother was born to be a mother and grandmother. I no longer focused on the stress associated with making sure I was fit to marry a woman who desperately wanted children to being thankful that this woman was going to help me be a parent, something I had always wanted.

I proposed not long after this realization, and the clock to parenthood started ticking. I knew that it would be at least a year after our marriage before we started trying because neither of us wanted to start a family until we were more secure financially. With my finishing business school, we decided to actually embrace the cliché of graduation day being the end of one chapter and the start of another.

[Because I am writing this section to couples contemplating IVF and/ or friends and family members who are trying to understand this process, I want to be very frank about my situation before I continue. As I said previously, I want to explain the side of IVF that is not strictly technical. I want to bring emotional insights, and it is not fair for me to bring this perspective without including some personal information about me. I embarked on this process as a 33 year old with two master's degrees, a high paying job, and no debt to my name. I was by no means rich, but I could pay for the procedure without assistance from a bank, friends, or family.

Also at the time of writing this section, you have realized that our going through IVF resulted in a beautiful baby. I mention these two facts because I can't help but believe that my recollections about the process are certainly influenced by my ability to pay for the procedure as well as by our success.]

My wife had decided that IVF was going to be the only way she could get pregnant long before we even met. After having an ovarian cyst and endometriosis in her early twenties, she was sure that getting pregnant would not be as easy for her as for other women. I don't think I realized how difficult this perspective was for her until we actually officially decided to do IVF. There had been a few times since we were married when someone said something to her about how easy it was for them to get pregnant. These comments offended her deeply because she carried the fear of infertility with her everyday. I could see how these comments were offensive, but I wasn't able to feel them in the same way as she did. It was only after we learned that I wasn't exactly a superstar in the fertility department either that I could begin to empathize with what she had been feeling all these years.

My wife and I will probably always disagree on how long we tried to get pregnant naturally. With her having been on the pill for so many years, I didn't really consider months 1-3 as trying because she wasn't even ovulating. I figured that ovulation was a pretty important part of this whole process☺ Nonetheless, month four of "trying" arrived, and she was ready to seek professional help. Well let me back up momentarily, she had already seen a doctor and made me give a sperm sample before we started trying to make sure that having a baby was even going to be possible.

I love my wife, and I know that she is not always the most rational. Part of the reason that I married her was because she relies much more on feelings that rational thoughts when it comes to making decisions. She scheduled an appointment with the doctor, and the process was underway. The OBGYN was not even able to open her mouth before my wife blurted out, "We are going to do IVF." I should have realized at the time that having a baby by whatever means necessary was my wife's ONLY objective. The years of worrying about what possible damage the endometriosis had caused to her uterus had warn

Dear Zoe || Love Dad

down her confidence in her getting pregnant naturally. I had a confidence problem too, but my issue was whether I would be a good father or not. I figured that taking our time in trying would at least help me ease into the idea of being a dad. She wanted to move fast, and I wanted to take things slow.

As I look back, I wish that I would have been more attuned to my wife's feelings. She was worried that she would never be able to have a baby and she had been worrying about this for quite some time. I think that I had severely underestimated how draining this worry had been on her. Having a baby was her main goal in life and each failed attempt was devastating to her. It might have only been three months, but each month only served to bolster her worst fears.

At the time, I thought that I was being tremendously supportive. I was at every appointment asking questions and helping plan a course of action. I also tried to make it clear that we WOULD have a baby by any means necessary. What I didn't realize was that calculating the probability of each course of action and then comparing its success rate to its cost was not what she needed. I was thinking like someone who had just graduated from business school and not like a future parent. I am surprised she didn't throw my computer out the window when I made a spreadsheet detailing which procedure resulted in the best bang for our buck. She needed emotion support not calculations.

She continued to press forward with the idea that IVF was the only option for us. My spreadsheet had not come to the same conclusion, but my love for her was strong enough that I was willing to lose this argument. We spoke to our OBGYN as well as the IVF specialist. In these meetings, my wife would hear what she wanted to hear and I would hear what I wanted to hear. It took awhile but I finally realized that there was no information that was going to make me believe that IVF was the right choice for us after trying naturally for only a few months. In turn, there was nothing that was going to convince my wife that we shouldn't do IVF.

I think that my thinking started to change when it was my turn to get retested by our new doctor in Pennsylvania. My sperm had already passed a test at our first appointment back in North Carolina, but our new doctor suggested that I have a more thorough exam. There wasn't any real room for me to argue given all of the things that my wife would be undertaking in the near future. My results came back, and they showed that not only did I have a low sperm count but I also had low quality sperm. I was scared. I had spent so much time worrying that I might not be able to handle being a father that I never even considered that I might not be able to even be a father. I never felt as if I was less of a man due to my "poor" sperm; my only worry was that I might never be able to have a child of my own. The more I thought about the situation the sadder I became.

Any fears of not being able to handle a child were temporarily pushed to the side. This news helped me realize how much I too wanted a child. With my wife wanting a child so bad, I don't think that I had ever spent the proper amount of time thinking about what I wanted. She had already made the decision about whether we were going to have children, and there was therefore nothing for me to consider except the actual raising of the child. I always jumped to the weeks after our child was born and my being nervous about whether he or she was breathing okay in the crib or whether he or she was safe from all the dangers that face children.

Now, I had to wonder whether I might never be able to have a child with my own DNA. The reframing of the situation allowed me to more fully realize that having a baby was something that I desperately wanted for myself as well as for my wife. We decided that I should get re-tested, and the time between the tests was very difficult for me. (The prostate exam was also a difficult time for me☺ When I consented to not only getting my sperm re-tested, but also submitting to a prostate exam, I knew how much I loved my wife and how badly I wanted a baby.) At first, I was simply upset by the idea that I might not be able to have a baby of my own, but I quickly began to think about my wife. She not only wanted to be a mom, but she also wanted to be pregnant. Many times I could remember her making it clear that she couldn't wait until she had a little child kicking away in her belly. With this new news, what would happen if I couldn't give her a baby? Would adoption be enough for her?

We never discussed what would happen if she couldn't get pregnant by me. At least, I don't remember if we did. It was hard knowing that I might have to make a decision to either adopt and therefore prevent my wife from both being pregnant and having her own child or to raise a baby whose father was an anonymous sperm donor. I kept these thoughts to myself. I tend to be fairly private by nature, and I didn't feel that there was anyone with whom I could really discuss this issue. As I waited for the second round of test results, I tried my best to face these fears on my own. Having OCD certainly didn't help as I was bombarded with unpleasant thoughts such as whether my wife would have ever wanted to marry me if she knew I couldn't have children. Or, what type of loving husband would prevent his wife from fulfilling her dream of having a child of her own if science could make it happen? I wasn't sure what was harder on me; knowing I might not be able to have a child of my own or knowing that I might not be able to give my wife the only gift she has ever truly wanted.

Fortunately, the second test showed that although my sperm count was low, it was better than originally thought. It might be a challenge for us to conceive naturally, but with a little help from doctors, I was going to be able to have a child who was my own flesh and blood. I remember having a difficult time after the burden of not knowing whether I would be able to father a child was temporarily lifted. My relief was accompanied by guilt. Did I feel that wanting to be able to have my "own" child meant that I would be closer to him or her than if I had adopted? Many couples who were going through this same process probably would end up adopting; did I somehow believe that their relationships would be less special? What if we still needed to adopt; IVF or any other treatment was certainly not guaranteed to work?

I am not sure whether all men and women struggling with fertility ask themselves these types of questions, or whether I was simply more affected by the process than most. It was hard to admit some of these questions to myself because I thought that a good father would never be concerned about such issues. There were definitely times when there was some incongruity between what I was feeling and what I thought I should be feeling.

I was realizing that my wife and I were beginning a long process that would be filled with great tension and anxiety. Each step along this process was probably going to be accompanied with a lot of soul searching. Any thoughts of having my wife surprise me with the news that she was pregnant one morning needed to be abandoned. This was not our reality. If we were going to be lucky enough to have a child, it was going to be the result of weeks of effort not one night.

I don't really remember ever making the decision to officially commit to doing IVF. I spent hours and hours thinking about what course of action would not only be best for us but more importantly best for my wife, but a truly defining moment fails to stand out in my memory. Once my wife and I started the journey, it seemed that there was a lot of inertia driving us to do IVF. Some of this invisible force was probably attributable to my wife who was making all the appointments with the various specialists. But, I do believe that the system kind of steered us in this direction as well. Once we started investigating fertility options, there always seemed to be another doctor who we should see for a consultation. The referring doctor must have put on our form that we were an IVF couple because many of these meetings began with the doctor assuming our decision was made. I still find it ridiculous that I, someone who researches all his decisions, can't remember making the biggest decision of my life, but it really is true.

When it was time for our first official appointment, it actually felt great to hand over the largest check that I had ever written. I am not being facetious either. I always find that it is easy to say what is important to you, but there is something affirming to actually doing something to prove it. I was proud that I could not only afford to pay this money, but also that I was also willing to spend this money for only a 40% chance of having a child. It wasn't logical what I was doing which only added to the specialness. My love for my wife and my hope for having a child allowed me to overcome my natural tendencies.

I didn't necessarily realize it at the time, but IVF was not only about my hope for a child but also about my love for my wife. There was only a 40% chance that this round of IVF would result in a healthy baby, but there was a 100% chance that my wife would know how committed I was to her and our future family. In my opinion, there is no greater gift that a husband can give his wife than a child that will always bind them together. It was always scary not knowing whether we were going to be able to conceive a child, but I took solace in having my wife know that I was 100% committed to the cause. The overly rational man she married was willing to take the leap of faith with her and pursue a child at whatever cost necessary.

[Walking through the hospital on the day of our first appointment was a very emotional experience. As a young twenty-something, I couldn't help but feel that I wasn't being paid enough at work. My late twenties brought feelings of sadness as I struggled to find a woman with whom I could really connect. Basically, I, like most people, have always found it very difficult to not compare myself to those who seemingly have it better than I. The last few months had once again been filled with some feelings of self-pity - why were so many people able to have babies without any assistance and yet we couldn't?

I don't remember any of the patients or visitors that I saw that first morning, but I do remember seeing many, many people whose lives certainly seemed more difficult than my own. Seeing the pain and sadness in many faces snapped me out of my feelings of self-pity. Of course going through IVF was going to be challenging, but my life had already been truly blessed. I said a prayer as I walked to the office thanking God for all that He had given me and asking for His help throughout this process.]

The deepening connection between my wife and me during the IVF process was definitely something that I had not originally expected. I mistakenly thought IVF was only about having a baby; the final outcome would be baby or no baby. I underestimated how the journey would impact me, my faith, and my marriage. It would always be about the baby, but it was also about much more.

For six straight weeks, I was consumed by the process. Each morning would begin with a very calm and emotional drive to the hospital to meet my wife who had already gone to secure her spot in the "first come first serve" line. Thinking about the gravity of the situation was simultaneously terrifying and uplifting. Fertility struggles had forced me to really think about what an amazing gift a child is. It was a great feeling to be so focused on the most worthwhile endeavor I could ever undertake. My life had more meaning than ever before.

The quiet drive each morning was filled a myriad of thoughts about life, love, marriage, religion, and many other things which I had too often pushed aside in favor of work deadlines and superficial desires. Often the radio needed to be turned off because I couldn't keep up with my many thoughts, listen to the radio, and drive at the same time. My mind raced from thoughts of why is having a baby so important to me to how would my marriage be impacted if we couldn't conceive as a couple. The thoughts were often not pleasant, but yet I wasn't scared. I was oddly at peace. Having OCD my whole life only made the tranquility that I was feeling that much more confusing. How could a situation that might result in deep sadness for me and my wife be causing me to feel this way?

[Reflecting on the situation over a year later has led me to believe that there were many things that were contributing to my happiness during this time. First, I was focused on something truly important. Sadly, this focus had often been missing as the daily minutiae of my life had often been elevated to a higher level of importance than was warranted. How important could any one PowerPoint presentation really be? My perspective had simply changed. Second, I was comforted by knowing that I needed God's help. There was nothing that I could do but pray and ask for His intercession. There had been many times in my life when I felt that I was alone and success rested solely on my shoulders. During IVF, I knew that only God could make a child and I couldn't succeed without His help. Third, I was completely attuned to my wife's feelings and emotions. I was being the husband that I wanted to be. Her needs were more important than my own, and I was proving it every day to her. Fourth, I was feeling emotions never felt previously. Essentially, I was living life to its fullest every single day by allowing myself to truly feel for the first time in a very long while.]

Once at the hospital, I would walk the halls looking at all the anonymous faces who were facing their own struggles. It was a very visceral experience for me. The hospital's harsh and sterile appearance only heightened my awareness of the pain in my midst. There was no way for me to ignore societal problems such as poverty, incurable disease, suffering, etc… when confronted by people embodying these issues. I would wonder why he was in a wheel chair. Who were they visiting? Did they have insurance? It was challenging to see any positives on this daily walk. It wasn't until weeks into our IVF journey that I realized something very special about the hospital. I finally realized that the hospital was one of the few places where humans were given permission to be themselves without fear of societal judgment. Emotions were on full display. Often, people simply did not have the energy to hide their anxieties, fears, and pain. The hospital also brought families together even if the circumstances were not the best.

By the time I reached the elevator, I would already be emotionally drained from the swirling thoughts in my head. Challenged by the realities of so many people in need, my worries and concerns were often put in a better perspective. My goal however was to make my wife my sole focus by the time I exited the elevator. I always tried to think about what she needed from me on this particular morning. Did she need me to be positive regardless of the news? Did she need me to ask a lot of questions to make sure that we were doing everything we could to have this child?

Entering the waiting room was almost always an uncomfortable experience. The room would be filled to capacity, but yet silence prevailed. I knew from my own experience that some days were tougher than others. I could only try to imagine what these other hopeful women were feeling as they tried to manage this emotional experience while being injected daily with rounds of hormones. As a husband and not a patient, I decided that I should just follow the norms established by these hopeful mothers.

Day after day, I sat in silence as I waited with my wife to be called back to her appointment. One thing that I clearly remember about these days was feeling a great sense of empathy or sympathy for these women. The experience was challenging for all. I did however think that it must have been harder for many of these women than it was for me. First, as I have already mentioned, my wife and I were in the fortunate position of being able to write an $8,400 check on the first morning. Second, we were going through our first round of IVF. We were not burdened with the doubts that inevitably haunt couples who have had failed attempts. Third, we were very close to the hospital having to drive only about fifteen minutes each morning. Fourth, I had a job that allowed my making each appointment so that my wife would not be going through this process alone. Looking around the room each morning, I knew that many if not all of these couples were not in the same situation. Without having a direct dialogue, I was forced to come to conclusions based only on what I saw. The sight of a woman's non-branded sneakers and modest clothing would lead me to believe that she was willing to sacrifice any and all money that she had for the chance to have a child. Women sitting alone would make me sad as I imagined the strain of having to handle the appointments alone. Did their husbands or significant others have employers who were not as understanding as mine; did they want to be here but simply couldn't? Maybe it was the setting or the state of my mind, but I really found myself trying to empathize and sympathize with these strangers. We all wanted the same thing so badly.

Dear Zoe || Love Dad

The first couple of appointments went very smoothly (outside of the incidents with appointment 1 which I detailed earlier) as I was still feeling the calm of having finally made the decision to move forward with the process. We knew that we would not be getting information from these appointments that would have the ability to derail our day. The questions we asked were very technical and straightforward. Does it matter whether we give this shot at the same time every day? How long do we leave the syringe in the skin before it is safe to pull out? There would be a time when the questions we asked would be about our probability of conceiving; these early days were not those days however. I tried very consciously to not look too far forward knowing that keeping myself as relaxed as possible would not only benefit me but also my wife whose stress level was already elevated.

Our daily routine of a shot and appointment in the morning followed by a shot at night began to feel very normal after only a few days. It was actually nice having dedicated times when I knew that my wife and I would be forced to slow down and connect. Between stresses at work and the digital invasion within our house, simply enjoying each other's company was not always on the agenda. Granted, giving her shots was not ideal, and I never got used to this element of the process. But, I will say that the process was intimate and helped strengthen our already solid bond. We were a team; we each had a role to play. With each successive shot, her stomach or butt became more and more tender. Finding virgin skin became harder as time went on. I found some solace however in really concentrating on becoming better and better at giving her these daily injections. I wanted to make them as painless as possible, and I tried to harness my competitive nature to make each subsequent shot less noticeable than the last.

Seeing my wife go through this process each day made me gain a better understanding of how much she wanted this baby. Never did she complain as her stomach began to swell from bruising, water retention, and swollen ovaries. Never did she question her decision. I had certainly never had any doubts that having a child and being a mom was her ultimate goal, but there was something special about seeing her commit to this process with daily sacrifices. Lifting up her shirt to expose her bruised stomach provided a daily reminder to me that my future child was going to have one tough mother who would love her or him with her whole being.

I grew in confidence about my ability to be a father each day. I wouldn't have been willing to initiate the IVF process if I didn't feel at least partially ready, but going through the fertility process gave me more assurance. I was definitely handling the stresses of IVF better than I would have anticipated, and I started thinking that being a dad would be something I could handle too. The parenting instinct of both love and protection were being honed as I ushered my wife through the process. I was both sensitive and loving to her while being ready to pounce on anyone who I felt was not treating her as she should have been. Maybe God wanted me to go through IVF to show me that I could be a father? Maybe having a child after one month of trying naturally would have been too much for me to handle?

With my confidence in my ability to be a dad increasing each day, my ability to focus on only the task at hand became more challenging. I wanted so badly to be a dad. Each "successful" appointment brought more hope which subsequently brought more anxiety. The early days were much easier as I could focus on my fears of giving a shot or my lack of knowledge about the other elements of this process. By the second week, I was confident that I could be a dad, I knew how to give shots, and I was starting to understand how to read the ultrasounds. I was no longer waiting for explanations from the doctor; I was reading the fuzzy black and white images myself. I would think, "The follicles didn't grow as much as I had expected since our last appointment." I started driving my wife crazy; she loved saying, "And, when did you get your medical degree?"

My wife had every right to be annoyed because I can have a little bit too much self-confidence at times. In this particular situation, I would like to think however that she found some comfort in my level of engagement. I didn't want her to have to worry about anything except getting rest and staying relaxed. Her worrying or being anxious would not be good for her or her eggs (I am not a medical doctor and that last statement might not be factual, but it is what I believed.) Making sure that she was getting the best care was my responsibility. Throughout our marriage, we have always tried to work as a team. Never before had this commitment to leveraging our respective strengths been more important. It was time for me to use my natural sense of curiosity and my assertive nature to challenge the doctors to provide their best. I knew that on any given day that our appointment was the most important thing happening in our lives; for the doctor, our appointment was one of many that they would be having. The possibility of this baby meant much more to me and my wife than it could have to any of the four doctors. I was going to do whatever needed to be done to give us the best chance of success.

Weeks of successful appointments had brought us to the point where we needed to harvest the eggs. I remember it dawning on me that I could actually be facing bad news for the first time. Up until this point, the news that we would get from the doctor was never going to derail our process. Maybe we would have to wait a couple more days for the follicles to more fully mature, but I never had any real fears that we would be given news that could put us back to square one. The egg retrieval was actually the first real step in the process. On the simplest level,

Dear Zoe || Love Dad

IVF involves retrieving eggs and sperm, marrying them together to create embryos, and then implanting embryos into the uterus. We were about to take the first major step.

When I think back to the day of the actual retrieval, I am still amazed at how one event seemingly triggered so many seemingly contradictory emotions and feelings. I distinctly remember being filled with paralyzing anxiety and complete tranquility. I remember being completely in tuned with my wife yet being totally enveloped in my own thoughts. I will try to explain as best I can, but I am afraid my words may fail me. With regards to my first point, there had never been a time when I had awoken with such a strong desire for a positive outcome (having my wife's follicles produce plenty of eggs). At the same time, I remember being at peace with God in a way that I had never previously experienced. I continued to pray to Him for his help on this day throughout the procedure, and I remember feeling as if He would do what was best for me regardless of what I wanted. I felt closer to God on that morning than I ever had in my life. Maybe it was because I knew I was doing something that He would want me to be doing. Maybe it took feeling completely helpless to admit that I needed Him. Regardless of the reason, I felt anxious and scared yet completely unafraid.

Regarding my feelings of being completely in tuned with my wife yet completed isolated in my own thoughts, I believe that most people can probably relate. Never had the bond between my wife and I been stronger than on that morning. As we both awaited news of whether the embryologists were finding eggs, we were united in hope that we would be successfully taking the first step toward having a baby. It was the most intimate experience that we had ever shared – especially with 4 other people in the room☺ At the same time, we were in two totally different places. She was fighting the physical pain of the procedure with the help of narcotics. She was conscious but far from completely lucid. I on the other hand was panic-stricken as I waited patiently for positive news from the embryologists knowing that everything my wife had ever wanted was up in the air. Not experiencing pain or sedation left me all too aware of what was at stake. When my wife would look to me and ask whether everything was okay – I knew that she needed me more than ever. At this moment in our lives, her emotions and needs supplanted my own to such a degree that I didn't have the extra bandwidth needed to process my own feelings. We were both focused on the same goal yet we were thinking about it completely differently.

[I have already detailed my persistence in having the doctor check both sides for follicles, and I therefore won't go into much detail about the situation here. I will however say that I still sometimes think about that moment and get frightened. I can't help but think,

Dear Zoe || Love Dad

"What if one of those momentarily forgotten follicles ended up providing the egg which became Zoe?"]

I don't think that I have ever shared with my wife or anyone for that matter how nervous I was heading back to the hospital later that morning to provide my sample. All the fears that I had had previously about not being able to give my wife a baby came flooding back on that fateful drive. The whole focus of IVF was on my wife. She was the person taking all the shots. She was the one having invasive check-ups each morning. Her stomach was bloated and bruised. All I had to do was ejaculate in a cup. I better be able to hold up my end of the bargain, right.

I was extremely thankful and appreciative that the doctors were able to find 11 eggs from the morning's retrieval, but it also made me feel an enormous amount of pressure. I felt that my wife had done way more than her fair share. I was hoping for around 5 to 7 and felt very blessed with the chance to fertilize 11. I didn't want all of her hard work to be wasted. I had seen her flat stomach transformed into a bloated, bruised mess. I had just seen her grimace and shriek in pain as the doctor performed an excruciating procedure. Her physical pain had been great, but it would pale in comparison to her emotional trauma if I wasn't able to fertilize these eggs.

She had exceeded expectations; I only hoped that I could meet them. I was about to perform the only act that I would do for the entire process. The tests that I had taken had shown that I could father a child, but it was now actually the moment of truth. I was petrified, but there was nothing that I could do at this point. I just had to pray, and praying about what I was about to do seemed really awkward☺

[I remember hoping at the time that all 11 eggs would fertilize and become embryos. My hope was not based on some need or desire to prove my virility, but rather I simply wanted to have the best chance of having a baby. All of my fears were about being able to help my wife have a child. Learning that we had five embryos was a wonderful relief. My biggest fear, an inability to produce a live embryo, was now able to be dismissed. I remember being attached to these five embryos in a way that I had never fathomed. As hard as it may be to believe, I already really felt like a parent. The embryos might have only been a single cell, but they were alive. I helped create life.

I certainly kept the two implanted embryos in my mind and prayers as we continued with the process and implantation. But, it actually wasn't until a couple of days after my daughter was born that I began to think about the embryos that we had stored for a later implantation. I had wanted all 11 eggs to fertilize so that we would have 11 chances at producing a full-term baby.

Dear Zoe || Love Dad

Something that I had never considered was what we would do with embryos if we had success on the first try. My wife and I had always discussed wanting to have two children. I began the IVF process wanting two children and knowing that this specific fertility treatment gave us the best odds of achieving this goal. What never even crossed my mind was what I would want to do if we were fortunate enough to have two kids before all of our embryos were implanted. What would happen to these unused embryos?

Before I try to address the question above, I must explain my thought process at that time. I have already explained how the IVF process triggered seemingly contradictory or mutually exclusive emotions and feelings in me on many occasions. There were times when I was terribly anxious on one level and completely at peace on another. One of the greatest contradictions, which was very relevant to my feelings about the number of embryos, was my ability to be optimistic about each step of IVF while being pessimistic that I would ever have a full-term baby. For someone as rational as I, I understand that the sentence above does not make complete sense; it is however how I felt. I went to every appointment and procedure with the belief that it was going to result in a positive outcome. However, I couldn't ever picture myself holding a healthy baby after a nine month pregnancy. Maybe I was subconsciously protecting myself from a level of sadness I had never known? Maybe it was impossible for me to see myself as a dad before I actually became one. Or, maybe our failed attempts, which resulted in our seeking fertility treatments, had eradicated the optimism I had once felt. Regardless of the reason, it was a challenging time.

My hope for as many embryos as possible can only be viewed in the context of my not having the confidence that I would ever be a dad. Having been told that your wife would have trouble conceiving and that your sperm was not ideal had begun the process of eroding a certain amount of my optimism. Researching various fertility treatments only made me more pessimistic as I began to grasp just how fragile the reproductive system can be. Even though giving my wife shots and then implanting her with embryos created "ideal" circumstances for a child to develop, our chances still only hovered around 40%. The odds were stacked against us. I knew that each embryo would provide a chance at having a baby, and I therefore wanted as many as possible.

It wasn't until we were blessed with a healthy daughter that I thought back to the frozen embryos. The embryos had been on my mind since they first fertilized, but I was so focused on my wife and unborn child throughout the pregnancy that any "serious" thought about these embryos was put on hiatus.

Holding my daughter in my arms the first few days in the hospital immediately led me to think about the other embryos. These embryos were not just my kids, but they were also her siblings. I knew immediately that we would eventually implant all three. My daughter was the greatest gift that I could ever be given; of course, I would want more. If we had 3 more kids then I would be thrilled with the blessing. Would there be challenges? Certainly, but my mother used to always say that there is an expression in Spain that says that every baby is born with a loaf of bread under each arm. When asked to explain, she said that you will always find a way to provide for your children even if it will be a challenge. My daughter was in the NICU and my wife had just gone through a very stressful 30 hour labor, and I knew that I was ready to try again.]

We received the call a few days later telling us that five eggs had in fact turned into embryos. So many thoughts immediately accompanied this news that I had to sit quietly for a moment in order to try and process. The questions arrived faster than I could provide answers. It was just a very overwhelming experience. Below is what I can best remember from those first few minutes after learning about the embryos.

- Five embryos mean that we have five chances to have a baby; this is great news.
- Five out of eleven; is my sperm really that bad.
- Thank God that my wife was able to produce so many eggs because I definitely couldn't be counted on.
- Was my wife happy with this news?
- Is my wife mad that I was only able to fertilize five eggs? Would she tell me if she was mad? Should I ask her?
- Wait, embryos are living beings. I'm a father. I can't believe it, I am a dad.
- Are all five going to be able to be implanted?
- I hope five will give us at least one healthy baby.
- Thank you God, for helping us this far.
- I wonder if one of the eggs that I had to tell the doctor about is one of these five.

I decided that it was important to just be thankful. There was no use in trying to predict what would happen with these embryos. And there was no value in being upset with myself for only being able to fertilize five of the eggs. God was in charge of this whole process; we just needed to keep moving forward with a positive attitude.

Now that we had actual embryos, we would only be waiting a few more days for the implantation to occur. I am not sure whether the doctors and nurses keep you intentionally in the dark about the IVF process, but it was shocking on many occasions to realize how little I knew about the next step we would be taking. Prior to the implantation, I hadn't realized that it is normal to wait two, three, or even more days to see which embryos are developing the best. The fact that these little guys and gals were being evaluated for cell development and cell structure was completely foreign to me until the morning of the implantation. I had assumed that the situation was binary – either there was or was not a viable embryo.

The doctor spoke with us on the morning of the implantation and told us why she had chosen the two embryos for implantation. We agreed with her rationale, and my wife was prepared for the procedure.

IVF is strange in the fact that there are such recognizable steps in the creation of a baby. My wife and I were "living" the chapter of human reproduction in a high school biology class. Our baby was going to be brought to this world only after following many discreet steps. More than a year later as I write this, I feel very fortunate that the creation of our daughter occurred in this manner. It really is an awesome experience and it helps me appreciate how lucky I am to have her. She had to fight so hard to become my baby, and I can see this attitude in her to this day. She is strong, and I will always be indebted to her.

A nurse walked into the room holding a little metal box and announced "here are your babies!" It was the first time that anyone had actually said "your babies" to my wife and me. What a truly magical moment. It was a moment that I will never forget for the rest of my life. (The IVF process allowed for us to have many "never forget" moments which is yet another reason I am thankful for having taken this route to fatherhood.)

I was being recognized as a dad for the first time, and I loved the feeling. I had been thinking about those embryos as my children, but I wasn't sure whether anyone else would feel the same way. Hearing the word "babies" associated with me really made all of these weird scientific processes feel personal.

The implantation was very simple as the doctor fed a tube with each embryo into the uterus. When she pulled out the tube to find one of the embryos still attached, I remember thinking about how difficult it is to have a child. I was so nervous that this situation was a bad sign. How could an 8-celled organism survive this process? How could he/she be forced off the tube and into the uterus and still be fine? I tried to remain positive, but it was a challenge. After hearing the nurse utter the word "babies", it really dawned on me how much I had to lose.

It was special for both my wife and I knowing that our little embryos would be leaving with us. I really did feel like a father. There was still plenty of work for these embryos to do, but I was happy knowing they would be with us. I looked at my wife differently from that moment forward. She was now not only my wife whom I loved with all my heart, but she was also the mother of my children. Even as I thought about the incredible challenge facing these embryos, I took some solace in the fact that my wife was ready to assist them. They would never be alone on this journey and I couldn't think of a better person for them to be with.

I remember leaving the hospital and not knowing where to go or what to do. I had just gone through the most significant experience of my entire life, but it was an experience that pointed toward another conclusion in two weeks. My ability to remain relatively calm and controlled was severely tested with each passing day. The clock had started. In two weeks, I would either be happier than I had ever been or sadder than I had ever been. Each appointment had always felt like a really critical appointment, but certainly, nothing would compare to the day when we would find out whether our babies had made it.

The next two weeks were by far the hardest of the whole IVF process. There were moments of complete joy as I imagined my little embryos growing and developing. There were also moments of severe doubt as I wondered how any babies are ever born IVF or not given the hurdles that must be overcome.

I wanted our babies to make it so badly that it was becoming harder and harder for me to be the "strong" one. It might sound odd given the fact that I actually have a master's degree in counseling, but I have never been one who likes to share his feelings. Growing up with OCD had made me somewhat ashamed to share some of the thoughts and emotions I faced. I knew that many of my thoughts were simply due to this disorder of the mind and my sharing them would have been too embarrassing. One of the great things about being truly in lovely and being married is never having to feel ashamed or embarrassed about how you are feeling. My wife and I have "never alone" etched into our wedding rings because it was so important to me that I overcome my tendency to stay closed-off from the world. Given the stress and pressures that we were both experiencing, I was starting to feel alone at times. It didn't seem fair to share any thoughts of doubt or fear with my wife who was going through the same emotions as me. I never really wanted to share much with friends, families, or co-workers because I have always felt that people's ability to be empathetic has definite limits. My main form of solace came from prayer. I continued to find a certain comfort in prayer that I had never experienced in my life. Through prayer, I felt that I could not only communicate with God but also my little babies. I truly felt that they understood how much I loved them even though at 6 and 8 cells this sentiment had no rational bases. (This belief continues today as I talk to my daughter all the time and know that there is some part of her that understand and appreciates it. She doesn't know what I am saying yet she comprehends the love I have for her.)

I continued to go through the motions at work knowing that only part of my mind was available at any given moment given the constant focus on our upcoming appointment. IVF is strange in many ways, but one of the main ways in which it differs from other pregnancies is the fact that it is pretty hard to "hide" from people. In order to be at all of my wife's appointments, I needed to miss many, many hours of work. These absences required an explanation, and I have always felt that "for personal reasons" creates more not less awkwardness. (I had little interest in my employer speculating as to why I was missing work. Was I sick? Was my wife sick? Was I getting divorced?) The telling of my boss led to another series of questions. If I tell my boss, shouldn't I tell the rest of my team? If I am telling the people with whom I only have a "working" relationship, don't I owe it to my family to tell them as well? I might as well tell my friends if it is no longer a big secret, right? For me, the telling of pretty much everyone in my life was not really a big deal. Although I am private about many things, I figured that there really wasn't any harm in others knowing. I decided that trying to "pretend" that my life was just as it always had been would be too exhausting given the other things I had on my mind. I also convinced myself that maybe I could be an inspiration to others who were having difficulty conceiving as well. The response from everyone was positive as I expected. There is certainly a lot of "wrongs" in this world, but I have generally found people, friends and strangers alike, to be supportive and caring when there is just cause. Hoping for a child certainly met this definition.

Even though many people knew what I was going through – the IVF process – I still kept them at a distance from what I was going through – the most emotionally challenging experience of my life. The only "Ones" who knew what I was dealing with were God and my embryos to whom I would write each night.

The pressure mounted with each passing day. My wife and I tried to occupy our minds as best we could, but our attempts were futile. It was impossible to focus on the mundane when were waiting to learn if we would be given the most profound gift we would ever receive.

I could only imagine what the situation was like for my wife who couldn't help but interpret each headache, stomach soreness, cramp, or pain as a potentially positive or negative sign. My nonchalant reaction to her comments about any of these physical manifestations was only to try and keep her calm. Inside, I was waiting until I could grab a free moment and search the internet for what these "signs" might be a harbinger for. Yes, prayer was still my main coping method, but the one-way dialogue often left me needing more immediate gratification. My ability to steer clear from the mountain of misinformation found on the internet had eroded. Many times I would search for the "answer" that I wanted to believe; a ritual that I knew was pointless yet managed to make me feel slightly better. There were times when I felt like an addict scouring the pages of the web trying to find his fix, an answer that would provide a momentary respite from my intense worry.

When the day that would have more impact on my future than any other day of my life arrived, I was totally emotionally drained. How do you really prepare for the possibility of having your entire life changed forever? How do you tell your wife that everything will be okay when you know bad news would completely devastate her? It was on this day that I realized how much "hope" had carried me over the last few months. My heart always believed 100% that we were going to be successful. My mind knew the odds were much lower, but there was always something inside me that made me think that my chances were different. Prayer had given my heart hope and my heart was winning the battle against my mind. Hope however would not be able to overcome truth. The results of the tests would be the final arbiter in this battle of heart and mind.

My strength was failing me as we left the doctor after completing my wife's blood work. The balance of power between my heart and mind had finally been tilted in favor of my rational mind. No longer capable of concealing my emotions from my wife, I admitted that I didn't think she was pregnant to her for the first time of the entire process. As I have already noted, the emotional elements of IVF both create closeness and distance from your spouse. At this moment, I needed closeness. I always tried to protect her as I knew she would be devastated if we were not successful. Once my mind started to convince me that she might not be pregnant, I realized I too would be completely devastated. We told each other all the "right/ optimistic" things during breakfast that day, but we both knew that there would be no solace if we learned she was not pregnant. It would be complete sadness. Even the thought of not having success had managed to cast a pall over all of my thoughts that morning.

I went numb. I sat frozen trying to digest what I was hearing. My wife was on the phone crying and yelling as she tried to successfully process the words coming through the phone. There was no sign of pain in these cries, and it was clear what she was being told. She was pregnant. IVF had worked.

The feeling was like none I had previously experienced. A peace washed over me. The burden I had been carrying these last months, weeks, and hours had been so intense. In an instant, all the stress had been eliminated by two of my wife's words, "I'm pregnant."

Dear Zoe || Love Dad

My wife and I had two very different reactions. She was crying and yelling in joy. I, on the other hand, continued sitting nearly paralyzed by the news. It was as if my body and mind were completely incapable of experiencing this much emotion.

The feeling was very unique for someone such as me who suffers from both OCD and anxiety issues. There are never times when my mind is at ease as thoughts and ruminations always run through my mind at a blistering pace. At that moment, my mind was completely calm. It was a euphoric feeling and one that I have not felt since.

I finally snapped out of this blissful trance and was able to say a short prayer thanking God for His assistance in this process. I then embraced my wife and told her how much I loved her and how I was very proud of her. Similarly to our engagement night, she couldn't wait to get on the phone and tell people whereas I just wanted to sit in silence taking in the moment. I was literally experiencing the greatest moment of my life, and I wanted to be as "present" as possible in it. Given that our journey had included the prayers and hopes of many others (as previously mentioned IVF is often a communal experience), I caved and began the process of informing friends and family.

The news was too big and too important to play any games. There would be no "pretending to be sad" only to surprise the person with the great news. As soon as the person would say "hello," we would immediately announce, "Gina is pregnant. We are going to have a baby!" My wife's mom received the first call, and you could feel the emotion through the phone as she too cried with joy. Next it was my mother, who said that she knew it would work as she had been praying everyday. The reactions were not unexpected as my wife's mom is very emotional and my mom is very religious. We continued making the happiest phone calls we would ever make. IVF had worked. We were going to have a baby.

Sustaining such a high level of emotion is not possible indefinitely. I knew that there would be a time for my worries to return as we continued along the journey to a healthy, live birth. I needed that day however to simply be about happiness, thankfulness, and love. My wife and I both needed an emotional break. The IVF process had gone remarkably well for both of us, but it was still exhausting and taxing.

On the day of the first ultrasound post-pregnancy, the nerves and anxiety returned. I knew how fragile and delicate the process was. We had been told that 20% of pregnancies end in miscarriages at the beginning of this journey and that number had loomed large in my mind following a few days of pure joy. I was also nervous to learn whether we would be having one or two babies. When the doctor found one beating heart, I felt a sense of relief that we still had a baby and a sense of sadness for the loss of the other embryo. It was sad because I already loved that other embryo. We started the process to have one baby, but things changed the moment the nurse brought in "our little babies" in the small, metal container. Thankfully, the beating heart helped me with this loss which was more upsetting than I would have realized.

What I had not originally grasped when we began the IVF process was how much it would impact my wife and me even after we learned that she was pregnant. We were having an IVF pregnancy which would result in an IVF baby. Our subsequent appointments were always preceded with a certain amount of gravity and anxiousness as we had spent so many hours thinking about the challenges involved in this awesome process. There was also an odd sense of "pride" as we had taken the financial and emotional risk and been rewarded. Finally, there was a true sense of appreciation that permeated my worldview as I thanked God as well as the doctors and nurses who were helping us fulfill our dream of becoming parents.

People often say that you appreciate "things" more when they are hard to get or are in danger of being taken away. Some might say that my feelings of appreciation for this pregnancy can simply be chalked up to this sentiment, but I disagree. What I think really made this pregnancy so special was (1) the relationships that I had with my wife, with God, and with the embryos and (2) the clear focus on what we were seeking – a baby.

Each day, I spent a very personal time with my wife. We were united in not only our love but also our desire to create a child that would bind us forever. Too often, we had simply let our routine of sitting together and watching TV dominate our relationship. With IVF, we were forced to not only spend time together, but also to converse about a subject we were both deeply invested in. Our relationship definitely grew during this time as we counted on each other for support and comfort. My relationship with God also improved as I finally felt at peace with my faith. There was a huge sense of relief when I realized that ultimately it was He and not I who was in charge of this process. The pressure I was feeling never left, but it was definitely lessened as I was able to share the burden with Him – someone Who could handle it.

I also believe that really focusing on what it means to have a baby made the entire process that much more special. I was completely engaged in every aspect of this process. With each appointment or progesterone shot, I was reminded of what this was all about – creating a baby who would hopefully go on to live a long and productive life. I spent countless hours thinking about why I wanted a baby, how I would raise him/her, what I would do if we weren't successful, etc.... Each day brought a deeper, richer understanding of why having a baby meant so much to me. I realized that I wanted to share this amazing world with a child. I wanted to raise a baby with the most wonderful woman I had ever known. I knew I was ready to make any and all sacrifices to have this child lead a happy life.

Once I knew that I was ready, I started thinking about this baby. Was I just being selfish bringing this child into the world? I was literally beginning a process that would hopefully result in a life not just a baby. Never before or again would I make such an important decision. I needed to assess our world and decide whether it would be suitable for a child. See, I realized that having a baby wasn't just about my desires or those of my wife. I needed to think of the future happiness of this child who would become a part of a world and society that was not always pleasant. What does it really mean to create life? I realized that the issue was too big for me to find resolution, but I found comfort in my faith. I might not understand the many calamities around the world, but I trusted God's vision.

Going through the IVF process was such a tremendously rewarding experience that I believe brought me closer to God, my wife, and my baby. I recognize how fortunate we were to have had success on our first try, and I can't help but believe that this success has certainly cast a positive glow over my memories. I also know that everyone will experience this process in a different manner unique to their situation. My experience was MY experience which I "own" and chose to share in the hope that it might help others thinking about starting this process.

Dear Zoe || Love Dad

Reflections on the NICU

I was very surprised when I received the call from my wife telling me to bring her "hospital bag" because we were having the baby that night. I said, "What do you mean? She isn't due for another five weeks. We can't have her yet." Our little girl decided that she wanted to see her dad a little sooner than expected which set off a chain of events the ultimately ended up with her being in the NICU for 20 days. The NICU can be both comforting and terrifying. Emotions of all kinds are constantly running high, and the lack of privacy only serves to catalyze them. There are plenty of books written by professionals about the NICU and what to expect, but I wanted to provide my experience so that parents and parents' loved ones could get a different, more personal perspective.

My wife's labor was long and arduous, and it finally came to an end with the performance of a C-section. I had been so nervous for both my wife and my baby that the sound of my daughter's first cry was the sweetest sound I had ever heard. Finally, I knew my wife and my little preemie were safe.

There had been some talk that my daughter might need to be taken immediately to the NICU given her early arrival. My wife was very concerned with the thought of the NICU because she wanted her baby with her at all times. I on the other hand harbored no such feelings; I was far from a confident parent and I just wanted help from whoever seemed capable. The NICU doctors and nurses certainly would have fallen into this category.

When it was time to finally perform the C-section, the OR was filled with medical personnel. Neonatologists joined the normal assembly of doctors, and I prepared myself for my daughter needing to be whisked away for additional support. Fortunately, the neo-natal doctors in the delivery room said that she was fine and thus sent her to the nursery.

Everything seemed fine until about an hour later when I tried to feed her a bottle for the first time. She was making a noise which I thought was odd, and I wanted to quickly return her to the nursery and inform the staff. My nerves were already frayed from the thirty hour labor which had caused my wife great pain and therefore me much anguish. My wife, who was completely drained both physically and emotionally from her preeclampsia, labor, and c-section, had told me explicitly that I needed to be with the baby at all. I tried to explain the situation, but she couldn't understand in her current state. Something inside me said that I needed to take her to the nursery which is exactly what I did even as it frustrated my wife. Never had I expected to be serving as the primary care giver for our little girl. My wife was the person with all the experience and instincts.

Dear Zoe || Love Dad

Exhausted in a way that was completely new to me, I laid down to take a short nap.

I awoke two hours later and saw my mom at the foot of my cot. She said, "Zoe stopped breathing; she had to be taken to the NICU." I was petrified. I couldn't believe that my little baby had stopped breathing. What if she had done that when there was no doctor or nurse in the room? I felt guilty. I was supposed to protect her. How could I have been sleeping?

I picked up the phone outside of the locked doors heading to the NICU. I said for the first time, "This is Zoe's dad; I would like to see my daughter." I heard the door unlock, a noise I would come to know well, and proceeded to the "scrub room." The situation was very intimidating for some with OCD. Everything seemed to be conspiring to make my OCD as bad as possible; I was already exhausted and stressed. Now, I was putting myself through a "cleaning ritual" that I had spent years overcoming. I felt something as a vigorously rubbed my arms on that first morning that I would experience many times. I felt a concern for not only my daughter but also for all the babies in the ward. I scrubbed and scrubbed not wanting to introduce any foreign germs into this fragile/ controlled environment.

I walked down the hallway until I reached a large open room containing around 30 cribs. The room was filled with an overwhelming amount of stimuli. Alarms and flashing lights were constantly going off. Nurses, doctors, and technicians roamed throughout the room it what seemed like controlled chaos. Being so tired and stressed, I didn't try to make sense of everything that I was experiencing. I simply wanted to see my little girl.

I continued walking until I located my daughter. In an instant, I was calm. The cacophony of alarms, cries, and bells faded away as I saw my beautiful child. It was truly a magical moment.

Her little body was covered with medical equipment ranging from a C-pap machine on her face to a slew of stickers and wires on her body, but I felt no fear. Her peaceful visage could easily be discerned behind the breathing mask, and I could experience anything but joy at being reunited with the daughter I had waited so long to see. It was the first of many, many times that she gave me strength and comfort rather than the other way around.

I spoke with her nurse who immediately instilled in me a great confidence. She was knowledgeable, self-assured, and kind. I felt very lucky to have her looking after my sweet baby. We talked about both what had happened and what was going to happen. It became clear that my little girl would not be going home in the near future as she had just started a 10 day antibiotic treatment. The regimen was presented to me as being pre-cautionary which I agreed was the right approach.

There we were; a dad and his little baby. I wasn't scared as I continued to stare at my little girl hooked up to all the various devices. I actually felt comforted by the monitors as it helped reassure me that she was getting the best possible care.

The NICU environment faded into the periphery as I enjoyed these first moments of fatherhood. I would reach into the crib and gently rub her foot or touch her hand. I tried my best to not disturb her from her peaceful sleep, but I wanted to feel connected to her. She needed to know that I was there for her.

The rest of the day, I would go to the NICU every couple of hours. The ritual of calling the triage nurse, scrubbing my arms, and speaking with Zoe's nurse felt natural after only a couple of visits. As much as I had never even considered my daughter having to go to the NICU, I had never really considered her coming home after a few days either. Having gone through IVF, I had been conditioned to not think too far in advance. This approach served me very well throughout my daughter's stay. Each challenge that arose was addressed in the order in which it arrived.

My wife continued to recover for the rest of the day. She was not doing well. The magnesium drip continued to cause her to be confused, hot, and irritated. The c-section contributed tremendous soreness. And, not having her baby with her in the room left her feeling sad and depressed. I tried to take care of both my wife and my baby. Many times, it seemed that my baby was doing much better than my wife; my daughter continued to look very serene during all of my visits whereas my wife was agitated and highly irritable.

With the magnesium drip finally removed, my wife woke me to take her to see our daughter. Her reaction was very different from mine. She hadn't even made it to the crib before her eyes became wet with tears. The medicines, exhaustion, and pain had clouded her thinking. Walking through the NICU en route to Zoe was the first time she truly comprehended the situation. She might have heard NICU, but she was picturing "nursery."

Her reaction as was a harbinger of things to come. Unlike me, she had clearly pictured a birthing sequence. Being separated from her child was terribly challenging for her. She of course wanted what was best for her baby, but it was readily apparent that she would not be happy into her baby was home with her. The last eight months of carrying her had created a bond that I, as a father, simply couldn't understand. She believed that a baby needed to be with her mom or dad at all times. She had been adamant on the night of our daughter's birth, and this belief was not going to go away.

My wife and I were different. Not only had the time spent carrying her created a closeness no man could truly understand, but she was also completely confident in her parenting abilities. From this first encounter, it was clear that God had made her to be a mother. I on the other hand lacked this innate parenting. I always hoped it would come to me, but I actually found comfort in the idea that my daughter was in the hands of trained professionals. We both wanted the absolute "best" for our baby; we just differed on how to define "best."

We continued to visit our daughter every couple of hours. Not ever having gone through any other births, I had no frame of reference for what it "could" or "should" be like on day one, two, three, etc… I therefore had the same "glow" that any new parent has. The pure joy of seeing my daughter each day outweighed any feelings of sadness that normally accompany parents of children in the NICU. I always believed Zoe would be a perfectly happy and healthy baby and that are NICU visit would be a simple blip on the timeline of her life.

Even as I continued to be ecstatic that I was a new dad, there were feelings of sadness each and every day. What I don't think that many people who haven't had a child in the NICU can comprehend is that the actual "environment" slowly erodes your ability to stay calm and happy. Most people who knew that Zoe was in the NICU focused only on the reports they would receive about Zoe. What level of oxygen was she on? How much did she eat? The experience of a NICU parent however cannot be summed up by the stats of their baby alone.

It hit me after about three visits. I had been hearing the beeps, cries, and alarms, I had been seeing the many cribs, crying parents, and medical equipment, but I had never taken the time to process these stimuli. My focus had to be completely on my daughter and her condition during these initial visits as I tried to understand what was happening to the most precious person in my world. Once, I became secure that I understood the challenges facing my own child, there was space in my mind to try and make sense of this unique environment.

I looked around as if for the first time. Everywhere I looked, I could see monitors, babies, nurses, and parents. It was unlike any place I had ever been. In a society where privacy is high, it was very odd having access to the most personal moments one could ever witness. No walls separated these little babies who by definition were fighting for their lives. Being human, I couldn't help but feel a connection to each of these little guys and gals as well as their loved ones.

Dear Zoe || Love Dad

As a human, it was impossible not to be moved by the plight of these children. Each day my wife and I got to know "our neighbors" better and better. There were some who broke our hearts because of their illnesses. Others broke our hearts by their lack of visitors. It quickly became apparent to each of us that being in the NICU is not simply about your own child. Being in the NICU is about being a parent. The world had changed the instant that we learned my wife was pregnant and it continued to change as we progressed through the pregnancy. We both reached a level of empathy and understanding previously unavailable. It was this empathy, understanding, and love that were constantly in high demand during these first three weeks of our daughter's life. We loved our child more than we knew possible, but we also had a type of "love" for all these kids.

Hour after hour, we sat holding our precious baby. As she slept peacefully in our arms, the babies surrounding us would often stop breathing, cry out in pain, or suffer some physical hardship. It was very challenging emotionally, and the plight of our "neighbors" weighed on each of us heavily. The environment created "healthy" babies and "unhealthy" parents as emotion and stress combined with complete physical exhaustion. It was never quiet. It was never dark. It was never peaceful. It was never private. Each parent was forced to deal with their own emotions amongst a whirlwind of activity.

I remember specifically one day when my love for my daughter and my caring for another patient collided. As my daughter was deemed to be progressing, she had been "paired up" with another baby who needed more attention. My wife had called me at work to tell me that Zoe was being ignored by her nurse. Zoe might have been "progressing" but she was still in the NICU for a very good reason – she was sick and needed constant monitoring. By the time I arrived at the hospital, I was already on edge. The days of sleeping minimally so that I could spend as much time with Zoe as possible while still getting all of my work completed had frayed my nerves. I sat watching Zoe in her crib for two hours and never even saw either of her nurses glance in her direction. My heart began to race as I my body began to reflect the agitation being experienced in my mind. Finally, I could no longer bite my tongue. I called the nurse over and told her very matter-of-factly that I understood the other baby needed a lot of support, but that I did not appreciate her ignoring my child. We argued momentarily, but I knew my point was delivered.

It was an awful moment that could only happen in the NICU. Day after day I waited for someone to visit the little boy next to Zoe. Day after day no one came. It broke my heart knowing that this little guy was going through this experience alone. The last thing that I would want to do was to take away the nurses, his only advocates, from him. At the same time, my daughter needed attention as well. It was situations such as this one that really defines what it means to be a parent of a NICU baby. Slowly but surely, the NICU begins to "break you down" emotionally. There is only so much sadness and stress a human can take.

I tried to stay strong for the benefit of both my baby and my wife. She was having a very difficult time dealing with the fact that our daughter was in the hospital. I distinctly remember trying my best to empathize with her ... to really understand what she was feeling. I tried to understand why she was so upset each time we needed to leave the NICU to get lunch or rest. What I have come to realize after spending a year with my daughter is that my wife had already spent eight months bonding with our child.

I question whether I could handle the NICU as well now as I did a year ago. (I don't know whether "well" is the right word? Maybe I should have tried to spend even more time with her. I know that if she were in the hospital today, as a one year old, I wouldn't leave her side.) My bond with Zoe is strengthened every day, and I couldn't imagine her being in the hospital without me. I thought I was bonding with Zoe while she was still in utero, but clearly the depth of our relationship was limited by the distance between us. My wife on the other hand had just spent at least the last three months feeling her kick, move, and twirl in her stomach. Of course, leaving her violated every maternal instinct she had. I am not knowledgeable about post-partum depression, but I don't believe my wife was suffering from this ailment. I think she was suffering because she loved our daughter in a way that only a mother can at that age. She already had a strong connection having provided for her these last eight months. She loved our daughter so much that the thought of her being all alone without her parents just tormented her.

Day by day, I could see the strain on both my wife and my mother in law (who had been with us since my wife started her labor). They were deteriorating both physically and emotionally. Many times I received phone calls at work asking that I come to the hospital to speak with a doctor or nurse. The hours at our daughter's bedside were beginning to cloud their judgment. Staring at your baby, who was hooked up to wires and monitors, all day and night was having a huge effect on them. Their ability to decipher what issues were truly important, tests from a head scan, and what issues were simply short-term nuisances was fading away. They tended to focus only on the most immediate of issues. Was she eating enough formula? When would her C-pap machine come off? When could she come home? It was my job to make sure that all the tests were being run properly and that we were being given the most accurate information possible. I would often say that they were responsible for her feeling loved and I was in charge of her getting healthy. Of course, this statement was simplistic and meant to be illustrative as all of us were concerned with both elements. The fact is however that there is certainly truth in those words.

We started to settle into our respective roles after a few days. Both my wife and mother in law are assertive people, but their physical and emotional exhaustion sapped their strength to fight or argue with the doctors or nurses. They were literally pouring all they had into loving our little baby; they didn't have any excess reserves available to fight. The calls to me began to focus not only on medical questions but also on personality conflicts with the hospital staff. Almost all of our interactions with the doctors, nurses, and techs were positive, but we were clearly overly sensitive. We had a baby in "intensive care" and our expectations of the staff were that they would provide intense care. Late lab results and misplaced IV's became my domain of concern. I always tried to keep in mind what end result I wanted. Regardless of whether I liked it or not, I was at the mercy of these people. I decided that I needed to be firm yet kind to ensure that my message would be received without any retribution. It was often a challenge as my tattered nerves usually made me more quick-tempered than sad. As I said, the staff was amazing, but they could never show as much care and concern for my daughter as I would have wanted as a new parent.

The stress and my new assertive nature started to bleed into all aspects of my life. The ability to simply compartmentalize the NICU was not really possible. The problems or issues that people would bring to me often seemed terribly trivial, and I was quick to assert as such. I got into a big blow up with the real estate agent representing the seller in our home transaction when he said that we owed him $60 because he had made a mistake. When a co-worker decided that telling me that some people in the office deemed me to be too direct and blunt knowing full well that my child was in a nearby hospital, she learned how blunt I could be. It was becoming clearer and clearer to me that the four of us, my wife, her mom, my daughter, and I, were living in our own world. If you weren't in the NICU every day with us, then you simply couldn't understand our plight.

The four of us were isolated not by choice but by circumstance. I make this distinction because both of our families and some of our friends began to grow frustrated with us. We weren't acting as they believed new parents should be acting. Why weren't we being ourselves? Why weren't we communicating as much as we had previously? The divide between the four of us and our respective families continued to widen throughout our stay as our focus had to be on taking care of ourselves. The four of us were dealing with a tremendous amount of "real" stress each and every day; we weren't going to deal with anyone adding "unnecessary, fabricated" stress.

Dear Zoe || Love Dad

To be honest, it wasn't until our daughter was out of the NICU and spending her first week at home that I fully understood what conversations had been taking place behind our backs. It took having one of the very few arguments I have ever had with my mother, someone who I know wants the best for me, my wife, and my baby, to fully grasp the situation. I don't think that she, nor anyone else, could really understand our situation without walking in our shoes, with our personalities, and with our fears and hopes.

I was completely caught off guard as I thought that I was doing a great job as not only a father but also as a son, brother, husband, and friend. Hearing that others were frustrated with me, my wife, or my mother in law infuriated me. Showing respect to my parents is something that I have always believed very strongly in, but I refused to accept this criticism. We should have been getting nothing but unconditional support NOT unconditional judgment. The three main issues that people had with us revolved around (A) not being fully informed (B) not bragging about our baby and (C) my wife's emotional state.

I was so mad at the time that I am not even sure whether I tried to present "my side" of the story. Why did I need to be justifying myself when I was the one going through the difficult time? For the purpose of this book, I definitely want to explain. My hope is that those reading this book who have been a parent of a NICU baby or a loved one of a NICU baby will find it helpful if any similar issues/ conflicts arise.

Not Being Fully Informed
There are many reasons why we didn't share every piece of information regarding our daughter. Some explanations are simple and some complex. The number one reason was the fact that cell phones aren't allowed in the NICU. When you are trying to spend as much time as possible with your newborn child, stepping outside to give an update is often not at the top of your list. For my wife, who also had to pump breast milk, clean the pump, and then feed our baby, there simply wasn't any available time. The lack of cell use was definitely a main factor during the early days, but I must admit that other reasons played an increasingly larger role.

When you child is in the NICU, he or she is being monitored every single second of his or her stay. It was this monitoring that provided both great comfort and great worry. Being analytical by nature, I always kept one eye on my daughter's "numbers" throughout my stay. Why was her hear rate rising? What was causing a dip in her blood oxygen levels? It was simply impossible to overlook given my proclivity for worrying. When you combine these stats with her feeding stats (30ml of formula this afternoon vs. 50ml this morning), there was plenty of information that could have been shared. It however quickly became too cumbersome to share as things were moving and changing each hour of the day. The sheer volume of information made sharing periodically impractical as too much had happened to be accurately conveyed. I just didn't have the strength to replay every detail which I knew would prompt additional questions which I may or may not be able to answer. I didn't always know what all the changes meant, and I knew that someone else in their living room a thousand miles away would have even less of an understanding. Why would I share only to get speculation on the other end of the line? Living in the moment was challenging enough; I couldn't afford to live in the past.

My daughter underwent several serious tests when she was in the NICU. Often, these tests were being performed even before I knew why they had been ordered. As I mentioned, things happen fast in the NICU. With my wife and mother in law being the primary care givers at the hospital, I often lacked a full understanding at any given moment. As I would learn about the tests, I didn't want to share information with anyone until I knew the results. My family is comprised of a lot of very bright people who rarely lack the confidence to make their own judgments or speculations. With respect to my daughter's health, I was in no mood to allow this to happen. The only people who could provide me with answers about her health were her doctors and nurses. And my only concern was the well being of both my daughter and my wife. There was nothing that anyone outside of the NICU could tell me that would ease my mind or alleviate any stress. Speculation would have only created more not less anxiety. When a doctor tells you that your daughter has a slight bleed in her brain or a small hole in her heart, I didn't want to hear about how this issue is common according to Wikipedia. Thankfully, the many tests that were administered came back with positive results. Armed with this information, I failed to see why I needed rehashing my past anxiety was warranted.

Given our situation, I decided to error on the side of what the four of us needed. I would do the same again. Others might seek comfort in sharing every bit of information, but I simply didn't. I made the decision to do what was best for my immediate family, and I stick by that decision.

Not Bragging Enough about Our Baby
I was simultaneously confused and offended when I was told that I was not bragging enough about my baby. I was confused because I didn't know that bragging about my baby was an important element of being a good dad. I was offended by the implication that I was not proud of my child, a child who had started her life in a petri dish, been transported in a little metal box, been artificially implanted, and had now been fighting in the NICU. How dare someone question my pride in her? Even as I write this a full year later, I can still feel my blood boil.

It was clear to me that my family just didn't understand what I had experienced over the last year and a half. My wife and I had desperately wanted a child. We had made the financial and emotional commitment to try a procedure with only a 40% success rate because our resolve to have a baby was extremely strong. Our daughter was born prematurely which led to her being in the NICU where she had to fight for her life. Over the last year, we had met many couples who had not gotten pregnant through IVF. We had seen babies in the NICU who didn't make it. Was I really supposed to "brag" about my child? The only emotions I felt were love and thankfulness. I felt more blessed than at any other time in my life. I was completely humbled by God's decision to bless me with her? I find the concept of bragging about my child as completely insensitive as I know that many people will never experience what I have felt over the last year. To this day, I never brag about her because I never want to make any other parent feel bad. I am sure they love their child as I love mine; elevating mine by definition "puts down" their child which is something I just won't do.

Secondly, I felt completely fulfilled when my daughter was born. There would have been nothing to gain from "bragging" about my little girl even if I didn't find the concept insensitive. She brought a happiness, peace, love, and joy to my life that had previously been inaccessible. No one could have made me feel any better; I just didn't need affirmation from anyone else.

<u>My Wife's Emotional State</u>
I think she is depressed.
Why hasn't she been calling your sister as much as she used to?
She doesn't seem like her normal self.

These were some of the comments various people were telling me about my wife. We were hundreds and/ or thousands of miles away from our various family members, but many people were trying to diagnose her with post-partum depression. I must say that I absolutely believe in post-partum depression and its seriousness. This section is therefore not meant to deny it in any way. What I do want to communicate is that being in the NICU is hard. Why is it so hard for people to acknowledge the challenges of having a baby in the NICU? We both felt that everyone's attempt to diagnose her with post-partum was yet another way to deny the natural sadness that accompanies having to leave your baby at the hospital when you are discharged.

Was my wife depressed? I am not sure. She was definitely sad. She was not able to breast feed our baby. She had to witness our child get poked and prodded on various occasions. She had to leave her at the hospital each night. She had to "call" the NICU nurses and then "scrub in" before gaining access to HER baby.

Our baby was in the Neonatal Intensive Care Unit. Your baby is not admitted to this unit unless he or she needs "intensive care." What parent would be unaffected by this situation? Of course my wife was not her normal self. She was caring for her first child who happened to be sick. What would have concerned me was if she was unaffected by the experience.

It made me very mad to have people continually deny the severity of our daughter's situation. It made me equally mad to have anyone question my wife's emotional state when she was an emotional rock for our daughter. She was going through a lot, but she was always there for my child. She was an amazing mother taking care of a sick child; any other views were simply wrong.

The clamor became loud enough that I actually found a section in a book, that my father had sent me regarding the NICU, which addressed how mothers often cope with a child in the NICU. I should have known better as the sharing of this passage led to a defensive reaction. "That passage is really talking about mothers whose babies are very sick and who will spend months not weeks in the NICU," I was told. The exchange only deepened my anger.

Reflections on the NICU – continued

I might have just listed the three main issues, but there were many more. I wish that I could say that our loved ones were also going through a tough-time with Zoe being in the hospital which had led to such erratic behavior, but I don't believe that was the case. No one was willing to take the time to walk in our shoes and accept that even having a relatively- healthy baby by NICU standards is still very difficult for first-time parents. Hurtful, ignorant things were said while my wife and I spent every waking moment thinking and caring for our little girl. It was a very strange time as I felt forced to become isolated from family and friends. My physical and emotional energy had to be saved for my daughter; I couldn't let my focus go from someone who needed me.

I however was able to quickly "get over" the situation. When someone had the audacity to suggest that Zoe was in the NICU not because she was sick but rather to simply fill a NICU bed so that the hospital could make money, the decision to leave the negativity behind was easy. Who would say something so asinine to a parent of a hospitalized child? We had a child that needed the help of a full medical staff to remain alive. My anger towards certain people changed to apathy as I lost the ability to relate to anyone who held such ridiculous views. My wife on the other hand continues to feel anger toward many people who were unwilling to accept that we had a child who was sick. It surprises me how much damage was done to so many relationships. It should have been a time when our family became closer not further apart. We were welcoming a miracle into the world. How the situation got so far out of hand remains a mystery to me to this day. Like I said, I let it go. I just feel too blessed each day when I hold Zoe to let anything make me feel sorry for myself.

The birth of my daughter, her stay in the NICU, and the changing dynamic in my family made me reevaluate the ways that I had treated loved ones in their various times of need. Zoe had and continues to have such a profound impact on me that I can't help but realize that I haven't always been the person that I now want to be. She brought a sense of balance, perspective, and depth to my life that has forced me to reflect on a lot of my actions. Thinking back to how I treated my brother and sister when they had their kids, it saddened me to realize that I had been on the sideline judging them.

When I was honest with myself, I realized that if Zoe were not my child that I might be one of those "people" talking about me behind my back. Conversations about others' abilities as a parent were certainly not new in my family as judgment not love too often seems to rule the day. There was definitely a lesson for me to learn. Rather the judge someone because he or she might not be doing exactly what you "think" you would do, help them resolve their issues in a manner suitable for him or her. It seems so simple to me now. Why spend time and energy making comments about someone rather than simply helping him. All those hours of making jokes about people could have been much better served by simply listening and showing genuine concern.

No one could understand what I was feeling and experiencing each day at the hospital, and I wish that someone would have simply acknowledged this fact as accurate. It wasn't up to anyone to tell me or my wife how we should be feeling or what we should be doing. Looking back, I am not convinced that I even fully understood how or what I was feeling at any given moment. Throughout this book, I have talked about the duality of my thoughts, and the days in the NICU were certainly filled with a lot of these contradictory emotions.

When I walked into the NICU for the first time, and I saw Zoe's nurse, Alissa, I was so happy. With my wife recovering, I knew that I loved Zoe and wanted the best for her but I was 100 percent convinced that I was not the person who could give her what she needed. The sight of a happy, experienced nurse brought tremendous relief. The interns, residents, and attendings also brought a certain amount of comfort to me. I had no confidence in myself. As Zoe's stay grew longer and longer, my thoughts began to change. It bothered me having to call the NICU each day and have them "buzz" me into the room to see MY DAUGHTER. It just didn't seem right that I was getting permission to see my own child. The few experiences with less than stellar nurses filled me with frustration that I wasn't in more control.

What people outside of the NICU have a hard time understanding was that I was a stranger in the NICU. I had no authority over the doctors, nurses, or hospital administrators. I was on their turf. It created a very challenging environment for a first time parent.

The NICU can be very intimidating when you first arrive. The lights, beeps, and hurried commotion create an unfriendly environment. For some, nurses and doctors, they have obviously acclimated to these surroundings as the NICU is simply their office. After a week or two, the NICU began to feel less and less intimidating. I knew what many of the beeps meant. I could easily I interpret the various monitors hooked up to Zoe. Clearly, I was not an expert in a few days, but I believe that God bestows parents with almost magical abilities when it comes to their drive to take care of their kids. What began to happen was that my growing confidence created a lot of tension. I was no longer able to simply "trust" the nurses and doctors as being the sole experts. They had many, many patients; I had only one daughter. My mind was focused solely on getting Zoe the best care, and I was very anxious when I felt she was not getting all the necessary resources.

I knew that Zoe needed to be in the NICU for her well-being, but it became increasingly hard to feel that you weren't in charge of your baby. We couldn't decide who her nurses or doctors would be. We couldn't decide in which room she would be housed. My wife would always say that our daughter needed to be at home with her family. At first, I had interpreted these words as meaning that she wanted all of us to simply be together in a more comfortable setting. Whether she meant it or not, I think this sentiment could also be expressing the general feeling that parenting a child in the NICU is hard. You never feel autonomy as your baby is being cared for by several strangers whose opinions – which were often contradictory- carried more weight than your own. I began to long for the day when I didn't need to constantly battle for my child. I wanted to simply love her, not fight for her.

Fighting was certainly a theme that ran through our journey from IVF to the NICU, and it was certainly not something that I had expected when I had previously thought about having a child. Bringing a child into this world is the greatest manifestation of love I can imagine. You love your spouse so much that you want to literally "create" another human being who is the expression of your union. You love life so much that you want to have someone experience it with all its ups and downs. You love your family so much that you want to add another person who will be indelibly tied to them for as long as they walk this planet. Never did I think about "fighting" when I imagined my journey to becoming a father. After many days in the NICU, fighting followed only love in terms of its relevance.

It really was a struggle every day after I became confident in my abilities as a parent. I lacked the skills and abilities to help my child medically, but I knew that I could impact her well being by ensuring that those with the knowledge and skill utilized the full force of their arsenal to their best ability. If it weren't such an emotional time, I probably would have found the attempt to coax maximum effort out of these relative strangers fascinating on a psychological level. I needed the medical staff at their best. I needed them to care about my daughter nearly as much as my wife and I did. It was a time of love and fighting. Zoe got unconditional love from me. I would hold her in my arms and try to make her feel the pure joy in my heart at having her in my life. Moments later, my wife would be holding her and I would be peppering the doctor with questions. The physician needed to do everything he could to make sure that my precious baby was continuing to recover nicely.

Shifting from hot to cold was exhausting. There was no time however for me to be weak. Our journey had always been a struggle. IVF presented challenge after challenge. It was during these early stages of the journey that I realized what an impact that I could have on the outcome of processes about which I understood very little. Whether it was finding "Little Mary" to show me where to give my wife her shot or telling the doctor to check again for more eggs, I had been able to influence the process even though I lacked any medical knowledge. These past successes helped buttress my confidence while in the NICU. The flipside however was that I felt an enormous amount of pressure. In my rational mind, I couldn't believe that I could have a positive impact on my daughter's care without also believing that a lack of action on my part could have a neutral or negative impact. When you mix in my OCD and anxiety issues, there were many days when the fight was very tough. Fortunately, my resolve was always fortified by the sight of my little girl and my beautiful wife. There was nothing that could stop me from supporting them.

I would continue to love my daughter and wife with all my heart while fighting for the well-being with any strength I had. I could see the physical and emotional stress wear down both my wife and my mother-in-law with each passing day, and I couldn't help but wonder whether they saw the same when they looked back at me. All the hours in the hospital where a wooden rocking chair amidst the disharmony of beeps, sirens, cries, and chatter served as the place where I would "unwind from a day at work." My wife's exhaustion manifested itself in tear after tear. My exhaustion made me more and more assertive and quick-tempered. My personality became less and less multidimensional. If you were my wife, mother-in-law, or daughter, you got love and patience from me. If you were not in that category, you would never know what you would be getting. I was often just too tired to be concerned with the mundane activities of those around me. When someone asked me where this "venom" had come from, it came from being the father of a child in the NICU. There was no "me" outside of being the father of a baby who was hospitalized. If you were wasting my time or wanting me to focus on anything other than my little girl, I quickly grew frustrated. My time had never before been so precious. It was unrealistic for me to believe that everyone would be able to keep my current situation at the forefront of their mind when addressing me, but it was equally unrealistic for them to think that my current situation would not impact all my reactions.

As our time in the NICU came closer and closer to being finished, there was always a bit of fear in my mind. I feared two things. I was afraid that Zoe would have another episode of some sort that would extend her stay in the NICU. My other fear was that Zoe would actually be released, and we would be taking her home. I was afraid of the only two possible outcomes available to me. The NICU was all I had ever known. I have just rattled off the many challenges of parenting a baby in the NICU, but it was at least a "known" situation to me. I had no idea how I would react to having such a little baby at our house without the 24 hour monitoring by both machines and medical professionals. Was I ready to be on my own? It was exhausting always feeling that I had to fight for her care, but at least she was getting great care?

I couldn't change the past, but I also couldn't forget it. Zoe was a miracle baby born 5 weeks early after being conceived through IVF. The medical community had played an enormous role in both the conception of Zoe and also her first weeks of care. I had grown accustomed to visiting the hospital and having my questions answered. My confidence in myself in these situations was now high, but it was also predicated on having the support of a full medical team. I wasn't so sure about how I would handle the first night at the house on my own. For three weeks, I had stared at her monitors always ready to alert a nurse or doctor if her "numbers" strayed from the normal range. Now, I would not only be without doctors and nurses, I would also be without monitors. It was terrifying.

I learned a lot by being the parent of a NICU baby. There were times when I felt very close to my fellow man, and there were times when I felt completely isolated. I gained exposure to the lives of many other families who, like us, were in the midst of the happiest and most stressful days of their lives. There was a "human" bond that too often gets ignored as people focus on differences rather than similarities. I also saw how others' ability to empathize was often quite limited as I felt the judgment of people who clearly could not understand what I was feeling and experiencing. Most importantly, I learned what the word unconditional love really means. I learned that unconditional love can make you stronger and happier than I would ever have been able to imagine.

Dear Zoe || Love Dad

<u>Reflections on IVF – Round 2</u>

It has been almost exactly two years to the day since my wife and I learned that she was pregnant with our first child. Utter ecstasy was the emotion of that day as our prayers had been answered. The stress associated with the many weeks of doctors' appointments faded to the background as we focused simply on the fact that IVF had worked. IVF was over; we could now focus on our fertility rather than infertility.

Fast forwarding to the present day, our fertility challenges have returned to the forefront of my mind. My wife and I have recently decided (my wife sent me a text message to be perfectly truthful) that it is time to implant our other little babies who have been resting comfortably if not coolly at the hospital for the last two years. Most things in life are easier the second time around, but I am more anxious about our second round of IVF than I was our first. My fear comes not so much from understanding the physical and emotional toll, but rather from the fact that I know how much is truly at stake.

Fatherhood is the greatest gift I have ever been given. The experience of having a child far exceeded any hopes or expectations I had been carrying two years ago when fatherhood was more of an abstract concept. I am so nervous about starting IVF again as I know what success will bring – a beautiful child destined to change my life forever.

I would be lying however if I said that it was only recently that I had begun to contemplate our IVF future. I distinctly remember sitting on a cot in the hospital discussing my frozen embryos with my mother while my newborn daughter was upstairs in the NICU. It was at this moment when I felt a renewed closeness to my three frozen children who were also housed within those hospital walls. The decision to implant all three of these embryos would be easy; the only question was the timing of said implantation.

Over the last few months, my wife has increasingly discussed her desire to have more children. She has said that if none of our three embryos are successfully carried to term that she would like to do another round of IVF. This decision is made as far as she is concerned. I however have struggled with this hypothetical question which may or may not ever materialize.

We started IVF with the hope of having two children. Knowing that there is a chance for us to have four as I write this, my hope is to have all four which would mean a set of triplets in the next year; a beautiful challenge I would welcome. If our next implantation does not result in a child, then I am not sure whether another round of IVF is what we should do. I can't help but think of what is realistically speaking a very extreme case where our next round of IVF results in 10 embryos all of which result in live births. Is it responsible for me to bring 10 new children into the world? I know that I would want to implant all embryos. I also know that I feel uncomfortable with the idea of giving up any of my children for adoption – even as am the uncle of the most beautiful adopted child.

Needless to say, I have found myself in somewhat of a mental quandary now that my focus is simply not on "having a baby" as it was in round one of IVF. My wife's determination also adds a layer of complexity to the situation as I don't want to disappoint her. She has proven to be a wonderful mother and any child would be blessed to join her brood. We have had a few discussions on the matter, but rarely have they lasted more than a few minutes before we decide that discussing/ arguing about the issue can wait until a later date. She isn't terribly interested in hearing any arguments as her mind is essentially made up already.

[I don't know if this is possible, but it would seem to be a logical answer to our quandary. My thought would be to freeze my wife's eggs and my sperm rather than fertilizing all the eggs and freezing the subsequent embryos. My method would allow for the number of embryos to be controlled. I would simply ask that the doctors in the andro lab fertilize my wife's eggs one at a time and stop after having fertilized two. At that point, those two eggs would be implanted with the hope of having twins. With success, the eggs and sperm could be destroyed as I don't have any moral or religious objections to the discarding of these two component parts. I really need to ask the doctors whether this is possible as I think it would help a lot of couples such as us who want children but have some unease with the current process.]

Because I don't know if another full round of IVF will be needed, I will postpone any more discussions of the unique challenges associated with it until a later date. I wanted to spend a little more time addressing the decision we recently made to implant the three frozen embryos.

My wife and I walked the route which had become so familiar two years ago. There were many changes since we last visited the IVF doctor including the construction of a new children's wing at the hospital and a few more pounds on my 5 foot nine inch frame. No change was as monumental as the fact that there were now three of us making this journey as Zoe sat comfortably in her stroller as we made the long walk. My emotions were many as the glass doors parted welcoming us to the sterile environment of the hospital which had been the home to our precious daughter for the first three weeks of her life. We continued through the halls as my mind replayed the many seminal events that had taken place on our IVF/NICU journey. By the time we reached the waiting room, I felt terribly unsettled. I wasn't really feeling nervous about the appointment at this time. I was nervous about Zoe. Never had I been in the waiting room with my child. This room had always been the place where I anxiously waited and prayed that I would someday become a dad. My mind was having a difficult time convincing itself that I was already a dad and had a beautiful, healthy child in the stroller in front of me.

I looked down at Zoe and just felt so very lucky. I had this sinking feeling in the pit of my stomach knowing that her birth had radically transformed every fiber of my being. As I sat in that room, I couldn't help but think that this moment might have never happened without God's blessing and the work of these magnificent doctors. She had brought more happiness in one year than I had experienced in my first 34. Her birth had been more inspiring and transformative than any other single experience I had ever felt.

I continued to try to reassure myself that Zoe was fine and that I was in fact her dad, but I was still tense. The only analogy that I think can accurately approach what I was experiencing is that terrible feeling that comes when one is almost in an accident. If you have ever been inches or seconds away from an accident, the shakiness felt while processing "what could have been" would probably be a close approximate to what I was feeling.

We followed the nurse back to a conference room where we met with Dr. Palmer, a doctor with whom we had first met two years ago. Zoe fidgeted in her stroller as we discussed our desire to move forward with implanting her siblings. I was surprised that Dr. Palmer did not "fuss" over Zoe. He had played such an integral role in her creation that I couldn't help but believe that he would be overcome with joy and emotion at the sight of her. His professional distance only served to solidify a belief that I had always had which was that no one would ever care about our IVF success as much as my wife and I. It was this realization early on during round 1 that gave me the confidence to tell Dr. Jones to keep looking for eggs when he said he didn't see any more. The doctors may have the medical knowledge and skill needed, but there is no substitute for the shear force of will of a hopeful parent.

My wife and I told Dr. Palmer that we were ready to once again begin IVF. I explained that we had a few questions that we wanted answered before we initiated the process. My wife and I had discussed whether we would be comfortable having triplets if God so chose and we both agreed that we would welcome the challenge. Our first question was to ask whether he would "thaw" out all three remaining embryos and be willing to implant all three embryos if they survived their unfreezing. He answered that "Yes, this would be his plan."

Dear Zoe || Love Dad

We then followed up our question by asking whether implanting all three posed any additional risks. We told him that we wanted to implant all three as long as implanting the three (1) did not reduce the chance of any given embryo surviving and (2) did not pose any additional risk to my wife. He gave the answer that we hoped for "Implanting all three did not pose risks to the embryos or my wife," but I became very sad and disconcerted.

While telling us that he did not believe that triplets posed any real additional risk, he also mentioned that never in his 27 years of practicing medicine had someone in our situation (three frozen embryos) resulted in three live births. I was caught off guard by my emotions. Even though my wife and I had always wanted 2 children only and we knew triplets would present a very difficult situation, I hated the idea of having any of my embryos not make it.

I looked to my right to see my beautiful daughter squirming and twisting in her stroller and I realized what these embryos could become. These embryos were my babies. They had the potential to grow into playful, rambunctious, loving, little people. It wasn't the place to address my feelings as the purpose of the meeting was to acquire some basic facts not wrestle with questions which I believe to be religious and philosophical in nature. Statistics and probabilities had been such a focus of mine during round one, but I didn't pay much attention as Dr. Palmer began saying "10% chance of X, and 30% chance of Y." I wanted all three babies to make it, and I wasn't interested in hearing any more about survival rates at this meeting. The decision had already been made to create embryos and there was nothing that I could do now except pray that God would grant us three little miracles.

I asked Dr. Palmer another question which was so unimportant to me that I can't even remember what it was as I write this. My mind had moved onto to thinking about my three embryos. Even though I knew there was nothing I could do to increase our chances of having all three survive, there was something terribly unsettling about knowing that we would be actively thawing these babies out and implanting them knowing that the odds of their survival were extremely low. I hated the idea of playing in part in their going back to heaven. My logic was definitely flawed, but I was struggling with the idea that I could ensure their continued existence if I had them remain frozen indefinitely. Surely, God's plan was not to have parents keep their 6-celled children frozen indefinitely, but I'm not sure He planned on IVF either.

I was beginning to understand how much more difficult round two of IVF would be when compared to round one. As challenging and stressful as round one had been, I was blinded by my complete focus on being the husband my wife needed me to be. Without the ability to comprehend what was truly at stake, I was able to want a baby with all my heart yet never lose sight of the need to comfort my wife. My emotions were those of a husband who desperately wanted to give his wife a baby, a gift she had dreamed about her whole life. I found comfort in my role as being a loving husband. Round 2 would be more about the babies than my wife (I mean this in a way that my wife would not find offensive.) Becoming a father was the greatest thing that had ever happened to me and loving my child and these embryos would forever be my main focus in life. Knowing what I had to gain or lose would make round 2 even more stressful. Round 2 was about me as much as it would be about my wife.

The meeting was continuing even as I tried to process everything that was happening. Dr. Palmer wouldn't be able to provide the answers I was searching for or eliminate my internal turmoil. He was however able to provide some answers to some additional medical concerns that I had. I decided that the only thing I could do was to set aside these larger issues and concentrate on gaining resolution to the few additional subjects that led to the making of this appointment.

I told Dr. Palmer that I was concerned about my wife's ability to carry these babies to term. Zoe had been induced due to my wife developing preeclampsia at week 35 of her pregnancy. Thankfully both my wife and daughter made it through the 30 hour labor with their health in tact. (Granted, Zoe had to go to the NICU and my wife had to suffer through 2.5 days of Magnesium, but for all intense and purposes, things went well.) I wanted to understand what risks were associated with my wife having these three embryos implanted.

Everything had happened so fast with the birth of our daughter that I never realized the seriousness of my wife's condition during delivery. The phone call telling me that she was going to be induced brought home the realization that I was about to become a father. I'm not sure whether I was taking cues from my wife, who will always care more about my daughter's health than her own, or whether I was just so nervous about the premature birth of my first child, but I never really worried about my wife's condition. Months after Zoe had left the NICU she came home from an appointment with her OBGYN regarding another matter only to tell me that she had never realized how serious a condition preeclampsia could be. She went on to tell me that the resident with whom she met had told her that her preeclampsia was progressing into a more serious condition known as HELP.

It became clear to me after a few minutes that she was under the impression that I had in fact known the full gravity of her situation. I had to tell her that I had severely underestimated the seriousness of her condition. From the time I received the call that she was being induced, my focus was always on Zoe who I hoped had spent enough time in the womb to be prepared to tackle the world. My main concern was on the lung development of my child knowing that being born at 35 weeks was right on the cusp of full long development.

At the time of Zoe's birth, I had mistakenly believed that the preeclampsia was not an issue due to the administration of magnesium and the decision to induce. Any concerns about short or long term health difficulties never really crossed my mind. The magnesium drip had caused great discomfort, but I knew that my wife gladly accepted any temporary discomfort for the lifelong joy brought on by the birth of her child.

I asked her what the resident had said, but I wasn't able to get a lot of answers. My wife has many, many great characteristics but an attention to detail is not one. Any questions I had would have to be investigated on the internet or at a follow up appointment.

I looked up at Dr. Palmer having tamed the whirlwind of emotions and thoughts about the three embryos and asked him about my wife's preeclampsia. I said that we would proceed with the implanting the three embryos, but I needed to know whether my wife was going physically capable of carrying these babies to term. Never had my wife and I discussed surrogacy and I think she was probably taken aback by my statement, but I felt that I needed to ensure the well-being of my wife and Zoe's mom. My wife loved being pregnant and any decision which would take this gift away from her would be devastating. Still, I wanted to know that I was not signing up for a procedure which could have dire consequences for anyone in my family.

Dr. Palmer said that he did see any reason why my wife should not carry these embryos. She was going to be treated as an at-risk patient due to her history and her chances of getting preeclampsia were definitely higher than the average patient. That being said, he went on to explain that women who had previously had preeclampsia will often get a "less powerful" form during future pregnancies. I was pleased on every level as I knew that my wife would have the chance to be pregnant again, that her health was not being irresponsibly jeopardized and that I would not be dealing with a very angry and sad spouse on the car ride home.

With all the major questions answered, it was time to speak about the more tactical elements of the process. How much would it cost? When should we start? What would it involve?

Much to my surprise – this part of the appointment yielded nothing but positive answers. The cost was going to be dramatically lessened from round one. The total cost was expected to be around $1,500 rather than $8,400. Similarly, the number of appointments would be reduced from around 20 to 4. Finally, we could begin at anytime. We simply needed to schedule an appointment with the IVF nurse to develop a schedule that would work for us and the medical staff.

We left the appointment with all questions answered. I walked with my wife and child while marinating in my own thoughts about what the next few months would entail. The only things that I was sure about was that this round was going to be harder than round one and that I had many prayers which needed to be said. My internal conversation was brought to an end when my wife said that she was going to call the IVF nurse, Janet, as soon as she got home. Clearly, she was not struggling with any of the religious and philosophical questions swimming in my head.

Her enthusiasm for starting round two immediately didn't result in any additional stress on my part however. It only made me love her that much more. She was such a beautiful person and her love of life and her love of being a mother only further solidified my belief that I could have never found a better woman to be my wife.

I don't know what the future holds. The odds of getting what I want, three healthy babies, are certainly stacked against me. Thankfully, I believe in heaven and I find some solace knowing that I will be reunited with my first embryo which didn't make it and any of my future embryos when my time on earth has passed.

Here we go.

www.ingramcontent.com/pod-product-compliance
Lightning Source LLC
Chambersburg PA
CBHW030215170426
43201CB00006B/95